TROY BETWEEN GREECE AND ROME

Troy between Greece and Rome

Local Tradition and Imperial Power

ANDREW ERSKINE

OXFORD

UNIVERSITY PRESS

OXFORD

UNIVERSITY PRESS

Great Clarendon Street, Oxford OX2 6DP

Oxford University Press is a department of the University of Oxford.
It furthers the University's objective of excellence in research, scholarship,
and education by publishing worldwide in

Oxford New York

Auckland Bangkok Buenos Aires Cape Town Chennai
Dar es Salaam Delhi Hong Kong Istanbul Karachi Kolkata
Kuala Lumpur Madrid Melbourne Mexico City Mumbai Nairobi
São Paulo Shanghai Singapore Taipei Tokyo Toronto

Oxford is a registered trade mark of Oxford University Press
in the UK and in certain other countries

Published in the United States
by Oxford University Press Inc., New York

First published 2001
First published in paperback 2003

British Library Cataloguing in Publication Data
Data available

Library of Congress Cataloging in Publication Data

Erskine, Andrew.
Troy between Greece and Rome: local tradition and imperial power / Andrew Erskine.
p.cm.
Includes bibliographical references and index.
1. Troy (Extinct city) 2. Trojan War. 3. Rome—History—To 510 B.C.
4. Rome—Civilization—Greek influences. 5. Mythology, Roman.
6. Greece—Civilization—To 146 B.C. I. Title: Troy between Greece & Rome. II. Title.
DF221.T8 E77 2001
939'.21—dc21   2001021925
ISBN 0-19-924033-7 (hbk)
ISBN 0-19-926580-1 (pbk)

1 3 5 7 9 10 8 6 4 2

Typeset by Regent Typesetting, London
Printed in Great Britain
on acid-free paper by
Biddles Ltd, Guildford and King's Lynn

For my father

νυνὶ δὲ μένει πίστις, ἐλπίς, ἀγάπη, τὰ τρία ταῦτα·
μείζων δὲ τούτων ἡ ἀγάπη.

Preface

This book is an accident. I had intended to write a book on Greek perceptions of the Romans, but somehow never got beyond the first chapter. Many debts have been incurred along the way. Much of it was written while I was a Humboldt Fellow at the Institut für Alte Geschichte in Munich. I am particularly grateful to my host, Hatto H. Schmitt, not only for his hospitality but also for his willingness to read and discuss my work. I have been lucky that so many have generously given up time to read all or part of the manuscript in its various incarnations, Paul Cartledge, Tim Cornell, Oliver Dany, Peter Derow, Martin Goodman, Dieter Hertel, Michael Lloyd, Keith Sidwell, Theresa Urbainczyk, and the still anonymous referees. Others too have helped with advice and conversation, Kai Brodersen, Tom Harrison, Peter Heslin, Llewelyn Morgan, and Manuel Schulte. My thanks are also due to Manfred Korfmann for giving me a tour of the Troad, to Brian Rose for taking me round Hellenistic Ilion, to Chris Hallett and Bert Smith for showing me the Sebasteion reliefs at Aphrodisias and to Christina Haywood, Ciarán Egan, and David Jennings for providing the maps. In the early stages George Forrest was there with his unerring ability to ask the necessary questions.

Underlying any formal list of acknowledgements are memories and associations, walking to Andechs, espresso coffee, the desks in the Institut für Klassiche Archäologie, West Stow, an invisible billiard-table, numerous Dublin restaurants, Coldharbour Lane, all relevant in some indefinable way.

Contents

Contents

Maps

Ancient Authors: Abbreviations and Glossary

Dates, often only approximate, are taken from *OCD³*. For convenience Greek names appear here in their traditional latinized form, although in the book itself I have chosen to transliterate Greek names rather than latinize them.

Aelian	Aelian (AD 165/70–230/5).
NA	*De natura animalium* (*On the Nature of Animals*).
VH	*Varia Historia.*
Aesch.	Aeschylus (?525/4–456/5 BC), Athenian tragedian.
Ag.	*Agamemnon.*
Pers.	*Persians.*
Aeschin.	Aeschines (*c*.397–*c*.322 BC), Athenian orator.
In Ctes.	*Against Ctesiphon.*
In Tim.	*Against Timarchus.*
[Aeschin.] *Epist.*	*Epistulae* (*Letters*).
Amm. Marc.	Ammianus Marcellinus (*c*. AD 330–95), historian.
Ampelius	Ampelius (3rd–4th cent. AD), *Liber memorialis.*
Anth. Pal.	*Anthologia Palatina* (*Palatine Anthology*).
Apoll. Rhod.	Apollonius Rhodius (3rd cent. BC), poet.
Arg.	*Argonautica.*
Apollod.	Apollodorus, mythographer.
Bibl.	*Bibliotheca.*
Epit.	*Epitome.*
App.	Appian (2nd cent. AD), Greek historian.
BC	*Bella civilia* (*Civil Wars*).
Hann.	Ἀννιβαϊκή (*Hannibalic War*).
Mith.	Μιθριδάτειος (*Mithridatic Wars*).
Sam.	Σαυνιτική (*Samnite Wars*), fragmentary.
Sic.	Σικελική (*Sicilian Wars*), fragmentary.
Syr.	Συριακή (*Syrian Wars*).

Arist.	Aristotle (384–322 BC), Greek philosopher.
Eth. Nic.	*Nicomachean Ethics.*
Poet.	*Poetics.*
Pol.	*Politics.*
[Arist.] *Ath. Pol.*	Ἀθηναίων πολιτεία (*Constitution of the Athenians*).
Mir. ausc.	*De mirabilibus auscultationibus.* (*On Marvellous Reports*).
Pepl.	*Peplus*, frag. 640 in V. Rose (ed.). *Aristotelis qui ferebantur librorum fragmenta.* Leipzig 1886.
Arnob.	Arnobius (late 2nd–early 3rd cent. AD), Christian, *Adversus nationes.*
Arr.	Arrian (*c.* AD 86–160), Greek historian.
Anab.	*Anabasis.*
Tact.	*Tactica.*
Athen.	Athenaeus (*c.* AD 200), *The Deipnosophists*, learned conversation at dinner.
Athenagoras	Athenagoras (2nd cent. AD), Christian apologist.
Leg.	*Legatio pro Christianis.*
August.	Augustine (AD 354–430).
De civ. D.	*De civitate Dei* (*The City of God*).
[Aur. Vict.] *De vir. ill.*	[Aurelius Victor], *De viri illustribus* (*On Famous Men*).
Caes.	Caesar, C. Iulius Caesar (100–44 BC).
BC	*Bellum Civile* (*The Civil War*).
[Caes.] *Alex.*	*Bellum Alexandrinum* (*The Alexandrian War*).
Cato	Cato the Elder, M. Porcius Cato (234–149 BC).
Orig.	*Origins* (ed. M. Chassignet, Paris 1986).
Catull.	Catullus (*c.*84–*c.*54 BC), Latin poet.
Cic.	Cicero, M. Tullius Cicero (106–43 BC).
Arch.	*Pro Archia.*
Att.	*Epistulae ad Atticum* (*Letters to Atticus*).
Balb.	*Pro Balbo.*

Brut.	*Brutus.*
Cael.	*Pro Caelio.*
Cat.	*In Catilinum.*
De or.	*De oratore* (*On the Orator*).
Div	*De divinatione* (*On Divination*).
Fam.	*Epistulae ad familiares* (*Letters to Friends*).
Fat.	*De fato* (*On Fate*).
Fin.	*De finibus* (*On Ends*).
Flac.	*Pro Flacco.*
Har. resp.	*De haruspicum responso* (*On the Reply of the Soothsayers*).
Leg.	*De legibus* (*On Laws*).
Mur.	*Pro Murena.*
Nat. D.	*De natura deorum* (*On the Nature of the Gods*).
Off.	*De officiis* (*On Duties*).
Phil.	*Philippics.*
Rep.	*De republica* (*On the Republic*).
Rosc. Am.	*Pro Sexto Roscio Amerino.*
Sen.	*De senectute* (*On Old Age*).
Tusc.	*Tusculan Disputations.*
Vat.	*In Vatinium.*
II *Verr.*	*In Verrem* (*Verrines*), Actio secunda.
[Cic.] *Rhet. ad Her.*	*Rhetorica ad Herennium.*
Claudian	Claudian (*c.*370–*c.*404), poet.
Laud. Ser.	*De laudibus Serenae reginae.*
Dem.	Demosthenes (384–322 BC), Athenian orator.
Dig.	*Digesta*, legal text, 6th cent. AD.
Dio	Cassius Dio (*c.* AD 164– after 229), Greek, *Roman History*.
Dio Chrys.	Dio Chrysostom (*c.* AD 40/50– after 110), Greek orator and philosopher.
Diod. Sic.	Diodorus Siculus (1st cent. BC), Sicilian author of a world history.
Diog. Laert.	Diogenes Laertius (probably early 3rd cent. AD), *Lives of the Philosophers*.
Dion. Hal.	Dionysius of Halicarnassus (later 1st cent. BC).
Ant. Rom.	*Roman Antiquities.*

Etym. Magn.	*Etymologicum Magnum* (ed. T. Gaisford, Oxford 1848).
Eur.	Euripides (*c.*480s–407/6 BC), Athenian tragedian.
Andr.	*Andromache.*
Bacch.	*Bacchae.*
Cyc.	*Cyclops.*
Hec.	*Hecuba (Hekabe).*
IA	*Iphigenia in Aulis.*
Or.	*Orestes.*
Phoen.	*Phoenissae.*
Tro.	*Troades (Trojan Women).*
Eustath. on Hom.	Eustathius, 12th cent. AD commentary on Homer's *Iliad* and *Odyssey.*
Eutrop.	Eutropius (4th cent. AD), historian, *Breviarum ab urbe condita.*
Festus	Festus (ed. W. M. Lindsay, Leipzig 1913).
Gorgias	Gorgias, in H. Diels and W. Kranz, *Fragmente der Vorsokratiker*, 6th edn. (Berlin 1952).
Hdt.	Herodotus of Halicarnassus (5th cent. BC), historian.
Hes. *Theog.*	Hesiod (*c.*700 BC?), Greek poet, *Theogony.*
Hippoc. *Aer.*	Hippocrates, medical writer, *Airs, Waters, Places.*
Hist. Aug. Alex. Sev.	*Historia Augusta: Alexander Severus.*
Hist. Aug. Prob.	*Historia Augusta: Probus.*
Hom.	Homer.
Il.	*Iliad.*
Od.	*Odyssey.*
Hor.	Horace (65–8 BC), Latin poet.
Carm. Saec.	*Carmen saeculare (Secular Hymn).*
Hyg. *Fab.*	Hyginus, *Fabulae.*
Isoc.	Isocrates (436–338 BC), Athenian orator.
Arch.	*Archidamus.*
Evag.	*Evagoras.*
Panath.	*Panathenaicus.*

Paneg.	*Panegyricus.*
Phil.	*Philippus.*
Jerome	Jerome, also Eusebius Hieronymus (AD 347–420), Christian writer.
Iov.	*Ad Iovinianum.*
Jos.	Josephus (1st cent. AD), historian.
AJ	*Antiquitates Judaicae.*
Ap.	*Contra Apionem.*
Julian	Julian 'the Apostate' (AD 331–63), emperor.
Epist.	*Epistulae* (ed. J. Bidez, Paris 1924).
Or.	*Orationes.*
Just. *Epit.*	Justin, *Epitome*, of the *Historiae Philippicae* of Pompeius Trogus.
Juv.	Juvenal (*c.* early 2nd cent. AD), *Satires.*
Lactant.	Lactantius (*c.* AD 240–*c.*320), Christian apologist.
Div. inst.	*Divinae institutiones.*
Livy	Livy (probably 59 BC–AD 17); history of Rome cited as 'Livy'.
Epit.	*Epitome.*
Per.	*Periochae.*
Lycurg.	Lycurgus (*c.*390–*c.*325/4 BC), Athenian orator.
Leoc.	*Against Leocrates.*
Lucan	Lucan, M. Annaeus Lucanus (AD 39–65), Latin poet, *De bello civili.*
Lucr.	Lucretius (1st cent. BC), Epicurean Latin poet, *De rerum natura* (*On the Nature of Things*).
Lycoph.	Lycophron, Hellenistic poet, *Alexandra.*
Macc.	Maccabees.
Macrob. *Sat.*	Macrobius (late empire), *Saturnalia.*
Min. Felix	Minucius Felix (early 3rd cent. AD), Christian apologist, *Octavius.*
Nepos	Cornelius Nepos (*c.*110–24 BC), Latin biographer.
Cato	*Life of Cato.*
OGR	*Origo gentis Romanae*, attributed to

	Aurelius Victor (ed. J.-C. Richard, Paris 1983).
Oros.	Orosius, Christian writer, 5th cent. AD.
Pag.	*Against the Pagans.*
Ovid	Ovid, Publius Ovidius Naso (43 BC–AD 17), Latin poet.
Met.	*Metamorphoses.*
Pont.	*Epistulae ex Ponto.*
Paus.	Pausanias (2nd cent. AD), Greek traveller, *Description of Greece*, cited according to the Teubner edn. of M. Rocha-Pereira (Leipzig 1973–81).
Philostr.	L. Flavius Philostratus (late 2nd cent. –240s AD), Greek.
Her.	*Heroicus.*
VA	*Vita Apollonii* (*Life of Apollonius of Tyana*).
Phot. *Lex.*	Photius (9th cent. AD), *Lexicon.*
Pind.	Pindar (late 6th–mid-5th cent. BC), Boeotian poet.
Isthm.	*Isthmian Odes.*
Nem.	*Nemean Odes.*
Ol.	*Olympian Odes.*
Pyth.	*Pythian Odes.*
Plato	Plato (*c.*429–347 BC), Athenian philosopher.
Apol.	*Apology.*
Hipp. Mai.	*Hippias Maior.*
Rep.	*Republic.*
[Plato] *Hipparch.*	*Hipparchus.*
Plaut.	Plautus (active late 3rd–early 2nd cent. BC), Latin comic playwright.
Bacch.	*Bacchides.*
Pseud.	*Pseudolus.*
Pliny	Pliny the Elder (AD 23/4–79).
HN	*Naturalis historia* (*Natural History*).
Plut.	Plutarch, Greek biographer and philosopher, mid-1st to 2nd cent. AD; *Lives* cited according to the Teubner edition of K. Ziegler (Leipzig).
Ages.	*Agesilaus.*

Alex.	*Alexander.*
Caes.	*Caesar.*
Cam.	*Camillus.*
Cato Min.	*Cato Minor (Cato the Younger).*
Cic.	*Cicero.*
Cim.	*Cimon.*
Cor.	*Coriolanus.*
Demetr.	*Demetrius.*
Fab.	*Fabius Maximus.*
Flam.	*Flamininus.*
Luc.	*Lucullus.*
Mor.	*Moralia.*
Nic.	*Nicias.*
Num.	*Numa.*
Per.	*Pericles.*
Pyrrh.	*Pyrrhus.*
Rom.	*Romulus.*
Them.	*Themistocles.*
Polyb.	Polybius (*c.*200–*c.*118 BC), Greek historian.
Prop.	Propertius (second half of 1st cent. BC), Latin poet.
Quint. Smyrn.	Quintus Smyrnaeus (probably 3rd cent. AD), Greek poet, *Posthomerica.*
RG	*Res gestae Divi Augusti.*
Sall.	Sallust, C. Sallustius Crispus (probably 86–35 BC), Latin historian.
Cat.	*Bellum Catilinae.*
Hist.	*Histories* (ed. B. Maurenbrecher, Leipzig 1891–2).
schol.	scholia.
Schol. Veron.	*Scholia Veronensia*, in H. Hagen, *Appendix Serviana* (Leipzig 1902)..
Serv.	Servius (4th cent. AD), commentator on Vergil.
Serv. Auct.	Servius Auctus.
Sid. Apoll.	Sidonius Apollonaris (5th cent. AD), *Carmina.*
Silius Italicus	Silius Italicus (*c.* AD 26–102), poet, *Punica.*

Solin.	Solinus (active early 3rd cent. AD), geographer.
Soph.	Sophocles (490s–406BC), Athenian tragedian.
Aj.	*Ajax.*
Phil.	*Philoctetes.*
Soz.	Sozomen (5th cent. AD), Greek ecclesiastical historian.
Stat.	Statius (second half of 1st cent. AD), Latin poet.
Silv.	*Silvae.*
Steph. Byz.	Stephanus of Byzantium (probably 6th cent. AD), *Ethnica.*
Strabo	Strabo (*c.*64 BC–after AD 21), *Geography.*
Suda	*Suda* (ed. A. Adler, Stuttgart 1928–38), a lexicon compiled in 10th cent. AD.
Suet.	Suetonius (*c.* AD 70–*c.*130), Latin biographer.
Aug.	*Divus Augustus.*
Claud.	*Divus Claudius.*
Iul.	*Divus Iulius.*
Tib.	*Tiberius.*
Synesius, *Calv. Enc.*	Synesius (*c.* AD 370–*c.*413), *Calvitii encomium.*
Tac.	Tacitus (*c.* AD 56–after *c.*118), Latin historian.
Ann.	*Annals.*
Tertullian	Tertullian (*c.* AD 160–*c.*240), Christian apologist.
Apol.	*Apologeticus.*
Theophr.	Theophrastus (late 370s–early 280s BC), Greek philosopher.
Char.	*Characters.*
Hist. pl.	*Historia plantarum.*
Thuc.	Thucydides (5th cent. BC), Athenian historian.
Tzetz.	Johannes Tzetzes (12th cent. AD), Byzantine commentator.
Chil.	*Historiarum variarum Chiliades.*

Val. Max.	Valerius Maximus (1st cent. AD), Latin writer.
Varro	Varro, M. Terentius Varro (116–27 BC).
Ling.	*De lingua Latina* (*On the Latin Language*).
Rust.	*De re rustica* (*On Farming*).
Vell. Pat.	Velleius Paterculus (early imperial), *Historiae Romanae.*
Verg.	Vergil or Virgil (70–19 BC), Latin poet.
Aen.	*Aeneid.*
Ecl.	*Eclogues.*
Xen.	Xenophon (*c.*430–mid-4th cent. BC), Athenian writer.
Ages.	*Agesilaus.*
Anab.	*Anabasis.*
Cyn.	*Cynegeticus* (*On Hunting*).
Hell.	*Hellenica.*
Symp.	*Symposium.*
Zonar.	Johannes Zonaras (12th cent. AD), Byzantine historian.
Zos.	Zosimus (late empire), Greek historian.

Reference Works: Abbreviations

AJArch.	*American Journal of Archaeology.*
AJPhil.	*American Journal of Philology.*
ANRW	*Aufstieg und Niedergang der römischen Welt.* Berlin. 1972– .
ASNP	*Annali della Scuola Normale Superiore di Pisa, Classe di Lettere e Filosofia.*
BCH	*Bulletin de Correspondance Hellénique.*
BÉ	*Bulletin épigraphique,* published in *REG.*
BICS	*Bulletin of the Institute of Classical Studies.*
BMC Peloponnese	Poole, R. S. *A Catalogue of the Greek Coins in the British Museum: Peloponnese.* London. 1887.
BMCRE i	Mattingly, H. *Coins of the Roman Empire in the British Museum.* Vol. i. London. 1923.
BMCRR	Grueber, H. A. *Coins of the Roman Republic in the British Museum.* London. 1910.
BMC Sicily	Poole, R. S. *A Catalogue of the Greek Coins in the British Museum: Sicily.* London. 1876.
BSA	*Annual of the British School at Athens.*
C.Phil.	*Classical Philology.*
CAH²	*Cambridge Ancient History.* 2nd edn. Cambridge, 1961– .
CCCA	Vermaseren, M. J. *Corpus Cultus Cybelae Attidisque.* Leiden. 1977–89.
CIL	*Corpus Inscriptionum Latinarum.* 1863– .
CJ	*Classical Journal.*
CQ	*Classical Quarterly.*
Davies *PMGF*	Davies, M. *Poetarum Melicorum Graecorum Fragmenta.* Oxford. 1991 (vol. i).
FGrH	Jacoby, F. *Fragmente der griechischen Historiker.* 1923– .
FPL	*Fragmenta Poetarum Latinorum epicorum et*

	lyricorum. 1st. edn. W. Morel, 1927. 2nd edn. C. Büchner, 1982. Leipzig.
GGM	Müller, C. *Geographici Graeci Minores*. Paris. 1855–61.
GRBS	*Greek, Roman and Byzantine Studies.*
Harv. Stud.	*Harvard Studies in Classical Philology.*
Harv. Theol. Rev.	*Harvard Theological Review.*
HRR	Peter, H. *Historicorum Romanorum Reliquiae*. Leipzig. 1906 (vol. 2). 1914 (vol. 1²).
I.Ilion	Frisch, P. *Die Inschriften von Ilion*. Bonn. 1975.
I.Lamp.	Frisch, P. *Die Inschriften von Lampsakos*. Bonn. 1978.
I.Magn.	Kern, O. *Die Inscriften von Magnesia am Maeander*. Berlin. 1900.
I.Perg.	Fränkel, M. *Die Inschriften von Pergamon*. Berlin. 1890 (vol. 1). 1895 (vol. 2).
I.Priene	Hiller von Gaertingen, F. *Die Inschriften von Priene*. Berlin. 1906.
IG	*Inscriptiones Graecae*. Berlin 1873– .
IGRR	Cagnat, R. *Inscriptiones Graecae ad res Romanas pertinentes*. Paris. 1906–27.
ILLRP	Degrassi, A. *Inscriptiones Latinae Liberae Rei Republicae*. Florence. 1963 (vol. 2). 1965 (vol. 1²).
ILS	Dessau, H. *Inscriptiones Latinae Selectae*. Berlin. 1892–1916.
Inscr. Ital.	*Inscriptiones Italiae*. Rome. 1931/2– .
JHS	*Journal of Hellenic Studies.*
JÖAI	*Jahreshefte des österreichischen archäologischen Instituts.*
JRS	*Journal of Roman Studies.*
LGPN	*Lexicon of Greek Personal Names*. Oxford. 1987– .
LIMC	*Lexicon Iconographicum Mythologiae Classicae*. Düsseldorf. 1981–99.
MDAI (I)	*Mitteilungen des deutschen archäologischen Instituts. Istanbulische Abteilung.*

MDAI (R)	*Mitteilungen des deutschen archäologischen Instituts. Römische Abteilung.*
ML	Meiggs, R. and Lewis, D. *A Selection of Greek Historical Inscriptions to the End of the Fifth Century BC.* Rev. edn. Oxford. 1988.
MRR	Broughton, T. R. S. *The Magistrates of the Roman Republic.* New York. 1951–2. Suppl. in 1986.
Müller *FHG*	Müller, C. *Fragmenta Historicorum Graecorum.* Paris. 1841–70.
OCD[3]	Hornblower, S. and Spawforth, A. *The Oxford Classical Dictionary.* 3rd edn. Oxford. 1996.
OGIS	Dittenberger, W. *Orientis Graeci Inscriptiones Selectae.* Leipzig. 1903–5.
PA	Kirchner, J. *Prosopographia Attica.* Berlin. 1901–3.
Page *PMG*	Page, D. L. *Poeticae Melici Graeci.* Oxford. 1962.
PCPS	*Proceedings of the Cambridge Philological Society.*
Poet. Lesb. Frag.	Lobel, E. and Page, D. L. *Poetarum Lesbiorum Fragmenta.* Oxford. 1955.
Radt *TrGF*	Radt, S. *Tragicorum Graecorum Fragmenta.* iii: *Aeschylus* (1985). iv: *Sophocles* (1977). Göttingen.
RC	Welles, C. B. *Royal Correspondence in the Hellenistic Period.* New Haven. 1934.
RDGE	Sherk, R. K. *Roman Documents from the Greek East:* Senatus Consulta *and* Epistulae *to the Age of Augustus.* Baltimore. 1969.
RE	A. Pauly, G. Wissowa, and W. Kroll, *Realencyclopädie des classischen Altertumswissenschaft.* 1893– .
REG	*Revue des études grecques.*
REL	*Revue des études latines.*
Ribbeck *TRF*	Ribbeck, O. *Tragicorum Romanorum Fragmenta.* In *Scaenicae Romanorum Poesis*

	Fragmenta. 3rd edn. Leipzig. 1897–8.
Roscher, *Lex.*	Roscher, W. H. *Ausführliches Lexikon des griechischen und römischen Mythologie.* Leipzig. 1884–1937.
SEG	*Supplementum Epigraphicum Graecum.* 1923– .
SIG³	Dittenberger, W. *Sylloge Inscriptionum Graecarum.* 3rd edn. Leipzig. 1915–24.
TAM	*Tituli Asiae Minoris.* 1901– .
TAPA	*Transactions and Proceedings of the American Philological Association.*
ZPE	*Zeitschrift für Papyrologie und Epigraphik.*

Introduction

I sing of arms and of the man, fated to be an exile, who long since left
the land of Troy and came to Italy to the shores of Lavinium; and a great
pounding he took by land and sea at the hands of the heavenly gods
because of the fierce and unforgetting anger of Juno. Great too were his
sufferings in war before he could found his city and carry his gods into
Latium. This was the beginning of the Latin race, the Alban fathers and
the high walls of Rome.

Verg. Aen. i. 1–7, trans. D. West 1990

In these first few lines of the *Aeneid* Vergil simply and succinctly
connects Rome and Troy. Here we read a Roman foundation
story told in Latin for an emperor who claimed descent from
Aeneas himself. Yet the origins of the tale are Greek. The Trojan
War was part of the mythical past of the Greeks, the subject of the
greatest of Greek epic poems, Homer's *Iliad*, written down centuries earlier and a partial model for Vergil's own work. Aeneas'
survival, although not his role in the foundation of Rome, was
already predicted by Poseidon in this poem. As a refugee from a
sacked city, he turned up all over the Mediterranean, helped on
his way by Greek story-telling. One stop was Rome. Troy, thus,
became the shared property of Greeks and Romans.

In a Greek world which was increasingly falling under Roman
influence the Trojan past of this emerging imperial power was not
a matter of mere academic interest. It was part of the new political order. Rome's Trojan origins have been the subject of many
studies by modern scholars, but the focus has tended to be on
Rome itself, especially the development of the myth there and in
central Italy. The Greek point of view, on the other hand, has
been relatively neglected, and where it is treated writers often
speak rather too freely of 'the Greeks', as if all Greeks thought and
acted in the same way.

Greeks are integral to an understanding of Rome's Trojan past.
To ignore them is to miss much that is of value. The aim of the
present book, therefore, is to consider the Trojan origins of Rome

from a Greek perspective and in a Greek context. This emphasis should allow a more nuanced picture to emerge. In the chapters that follow I stress the variety of the Greek response and the importance of local tradition in shaping that response. The myth, I argue, is best understood not as a Roman myth but as a Graeco-Roman myth, a collaboration that acquires its force and meaning in the interaction between Greeks and Romans. Far from a monolithic reaction, there was no uniformity; what the myth represented and how it could be used varied with time and place. This study explores the period from the Greeks' earliest contacts with Italy up until the point when the emperor Augustus is acclaimed as the descendant of Trojan Aeneas.

1. MYTH AND LOCAL TRADITION

Greeks told many stories of Agamemnon's ten-year campaign against Troy, a city in the north-western corner of Asia Minor. Here on the plain of Troy hero fought against hero, often hindered or helped by the intervention of interested gods and goddesses. The Trojan War is inseparable now from Homer's *Iliad*, yet many of the most celebrated stories are at best only alluded to in the poem.[1] Largely absent, for instance, are the judgement of Paris, the abduction of Helen, the sacrifice of Iphigeneia, the suicide of Aias, the making of the Wooden Horse and the resulting capture of the city, stories which have to be found elsewhere in Greek literature and art. The *Iliad* itself tells of Achilles' quarrel with Agamemnon, his withdrawal from the fighting, and his eventual return to avenge the death of his friend Patroklos, events that take place over a period of only a couple of months in the last year of the war.[2] All these tales together form one part of a much more extensive set of Greek myths, that is to say traditional stories of gods and heroes linked by common characters and complex genealogies.[3]

In what follows I will often refer to the Trojan War and related

---

[1] *OCD*[3] s.v. 'Trojan War' reads simply 'See HOMER; TROY.'

[2] For a full survey of Trojan War myths, Gantz 1993: 557–717.

[3] Cf. Burkert's (1979: 23) influential definition of myth as 'a traditional tale with secondary, partial reference to something of collective importance' or Bremmer 1987a: 7, 'traditional tales relevant to society'. The present discussion places particular emphasis on the importance of social context for understanding myth, cf. Buxton 1994. This is, of course, not the only approach; for a useful survey, Edmunds 1990.

stories as mythical. In doing so I am adopting a modern perspective, one which distinguishes myth from history, but it is
important to remember that Greeks would not have made this
distinction.[4] For them heroes such as Agamemnon, Achilles,
Hektor all existed, and the Trojan War was a historical event.
Historians and intellectuals in the ancient world could certainly
have reservations about these stories, but what they did was to
rationalize them, for instance by removing the gods and divesting
the heroes of their divine ancestry.[5] Thucydides' analysis of the
early history of the Peloponnese up to the time of the Trojan War
is a model of this sort of approach: Pelops is the founder of the
dynasty, Agamemnon the powerful warlord, followed more out of
fear than loyalty.[6] The historicity of the war was further affirmed
by the Alexandrian scholar, Eratosthenes, who began his *Chronological Tables* with the fall of Troy, dating it to 1184/3 BC.[7] Doubts
could arise but the substance of the war remained intact, as
Pausanias shows when he describes a bronze statue of the Wooden
Horse to be found on the Acropolis of Athens: 'Anybody who
does not think that Phrygians [i.e. Trojans] are completely simple-
minded knows that what Epeios constructed was a siege engine
for breaking through the wall.'[8] In modern times too there have
been scholars who have accepted the historicity of the Trojan
War, or at least believed that the story represents an actual event,
albeit much elaborated.[9] Whatever its historical basis, however,
the story of the war came to be incorporated into the wider network of Greek myths.

Populated by gods and heroes, this mythical world was rather
different from the society inhabited by historical Greeks, but it
was not autonomous and free-floating. It was a past closely connected to the present. The gods were the same ones that were the
objects of cult throughout the Greek world. The stories were
located in specific, usually identifiable, places, such as Athens,
Sparta, Thebes, Troy, and Argos. Cities would remember the

---

[4] On myth and history, Brillante 1990, Cartledge 1993: 18–35, P. Green 1997: 35–45.
[5] Veyne 1988: 41–57.
[6] Thuc. 1. 9–11.
[7] Fraser 1972: i. 456–7, Jacoby 1904: 146–9 who gives a full survey of all the ancient dates
for the fall of Troy, beginning with Douris' date of 1334/3 BC, cf. also Burkert 1995.
[8] Paus. 1. 23. 8, cf. Serv. on Verg. *Aen.* 2. 15.
[9] For the debate on historicity, Blegen 1963: 20, Finley *et al.* 1964, Davies and Foxhall
1984, Dowden 1992: 65–8.

part played by this or that hero in their own past, perhaps as a founder or visitor. Local people might point out a tomb or some other landmark associated with the hero, or a temple may contain objects dedicated by a hero such as Philoktetes. This sense of continuity is especially evident on the Parian Marble, a stone stele inscribed with a lengthy list of dated events, beginning in 1581/0 BC with the legendary Kekrops, king of Athens, and ending in 264/3 BC. In between lie such events as the invasion of Attika by the Amazons (1256/5), the fall of Troy (1209/8), the battle of Plataia (479/8) and the death of Alexander (324/3).[10] Myth here flows into history.

All Greek communities shared in this mythical world; it was part of their past. Local tradition, therefore, included stories not only about the historical past but also about events which we would class as mythical. Often the stories were aetiological; they might, for instance, explain the origins of a festival or the foundation of a city, or they might relate how a mountain, river or lake acquired its name. In this way a city and its landscape could be located in a common Greek past.

A fascinating insight into civic pride and local tradition is offered by a recently discovered verse inscription from second-century BC Halikarnassos, or, more accurately, from the nearby promontory of Salmakis. The poem begins with a question to Aphrodite, whose temple is believed to have been in the vicinity: 'What is it that brings honour to Halikarnassos?' The answer comes in two parts. Rather self-referentially the poet, albeit with the voice of Aphrodite, highlights the achievements of the city's poets and historians, but first he relates a series of episodes involving gods and heroes. This was the place where Zeus was born and protected from his father, and here too the nymph Salmakis met Hermaphroditos. Then follows a list of heroes who had some role in settling the land, Bellerophontes, Kranaos, Endymion, and probably Anthes.[11] Familiar, or moderately familiar, figures are thus localized in Halikarnassos. A poem that celebrates poets might be expected to have a predilection for mythical material, but such preoccupations can be observed elsewhere when cities reflect on their past. An inscription from Lykian Xanthos reports

---

[10] Jacoby 1904.

[11] Text and commentary, Isager 1998, Lloyd-Jones 1999 (whose translation is given here).

the elaborate mythological arguments used by the city of Kytinion in mainland Greece when it asked the Lykians for financial assistance. These efforts to establish ties of kinship and goodwill show that the Kytinians had a substantial mythical past to exploit. Their ambassadors could point to their connections with Asklepios, to their descent from Aiolos and Doros, and to the exploits of the Heraklids.[12] In both these examples the mythical past speaks to people outside the city, whether through shared genealogy or shared knowledge.

Each Greek city, although participating in the common mythology, had its own version, which not unnaturally tended to make itself the central character. Much of the material in the Halikarnassos inscription, for instance, is unique to Halikarnassos. Nowhere else do we hear that Zeus was born and brought up in this area, although such a claim was not unusual; as Pausanias says, 'even someone determined would find it impossible to count up all the peoples who maintain that Zeus was born and reared amongst them'. Nor do novelties end here. In a rather sanitized version of the Salmakis story, Hermaphroditos appears as the inventor of lawful marriage, an otherwise unattested achievement. Furthermore, of the four settlers named only Anthes had previously been associated with the foundation of Halikarnassos.[13] No doubt even within the city there was variety as families or villages gave their own account of local history. As the stories passed down through the generations, so they would change yet again, adapting to suit present circumstances.

There was no one, canonical, accepted version of any myth. Not even the introduction of writing could bring order to the mass of inconsistent myths and legendary genealogies. The sixth-century author of the Hesiodic *Catalogue of Women* appears to have made an attempt with his very full listing of heroic genealogies, but early mythographers such as Hekataios of Miletos, writing perhaps a hundred years later, do not seem to have felt unduly constrained.[14] Variants continued to be reported and develop. One reason for this was the very vitality of the mythic tradition as it adapted to time and place, resulting in a multiplicity of different versions of the same story. It was the living past of cities, rehearsed

---

[12] Xanthos text quoted in full and discussed, Ch. 7.1.

[13] Isager 1998: 12–15, Paus. 4. 33. 1; Anthes: Strabo 8. 6. 14, 14. 2. 6.

[14] Fowler 1998, esp. 18–19.

in rituals and festivals, presented to outsiders in diplomatic dealings, and to themselves as a way of understanding their present and past. Myth could both assert a city's distinctiveness and link it to other Greeks.

Local traditions play a prominent role in this book, especially those concerning Troy. There are two principal reasons why they are of relevance to an examination of the Greek reaction to Rome's Trojan ancestry. First, if that reaction is to be satisfactorily understood, it is necessary to gain some sense of the way in which Trojans in general were viewed by the Greeks. What sort of preconceptions might the Greeks have had when faced with the Romans? To focus simply on the portrayal of Trojans in Greek literature, however, would result in too partial and unrepresentative a picture. What survives of classical and Hellenistic literature is the product of a small number of people in a small number of cities. The gulf between this and the hundreds of cities that had to come to terms with Rome as a new power in the Greek world is just too large. The study of local traditions, on the other hand, offers one way into these many cities, some well known, others obscure. The second reason for my interest in local tradition is that it helps the understanding of those cities that do use the Trojan myth in their dealings with Rome. It becomes possible to see what traditions they are drawing on as they seek to establish common ground. Significantly, although cities may shape their Trojan past to suit the Romans, there is no sign that they simply invent it.[15]

2. GREEKS, TROJANS, AND BARBARIANS

There is an assumption that runs through much modern scholarship on Rome's Trojan ancestry that goes something like this: 'If the Romans were descended from the Trojans, they were barbarians and enemies of the Greeks.' This works its way into the scholarly literature in various forms. It is suggested, for instance, that such thinking must have coloured Greek views of Rome; that Trojan ancestry must have handicapped the Romans as they sought to win friends and influence in the Greek world; that it

---

[15] Perret 1942 is the most extreme advocate of invention (pp. 8–10) e.g., p. 52: 'La légende troyenne d'Arcadie rentre donc dans la catégorie fort commune des légendes artificiellement créées à partir du IIᵉ siècle pour courtiser les Romains'.

would have made potent anti-Roman propaganda, reinforcing Rome's barbarian image and recalling the Trojan War; or even that it would have appealed to the Romans themselves, because it emphasized Roman distinctiveness, asserting that they were not Greeks. The assumption that underlies all these positions is usually felt to be so self-evident that no justification is required.[16]

Some Greeks probably did view the Romans in this way, but the evidence is poor and certainly insufficient to support any kind of generalization. The reason that this modern assumption has had such a tenacious hold on the scholarly imagination has less to do with evidence and more to do with a presumed Greek antagonism to anything Trojan. This is all the more surprising because what evidence there is tends to tell of the role played by Troy in diplomacy between Greeks and Romans, where its purpose was to bring the two parties together rather than to divide them. Some scholars have sought to explain this apparent inconsistency, for instance by arguing that Rome's heroic past compensated for its inherited barbarian character or that Aineias was a sufficiently ambiguous figure to make the Trojan past acceptable.[17] Yet, perhaps the problem is more imagined than real, a consequence of an assumption that is never tested.

The present book starts afresh by asking how the Greeks viewed the Trojans. Part II in particular explores the many different ways in which they approached the Trojan past. Only when this has been done is it possible to understand what Rome's Trojan ancestry may have meant to the Greeks. Local traditions are especially valuable in such an inquiry, because they allow one to look beyond the fairly narrow range of available literary texts. What results is a sense of tremendous variety. Antagonism was certainly one Greek response to the Trojans, but it was only one response among many and hardly the most typical. It was much more localized and context dependent than it might first appear.

It is in fifth-century Athens that the barbarian Trojan, enemy

---

[16] In various formulations, e.g. Norden 1901: 326–7, Jüthner 1923: 70–2 ('Äneas war ein Trojaner, also ein Barbar'), Perret 1942: 412 ('une nouvelle croisade contre le Barbare, une nouvelle guerre de Troie'), Bömer 1951: 44–5 ('die erklärten Feinde der Griechen'), Gruen 1992: 6 ('a people perceived as the pre-eminent foe of Hellas'), 43 (though contrast p. 49), Malkin 1998: 202–3, 209, C. P. Jones 1999: 81–8, esp. 88. Such ethnic preoccupations are found in reverse in Gabba 1974: 633, who sees Trojan ancestry as saving the Romans from the charge of barbarism, cf. Gruen 1992: 49.

[17] Jüthner 1923: 70–2 for heroic past, C. P. Jones 1999: 88 for Aineias.

of the Greeks, is most evident, but it is essential to appreciate the anti-Persian context. In the aftermath of the Persian invasions the Trojan War seemed to offer a mythical parallel for the struggle with Persia; here was a Greek victory over a powerful eastern kingdom. In imitation of the Persians the Trojans came to be called 'barbarians' (*barbaroi*), that derogatory term for all who were not Greek. Nonetheless, a reading of Homer and a study of the local traditions of the wider Greek world show how unrepresentative this is. Even in Athens, a city that would appear to offer the strongest case for this image of the Trojan, important qualifications have to be made, as Chapter Three will argue.

Yet the influence of classical Athens has been so great that it has shaped the subsequent literary and intellectual tradition, both ancient and modern. Where Homer spoke of 'Achaians' and 'Trojans', his ancient commentators, well-versed in Athenian literature, wrote of 'Greeks' and 'barbarians' and depicted them accordingly.[18] Modern commentators have often adopted rather similar interpretations, although generally refraining from using the term 'barbarian'.[19] Ancient scholarly traditions combine with a more modern ambivalence towards the east. William Mure captures the tone in his mid-nineteenth-century history of Greek literature:

Allusion has already been made to certain defects in the character of the Trojans incidentally stigmatised in the *Iliad*, either by Homer himself or his heroes; to their want of moral principle, to the levity and treachery of their international dealings, to the palpable injustice of their cause, to their obstinacy in upholding it, and to the profligacy of their domestic manners. How far these defects, as compared with the rightful motives, fair dealing, and primitive habits of their adversaries, may be laid to account of Homer's national partialities, how far they may rest on a historical basis, are questions on which it were little profit to enlarge. The contrast itself may, at least, be considered shadowing forth certain fundamental features of distinction, which have always been more or less observable between the European and Asiatic races.[20]

---

[18] See Epilogue. It also permeates through to Roman literary circles, cf. Verg. *Aen.* 2. 504, 11. 768–80 and further references in Galinsky 1969: 98 n. 94.

[19] E. Hall 1989: 22 on Bowra 1930: 241 is hardly justified.

[20] Mure 1854: 340–1, cf. description of Priam's court as 'an interesting combination of patriarchal simplicity with Oriental licentiousness' (p. 342). For such 19th-cent. Western attitudes to the East, Said 1978. Mure's history was 'something of a standard work', Jenkyns 1980: 208.

More recent writing may not be as harsh, but the underlying assumption that the Trojan is a barbarian can still be found. Jasper Griffin may stay strictly with Achaian/Trojan nomenclature, but barbarian stereotypes are again evident: 'The Trojans lose because they are the sort of people they are—glamorous, reckless, frivolous, undisciplined.' Marchinus van der Valk can present the *Iliad* as a nationalistic epic, exemplifying Greek superiority. M. W. Edwards can write of the Trojan War as 'a mighty Greek achievement against a foreign foe', while there is no equivocation apparent in the words of Fernand Robert: 'L'*Iliade* est un poème de l'hellenisme uni contre le Barbare.'[21] Even the more restrained frequently turn Homer's Achaians into Greeks and thus implicitly turn his Trojans into enemies of the Greeks.[22] It is little wonder, then, that modern historians of Rome's Trojan ancestry should also assume that Greeks in general characterized the Trojans as barbarians and enemies. The historians too are falling under the influence of Athens.[23]

Elsewhere, however, a different picture emerges. Scattered round the Greek world were the tombs of famous Trojans, cities with Trojan founders, temples with Trojan relics, and even Greeks with Trojan names. All this made the Trojan past part of the Greek present. Rather than identifying totally with one side and rejecting the other as alien, Greek cities would often look to both sides in the conflict. It was one of the great wars of the heroic age, a war not between Greeks and barbarians but one between heroes. Even if the majority of Greeks did tend to identify more closely with the Achaians than the Trojans, the heroic past and heroic ancestry were always things to be valued.[24]

This willingness to embrace the Trojan rather than to anathematize it and celebrate victory over it finds expression in a passage of the *Odyssey*. Odysseus, a guest at the court of the Phaiakians, asks the bard Demodokos to sing of the fall of Troy:

He sang how the sons of the Achaians laid waste the town of Troy,

---

[21] J. Griffin 1980: 5–6, Van der Valk 1953, Edwards 1987: 173, F. Robert 1950: 310 ('The *Iliad* is a poem about Hellenism united against the Barbarian').

[22] For instance de Jong 1987: e.g. 57, 160, Stanley 1993; the Oxford commentary on the *Iliad* varies from volume to volume, Kirk, Hainsworth (Achaians), Janko, Edwards (Greeks).

[23] When the assumption is justified, reference is usually made to the 5th-cent. Athenian tragedy and/or historiography, cf. Perret 1942: 419–21, Malkin 1998: 203.

[24] See Ch. 4.

pouring out of the horse, abandoning their hollow ambush. He sang how they sacked that lofty city, one going one way, one another; how Odysseus, accompanied by great Menelaos, went like Ares to the house of Deiphobos. There, he said, Odysseus braved a most dreadful fight but with the help of great-hearted Athena he emerged the victor.

These things the famous minstrel sang. Odysseus melted and below his eyes tears moistened his cheeks. Imagine a woman wailing as she falls to embrace her beloved husband, who fell in battle before his city and his people, trying to protect his town and his children from destruction. Seeing him dying and struggling to breath she clasps him and howls loudly. As she does so, men behind her beat her back and shoulders with their spears and lead her into slavery, to a life of labour and misery. Her cheeks are ravaged by the most piteous grief. Just so did Odysseus let fall piteous tears from beneath his brows.

Through this stark and striking image Homer conflates Odysseus' reaction to the song with the suffering of the people in the captured city. Odysseus becomes at once the sacker and the sacked, the victor and the victim.[25]

Augustus determines the chronological limit of the book, because his vigorous promotion of the Trojan myth changed its whole status in the Roman Empire. He also offers a suitable starting point, and for rather similar reasons. Augustus and the nature of the Trojan myth in Rome are the subject of Part I, because so much of the evidence for the earlier period is a product of a world formed by Augustus. His influence must, therefore, be confronted at the beginning of this book. It will be seen that knowledge of the myth both in Rome and among the Greeks was probably more limited and more scattered than often imagined. Augustus himself will be a recurring presence throughout the book.

Part II focuses on more exclusively Greek concerns. In order to understand what Rome's Trojan past may have meant to the Greeks, it is necessary to consider the place of Troy and the Trojans in the Greek world. Chapter Two, 'Homer and the Archaic Age', therefore, examines Homer's work and its potential for allowing different and often conflicting interpretations. Something of these various interpretations can be observed in the chapters that follow. Here the subject is not merely the well-recorded case of Athens with all its art and literature but the local traditions of numerous, rather more poorly documented cities.

[25] Hom. *Od.* 8. 516–31, a passage which has provoked many interpretations, M. Lloyd 1987: 87–9.

What results is a remarkable diversity and an assertion of the individuality of Greek cities, however obscure they may be.

Building on these first two parts, Part III explores the role of the myth in the relationship between Greeks and Romans. Initially the story of Rome's Trojan past developed out of the interplay of Greek and Roman in Italy, the theme of 'Troy and the Western Greeks', the opening chapter of Part III. I then go on to examine the way in which this Trojan ancestry was used in diplomacy, the part it played in the introduction to Rome of two new gods, Venus Erycina and the Magna Mater, and finally the significance of the city of Ilion itself for both Greeks and Romans. Repeatedly Troy can be seen to perform a mediating role, not in a general sense, but specifically between the Romans and those Greeks who themselves could look to some form of Trojan past.

Throughout this whole period Rome and its relations with the Greeks underwent considerable change, so it is useful to outline at this point the historical background. The many Greek colonies in southern Italy, some dating from as early as the eighth century BC, meant that Rome had long been on the edge of the Greek world. By the early third century increasing control of the Italian peninsula brought Rome into conflict with southern Italian Greeks, who called upon the Epirote king, Pyrrhos, to assist them in their struggle. His failure allowed the Romans to complete their takeover of Italy. Nonetheless, Rome's major concern in the third century was not with Greeks but with the North African city of Carthage, its opponent in two destructive and lengthy wars. During this time Rome was not uninvolved with the Greek world across the Adriatic, as several brief incursions in the latter part of the third century demonstrate, but anything more substantial had to wait until after the defeat of Carthage in 202.

At the beginning of the second century the Greek east and its cities were ruled by four main kingdoms, the Antigonids in Macedon, the Seleukids in Syria, the Ptolemies in Egypt, and the newer, upstart dynasty of the Attalids in Asia Minor. By the time the century was hardly more than a decade old, Rome had already defeated two of these once-great kingdoms, first Carthage's former ally Philip V of Macedon, and not long afterwards the Seleukid king Antiochos the Great. The Greek cities of the eastern Mediterranean increasingly had to address themselves to the question of the growing power of Rome. By the end of the second century Macedon and Asia had become Roman provinces, while the Seleukids and Ptolemies had little choice but to recognize Roman authority. The following century would see the disappearance of both these kingdoms, Egypt becoming the personal property of Augustus.

My stress on the Greek context has meant that I have tried to avoid becoming too entangled in the numerous debates about the myth in early Rome, Latium, and Etruria. Instead I have sought to keep the Greek viewpoint in the forefront and have concentrated only on those issues that seemed particularly relevant, notably in Chapter One, 'The Recovery of Trojan Rome', and Chapter Five, 'Troy and the Western Greeks'. A similar concern is reflected in my decision to transliterate Greek names rather than latinize them, at least in so far as is reasonable, except in those sections that clearly deal with Latin texts or a Roman context (thus usually Aineias rather than Aeneas, Ilion rather than Ilium).[26] This will, I hope, give extra emphasis to the search for a Greek perspective and in general reinforce the Greekness of the subject matter, but the enormous influence of Augustus means that a beginning needs to be made in Rome itself.

[26] In this I largely follow the conventions of *Der kleine Pauly: Lexikon der Antike*, ed. K. Ziegler and W. Sontheimer (Stuttgart 1964–75).

Part I

Rome

1

The Recovery of Trojan Rome

After the fall of Troy Aeneas and his band of Trojan survivors fled westwards. Their wanderings stopped only when they had arrived in central Italy, where they founded two settlements, Lavinium and Alba Longa. Later, and more importantly, the descendants of these Trojan refugees in the persons of Romulus and Remus established a third settlement in Latium, the city of Rome. Trojan origins are here an essential feature of the foundation story of Rome.

The fullest surviving accounts of this story date from the reign of Augustus, the work of Vergil, Livy, and Dionysios of Halikarnassos.[1] It is no coincidence that they all come from this period. This was a time when the rulers of Rome, Augustus and his predecessor Caesar, were promoting their family's Trojan descent. This family, the Iulii, claimed Trojan ancestry through Aeneas and Aeneas' son or grandson, Iulus, and divine ancestry through Aeneas' mother, Venus. It was a good pedigree. Augustus like Caesar had acquired his pre-eminent position as a result of civil war. He could exploit Aeneas to justify and legitimize his dominance of Roman politics. It showed that his rule was based not simply on military force but on ancestry as well. Augustus had 'restored the Republic', so it was only appropriate that his ancestors should have been among the founding figures of the state. Troy and Aeneas were part of the ideology of the new regime, symbolizing the refoundation and regeneration of Rome after the destruction of the civil wars.

This, however, raises questions. What was the situation before the Iulii came to power? How important was this myth of Trojan origins before Augustus and Caesar started promoting it? For many scholars it was already an essential element of the Roman sense of their own identity, that is to say their sense of what it was

---

[1] Verg. *Aen.*, Livy 1. 1–7, Dion. Hal. *Ant. Rom.* 1. 45–89; other roughly contemporary accounts are Strabo 5. 3. 2, Diod. Sic. 7. 4–6 (somewhat mutilated), and Pompeius Trogus as epitomized by Just. *Epit.* 43. 1–3.

to be Roman. This conception of the centrality of the myth was well expressed by E. J. Bickerman when he described 'the belief in the Trojan parentage of the city' as 'an article of the Roman national creed'. Debate has tended to focus not on whether this is correct but rather on when and in what circumstances it came about. Erich Gruen has written: 'The Trojan connection had entrenched itself in Roman consciousness by the early third century.' Arnaldo Momigliano went earlier still: 'the Trojan legend appears to have taken root in Rome and in the rest of Latium not later than the early fourth century BC'. Andreas Alföldi would, nonetheless, push the date back a century or so; the myth was brought to Latium, and thus to Rome, by Etruscan rule over the region in the sixth century BC.[2] It is worth considering the words being used in these examples: 'Roman national creed', 'entrenched', 'taken root'. There is nothing superficial here about the Roman adoption of a myth of Trojan origins; it is envisaged as a fundamental feature of the Roman view of themselves. There are exceptions to this comparative consensus. Jacques Perret argued that the whole story was invented by the Epirote king Pyrrhos during his war with Rome in the third century BC; Pyrrhos wanted to be the new Achilles, so he made the Romans his Trojans. The idea proved attractive to the Romans, at least for a while, although it finally fell into abeyance until revived by Caesar.[3]

Too often modern discussions have given insufficient attention to the impact of the Iulii on our knowledge of Republican traditions about Troy.[4] Consequently there has been a tendency to overestimate the importance of Troy in the self-image of Republican Rome. The present chapter seeks to reassess this picture. It is, therefore, necessary to begin with the Iulii in order to see how they may have influenced our understanding of the place of the myth in the Republic.

---

[2] Bickerman 1952: 67, Gruen 1992: 31, Momigliano 1984: 448, Alföldi 1957: 14–19, 1965: 278–87, cf. Cornell 1995: 68, who tentatively accepts the possibility of the 6th cent., although Cornell 1977: 82–3 doubted that it was known in Rome before the 3rd cent.

[3] Perret 1942; this enormous and comprehensive work often appears in footnotes but its insights can get lost in his rather perverse insistence on holding Pyrrhos responsible for everything, cf. the important reviews by Boyancé 1943 and Momigliano 1945.

[4] An important exception is Horsfall 1987: 20–4.

I. TROY AND THE IULII

Under the patronage of Augustus' friend, Maecenas, Vergil made Aeneas the subject of an epic poem to rival Homer's *Iliad* and *Odyssey* combined. The *Aeneid* told the story of Aeneas' flight from Troy and his battle to establish himself and his refugee Trojans in a new home in Italy. The choice of Aeneas as the central figure can be seen as being in harmony with Augustus' own public image as a descendant of the Trojan hero.[5] Even without direct references the poem's relevance to Augustus would have been clear. Vergil, nevertheless, removes any doubt by the inclusion of several passages that prophesy the future glory not only of the Romans but of the Iulii and Augustus in particular. Just as it is the destiny of Aeneas to reach Italy, so it is the destiny of his descendant Augustus to rule Rome. Nor does Vergil delay in making this point; it is made in the very first book and given especial authority by being placed in the mouth of Jupiter himself.[6] Later in the poem, when Vulcan makes a shield for Aeneas, it is intricately decorated with events which are destined to happen during the course of Rome's history. The centrepiece is Augustus' victory at the battle of Actium and the triumphs that followed, to which fifty-four of the one hundred lines are devoted.[7] But the most vivid presentation of future Roman greatness occurs when Aeneas' father, Anchises, now a permanent resident in the underworld, seeks to boost the morale of his visiting son by showing him the souls of great Romans yet to be born. After Romulus come the Iulii:

Now turn your two eyes in this direction and look at this family of yours, your own Romans. Here is Caesar, and all the sons of Iulus about to come under the great vault of the sky. Here is the man whose coming you so often hear prophesied, here he is, Augustus Caesar, son of a god, the man who will bring back the golden years to the fields of Latium once ruled over by Saturn, and extend Rome's empire beyond the Indians and the Garamantes.[8]

[5] The political character of the *Aeneid* and Augustan poetry in general has been the subject of much debate, see esp. J. Griffin 1984, G. Williams 1990, the articles collected in Powell 1992 (esp. Powell's own contribution), and White 1993.

[6] Verg. *Aen.* 1. 257–96.

[7] For the shield: Verg. *Aen.* 8. 608–731; Augustus and Actium: 8. 675–728, on which Hardie 1986, Gurval 1995: 209–47.

[8] Verg. *Aen.* 6. 788–95, trans. D. West 1990.

Just as Actium is the centrepiece of the shield, so this parade of great Romans is located at the centre of the *Aeneid*.

Nowadays Vergil's *Aeneid* may be treated as the embodiment of Rome and Augustus' Trojan past, but it was only one aspect of a much wider celebration of the Trojan myth, all with a particular focus on Aeneas, son of Venus and ancestor of the Iulii. It features in literature, relief sculpture, statuary, paintings, and coins; sometimes it was produced on the initiative of Augustus, at other times it was a reflection of this official stance, although this is a distinction that it is often hard to make in practice.

The new Forum of Augustus emphasized the importance of the Iulii and their links with Aeneas. The temple of Mars Ultor, which was built as a result of a vow Augustus had made at the battle of Philippi, was the focus of the Forum and contained cult statues of Mars, Venus, and the deified Caesar. On either side of the Forum there was a colonnade. In one there was a statue of Aeneas carrying his father Anchises and holding his son by the hand. Alongside Aeneas are the kings of Alba Longa and statues of the Iulian family. Facing them in the other colonnade are Romulus and famous men of Rome's past, such as Scipio Aemilianus, Sulla, Pompey and Lucullus, wearing triumphal dress. Placing the Iulii opposite the rest of Rome's great men asserted the superiority of the Iulii, and the presence of Aeneas and his family among them justified that superiority.[9] A similar balance is to be found in the Ara Pacis, erected by the Senate in honour of Augustus. On one side are the assembled senators, on the other Augustus and his family. Around the corner from Augustus is Aeneas sacrificing a sow, an act that happened on the spot where Lavinium was founded, thus drawing attention to the role of Aeneas as a founder and by association to Augustus as a new founder.[10]

Augustus' sponsorship of Aeneas and the Trojan myth is evident throughout his career, initially perhaps as a means of emphasizing his relationship with Caesar. Already in 42 BC, only two years after the murder of his adoptive father, Octavian was minting coins with his own head on one side and Aeneas carrying Anchises on the other. The same year also saw the appearance of

---

[9] Suet. *Aug.* 29. 1–2, 31. 5, Ovid, *Fasti* 5. 545–78, Pliny *HN* 22. 13, *Hist. Aug. Alex. Sev.* 28. 6, *Inscr. Ital.* 13. 3, pp. 1–36, Zanker 1988: 192–215, setting the Forum within the context of Augustan ideology.

[10] Ara Pacis: Simon 1967, Zanker 1988: 203–6, Galinsky 1996: 141–55; cf. the Belvedere Altar for the same theme in a less elevated form: Zanker 1969, Galinsky 1996: 319–21.

the goddess Venus on his coinage.[11] Later Trojan ancestry could reinforce his image as the new founder of Rome. When Horace was commissioned to write his *Secular Hymn* for the games which were to inaugurate a new era in 17 BC, he appropriately devoted several stanzas to celebrating the Trojan origins of Rome and Augustus.[12] Doubtless, too, Augustus encouraged the work of his freedman C. Iulius Hyginus, whose book on Trojan families, *De familiis Troianis*, would have proved a useful reference manual when planning such things as the colonnades of the Forum of Augustus.[13]

The direction had already been set by Caesar, who placed great emphasis on his own relationship with Venus.[14] The temple of Venus Genetrix was built as the focal point of his new Forum Iulium. The bust of Venus appears on the obverse of several coins issued by Caesar in the forties; in one instance she is backed by Aeneas carrying Anchises and the Palladium, the sacred image rescued from Troy.[15] So close was Caesar's association with Venus that even as early as March 49 M. Caelius Rufus could write to Cicero and refer to Caesar simply as *Venere prognatus*, offspring of Venus.[16] It was also said that 'Venus' was used by Caesar as the password at the battle of Munda in 45.[17] The Trojan character of Venus was emphasized not only by the juxtaposition of Venus and Aeneas on the same coin, but also by the revival of the Troy Game, *lusus Troiae*, in the context of the dedication of the Temple of Venus in 46.[18] The origins of this equestrian game for young patricians are obscure, but Vergil would later locate its roots in the funeral games organized by Aeneas for his father Anchises.[19] Augustus was to make much of the *lusus Troiae*, putting members

[11] Aeneas: Crawford 1974: 502, *BMCRR* i, nos. 4257–8, Fuchs 1973: 626; Venus: Crawford 1974: 503, *BMCRR* i, no. 4277, cf. later, *BMCRE* i, nos. 98–9 (16 BC). The dates given in the text are those of Crawford, *BMCRR* give *c*.39 and *c*.38 respectively.

[12] Hor. *Carm. Saec.* esp. lines 37–52; on the games as the inauguration of a new era, Zanker 1988: 167–72 and the more restrained Galinsky 1996: 100–6.

[13] Peter *HRR* 2 F14, cf. Varro's earlier work on the same subject, Peter *HRR* 2, xxxii–xxxiii; on both Toohey 1984.

[14] Weinstock 1971: 80–91, cf. Suet. *Iul.* 6, App. *BC* 2. 68, Dio 43. 43. 3.

[15] Weinstock 1971: plate 6.10–12, Crawford 1974: 471, 479, 493–5; on Aeneas and Anchises motif, Fuchs 1973: 624–7.

[16] Caelius in Cic. *Fam.* 8. 15. 2.

[17] App. *BC* 2. 104, cf. 2. 76, Serv. on *Aen.* 7. 637, Weinstock 1971: 83.

[18] Dio 43. 22, Suet. *Iul.* 39. 2; for later examples, Suet. *Aug.* 43. 2, Dio 49. 43. 3, 51. 22. 4, 54. 26. 1; on the Troy Game, Weinstock 1971: 88–9, Weeber 1974.

[19] Verg. *Aen.* 5. 503–603.

of his family such as his stepson Tiberius and his grandsons C. Caesar and Agrippa Postumus in important roles.[20]

After defeating Pompey at Pharsalos in 48 Caesar bestowed various privileges upon Ilion, a city that, like himself, claimed descent from the Troy of Homer.[21] The cities of Asia Minor took note and accordingly honoured Caesar as 'descendant of Ares and Aphrodite'.[22] In Rome rumours may have circulated that Caesar intended to transfer the capital to Ilion.[23] Desire to imitate Alexander or to promote his family's Trojan origin for Roman domestic consumption may have played their part, but Caesar's treatment of Ilion should also be understood within the context of the Greek east, which had largely supported the wrong side in the civil war. Caesar was one of a series of leaders, stretching back to Xerxes, who sought support in the Greek world by showing their respect for Ilion.[24]

Caesar's use of Venus and Troy emphasized the antiquity and importance of his family, and divine ancestry would have given him a certain numinous aura. But more specific use was also made of this Trojan past. Dionysios of Halikarnassos tells of a dispute over the succession to Ascanius between Silvius, Ascanius' brother, and Iulus, Ascanius' son. The conflict was resolved by a vote of the people; Silvius was made king, but Iulus was given special religious authority, which according to Dionysios was still held by Iulus' descendants.[25] This religious authority is surely the office of Pontifex Maximus, held by Caesar since 63 and Augustus since 12 BC. The story was already current by about 30 BC, when Diodoros included a version in his history.[26] Caesar may well have been using Iulus to boost his credibility as Pontifex Maximus, perhaps during his election campaign of 63. A very junior candidate for the post, he was alleged to have been successful only because he was so generous with his bribes.[27] Alternatively, the story may have emerged in the thirties, when there was pressure to depose the incumbent Pontifex Maximus and replace him with Octavian.[28]

[20] Suet. *Tib.* 6. 4, Dio 54. 26. 1, 55. 10. 6.   [21] Strabo 13. 1. 27.
[22] *SIG*³ 760.   [23] Suet. *Iul.* 79. 3 or to Alexandria.
[24] See below, Ch. 9.   [25] Dion. Hal. *Ant. Rom.* 1. 70.
[26] Diod. Sic. 7. 5. 8, known only through an Armenian translation of Eusebios' *Chronicle*. On date of Diodoros' history, Sacks 1990: 161.
[27] Plut. *Caes.* 7. 1–4, Suet. *Iul.* 13, Gelzer 1960: 42, Meier 1982: 205–6.
[28] Cf. Dio 49. 15.3, 54. 15, 54. 27. 2.

Caesar was not the first of the Iulii to highlight his Trojan roots. Venus in a chariot, or to be more precise a *biga*, appears on the reverse of denarii minted by Sex. Iulius Caesar in 129 and again on the denarii of L. Iulius Caesar in 103 BC, although here the link with Troy is implicit rather than explicit.[29] In alluding to their ancestry in this way the Iulii were following a practice which had become increasingly common among Roman moneyers from the mid-second century onwards.[30] Furthermore, epigraphic evidence from Ilion reveals at least one member of the family to have been a benefactor of the city.[31] So, even before Caesar, Iulii are found showing respect for both Venus and Ilion, but one should be wary of concluding from this that they were already presenting themselves as descendants of Venus. Another Roman family, the Memmii, provides a useful comparison. In the late second and early first century BC moneyers from a fairly obscure part of this family put Venus on their coins, but the only evidence for their ancestry suggests that, although they claimed Trojan origins, it was not from Aeneas but from his companion Mnestheus, descendant of Assaracus.[32] The presence of Venus on their coins can be explained not as a claim to divine descent, but as an allusion to Venus' role as protector of the Trojans and therefore to the family's Trojan background.

Heroic ancestry was not uncommon among the Roman aristocracy. The Mamilii traced their family back to Odysseus and Circe, the Fabii to Hercules, and the Caecilii to Caeculus, son of Vulcan.[33] Trojan ancestry was one of many such legendary genealogies. In the competitive world of the Republican aristocrat these mythical ancestors not only asserted the antiquity of the family but also conferred distinction and prestige. How many began their family tree in Troy is difficult to determine. It might

---

[29] Weinstock 1971: 17, pl. 3. 1–2, Crawford 1974: 284, 325, identified as *RE* Iulius 150 and 142 respectively. Dates are Crawford's.

[30] Wikander 1993: 78–80.

[31] *I.Ilion* 10. 3–6, 71, 72, see Ch. 9.4 below.

[32] Weinstock 1971: 23–4, Crawford 1974: 322–3 (106 BC), 363–4 (87 BC); Trojan ancestry is also alluded to in Lucr. 1.1–2; Mnestheus: Verg. *Aen.* 5.116–17 with Serv. ad loc., cf. Verg. *Aen.* 5. 184, 12. 127. Evans 1992: 28, however, thinks the Venus coins mean that the Memmii too claimed divine descent.

[33] Mamilii: Livy 1. 49. 9, Dion. Hal. *Ant. Rom.* 4. 45. 1, Crawford 1974: 219–20, 375–7; Ogilvie 1965: 199; Fabii: Festus 77L, s.v. 'Fovi', Plut. *Fab.* 1. 2; Caecilii: Solin. 2. 9, Cato *Orig.* bk. 2 F29, Serv. on Verg. *Aen.* 7. 678, Festus 38L. On these and others, Wiseman 1974, cf. also Wikander 1993.

be tempting to infer from the size of Varro's lost four-volume work on Trojan families that it was a fair number, but many of these Trojan genealogies may have been of recent date, a consequence of increased late Republican interest, or, more particularly, of Caesar's promotion of his own Trojan past. At some point, for instance, the Caecilii abandoned their former legendary ties for more fashionable Trojan ancestors.[34] The evidence for these Trojan families tends to be Augustan or later; they include the Sergii, the Cluentii, the Aemilii, and the Iunii.[35] Dionysios of Halikarnassos can say that there were fifty Trojan families in Rome in his own time, a figure perhaps gleaned from a reading of the work of Varro or Hyginus.[36]

What distinguished the Iulii, however, was their claim to be related to Aeneas himself and in turn to Venus. The divine descent of the Iulii is first attested in C. Iulius Caesar's funeral *laudatio* for his aunt Iulia in 69 BC.[37] Fundamental to this claim was the shadowy figure of Iulus. Some writers such as Vergil seem to have chosen the awkward expedient of saying that Iulus was merely another name for Ascanius, thus making him the son of Aeneas and ruler of Alba Longa.[38] Others preferred to add Iulus as an extra son of Ascanius who gained no political power, although he did acquire priestly power.[39] Both positions reveal Iulus to have been a late addition to the family tree of Aeneas, although the date of this addition remains obscure. The first to commit the Iulus/Ascanius identification to writing may have been a certain L. Iulius Caesar, author of a work, now lost and without a title, which appears to have dealt with early Rome.

---

[34] For Varro's *De familiis Troianis*, Peter *HRR* 2, xxxii–xxxiii, cf. Hyginus' later work, see n. 13 above with accompanying text. On families changing genealogical allegiance, Wiseman 1974: 158.

[35] Peter *HRR* 2, xxxii–xxxiii, who notes, in addition to the Memmii, the Sergii, the Cluentii (Verg. *Aen.* 5. 117–22), the Geganii (Serv. on *Aen.* 5. 119), the Iunii (Dion. Hal. *Ant. Rom.* 4. 68. 1), the Aemilii (Festus 22L), the Caecilii (Festus 38L), the Cloelii (Festus 48L). On Trojan families, see also Wiseman 1974, Toohey 1984, Weinstock in *RE* 19. 1, col. 446–7, s.v. 'Penates'.

[36] Dion. Hal. *Ant. Rom.* 1. 85. 3.

[37] Suet. *Iul.* 6. 1.

[38] 'Puer Ascanius, cui nunc cognomen Iulo additur', Verg. *Aen.* 1. 267 with Serv. ad loc. Vergil uses 'Iulus' 35 times and 'Ascanius' 41 times, Austin 1964: 216, 1971: 103–4. Ascanius was something of a chameleon; Dion. Hal. *Ant. Rom.* 1. 65. 1 notes that he was originally called Euryleon but changed his name on the flight from Troy. No wonder Dionysios preferred to have Iulus as the son of Ascanius.

[39] Dion. Hal. *Ant. Rom.* 1. 70; priestly power, see nn. 25–8 above with accompanying text.

Perhaps the consul of 64, he is said to have written that Ascanius changed his name to Iulus after his killing of Mezentius. It is possible but less likely that the identification had earlier been made by Cato in his *Origins*.[40] Whichever is the case, the Iulii clearly played an important and self-interested role in propagating this version of the story. Grafting themselves onto the family tree of Aeneas, they transformed themselves from ordinary Trojan Romans into élite Trojans.

2. THE MYTH BEFORE THE IULII: NEUTRAL CITATIONS?

The myth of Aeneas and Rome's Trojan origins was of central importance in Augustan propaganda. The Iulii exploited it to elevate themselves, but a corollary of this may have been that the myth itself was elevated to a prominence which it had never possessed previously. In the years that followed it became accepted throughout the Greek and Roman world as the standard version of the origins of Rome, but what about the early history of the myth?

Here the Augustan age presents a major problem, because it skews the evidence for the period that precedes it. Many pre-Augustan writers are said to have mentioned Troy's role in Rome's origins. These include the Greek historians Hellanikos, Hegesianax of Alexandreia Troas, Diokles of Peparethos, the Roman historians Q. Fabius Pictor, Cato the Elder, L. Cassius Hemina, Q. Fabius Maximus, L. Calpurnius Piso Frugi, Q. Lutatius Catulus, L. Coelius Antipater, A. Postumius Albinus, the Arkadian poet Agathyllos, the Latin poets Ennius and Naevius.[41]

---

[40] Serv. Auct. on *Aen.* 1. 267 explicitly attributes its information about the name-change to Caesar, but the shorter Servius omits Caesar's name and thus implies that Cato, who had earlier been cited, is the source, Cato *Orig.* bk. 1 F9a (for the greater reliability of Servius Auctus' citations, R. B. Lloyd 1961; see sect. 2 below on Servius). In the context of Ascanius' name-change (with a different explanation) *OGR* 15. 5 refers to Caesar and Cato but two points must be made: first, *OGR* only explicitly cites them for the Iulian descent from Iulus; secondly the citation of Cato may come from Caesar (*OGR* cites Caesar 9 times, Cato 2), so it becomes even less clear what Cato actually wrote, Momigliano 1958: 69 with n. 56. On the debate and etymologies of Iulus, Weinstock 1971: 9–11, Richard 1983a. On *OGR*, see next section.

[41] Hellanikos: Dion. Hal. *Ant. Rom.* 1. 72. 2 (*FGrH* 4F84); Hegesianax: Dion. Hal. *Ant. Rom.* 1. 72. 1 (*FGrH* 45F9); Diokles: Plut. *Rom.* 3. 1–2 (*FGrH* 820); Fabius Pictor: Cic. *Div.* 1. 43, Diod. Sic. 7. 5, Plut. *Rom.* 3. 1–2 (*FGrH* 809F1, 2, 4); Cato: Frags. of *Origins* bk 1, nos. 6–14; Cassius, Fabius Maximus, Piso, Lutatius, Coelius, Postumius, see n. 56 below; Agathyllos: Dion. Hal. *Ant. Rom.* 1. 49. 2 (*FGrH* 321F2); Ennius: Frags. of *Annals* bk 1

This is a formidable and varied list of authorities, but for all their diversity these writers have one thing in common: their discussions of Rome's Trojan past are lost, a circumstance that gives much scope to speculation. Indeed with the sole exception of Cato's not a single work by any of these many writers survives today.

Our knowledge of them has to depend largely on citations made in the Augustan period or later. The selection of material, therefore, reflects not the concerns of the original writers but those of Augustan Rome. Without the Augustan emphasis on the myth very little of this would have survived at all. Nor can we be sure that the citations are accurate representations of what was originally written. Quotations are rare, so usually we must be satisfied with the gist of what was written.[42] Yet, a thorough knowledge of the *Aeneid* might have contaminated a reading of Cato and led an incautious or overenthusiastic reader to fill in the gaps.

An exhaustive examination of all these later writers who yield glimpses of their predecessors is not possible here, but two examples will serve to demonstrate the nature of the problem. The first will be Dionysios of Halikarnassos, a Greek historian living in Rome during the reign of Augustus. The second will be the ancient commentators on Vergil's *Aeneid*, who often cite now lost writers in order to illuminate their chosen text.

Dionysios devotes the first book of his *Roman Antiquities* to the prehistory of Rome, that is to say the events leading up to the foundation of Rome. In the course of this book he cites a very large number of Greek and Roman writers on early Italian and Roman history. It is curious that, although he cites many Roman authors in his first book, none is included by name in the long section on Rome's Trojan past. This could be evidence for a lack of material on the subject in earlier Roman authors, but it could also be that where Dionysios had a choice between Greek and Roman authors he preferred Greeks, perhaps believing them to be more reliable, or perhaps because of a simple chauvinistic preference for anything Greek. It can hardly be a linguistic preference,

---

(Skutsch); Naevius: frags. of *Bellum Punicum* collected in *FPL*. These and other lost writers on events leading up to foundation of Rome can be found collected in *FGrH* 840, Plut. *Rom.* 2–3, Festus 326–8L, Serv. Auct. on *Aen.* 1. 273. Many are translated in the appendix to Wiseman 1995.

[42] See the important cautionary remarks of Brunt 1980.

because Fabius Pictor and other early Roman historians did write their histories in Greek.[43] Or he may be using Roman sources without acknowledgement.[44] With the story of Romulus and Remus, however, Roman historians begin to displace Greeks in the text. Reference is made to Q. Fabius Pictor, L. Cincius Alimentus, M. Porcius Cato, L. Calpurnius Piso, Q. Aelius Tubero.[45] Perhaps this is a sign that Romulus was more important than Aeneas to Romans of the Republic, but it could equally be that this was the point at which Greek historians lost interest.

The purpose of Dionysios' history was to prove that the Romans were really Greeks.[46] This may have been an idiosyncratic project, but the way he goes about it was thoroughly in keeping with his time, reflecting the contemporary Augustan interest in the Trojan myth and the foundation of Rome. The Trojan origins of Rome were potentially damaging to his thesis that the Romans were Greeks, so he might have been expected to minimize them or even deny them altogether, but, on the contrary, he accepts and even elaborates them. He neatly circumvents any objection this might pose to his thesis by arguing that the Trojans were Greeks too, whose ancestor Dardanos originally came to the Troad from Arkadia.[47] With the Trojans safely Hellenized, approximately one-third of the first book is concerned with Trojans, and Aeneas in particular.[48]

Much of this Trojan section is not relevant to his carefully constructed argument to show the succession of Greek peoples who emigrated to Italy, but it does reflect the Augustan preoccupation with Aeneas. Many ancient writers are introduced into his discussions about how Aeneas escaped from Troy, his route to Italy and especially on the foundation of Rome itself. Thus, Hellanikos' *Troika* is cited for Aeneas' escape from Troy, Menekrates of

[43] Badian 1966: 2–7; Dion. Hal. *Ant. Rom.* 1. 73 cites several Roman accounts of the Trojan prehistory of Rome, but does not name authorities. Significantly one ch. is sufficient.

[44] Varro, for instance, has often been suggested for Dion. Hal.'s account (1. 49–53) of Aeneas' wanderings, cf. Perret 1942: 582–96, but see Poucet 1989*b*.

[45] Pictor, Alimentus, Cato: 1. 74. 1, 79. 4; Piso: 79. 4; Tubero: 80. 1.

[46] Dion. Hal. *Ant. Rom.* 1. 5, 1. 89–90, 4. 26. 5, 7. 70, 7. 72. 18, Gabba 1991: 93–147.

[47] Dion. Hal. *Ant. Rom.* 1. 61–2; Dionysios is perhaps aware that this is not wholly convincing—thus they form only one part of Greek emigration to Italy. Vergil, on the other hand, gives Dardanus an Italian origin, *Aen.* 1. 380, 3. 167–8, 7. 205–8, 240, Austin 1971: 137.

[48] Dion. Hal. *Ant. Rom.* 1. 45–73, out of 90 chapters.

Xanthos for his betrayal of Troy, Hegesianax of Alexandreia Troas and Hegesippos for Aeneas' death in Thrace, Ariaithos and Agathyllos for his time in Arkadia, Timaios for sacred objects in Lavinium.[49] There is also the 'author of the history of the priestesses at Argos', usually identified with Hellanikos, who controversially has Aeneas come to Italy from the land of the Molossians and found Rome with or after Odysseus.[50] Nevertheless, these authorities will not have been as interested in Aeneas and the foundation of Rome as Dionysios and his contemporaries. For these earlier writers Aeneas was relevant but marginal. In Augustan Rome he was central, a distinguished ancestor of the ruler, as Dionysios was aware.[51] Scholars studying lost historians and the mythology of early Rome have so little to work with that they are often tempted to extract as much as possible from Dionysios and overinterpret his sometimes rather sketchy citations. Yet in doing this they may be doing exactly what Dionysios himself was doing to his own sources.[52]

Dionysios was writing in Rome and largely followed the prevailing view there,[53] but he was also a Greek and he knew that many Greeks were unaware of or even rejected stories of Aeneas' role in the development of Rome. The ignorance or scepticism of historians about the arrival of Aeneas in Italy is the subject of repeated complaints from Dionysios.[54] So the emphasis on Aeneas in book one appears to be the result of a determination on Dionysios' part to persuade his Greek audience that the Augustan version of Rome's past is the right one.[55] Consequently, even when Dionysios gathers together alternative versions, as he does

---

[49] Hellanikos: 1. 48. 1 (*FGrH* 4F31), Menekrates: 1. 48. 3 (*FGrH* 769F3), Hegesianax (in the guise of Kephalon of Gergis) and Hegesippos: 1. 49. 1 (*FGrH* 45F7, 391F5), Ariaithos and Agathyllos: 1. 49. 1–2 (*FGrH* 316F1, 321F2), Timaios: 1. 67. 4 (*FGrH* 566F59).

[50] Dion. Hal. *Ant. Rom.* 72. 2 (*FGrH* 4F84); this tangled text (μετ' Ὀδυσσέως or Ὀδυσσέα?) is treated sceptically by Horsfall 1979*b*: 379–83, 1987: 15–16, in contrast to Solmsen 1986. It may also mean that Aeneas arrived with/after Odysseus.

[51] Dion. Hal. *Ant. Rom.* 1. 70. 4; whether Dionysios is pro- or anti-Augustan is not relevant; Gabba 1991: 212–13 is sceptical of the pro-Augustan Dionysios of Martin (1971).

[52] The belief of Pearson (1939: 187–92) that much of Dionysios' Trojan section is Hellanikos is rightly criticized by Horsfall 1979*b*: 377, cf. also n. 50 above.

[53] This is not to say that all Augustan writers agreed on everything, cf. Hill 1961, Gabba 1991: 116–18, Vanotti 1995: 81–98.

[54] Dion. Hal. *Ant. Rom.* 1. 45. 4, some historians do not know of Aeneas' arrival in Italy; 1. 53. 4, some historians say that Aeneas never came to Italy, cf. Hegesianax and Hegesippos at 1. 49. 1; 1. 54. 3, Dionysios cites evidence for Aeneas' presence in Italy; 1. 72. 1 on the disagreement over the founders of Rome.

[55] On audience, Gabba 1991: 79–80.

in 1.72, where nine different writers, including Hegesianax, Agathyllos, Aristotle, and Xenophanes, are cited, it is only part of the contemporary debate, without which they would probably never have been mentioned.

A similar problem occurs with another major source for pre-Augustan authors, the commentaries on Vergil's *Aeneid*. The writers of these commentaries searched Republican literature, both history and poetry, for anything that might illuminate the text of Vergil. Without the *Aeneid* none of these citations would have been made. Again, therefore, it is Augustan priorities which are to the fore, dictating the nature of our knowledge of the myth. The commentaries provide virtually our sole evidence for statements by L. Coelius Antipater, Q. Fabius Maximus, A. Postumius Albinus, C. Cassius Hemina, L. Cornelius Sisenna and Q. Aelius Tubero about Troy and Trojan involvement in Italy.[56] The main commentary to survive from antiquity was composed in the fourth century AD by Servius, but there is also an expanded version of Servius, known as Servius Auctus or Servius Danielis. The latter was probably compiled in the seventh or eighth century by augmenting Servius with material from an older commentary, usually thought to be that of Donatus. The expanded Servius is not only more precise in its references to earlier authors, it also contains a greater number of such citations. Also relevant is the *Saturnalia* of Macrobius. This is not strictly speaking a commentary but rather a series of dialogues set during the festival of the Saturnalia. Nevertheless, the discussion, which features Servius as a participant, focuses heavily on Vergil. Here again citations of Republican writers are to be found.[57]

Cato's lost *Origins*, written in the mid-second century BC,

[56] Coelius Antipater: Peter *HRR* F52 = Serv. Auct. on *Aen.* 10. 145; Fabius: *HRR* F1 = Serv. Auct. on *Aen.* 1. 3; Postumius: *HRR* F3 = Serv. Auct. on *Aen.* 9. 707; Cassius Hemina: *HRR* F5 = *Schol. Veron.* on *Aen.* 2. 717, *HRR* F6 = Serv. Auct. on *Aen* 1. 378, Macrob. *Sat.* 3. 4. 9 (all three are 'multiple manifestations of the same fragment', according to Forsythe 1990: 337); Sisenna: *HRR* F1 = Serv. on *Aen.* 1. 242, F2 = ibid. 11. 316; Tubero: *HRR* F2 = Serv. on *Aen.* 2. 15. Cassius also appears in Solin. 2. 14 (*HRR* F7), Postumius and Tubero also in *OGR* 15. 4, 17. 3. Q. Lutatius Catulus on Troy occurs once in the commentaries (*HRR* F8 = Serv. Auct. on *Aen.* 9. 707), but several times in *OGR* (9. 2, 10. 2, 11. 3, 13. 7, 18. 1), similarly L. Calpurnius Piso (*HRR* F2 = *Schol. Veron.* on *Aen.* 2.717; *OGR* 10. 2, 13. 8). On *OGR* see next paragraph but one. Note the new editions of the fragments of Cassius Hemina and Piso with discussions, by Santini 1995 (esp. 76–80, 128–44) and Forsythe 1994 (esp. 90–113, 428–31) respectively.

[57] On the relationship between Servius and Servius Auctus: Goold 1970, esp. 102–30, though Daintree 1990 has made a strong case against the Donatus interpretation; on the

provide a useful example. It was a work much cited in antiquity. There remain forty-eight references to the first book, collected together from eighteen different sources.[58] Of these forty-eight citations fifteen are about the Trojan myth, which suggests at first sight that the myth played a fairly important part in the first book of the *Origins*. This is almost a third of the citations after all. Yet, in contrast to the variety of sources for the rest of book one, all but two of these fifteen are to be found in commentaries or discussions of Vergil's *Aeneid*.[59] So if Augustus had not existed, our editions of book one of Cato's *Origins* would look very different from the way they do now—or more properly our editions of the fragments of book one.[60] We would have over thirty citations, but only two would mention either Aeneas or Troy, a very small proportion. Such a proportion suggests the very opposite of the earlier set of statistics, which included the commentaries on Vergil. Maybe more attention should be paid to Cornelius Nepos. When Nepos wrote his study of Cato in the first century BC, he summarized the contents of the seven books of the *Origins*: 'the first book included the achievements of the kings of the Roman People'. This succinct summary has been criticized for ignoring what Cato had to say about the period before the foundation of Rome, but perhaps Nepos is reflecting the substance of the book, whereas our evidence has been distorted by the interests of later ages.[61]

Together these writers on Vergil form the most important source of information about Republican Roman history writing on Rome's Trojan past, but it is perhaps helpful here to look briefly at the *Origo gentis Romanae*. This short and controversial booklet, probably composed in the fourth century AD using a work

relative quality of citations: R. B. Lloyd 1961, esp. 299–302 on historians; on Servius: Kaster 1988: 169–97. Other briefer, non-Servian commentaries, such as the *Scholia Veronensia*, do survive, *Enciclopedia Vergiliana*, s.v. 'Scholia, non-serviana'. Macrobius: P. V. Davies 1969: 17–23, Kaster 1988: 60–2.

[58] Following the edition of Schröder 1971.

[59] i.e. Servius, Servius Auctus., Macrobius; the exceptions are both from *OGR* 12. 5, 15. 5 (Cato *Orig.* bk. 1 F14b, 9b). Cf. also in *Origins*, Politorium in Latium founded by Polites, son of Priam (bk. 2 F24, Serv. on *Aen.* 5. 564) and Veneti by Trojans (bk. 2 F12, Pliny *HN* 3. 130).

[60] Even 'fragments' is too strong a word since it suggests quotation which these citations rarely are, cf. Brunt 1980.

[61] Nepos, *Cato* 3. 3: 'primus continet res gestas regum populi Romani'; cf. Chassignet 1986: p. xi for criticism of Nepos. For a more positive account of the value of the Vergilian commentaries, see Cornell 1995: 22–3.

from the early empire, contains the bulk of the remaining citations of Republican historians on the subject. In the fourteen chapters covering the period from Aeneas' escape from Troy to the foundation of Rome the anonymous author manages to cite almost twenty different Republican historians, an impressive display of learning. The authenticity of these citations, however, has been a matter of considerable dispute, so great in fact that Hermann Peter excluded them altogether from his *Historicorum Romanorum Reliquiae*, in which he collected the remains of lost Roman historians. More recently they have been accepted as citations made in good faith, albeit marred by occasional errors.[62] In spite of all its references to lost Republican writing the *Origo gentis Romanae* is very much a post-Augustan text, that is to say the product of a world in which Augustus had defined the shape of Rome's prehistory. The work opens with the quotation and discussion of a number of passages of Vergil as the author surveys the reigns of Ianus, Saturn, Picus, and Faunus. Only as the author approaches the arrival of Aeneas is Vergil dropped in favour of more historically grounded writers, but the Vergilian starting point is already clear.[63] Later, the description of Aeneas and his family recalls the statue group in the Forum of Augustus as well as containing echoes of the *Aeneid*.[64] Finally, by far the most frequently cited authority in the work is an unidentified 'Caesar', perhaps L. Iulius Caesar, the consul of 64 BC, although some have argued for the dictator.[65]

The two examples studied here, Dionysios of Halikarnassos and the Vergilian commentators, help to demonstrate the extent to which our knowledge of earlier traditions is dependent on Augustan priorities. This dependence, however, is not limited solely to the literary arena, but can also be observed in the visual arts. Here one of the most common depictions of Aeneas shows him during his escape from Troy. Aeneas is leading his son Ascanius by the right hand, while his father Anchises sits perched

[62] Momigliano 1958 did much to rehabilitate the *OGR*; subsequent debate is summed up in the Richard 1983*b* Budé ed.

[63] On structure, Momigliano 1958: 70, Richard 1983*b*: 48–53.

[64] *OGR* 9. 1: 'prae se deos penates patremque Anchisen humeris gestans nec non et parvulum filium manu trahens' ([Aeneas] carrying the Penates before him and Anchises on his shoulders, and also leading his small son by the hand); Forum group: see next paragraph; Richard 1983*b*: 135 sees Vergilian echoes, cf. *Aen.* 2. 320–1, 707–8, 804.

[65] Cited 9 times, 6 as 'Caesar' alone, 2 as L. Caesar, 1 as C. Caesar. On this Richard 1983*b*: 139.

upon his left shoulder. This image has been found in many parts of the empire on coins, finger rings, and lamps, in painting, relief sculpture, and statuary, and the most likely explanation for this uniformity is that they are all based on a common model, namely the statue of Aeneas in the Forum of Augustus.[66] A contrast can be made with the earlier representation of Aeneas' flight as it appeared on the coins of Caesar, where Ascanius was absent and in his place Aeneas carried the Palladium.[67] Caesar may have established the precedent but it is the Augustan period that is responsible for the multiplicity of later images.

So the Augustan age seriously warps the evidence for earlier Roman representations of the Trojan myth, both Greek and Roman. In no way are these neutral citations.

3. REPUBLICAN SURVIVORS: THE INSIDE VIEW

Rather than trying to reconstruct these lost writers, therefore, it might be more valuable to look at what does survive from the Republican period. My concern in this section is with Roman writers, the insider's view rather than the outsider's view which is presented in Greek literature. It is these writers who will reveal what the Romans thought about themselves, not merely because they were Romans, but because the audience for these texts was other Romans, other Latin speakers. When these extant Republican writers are examined, there is little to suggest that Aeneas or even the Trojans were central to the Roman sense of their own identity. Romans themselves paid far more attention to Romulus than to any Trojan ancestors of the Romans.

An examination of the copious writings of Cicero suggests that the Republican picture of the origins of Rome was very different from the Augustan one. Over some forty years of the first century BC Cicero produced the largest body of surviving Republican literature; this included political and forensic speeches, philosophical and rhetorical treatises, and letters. Here some distinctions need to be made between the treatises, on the one hand, and the speeches on the other. Cicero's philosophical and rhetorical treatises are more learned and are more reliant on the writings of Greek intellectuals, whereas the speeches are more likely to reflect

---

[66] Galinsky 1969: 8–9, Fuchs 1973: 629–31, Zanker 1988: 200–10, see sect. 1 above.
[67] Galinsky 1969: 5, see also n. 15 above.

the general body of knowledge among Romans—and for the most part these will have been upper-class Romans, although some of the speeches were addressed to the People. Letters are not so readily categorized, because their tone will change with the recipient. In this huge corpus of work Troy is sometimes mentioned, but it is significant that almost all Cicero's references to Troy and Trojans are limited to the course of the Trojan War itself. Little is said about the post-war adventures of the Trojan survivors.

An exception is to be found in Cicero's undelivered prosecution speech for the trial of Verres in 70 BC. Among Verres' victims during his notorious governorship of Sicily was the city of Segesta: 'Segesta is a very ancient town in Sicily, gentlemen, which they say was founded by Aeneas when he fled from Troy and arrived in this area. Therefore the Segestans consider themselves to be bound to the Roman People not only by permanent alliance and friendship but also by kinship.'[68] Cicero expects his audience of educated Romans to know about Aeneas' links with Rome, but he does not presume any knowledge of Aeneas' role in the foundation of Segesta; there is even a hint of scepticism. Kinship between the two cities, however, suits Cicero's purpose, making the actions of Verres all the more reprehensible. This is the only occasion on which Cicero connects Troy with Rome, although there is a passage in his *On Divination* that alludes to stories of Rome's Trojan past. There he cites a prophetic dream of Aeneas, which he says was recorded in the Greek annals of Fabius Pictor.[69] The very precise way in which he gives Fabius as his source suggests that the dream would not have been well known to his audience. This was not one of those things about the past that all Romans could be expected to know, not even the educated readers of a treatise such as *On Divination*. Nor was it a story that could be found in *any* book on Rome's past but rather it was in Fabius' Greek annals. However well known Aeneas may have been in Rome, this dream surely was not. These two passages are as much as Cicero has to say about Rome's Trojan past.[70] It is the war itself that makes up the majority of Cicero's Trojan references.

The contrast between the treatises and the speeches is evident from the kind of examples that he cites. In the treatises his

---

[68] Cic. II *Verr.* 4. 72, on which see further Ch. 7. 2 below.

[69] Cic. *Div.* 1. 43 = *FGrH* 809F1.

[70] Aeneas appears as an example of piety in the spurious *Rhet. ad Her.* 4. 46 (early 1st cent. BC?).

examples tend to imply a greater knowledge on the part of the audience and are often more detailed. He refers, for instance, to the death of Hector, Agamemnon's sacrifice of Iphigenia, the prophetic powers of Calchas, Hector's last-minute prophecy of Achilles' death. In *On Fate* he argues that Hecuba was not the cause of the death of Trojans just because she gave birth to Alexander, an example that assumes a fair knowledge of the war. Frequently Homer is cited, but also other writers such as Sophocles and Accius; sometimes Cicero even provides his own translations of Homer.[71] These, then, are learned works for an educated readership, which is expected to be familiar with the classics of Greek and Roman literature, but it is a readership that was hardly typical even of the Roman upper classes.

Cicero had read Homer and knew his work well, but it is apparent from his speeches that he did not expect the same of other Romans. Here, in contrast to his treatises, only a basic knowledge of the Trojan War was required. It was enough to know that Helen started it and the Trojan Horse ended it.[72] Thus in the *Philippics* Antony is to the Republic what Helen was to the Trojans. But it is the Trojan Horse that appeals most to Cicero; it finds its way into the *Verrines*, *Pro Murena*, *Pro Caelio*, and *Philippics*. Sometimes it is a good thing, at other times bad; in the *Pro Murena* the Catilinarians are like the horse within the city, but Cicero is ever alert; so the Catilinarians represent the Greeks and Cicero represents the Trojans. In the *Philippics*, however, the whole analogy is reversed: Cicero himself is in the horse along with the conspirators as they seek to undermine Antony. Such flexibility does not suggest a particularly strong identification with the Trojans. This Roman knowledge of the Trojan Horse may be traced back to earlier Roman plays on the theme. Both Naevius and Livius Andronicus are reported to have written plays entitled *The Trojan Horse*.[73] Later, Plautus subjected the Trojan Horse and the sack of

[71] Hector's death: Cic. *Tusc.* 1. 105 (Accius); Iphigenia: *Off.* 3. 95; Calchas: *Div.* 1. 72, 87 (Homer); Achilles' death: *Div.* 1. 65; Hecuba: *Fat.* 34; Homer: *Div.* 1. 89, *Sen.* 31; translations: *Div.* 2. 63–4, *Fin.* 5. 49; Sophocles: *Tusc.* 3. 71. These are only a selection.

[72] Helen: Cic. *Phil.* 2. 55; Horse: II *Verr.* 4. 52, *Mur.* 78, *Cael.* 67, *Phil.* 2. 32 (cf. *De or.* 2. 94), Austin 1959: 17. Cf. also Priam as example of old man in (*Rosc. Am.* 90), and Telephus guiding Agamemnon (*Flac.* 72); the latter is more obscure, but it is in the context of a defence of a governor of Asia.

[73] Andronicus: Nonius 475M; Naevius: Macrob. *Sat.* 6. 1. 38; both quoted in Ribbeck *TRF*; Cicero twice mentions a play of this name, *Fam.* 7. 1. 2, 7. 16. 1; on Trojan horse plays in Rome: Erskine 1998.

Troy to an elaborate parody in the *Bacchides*, a play which does survive and thus offers one of the few insights into the Trojan myth in second-century BC Rome. Yet, there is no hint in Plautus that the sack of Troy had any special relevance to the Romans at all. Indeed the story is presented from the Greek perspective, the perspective of the sackers rather than that of the simple-minded victims. It is hard to imagine that the Romans identified themselves with the credulous old man of Plautus' play.[74]

The Trojans thus feature in Cicero's writings, but there is no sign that they are especially significant to the Romans. Aeneas himself is almost invisible. Cicero's treatment of Romulus, however, is markedly different. The importance of Romulus is apparent from the repeated mentions of him in *On the Republic*, Cicero's meditation on the ideal state. In contrast to Plato's *Republic* this work has much to say about existing states, in particular about Rome, the state that comes closest to the perfect state.[75] In book two Cicero is concerned with 'the origin of the Roman people', *populi Romani origo*, a phrase that recalls Cato's *Origins*.[76] Here the emphasis is firmly on Romulus, a man celebrated as the founding figure of the state and establisher of the Senate and augurate.[77] A series of comparisons with the Spartan lawgiver Lycurgus enhance Romulus' standing still further.[78] But nowhere in book two or anywhere else in the surviving parts of *On the Republic* is there any mention of Aeneas or even of Trojans. Cicero's opinion of Rome did not always reach the heightened terms of *On the Republic*; in the more relaxed context of a letter to Atticus he contrasts Plato's *Republic* with Romulus' cesspit, *Romuli faece*,[79] but there is still the close identification of the Roman state with Romulus. As Cicero puts it in *On Divination*, Romulus is 'father of the city', *huius urbis parens*.[80]

[74] Plaut. *Bacch.* 925–1075 (cf. *Pseud.* 1244), on which Barsby 1986: 173–81. In order to save the Trojans from imbecility Paus. 1. 23. 8 (cf. Serv. on *Aen.* 2. 15) interprets the Trojan Horse as a siege engine.

[75] Cic. *Rep.* 1. 70.

[76] Cic. *Rep.* 2. 3. 1.

[77] Cic. *Rep.* 2. 4–20, 22–3, 25–6, 50–2, cf. 1. 25, 58, 64, 3. 47, 6. 24; on Romulus in *Rep.* see Zetzel 1995: 160–78; Senate and augurate: *Rep.* 2. 14–17; elsewhere on Romulus and augurate: *Div.* 1. 3, 30, 107, 2. 70, 73, 80, *Vat.* 20.

[78] Cic. *Rep.* 2. 2, 15, 18–19, 24, 50.

[79] Cic. *Att.* 2. 1. 8.

[80] Cic. *Div.* 1. 3, cf. Romulus as founder, *Balb.* 31, *Leg.* 2. 33, *Off.* 3. 41, *Paradoxa Stoicorum* 1. 11, where Roman history starts with Romulus or the liberators.

A similar emphasis can be found in the poetry of Cicero's contemporary, Catullus. There are four poems that contain references to Romulus and the identification between Romulus, and Rome is again clear.[81] The Romans are 'the race of Romulus' or 'the descendants of Romulus.'[82] Troy, on the other hand, is mentioned only in one poem and is presented in a very negative manner. This common burial ground of Greeks and Trojans is also where Catullus' brother is buried, an alien, foreign, and unpleasant place:

> quem nunc tam longe non inter nota sepulcra
> nec prope cognatos compositum cineres,
> sed Troia obscena, Troia infelice sepultum
> detinet extremo terra aliena solo.
>
> Whom now so far away and not among familiar tombs
> nor laid to rest among the ashes of your kin
> but buried in hateful Troy, ill-omened Troy
> a foreign land holds in a distant soil.[83]

These lines of Catullus do reflect the bitterness of grief, but at the same time the complete lack of identification with Troy is striking. Troy is *obscena, aliena*, an inappropriate place to be buried. Catullus chose Troy not as a Roman homeland, but as a place of death and alienation, which is far from kin.

Aeneas and Rome's Trojan prehistory do occur occasionally in the surviving literature of the Republic. Lucretius begins his *On the Nature of Things* with an address to Venus as *Aeneadum genetrix*, mother of Aeneas and his descendants, but this is no innocent invocation of Venus as mother of the Roman people. Lucretius' poem, probably published by the mid-fifties BC, was dedicated to C. Memmius, an aristocrat from one of the old Trojan families of Rome, who could claim Venus as his protecting goddess.[84] The opening lines can thus allude both to Rome's Trojan past and to Memmius' own Trojan ancestry;[85] in doing so they present Roman history as the Memmii told it.

[81] Catull. 28. 15, 29. 5 and 9, 34. 22, 49. 1.
[82] Catull. 34. 22, 49. 1.
[83] Catull. 68. 97–100. Text and trans. G. P. Goold 1983.
[84] Lucr. 1. 1–2; the only other reference to Troy in the poem is 1. 464–82, where it is used as an example. On date, see D. Fowler, *OCD³* s.v. 'Lucretius'. For Memmii, sect. 1 above. Lucretius himself refers to Venus' patronage of Memmius, 1. 25–7.
[85] Cf. Feeney 1998: 16.

Other examples from the Republic tend to be rather later and perhaps under the influence of Caesar. Varro in his *On the Latin Language* tells of the sow that escaped from Aeneas' ship and gave birth to thirty piglets, a sign that there would be thirty years between the foundation of Lavinium and that of Alba Longa. But this and one briefer appearance by Aeneas in the same volume must be balanced by the thirteen mentions of Romulus.[86] Varro becomes a more important figure in the transmission of the Aeneas story if his lost writings are included. Not only did he write four books on Trojan families, but he also discussed Aeneas in the second book of his lengthy *Antiquitates rerum humanarum et divinarum*; six relevant citations of book two are preserved, all courtesy of the Vergilian commentators.[87] Varro's dependence on Caesar in the 40s, however, may have had some bearing on his interest in the Trojan past; the second half of the *Antiquitates* was dedicated to Caesar as Pontifex Maximus.[88] The Iulian connection may have continued beyond Caesar's death if it is correct that Varro subsequently aligned himself with Octavian.[89] As a good Caesarian the historian Sallust too knew and accepted the story of Aeneas' involvement in the founding of Rome, although what he knew is a little obscure: 'The city of Rome, as I believe (*sicuti ego accepi*), was founded and occupied initially by the Trojans, who under the leadership of Aeneas wandered about as refugees with no fixed abode, and together with them by the Aborigines, a country people, who lived without laws or government, free and unrestrained.' Sometimes Sallust is interpreted to mean that it was Aeneas who founded Rome, but it is more probable that this is merely a compressed way of identifying the Trojans who were eventually to found Rome.[90] Whatever his meaning his interpretation of Rome's past was not universally accepted; *sicuti ego accepi*

[86] Aeneas: Varro, *Ling.* 5. 144, 6. 60, cf. *Rust.* 2. 4. 18; Romulus: *Ling.* 5. 9, 33, 46, 54, 55, 144, 149, 8. 18, 45, 80, 9. 34, 50, 10. 15.

[87] Varro F10–12, 14–16 (Semi); Aeneas appears twice elsewhere in the 41-book work, F119 from Augustine, and F124 from Servius.

[88] On Varro and Caesar with discussion of chronology, Horsfall 1972, Toohey 1984: 6–8; R. Kaster, *OCD*³ s.v. 'Varro', dates *Antiquitates* to 47 BC (though some prefer *c.*56 for *res humanae*), *Ling.* to 43 BC, *Rust.* to 37 BC (intended to 'further Octavian's agrarian policy'? So L. R. Taylor 1934: 229). Toohey dates *De familiis Troianis* to mid-40s BC.

[89] L. R. Taylor 1934, Horsfall 1972.

[90] Sall. *Cat.* 6. 1: 'Urbem Romam, sicuti ego accepi, condidere atque habuere initio Troiani, qui Aenea duce profugi sedibus incertis vagabantur cumque eis Aborigines, genus hominum agreste, sine legibus, sine imperio, liberum atque solutum'; on which Schröder 1971: 69, Cornell 1975: 13, Momigliano 1984: 447, Gruen 1992: 23 n. 78.

implies the existence of alternative versions which he is not following.[91]

Extant Republican literature emphasizes Romulus rather than the Trojans. Romulus was more embedded in the self-image of the Roman state. He was the father of the country. A representation of Romulus and Remus with the wolf was set up in Rome as early as 296.[92] By the early 260s this family group had appeared on Roman coins,[93] whereas Aeneas made no such numismatic appearance until the mid-first century BC, and then it was only with the assistance of his descendant Caesar. Romulus features in Cicero's speeches, whether they are to the upper classes or to the People. Troy, on the other hand, appears to be reserved for the upper classes alone and even to them Cicero speaks not of Trojan ancestry but rather of the Trojan War.[94] Troy in any form makes not a single appearance in any of Cicero's surviving speeches to the People. Was this because the People were felt to know little, if anything, about Troy, whereas Romulus was instantly recognizable? There is a sense in which the myth of Troy and Aeneas in the Republican period fails to be a popular myth.[95]

The purpose of this section has not been to deny Roman familiarity with the story of Rome's Trojan origins, but rather to emphasize its limitations. Augustan and post-Augustan writers may give the impression that the myth was more widely accepted and better known than it in fact was. A study of extant Republican authors suggests, however, that even by the time of Cicero Troy was not yet an integral part of the Roman self-image. Instead, the meaning and function of the myth before the Iulii must be sought outside Rome. As the next section will argue, the myth is most readily understood not as a Roman myth but as a Graeco-Roman myth, the product of interaction between Greeks and Romans, whether direct or indirect.

---

[91] McGushin 1977: 70.

[92] Livy 10. 23. 12, Momigliano 1984: 439–40, Wiseman 1995: 72–6.

[93] Crawford 1974: 137, 150, 714 .

[94] Romulus to People: *Pro Rabirio perduellionis reo* 13, *Cat.* 3. 19; Romulus to upper classes: *Cat.* 1.33, *Vat.* 20, *Balb.* 31; Troy in general to upper classes: II*Verr.* 4. 52, 4. 72, *Mur.* 78, *Cael.* 67, *Phil.* 2. 33, 2. 55, *Flac.* 72, *Rosc. Am.* 90—only II*Verr.* 4.72 concerns Aeneas. It is true that this is a fairly small sample and therefore dangerous to build too much on.

[95] Cf. Cornell 1977: 83.

4. THE MYTH IN CONTEXT

Aeneas was a central part of the foundation story of Rome, yet he is almost absent from the surviving Latin literature of the Republic. This hardly constitutes a myth that is an essential feature of the Roman self-image, an article of the national creed. It would be mistaken, however, to conclude that the myth of Rome's Trojan origins was unimportant in the Republic and that it became significant only with the arrival of the Iulii. The choice does not lie between two such extremes. In understanding the myth what is relevant is the context in which it is used, and not used. What follows anticipates to some extent the discussions of Part III, but it is nonetheless valuable at this point to outline the Graeco-Roman setting of the myth, which should offer an important complement to the Troyless Rome that has been observed so far.

In the Republic the myth does not generally appear when Romans are addressing other Romans. This may be something of an oversimplification, but it is the implication of the Republican literature discussed in the previous section. In that context the myth had little to offer, because the Romans already had a founder, Romulus. The history of their city, therefore, started with Romulus, whereas Aeneas and the Trojans were part of what could be called prehistory. For Romans addressing each other, Rome was a self-contained unit that could be understood on its own terms, beginning with Romulus, hence the repeated references to Romulus in the surviving literature of the Republic and the relative disregard of Aeneas. There was no need for infinite regress.

Outside Rome, however, Romulus is unfamiliar, a figure who will elicit only limited comprehension. It was here that Aeneas and the Trojans were of value, because they rooted Rome in the mythical past, the age of the heroes of Homer. In this way Rome was linked to the world beyond Rome, in particular to the Greek world. It is in the interaction with Greeks and things Greek that the Trojan myth is primarily found. It was in this context that it was meaningful, because it provided the Romans and the Greeks with a common past that they could look back to and exploit in order to understand and validate their relationship in the present.

It was a myth that worked in both directions, serving both the Romans looking out at the Greek world beyond and the Greeks looking in from the outside. This may have been more important for the Greeks than for the Romans, since the tradition that it was based on was Greek, not Roman, but at the same time it did give both Greeks and Romans a shared past, a common language. It integrated Romulus and therefore the Romans into the world outside Rome. It was not, however, uncomplicated. Because their ancestors had been on opposing sides in the Trojan War, the myth could also embody the tension that existed between Greeks and Romans.

Some examples will help to demonstrate how this myth of Rome's Trojan origins could operate within the context of inter-action between Greeks and Romans. It was not limited purely to diplomacy and interstate relations, but could play a part in any form of interaction, whether on a political or cultural level.

The 'fragmentary' Roman evidence that is preserved in Augustan and later writers suggests that the myth was the sphere of historians and poets, those who would be using Greek forms or even writing in Greek. Fabius Pictor famously inaugurated Roman historiography by writing his history of Rome in Greek, an example followed by his successors, A. Postumius Albinus, C. Acilius, and L. Cincius Alimentus.[96] Thus, if the myth did appear in Rome, it tended to be in what are essentially Greek genres, contexts in which the writers were already part-way between Greek and Roman culture. In contrast, Cicero when addressing the Senate was under no such pressure. Nevertheless, even in the cases of these poets and historians, their works now lost, the emphasis has probably been distorted by Augustan preoccupations. What little the poet Ennius is reported to have written in his *Annals* about the Trojan past survives in imperial texts, but some substantial passages on Romulus are to be found in the Republican Cicero.[97] Thus the selections reflect the priori-ties and views of their age.

[96] Fabius: *FGrH* 809 with n. 41 above; Albinus: *FGrH* 812; Acilius: *FGrH* 813; Cincius: *FGrH* 810; Badian 1966: 2–7. For the poets, Naevius and Ennius, see n. 41 above; note also the *Aeneadae vel Decius* of Accius, which probably took the battle of Sentinum in 295 as its theme, Ribbeck *TRF* 326–8, J. Dangel's Budé ed. of Accius, pp. 230–42.

[97] On Trojans, note in particular Ennius, lines 14–19, 28–9 (Skutsch); on Romulus, lines 72–91, 105–9 (Skutsch) = Cic. *Div.* 1. 107, *Rep.* 1. 64. Ennius' quotations are often so short that it is no easy matter to know what they are about, Cornell 1986: 248–9, a review of Skutsch.

The importance of a Greek context is also evident in an occurrence of the myth in Rome during the war against Hannibal. According to Livy a stir was caused in Rome in 212 BC by the belated discovery of some prophecies of the seer Marcius, one of which had (if they had but known) predicted Cannae, the disastrous battle of 216: 'Flee the River Canna, O offspring of Troy (*Troiugena*), and don't let men of foreign birth compel you to fight on the plain of Diomedes.'[98] Whether or not this is an authentic prophecy, the Greek tone is clear: not only are the Romans addressed as *Troiugena*, a term of Greek derivation, but the battle-site of Cannae is located by reference to the plain of the Greek hero Diomedes.[99] The Hellenic context continued in the second prophecy which recommended the introduction of a festival of Apollo together with the sacrifice of victims according to Greek rite.[100] This Trojan prophecy has been used to demonstrate that Rome's Trojan origins were well known in late-third-century Rome,[101] but such an argument is far from convincing. Since prophecies and oracles are usually cryptic and enigmatic, one could equally maintain that the occurrence of the term *Troiugena* is evidence for the lack of familiarity with the myth in Rome.

On the Greek side evidence for the myth of Rome's Trojan origins is better, perhaps inevitably since any reference to Rome is some form of interaction between Greek and Roman. So, if a writer is to discuss Rome, it might suit him to introduce the myth in order to tie Rome into the Greek world of his reader.[102] The myth was familiar to Lykophron, Timaios, and Polybios, all writers who were active in the third or second centuries BC. It is, however, also clear that many Greeks were ignorant of the myth and continued to be so, even in the late first century BC when Dionysios of Halikarnassos was writing.[103]

[98] Livy 25. 12. 1–7: 'amnem, Troiugena, fuge Cannam, ne te alienagenae cogant in campo Diomedis conserere manus'. Galinsky 1969: 177–8 rightly rejects the Perret 1942: 454–7 supposition that the lines reflect hostility between Greeks and Trojans.

[99] On authenticity, Perret 1942: 454–7. On *Troiugena*, cf. the description of the Romans as Τρώων γενεά in a Greek oracle, perhaps from the 2nd cent. BC, Plut. *Mor.* 399cd. The story also appears in Zonar. 9. 1, with discussion of the plain of Diomedes; on the latter, see also Tzetzes on Lycoph. 602, Tzetz. *Chil.* 1. 757–9; all three are collected at the beginning of frags. of Dio bk. 15.

[100] Livy 25. 12. 9–10, *Graeco ritu.*

[101] Perret 1942: 457, Gruen 1990: 14.

[102] For the Greek habit of seeing the rest of the world as an extension of the Greek world, Bickerman 1952.

[103] Dion. Hal. *Ant. Rom.*, see n. 54 above.

The area of diplomatic relations produces valuable evidence for the use of the myth in the centuries BC. Significantly one of the few allusions to Rome's Trojan origins in surviving Roman literature of the period is concerned with interstate relations, Cicero's remark that the Segestans felt a particular affinity with the Romans because of their shared Trojan ancestry. There is also definite and contemporary evidence for Greek cities in the Troad making use of the Trojan connection in their diplomatic relations with Rome. In the 190s Lampsakos, perhaps under pressure from Antiochos the Great, appealed to Rome for help; to support their case the Lampsakenes placed considerable emphasis on their kinship with the Romans, as a decree honouring one of the ambassadors attests. A few years later, according to Polybios, the people of Ilion, a city that claimed to be a descendant of old Troy, interceded with the Romans on behalf of the Lykians. In doing so they drew attention to their kinship with the Romans. Other instances can be found, though in later and less reliable sources: the Akarnanians, when they sought the help of the Romans, ingeniously pointed out that their ancestors had *not* joined the expedition against Troy, or the famous letter in which the Romans asked a certain King Seleukos not to tax their kinsmen, the people of Ilion. Such claims go further than a shared heroic past, but this was diplomacy, and kinship had always been considered a useful argument in Greek diplomacy.[104]

Two final examples serve to illustrate the way in which the myth is very much a collaboration between Greeks and Romans. Its significance lies in its acceptance by both parties, as its use in diplomacy suggests.

Painted in red on the wall of a building in Tauromenion in Sicily in the late second century BC were brief biographies of famous writers. This novel decoration may have been part of the portico of a gymnasium, perhaps even a gymnasium with a library. The damaged biographies of three historians survive—Kallisthenes of Olynthos, Philistos of Syracuse, and the Roman Fabius Pictor—and of one philosopher, Anaximander of Miletos. Before breaking off, the Fabius biography outlines the early part of his history: the arrival of Herakles in Italy, something unclear

---

[104] Segesta: Cic. II *Verr.* 4. 72; Lampsakos: *SIG*³ 591; Ilion and Lykia: Polyb. 22. 5. 1–4; Akarnania: Just. *Epit.* 28. 1. 6; Seleukos: Suet. *Claud.* 25. 10; all these are discussed in detail in Ch. 7 below.

about Lanoïos, ally of Aineias and Askanios, the birth of Romulus and Remus, and the foundation of Rome by Romulus.[105] By writing his history in Greek, Fabius was, whether intentionally or not, reaching out to a Greek audience and he had surely found at least one reader in Sicily. Acceptance of the Fabian version of Rome's origins by the Tauromenians is implied, first, by their decision to include Fabius at all, secondly, by their reporting the beginning of his history. Neither was necessary: what remains of the biographical sketch of Philistos concentrates not on his writings but his political activities. Nevertheless, in presenting the Fabian version the Tauromenians were also making it their own by selecting what was of particular interest to themselves. This is the only report of Fabius to mention Herakles, a result perhaps of the special reverence for Herakles in Sicily.[106] More relevant, however, is the attention paid to the otherwise unknown Lanoïos; this figure has been most plausibly interpreted as a hero from eastern Sicily, who travelled to Latium and founded the city of Lanuvium.[107] Thus although the Tauromenians acknowledge the place of Aineias in the story, they adjust the emphasis to create a 'Sicilian' Fabius, who affirms the bond between themselves and the Latins. Another city with a different set of traditions would in all likelihood have produced its own image of Fabius. Each city, therefore, will engage with the story of Rome's origins in its own way, a situation that will encourage variety rather than uniformity.

At some point in the 190s after the conclusion of the Second Macedonian War Titus Quinctius Flamininus dedicated some shields and a gold wreath at Delphi. Two verse inscriptions were added, both of which emphasized the Trojan ancestry of the Romans:

O sons of Zeus who take pleasure in swift horsemanship, O Tyndaridai,

---

[105] [Κόι]ντος Φάβιος ὁ Πι[κτω]ρῖνος ἐπικαλού[μεν]ος, Ῥωμαῖος, Γαίου [υἱό]ς. [ὃς] ἱστόρηκεν τὴν [Ἡρ]ακλέους ἄφιξιν [εἰς] Ἰταλίαν καὶ δ'ἔτι [νόσ]τον Λανοΐου συμ[μάχ]ου τε Αἰνεία καὶ [Ἀσκα]νίου. πολι ὕστε[ρον ἐ]γένοντο Ῥωμύλος [καὶ Ῥ]έμος καὶ Ῥώμης [κτίσις ὑ]πὸ Ῥωμύλου, [ὃς πρῶτ]ος βεβασί[λευκεν. All three texts published in Manganaro 1974 and 1976 (the 1976 article was in fact written first). Until the recent discovery of the Anaximander fragment (Blanck 1997) the wall was thought to have been devoted to historians.

[106] Diod. Sic. 4. 23. 4–24. 6, Hdt. 5. 43, Dion. Hal. *Ant. Rom.* 1. 44. 1, Malkin 1994: 203–18.

[107] Manganaro 1976: 87–8, which includes the text of an inscription, recording kinship between the Sicel town of Kentoripa and Lanuvium, the latter said in the inscription to be a colony of Kentoripa, something which could only be true in a mythical sense.

princes of Sparta, Titus, descendant of Aineias, has presented a very splendid gift to you, he who won freedom for the children of Greece.

and:

It is fitting, son of Leto, that this golden crown, which is given by the great commander of the descendants of Aineias, should sit on your ambrosial locks. Apollo, grant to the divine (*theios*) Titus the glory due to his prowess.[108]

The dedication of the shields and the wreath was a friendly gesture of goodwill by a Roman commander at a major Greek sanctuary, a place where politics and religion met. The explicit reference to the Trojan ancestry of the Romans reinforces the sense of common ground between Greeks and Romans, peoples who shared in a common past. The inscriptions were in Greek and this was an appropriate thing to say in Greek. According to Plutarch Flamininus himself was responsible for the inscriptions and most scholars seem to accept this.[109] These verses, therefore, could be interpreted as examples of a Roman commander using the myth to integrate himself and the Romans into the Greek world. It is, however, possible that the verses were never written by Flamininus at all; Plutarch simply assumed that they were. The second dedication is especially striking. Would Flamininus really have described himself as *theios*, especially when addressing Apollo? Whether *theios* is translated as 'godlike' or 'divine', this seems most improbable. The use of the term here reflects not Flamininus' high self-esteem but rather the Greek view of Flamininus at a time when numerous Greek cities were honouring the Roman general, and some were even making him the object of cult worship.[110] Perhaps the Greeks were composing what they thought would please Flamininus, in which case the text of the dedication would itself be a joint effort. Whoever composed the verses, they show that it is in the context of exchange between Greeks and Romans that the Trojan myth is meaningful.

This Chapter has been concerned to make three main points. First, Augustus' promotion of the myth of Rome's Trojan

---

[108] Plut. *Flam.* 12.

[109] e.g. Balsdon 1951: 8, Bickerman 1952: 68, Walbank 1967: 182–3, Ferrary 1988: 223, Gruen 1992: 48.

[110] Honours: *IG* 12. 9. 931, *SEG* 22. 214, *SIG*³ 616; cult: *SIG*³ 592, *SEG* 11. 923, lines 11–12, Plut. *Flam.* 16.

ancestry shapes and distorts our perception of this myth in pre-Augustan times. Knowledge of this myth both within Rome and outside it may have been more limited and scattered than the Augustan picture suggests. Secondly, the myth was not a significant part of the Roman self-image until the Iulii put themselves and the myth at the centre of Roman politics. Thirdly, Rome's Trojan ancestry cannot be understood separately from the Greek world that directly or indirectly produced the myth. It is Troy's role in this interaction between Greeks and Romans that is the subject of this book, but before looking more closely at this it is important to consider the place of Troy and the Trojans in the Greek world.

Part II

Greece

2

Homer and the Archaic Age

At the very same time that one Greek city was revering a Trojan as its eponymous founder, another was transforming the Trojans into barbarian precursors of the Persians. The former was the obscure northern town of Aineia, the latter was Athens as it recovered from the Persian Wars.[1] These two examples represent opposite poles and help to demonstrate that there was no one image of the Trojans current among the Greeks. Instead, the Greek relationship with the mythical Trojans was complex and changing, responding to situation and circumstances. The alien, non-Greek Trojan that can be observed in Athens has perhaps acquired greater prominence than it should have, and this is for two reasons. First, the very Athenocentric nature of our evidence tends to mean that the shift from 'Athenian' to 'Greek' is all too easily made; secondly, Athens' role as the cultural centre of the Greek world led later intellectuals to adopt readily an Athenian perspective.

The next three chapters aim to explore these various images of the Trojans and emphasize their overall complexity in order to provide a suitable background for the coming of the Romans. The Trojans of Homer and the archaic age will be seen to be very different from the later Athenian model. Nor can Athens be considered typical. The polemical interpretation to be found there was just one of many ways of understanding the Trojan War. More emphasis, instead, should be placed on the widespread, if somewhat random, evidence of local tradition, cults, and names, often from much less celebrated cities than Athens. These reveal that in many places the Trojan past played a positive part in civic life. The Trojan myth was a very flexible motif which could be adapted to suit different times and places. The focus in this part of the book will be on the Greeks of the eastern Mediterranean, whose traditions were already well developed before the arrival of the Romans. The Greeks of Italy and Sicily, however, will be

---

[1] Aineia: Ch. 4.1; Athens: Ch. 3.

delayed until Part III, because here Troy's mediating role is not so much a consequence of these traditions as a part of them.

1. THE IMPORTANCE OF HOMER

Homer's *Iliad* is fundamental to any study of Troy and the Trojans. The poet probably lived in the eighth or early seventh century BC, although it may not have been until the sixth century that the poem itself took on a written form.[2] The *Iliad*'s importance for the purpose of this book is twofold. First, it is the earliest surviving literary representation of the Trojans, so it gives us a valuable indication of how they were depicted before the Persian Wars. Secondly, the *Iliad* had a continuing influence right through to the end of the ancient world. Consequently, the significance of its representation of the Trojans is not limited to the archaic period. Even under the Roman Empire, then, local images of the Trojans are likely to have been weighed against their depiction in the *Iliad*.

The influence of the *Iliad* and its companion poem, the *Odyssey*, was no mere literary phenomenon. Rather, they were central texts in Greek culture, the *Iliad* in particular.[3] They could be cited as evidence, not only for the historicity of the Trojan War, but also for minor and even fairly esoteric facts. Thus Herodotos, after suggesting that cattle in Skythia have no horns because of the cold, quotes a line of the *Odyssey* to prove that horns grow faster in hot climates, 'Libya, where lambs develop horns quickly'.[4] These texts might also be used to justify behaviour or even to provide moral guidance; a jury would not be surprised to find a defendant or prosecutor citing lines of Homer.[5] From as early as the sixth century rhapsodes could be found engaging in competitive recitations of Homeric epic, such as at the Panathenaia in Athens;[6] at that time 'Homeric' may have included almost any epic narrative poem but by the late fourth century this had been whittled

[2] For discussion of the problem: Kirk 1985: 1–16, Taplin 1992: 31–44, Nagy 1996: 65–112.

[3] Lamberton 1997 offers a convenient survey.

[4] Trojan War: Thuc. 1. 3–10; cattle: Hdt. 4. 29, quoting Hom. *Od.* 4. 85.

[5] Aeschin. *In Tim.* 144, 148–50, Lycurg. *Leoc.* 103.

[6] On rhapsodes: Pfeiffer 1968: 8–10, Taplin 1992: 28–9; in Athens: Plato *Ion* 530b, [Plato] *Hipparch.* 228b, Diog. Laert. 1. 57, Lycurg. *Leoc.* 102, Isoc. *Paneg.* 159, Plut. *Per.* 13. 6, cf. Xen. *Symp.* 3. 6; Davison 1955: 7–15, 1958: 38–9, Neils 1992: 72–5. At Sikyon, Hdt. 5. 67. 1, Cingano 1985.

down to the *Iliad,* the *Odyssey* and a now lost poem, the *Margites.*[7] Amongst the élite the sophists promoted the educational value of Homer's works and offered to interpret them for those with the money to listen.[8] The Athenian politician Nikias made his son learn the complete works of Homer, in the belief that it would make him into a good man.[9] Most levels of society, therefore, would have had some contact with Homer.

Not all were happy that Homer had this degree of influence. In Plato's *Republic* Sokrates finds himself saying,

> So, Glaukon, when you meet admirers of Homer who say that this poet has educated Greece, and that in the management and education of human affairs one should study his poems and arrange one's whole life according to this poet, then you should treat them in a friendly way, since they are doing the best they can.

Such idolization was much to the chagrin of Plato who proposed to ban Homer's poetry from the ideal state of the *Republic,* but even as he did this he could acknowledge that 'Homer is the best of poets and first of tragedians'.[10] Yet the argument of the *Republic* and the practice of Plato were two different things. Plato himself frequently chooses to quote lines of Homer in his works. In the *Apology* Sokrates compares himself to Achilles, reciting some lines from the *Iliad* to justify his decision to stand by his principles and die rather than abandon them and live.[11] Perhaps Plato intended to copy the format of speeches in the jury courts, but nonetheless it is significant that at such a crucial point Sokrates should be presented in this manner.

As the corpus of works attributed to Homer diminished, so his reputation increased. By the Hellenistic period Homer was 'The Poet',[12] Alexander had famously kept his copy of the *Iliad* under his pillow while on campaign, considering it to be 'a guide to the art of war',[13] and editing Homer had become a major intellectual

---

[7] Pfeiffer 1968: 43–4, 73–4. When Aischylos said (if he did) that his tragedies were 'slices from mighty meals of Homer', he surely had in mind the whole epic cycle (Athen. 8. 347e). The food analogy continues, less tastefully, in the work of the painter Galaton who presented Homer vomiting and the other poets collecting the vomit, Aelian *VH* 13. 22.

[8] Richardson 1975.

[9] Xen. *Symp.* 3. 5, specifying the *Iliad* and the *Odyssey.*

[10] Plato *Rep.* 10. 606e–7d.

[11] Plato *Apol.* 28cd, quoting and paraphrasing *Iliad* 18. 94–106; for examples, Howes 1895 and Labarbe 1949.　　　　　　　　　　　　　　　[12] Harmon 1923, Brink 1972.

[13] Plut. *Alex.* 8. 2, cf. Strabo 13. 1. 27, Plut. *Alex.* 26. 1–2, Pliny, *HN* 7. 107–8, Plut. *Mor.* 327F. Dio Chrys. 4. 39 claims that Alexander knew the *Iliad* by heart.

industry in Alexandria.[14] Ptolemy IV Philopator even set up a temple to Homer in Alexandria in the late third century BC; a statue of Homer was seated in the sanctuary and around him in a circle were placed representations of all the cities which laid claim to Homer. Nor was Alexandria the only city to have a cult of Homer; Argos, Chios, Ios, and Smyrna all paid their respects in this way.[15] Texts of Homer used in the Library of Alexandria appear to have come from as far afield as Massalia in southern France, Argos in the Peloponnese, Chios in the Aegean, and Sinope on the Black Sea, indicating how widespread Homer's readership was, from one end of the Mediterranean world to the other.[16] Further evidence for the enormous popularity of Homer comes from Egyptian papyri finds, among which Homer far out-weighs any other author.[17]

The *Iliad*, of course, was not the only poem to take the Trojan War as its subject. There were other, now lost, poems, known collectively as the epic cycle, dating from the seventh and sixth centuries, which narrated different episodes from the war, many of them originally ascribed to Homer himself. These included poems such as *Kypria*, which concerned the beginnings of the war, the *Iliou Persis* on the fall of Troy, the *Little Iliad* or *Mikra Ilias*, which deals with the end of the war, the *Aithiopis*, in which Achilles dies. Comparable to the *Odyssey* are the *Nostoi* which tell the story of the returning heroes.[18] The strength of the Homeric model may have been weaker in the fifth and fourth centuries when these other poems appear to have been read more widely than they were later. Tragedy, for instance, ransacked the whole mythological corpus for suitable material.[19] The lack of papyrus finds for the poems of the epic cycle is in marked contrast to those of Homer and is a sign of the decline in their popularity by the Hellenistic period.[20]

[14] Pfeiffer 1968: 105–233, Fraser 1972: i. 447–79, A. Erskine 1995*b*, esp. 45–6.

[15] Brink 1972: 549–52; on Alexandria, Aelian *VH* 13. 22.

[16] Adopting the interpretation of the scholiast's provenance labels in Fraser 1972: i. 328, also ii. 483 n. 163.   [17] Haslam 1997: 60–1.

[18] There is disagreement on the date; M. Davies 1989*b* would place the majority in the late 6th cent. but others, such as J. Griffin 1977: 39 n. 9, would go back as far as the late 7th. For general discussion of the cycle and individual poems, M. Davies 1989*a*. For the text, M. Davies 1988. Burgess 1996 argues that the epic cycle is 'independent in content and even form from the Homeric poems' (i.e. the *Iliad* and *Odyssey*); for ancient comparison of Homeric poems with the epic cycle, Arist. *Poet.* 23.

[19] Cf. Herington 1985: 133–6, E. Hall 1989: 32–3.

[20] According to M. L. West, *OCD*[3] s.v. 'Epic Cycle', 'no papyrus fragment of them has been identified'.

The centrality of Homer in ancient Greek culture means that later representations of the Trojans could never be entirely independent of the Homeric model. Even when there was no direct reference to the *Iliad* or the *Odyssey*, Homer was always there in the background, as comparison and support. Greeks could look to Homer's *Iliad* to underpin their conception of the Trojans, whether favourable or not. It is a text that responds to the prejudices and wishes of its readers, both ancient and modern. The present study is not concerned with a full analysis of the *Iliad*'s representation of the Trojans but rather with its potential for allowing varying interpretations.

2. BARBARIAN TROJANS IN THE *ILIAD*?

I think that the poetry of Homer achieved greater fame, because he nobly glorified those who fought against the barbarians; it was for this reason that our ancestors decided to give his art a place of honour in the music contests and in the education of our young, so that by hearing the verses again and again we might grasp fully the animosity which exists towards the barbarians and by admiring the courageous conduct of those who went on the campaign [against Troy] we might desire to emulate them.[21]

For the fourth-century Athenian orator and anti-Persian propagandist Isokrates, Homer's *Iliad* was an inspirational text in the ongoing struggle between Greek and barbarian. The victorious Greeks had burnt the city of Troy, and the barbarian Trojans had been all but annihilated. The new Trojans were the Persians and the past could be repeated. Isokrates' interpretation of Homer was not unique; a similar attitude to the Trojans can be found in much fifth- and fourth-century BC literature.

Yet, such a partisan interpretation is not the only possible interpretation, nor indeed is it the most obvious. A study of the *Iliad* itself offers little by way of confirmation. Instead, both the warring sides in this national epic of the Greeks are given surprisingly equal treatment. In spite of Isokrates' rhetorical flourishes there are no 'Hellenes' and 'barbarians' here, with all the notions of Greek superiority and exclusivity that those terms imply. Such overt polarization is absent from Homer. There is not even any consistency in the collective descriptions of what we tend to call

[21] Isoc. *Paneg.* 159.

the 'Greek' side; at one moment they are 'Achaians', at another they are 'Argives' or 'Danaans' or even 'Panachaians'.[22] These terms, for all their variety, do lead to a hazy sense of unity, but it need not be cultural or ethnic; they may simply be convenient ways of designating the whole invading force, whose unity is based on Agamemnon's role as commander-in-chief. Hellas, on the other hand, is used in a very narrow sense to refer to a part of Thessaly,[23] but there is no hint of its later broader meaning, except perhaps the single occurrence of Panhellenes.[24]

Similarly the Trojan forces are not designated as barbarians. They are a fairly loose grouping, often 'Trojans, Dardanians, and their allies' or 'Trojans, Lykians, and Dardanians';[25] at other times, especially when opposed to the 'Achaian' side, 'Trojans' might stand for all those on the defending side.[26] Thucydides asserted that the term 'barbarian' did not occur in Homer, which is true, although the catalogue of Trojan forces in book two does call the Karians *barbarophonoi*, 'of foreign speech'.[27] Apart from this one reference to Karians none on the Trojan side is termed either *barbaros* or *barbarophonos*. This is later to be of crucial importance for the Greeks of Asia Minor, because they could look back to the Trojans as predecessors without compromising their own Greekness.

Of course, even without speaking explicitly of Greeks and barbarians, it would still have been possible for Homer to present his Trojans in the manner of barbarians. If their behaviour, customs, and political organization conformed to a barbarian stereotype, then they would effectively be marked out as non-Greek or barbarian. Ancient commentators on Homer were certainly convinced of the barbarian character of the Trojans, but it is a position that is hard to sustain. In recent times several

---

[22] The point is made with great clarity by Thuc. 1. 3, cf. E. Hall 1989: 7–8, Lévy 1991: 52–7.

[23] e.g. Hom. *Il.* 2. 683 (and 684 for Ἕλληνες), 9. 395, 447, Kirk 1985: 229, Hainsworth 1993: 115.

[24] Hom. *Il.* 2. 530, E. Hall 1989: 7.

[25] Trojans, Dardanians, and their allies: Hom. *Il.* 3. 456, 7. 348, 368, 8. 497; Trojans, Lykians, and Dardanians: 8. 173, 13. 150, 17. 184; also Trojans and Dardanians: 7. 414, 8. 154.

[26] e.g. Hom. *Il.* 3. 99: Argives and Trojans; 3. 111: Achaians and Trojans; or cf. 8. 172 where 'Trojans' clearly includes the Trojans, Lykians, and Dardanians, or 8. 496, where it includes the Trojans, Dardanians, and their allies.

[27] Thuc. 1. 3. 3, Hom. *Il.* 2. 867.

careful studies of the text have revealed no significant ethnic differences; instead, the characterization of the opposing sides is remarkably similar.[28] Thus, far from being two separate and exclusive groups, they are linked to each other by a network of guest friendships, something brought out clearly when Diomedes and Glaukos meet on the battlefield and exchange family trees.[29] Both sides also share the same form of political organization: kings rule with the advice of a council of elders and some part is played by a popular assembly.[30] In general the behaviour of the Trojans is no more nor less barbarian than that of the Achaians. Both sides have a penchant for mutilating corpses, a practice considered to be barbarian in classical times.[31] It is Achilles who comes closest to the stereotype of the barbarian, with his excessive grief, his cruel sacrifice of twelve Trojans on Patroklos' funeral pyre and his extreme abuse of Hektor's corpse.[32] Agamemnon's chronic defeatism is also curious.[33] Nor would the reader of the *Iliad* find that the Trojans are devotees of strange and alien gods; on the contrary their prayers and sacrifices are to familiar Greek deities, such as Zeus, Apollo, and Athena.[34]

Nevertheless, however fair the *Iliad* may appear to some of its readers, it does have the potential for alternative interpretations. Someone like Isokrates whose sympathies were already firmly with the Greeks could find material to support a pro-Greek, anti-barbarian interpretation, and so too could the ancient commentators.[35] Cowardice, for instance, was a typically barbarian character trait, and it is noticeable that it is only those on the Trojan side who show cowardice in the face of death; Lykaon, son of Priam, vainly grasps Achilles' knees, the petrified and treacherous Dolon attempts to obtain mercy from Diomedes, the sons of

---

[28] Kakridis 1971: 54–67, E. Hall 1989: 19–47, Taplin 1992: 110–15. Mackie 1996, esp. 7–10, while accepting that there are few signs of barbarian stereotyping, does detect other differences between Achaians and Trojans.

[29] Hom. *Il.* 6. 120–236; van Wees 1992: 169–71.

[30] E. Hall 1989: 14–16, van Wees 1992: 31–6.

[31] E. Hall 1989: 25–6, Hdt. 9. 78–9.

[32] Grief: Hom. *Il.* 22. 22–125; human sacrifice: 22. 175–83; abuse: 22. 395–405.

[33] Hom. *Il.* 9. 1–51, brought back into line by Diomedes; Hom. *Il.* 14. 64–108, by Odysseus; what he is doing with his test of the troops at the beginning of bk. 2 is a mystery to me.

[34] e.g. Hom. *Il.* 6. 297–312, 7. 76–83, 24. 306–14.

[35] On scholia, Kakridis 1971: 54–5, E. Hall 1989: 23–5. More in sympathy with the scholiasts is J. Griffin 1980: 3–6, who contrasts the two sides more sharply, often citing the scholiasts in support of his position.

Antimachos plead with Agamemnon.[36] Barbarian disrespect for oaths could be seen in the way in which the Lykian Pandaros breaks the truce, but, as it is the sole instance and involves a Lykian, not a Trojan, it would be unwise to generalize.[37] The behaviour of the Achaian and Trojan forces in battle is at times sharply contrasted; the Achaians advance silently towards the enemy, whereas the Trojan forces make a tremendous racket, on one occasion sounding like squawking birds, on another like bleating sheep.[38] Such descriptions could recall a common image of noisy, undisciplined barbarians,[39] but it should also be noted that when the Trojans make a successful assault they too are silent.[40]

An advocate of a barbarian interpretation of the *Iliad* could also point out that unlike the Achaians the Trojan side spoke many, different languages, and it was language, among other things, that marked out the barbarian.[41] The *Iliad* does not indicate the language of the Trojans themselves, so their language is left to be filled in by the preconceptions of the listener. It is, however, assumed that the nobility of both sides will have no difficulty communicating with each other. Priam can speak directly to Achilles when asking for the return of Hektor's body, while warriors regularly address one another on the battlefield. Selective use of evidence could produce a barbarian Trojan in the *Iliad*, but such arguments would fail to show that barbarian stereotyping is a consistent feature of the poem. Rather, the overall impression given is the opposite.

3. Enemies of the Greeks?

For Isokrates the *Iliad* was a poem that took sides; yet other more balanced interpretations are possible. These Trojans are not

[36] Cowardice as a barbarian characteristic: Hippoc. *Aer.* 16, Arist. *Pol.* 1327^{b}27–8, Hdt. 5. 49.3, cf. Long 1986: 141 on cowardly Phrygians; Lykaon: Hom. *Il.* 21. 64–116; Dolon: 10. 454–6; sons: 11. 130–7.

[37] Hom. *Il.* 4. 50–126, though the treachery of Paris is behind the *Iliad*. Both significantly are archers, cf. Thuc. 4. 40. 2, S. Hornblower 1996: 196.

[38] Hom. *Il.* 3. 2–9, 4. 433–6.

[39] Hdt. 4. 134. 1, 9. 59. 2, Polyb. 2. 29, cf. Xen. *Anab.* 1.8, where barbarians confound expectations by their silence and the noisy Greeks lose.

[40] Hom. *Il.* 13. 41, E. Hall 1989: 30, and at 14. 400 both are noisy, Taplin 1992: 113.

[41] Hom. *Il.* 2. 804, 4. 437–8, cf. 2. 867 on the Karians. In the *Hymn to Aphrodite* (113–17) Aphrodite claims to recognize that Anchises comes from Troy by his γλῶσσα, but this could be either language or dialect. For language as a marker of Greekness, Hdt. 8. 144. 2, though note the qualifications of J. Hall 1995a: 92–5 and Harrison 1998.

stereotypical enemies, who might be represented as fodder for Achaian javelins and swords. The careful description of life within the besieged city could even have engendered feelings of pity among the listeners. Hektor is not only presented as a killer of Achaians; he is also seen in his domestic environment during a break from battle, playing with his infant son and reassuring his anxious wife Andromache, all of which increases the pathos of his death, especially as this is the last time he will see his family.[42] Elsewhere Achilles' grief for his friend Patroklos is matched by Priam's grief for his son. The gods themselves are frequently anguished and tormented at the imminent death of a Trojan favourite, such as Hektor or Sarpedon.[43] The city of Troy is said to be particularly close to Zeus' heart.[44]

Nor is the perspective within the poem solely from the Achaian side, but, rather, it is constantly shifting; sometimes it is from the viewpoint of the gods, sometimes the Achaians, and sometimes the Trojans. The Trojan perspective is at its most vivid when the listener stands with the besieged on the battlements looking outwards. Thus Priam points out the most distinctive Achaian warriors as they move beneath the city walls, while Helen, sitting beside him, identifies each of them, Agamemnon, Odysseus, Aias, and Idomeneus.[45] This shifting perspective is deployed to powerful effect on the death of Hektor. All the gods watch in silence as Achilles chases Hektor. After Achilles' victory the Achaian warriors stand around the body, both taunting and admiring it. But, when it comes to the final outrage, as Achilles drags Hektor's body around the walls of Troy, the viewpoint shifts yet again; this time to the Trojans within the city. They stand on the city walls watching this mistreatment of the body; the Trojan people, Hekabe, Priam, and finally Andromache all witness it. It is the Trojan, not the Achaian, reaction to Hektor's death that receives the greatest emphasis, grief rather than celebration. The taunting of the Achaians contrasts poorly with the lamentations of the Trojans.[46]

Yet, there are aspects of the poem that do favour the Achaians and that would no doubt have appealed especially to Isokrates.

---

[42] Hom. *Il.* 6. 370–502, E. Hall 1989: 31, Taplin 1992: 115–27.

[43] Hektor: Hom. *Il.* 22. 167–76; Sarpedon: 16. 431–8.

[44] Hom. *Il.* 4. 44–7.   [45] Hom. *Il.* 3. 146–244.

[46] Gods: Hom. *Il.* 22. 165–7; Achaian warriors: 22. 367–75; Trojans: 22. 405–515. For a narratological study of the *Iliad*, de Jong 1987.

Warriors on the Trojan side, for instance, are more likely to die in battle than their opponents; over three times as many named Trojans are killed as named Achaians.[47] There are also self-contained stories in which a contrast between Achaians and Trojans works in favour of the Achaians. Twice a Trojan challenges an Achaian to a duel in front of the assembled army and on both occasions it is the Achaian who is successful. Thus Aias gets the better of Hektor until bad light ends play,[48] and earlier Paris was saved from Menelaos only by the intervention of Aphrodite.[49] Book 10 presents two small expeditions which venture out into enemy territory on the same night, one from the Trojan camp, the other from the Achaian. The contrast is clear. The expedition of the Trojan Dolon ends in cowardly failure, whereas the Achaians Odysseus and Diomedes are successful.[50] Another example occurs when Diomedes and the Lykian Glaukos meet in battle. On addressing each other they discover that they are guest friends and so exchange gifts, but 'Zeus, son of Kronos, robbed Glaukos of his wits, and he exchanged with Diomedes, son of Tydeus, golden armour for bronze, a hundred oxen worth for nine'.[51] Is it just chance that it is Glaukos who looks foolish? It is true that he is a Lykian, not a Trojan, but he is on the Trojan side. Nevertheless these elements exist alongside, or even within, an approach which is generally sympathetic to the Trojans.

Passages such as those in which the Achaians fare better or in which an element of barbarism can be detected may reflect the different stages of composition of the *Iliad*. Thus the treatment of the Trojans may vary in different parts of the text. The audience too may have been relevant; perhaps some parts were specifically written with a mainland audience in mind, others for an audience in the Troad which would, therefore, have felt a closer identification with the Trojans.[52] It is important, however, to see that the

[47] Kakridis 1971: 63.

[48] Hom. *Il.* 7. 54–312 with 7. 312 on Aias' victory.

[49] Hom. *Il.* 3. 58–120, 324–82 (rescue by Aphrodite at 373–82), 448–61 (Menelaos described as victorious).

[50] Bk. 10, the Doloneia, is often seen as a later addition, cf. Taplin 1992: 11, 152–3, for whom it manifests 'a pro-Greek chauvinism . . . which is not characteristic of the *Iliad* as a whole'.

[51] Hom. *Il.* 6. 234–6; for another contrast note Aineias and Pandaros versus Diomedes and Sthenelos, 5. 166–327.

[52] It has, for instance, been suggested that the Aineias theme of bk 20 was composed for performance in the Troad, Reinhardt 1961: 450–2, 507, rejected by P. M. Smith 1981.

Trojans are not anathematized nor are they presented as the natural enemies of the Greeks. Indeed there are no clearly defined Greeks in the poem; rather it is open to later readers to designate one group as Greek and the other as non-Greek or even barbarian. Rather than a war between peoples the Trojan War of the *Iliad* is a war between individuals together with their followers.

The representation of the Greeks and Trojans in the *Iliad* has provoked considerable scholarly disagreement in modern times. While some have followed Isokrates in seeing it as a nationalist epic,[53] others have argued that Homer gives a very balanced picture of both sides, one that contrasts sharply with the barbarized Trojans of later tragedy.[54] On the other hand, the contrast with tragedy can make the *Iliad* seem more balanced than it actually is. The varied responses cannot simply be put down to the prejudices of the readers or listeners. These widely differing interpretations, both ancient and modern, are in part also the result of the ambiguities of the *Iliad* itself.

4. OTHER ARCHAIC REPRESENTATIONS

But how typical of the archaic period is the *Iliad*'s depiction of the Trojans? Some might say that the *Iliad* is a great and unique literary work, crafted with immense subtlety, so hardly likely to provide a fair reflection of the attitudes prevailing in Greece before the Persian Wars. Nevertheless, roughly contemporary evidence from the seventh and sixth centuries tends to concur with the evenly balanced picture found in the *Iliad*. Sappho's verses on the marriage of Hektor and Andromache, for instance, nicely complement the Homeric image of their relationship.[55] It is hard to make a judgement about the poems of the epic cycle, because only a meagre 120 lines or so survive.[56] The more plentiful evidence of art and of vase-painting, however, does tend to confirm the conclusions reached so far about the representation of Trojans in Homer.

Themes from the Trojan War appear in Greek art from as early as 700 B.C.[57] The famous Mykonos pithos of *c.*675 depicts in

---

[53] Van der Valk 1953, criticized by Kakridis 1971.

[54] See n. 28 above.

[55] *Poet. Lesb. Frag.* Sappho F44.

[56] According to E. Hall 1989: 33–7 here too there were no overt ethnic distinctions.

[57] For the Trojan War in archaic art, see esp. Johansen 1967, Ahlberg-Cornell 1992: 58–85.

relief several scenes from the sack of the city, the wooden horse, Menelaos' recovery of Helen, the death of Astyanax.[58] Troy's capture, along with other incidents from the war, features also on some shield reliefs from Olympia, which can be dated to the sixth and early fifth centuries.[59] The bulk of Trojan War scenes, however, come from the vase-painters of the second half of the sixth century.[60] In none of this archaic material is there any sign of ethnic distinction between Achaians and Trojans; there is no difference in armour, clothes, weapons, or physical characterization. The Trojan warriors could be any Greek hoplite; it is only the identifying inscriptions that betray their Trojan roots. The similarity between the two sides is brought out most clearly in duel scenes. A Rhodian plate of the late seventh century shows Hektor fighting Menelaos over the body of Euphorbos; the Trojan warrior is almost the mirror image of his Achaian opponent. The same can be observed in the common Hektor versus Achilles duels that decorate Attic vases of the late sixth century and early fifth century. The Achaians and Trojans are interchangeable in these duels; both are warriors and heroes and are depicted as such.[61] Sixth-century vase-painters were certainly aware of ethnic differences as their representations of Skythians, Thracians, and Kimmerians demonstrate. Sometimes Skythians and Thracians appear together, making the contrast clear; the Skythians have a distinctive cap, either pointed or with a bulging crown, and close-fitting trousers, while the Thracians have a foxskin cap with a tail, a mantle, and are trouserless.[62] The Trojans, on the other hand, are represented as if they were Greeks.

Thus archaic art shares its perspective with Homer. This cannot be explained by arguing that the art is illustrating Homer and therefore adopting the Homeric view. The majority of Trojan War scenes that appear in archaic vase-painting do not occur in the *Iliad* or the *Odyssey* at all.[63] Common non-Homeric scenes

[58] Ervin 1963 with plates, Anderson 1997: 183–91.

[59] Kunze 1950: 139–67, Bol 1989: 139–67.

[60] See nn. 61, 63, 64 below.

[61] Hektor v. Menelaos: Galinsky 1969: 93–4, plate 80, *LIMC* Euphorbos I no. 1. Hektor v. Achilles: *LIMC* Achilleus, sect. XIX, esp. no. 565, cf. *LIMC* Hektor no. 60; also Achilles fighting Aineias over Troilos, Carpenter 1991: no. 34, *c*.510 BC. Sometimes one is naked, the other in hoplite dress, but it could be either figure, Knittlmayer 1997: 55.

[62] Vos 1963: 40–5, Galinsky 1969: 94–5. Hdt. 7. 60–80 later outlines the various costumes of the different peoples in Xerxes' army; headgear is an important distinguishing feature.

[63] Wiencke 1954: 285, Johansen 1967: 38–9.

include Neoptolemos' killing of Astyanax and Priam, the death of Troilos, the judgement of Paris, Aias' rape of Kassandra, and Aineias fleeing with Anchises.[64] These episodes occurred in other poems of the epic cycle, such as the *Kypria*, the *Little Iliad*, and the *Iliou Persis*. The manner of their depiction in vase-painting does suggest that the approach of the epic cycle was similar to that of Homer, but it would probably be wrong to imagine that the vase-painters were directly illustrating particular epic poems. Rather, both vase-painting and epic poetry were merely the more polished expressions of a rich store of popular mythology, probably encountered first in childhood with parents or nurses as narrators.[65]

Nor is it only vase-painting that represents the Trojans in this way; public, monumental art appears to have been no different. The east frieze of the Siphnian treasury at Delphi, dating from *c*.525, presents a fight between Achaians and Trojans. The whole scene is carefully balanced; in the centre lies the body of Antilochos, separating the fighting Achaian and Trojan warriors, two on each side; beyond them, framing the scene stand the waiting charioteers and their teams of horses. Again the Trojan side is virtually a mirror image of the Achaian.[66]

In the world of archaic poets and artists, therefore, the Trojans were warriors and heroes, no different from their Achaian counterparts except that they were always destined to lose. These archaic myths of the Trojan War had the potential to be claimed by many, each in their own way. They did not preclude any one interpretation. The Athenians in the aftermath of the Persian Wars could see the Trojans as barbarian precursors of the Persians and depict them accordingly. The inhabitants of Asia Minor could still view the Persians as barbarians but have no problem incorporating the Trojans into their traditions, even as

---

[64] Neoptolemos: Wiencke 1954: 285–306, Anderson 1997: 192–9; Troilos: Knittlmayer 1997: 80–99, Carpenter 1991: 17–21, *LIMC* Achilleus, sect. VII; Paris: Clairmont 1951, Raab 1972, *LIMC* Paridis Iudicium; Aias: Anderson 1997: 199–202, *LIMC* Aias II; Aineias: Schauenburg 1960, Woodford and Loudon 1980, *LIMC* Aineias, section M.

[65] R. M. Cook 1983, Ahlberg-Cornell 1992: 184–8, Hedreen 1996, who succinctly sums up the arguments for this position (154–6). Snodgrass 1998 argues in detail that Homer had little impact on early Greek art.

[66] Stewart 1990: 128–9. The figures, who include Achilles and Memnon, are identified by inscriptions, Brinkmann 1985, whose argument affects the interpretation of Watrous 1982. The Greeks do not even get the best position as Stewart 1990: 129 notes: 'The ill-omened position of the Greek side (on the proper left side—spectators right) subtly hints at the eventual outcome.'

ancestors. The western Greeks of Sicily and South Italy may have felt a closer identification with the 'Greek' side but they could see the Trojans as representatives of the heroic age, a suitable antecedent for neighbouring non-Greeks. All these groups will develop their own image of the Trojans.[67]

[67] Athens: Ch. 3; Asia Minor: Ch. 4; West: Ch. 5.

3

The Persian Wars and the Denigration
of the Trojans

In Euripides' *Andromache* Hermione, the wife of Neoptolemos, delivers an angry tirade against her Trojan rival:

There is no Hektor here, nor Priam with his gold, but instead it is a Greek city. Yet you have reached such a depth of ignorance, you wretched woman, that you can bear to sleep with the son of the man who killed your husband and to have children by the murderers of your kin. The whole barbarian race is like that. Fathers have sex with daughters, sons with mothers, sisters with brothers, the nearest and dearest murder each other, and law prevents none of this. Do not introduce such things here.

Something has happened between Homer and this diatribe. For Hermione Trojans are typical barbarians, incestuous, internecine, and lawless, the very opposite of what it is to be Greek.[1] The fifth century BC was a time when such a depiction of the Trojans was possible. Hermione may present the Trojan as barbarian in a particularly extreme form, but the idea itself was not exceptional.

This new image, very different from the Homeric picture, flourished especially in fifth-century Athens. Fundamental to the changed representation of the Trojans were the Persian Wars. In the years that followed, the Trojans became transformed into barbarians and natural enemies of the Greeks, the mythical forerunners of the Persians. Yet, even in Athens, where this equation of Trojan and barbarian was most pronounced, there was considerable ambiguity. Public art could emphasize the parallels between the Persian Wars and the Trojan War, but the more private medium of vase-painting held back. In the theatre Athenian audiences would have watched Trojans who had much in common with contemporary Persians, but the identification was far from unequivocal: there Trojans could at times behave like Greeks,

[1] Eur. *Andr.* 168–77; it does, nevertheless, read like the plot of a typical Greek tragedy.

while their Greek counterparts could behave like barbarians. The present chapter is concerned with the causes and implications of the Trojan's metamorphosis into a barbarian, but also with its limitations.

1. Aigina, the Aiakids, and Salamis

The earliest evidence for the analogy between the Trojan War and the Persian Wars comes not from Athens but from nearby Aigina. This island state played a prominent part in the naval victory over the Persians at Salamis in 480. Nor was this all. Local Aiginetan heroes, the Aiakids, who had earlier distinguished themselves at Troy, lent vital supernatural support to the Greek forces in the battle. The Aiakids were crucial to the development of early parallels between the two wars. Adorning Aigina's temple of Aphaia and featuring in Pindar's poems in praise of Aiginetan athletes, they offered a mythological model for the Aiginetan struggle against the Persians.

The Greek fleet at Salamis had been composed of ships from many different states and afterwards there was considerable competition to claim credit for the victory. The Athenians were particularly sensitive on this issue; they accused the Corinthians of fleeing from the battle and squabbled with Aiginetans over which had been the first to go into action.[2] Nevertheless, the general view, at least according to Herodotos, was that the Aiginetans had performed best in the sea battle while the Athenians were in second place. Such a judgement must have rankled with the Athenians, especially as they had recently been at war with Aigina.[3]

Greek naval forces were supplemented by more supernatural forces. Stories circulated of phantom women, disembodied voices, the hero Kychreus appearing in the form of a serpent, a ghost ship, and, most important of all, the assistance of the Aiakids, the family of Aiakos.[4] Herodotos tells how the Aiakids were summoned by the Greeks to be allies in the ensuing battle. Aias and Telamon were based at Salamis and so in effect already present. Aiakos and his other sons had to be fetched from Aigina.[5] Plutarch

[2] Hdt. 8. 94, 8. 84. 2.   [3] Hdt. 8. 93. 1.
[4] Women: Hdt. 8. 84. 2; voice: Hdt. 8. 65; serpent: Paus. 1. 36. 1; ship: Hdt. 8. 94; Aiakids: Hdt. 8. 64, Plut. *Them.* 15. 2, cf. Hdt. 8. 83. 2, 8. 84. 2.
[5] Burkert 1977: 317 suggests couches were placed on the ship for the invisible heroes, though perhaps the ship carried statues of the heroes.

adds that ghostly armed men were seen coming from Aigina with their arms outstretched to protect the Greek fleet.

There is no reason to doubt that the Aiakids were invoked at Salamis. They had been shipped over to help the Thebans some years previously, so such activity was not unprecedented.[6] Their presence in the neighbourhood of Salamis made them an obvious choice for anyone seeking supernatural assistance in battle. Nevertheless, there may have been more to the invocation than mere convenience. Even at this early stage the analogy between Troy and Persia may have been emerging as an element of anti-Persian propaganda. The Aiakids had taken part in two successful assaults against the eastern city of Troy, first Herakles' swift campaign against the city when it was ruled by Laomedon, then later Agamemnon's more drawn-out siege of Priam's city.[7] In these circumstances the mythology of the Trojan War would have provided an appropriate and powerful means of boosting morale.[8] Pindar's *Sixth Isthmian* which was composed in the 480s, perhaps even as late as 480,[9] in honour of an Aiginetan athlete, focuses heavily on the Aiakids' first campaign against Troy. Their fame is such that the whole world knows about them: 'There is no city so barbarian or backward of speech it knows nothing of the heroic fame of Peleus, blessed son-in-law of the gods, no city that knows not of Telamonian Aias and his father.'[10] This very early use of 'barbarian', its only occurrence in Pindar, suggests a context of developing alienation between Greek and non-Greek. Is this part of the psychological preparation for battle?

The Aiakid intervention opened up a mythological battleground with Aigina on the one side and Athens on the other. The Aiginetans could point to the close association between their island and Aiakos and his family. Not only were the Aiakids the objects of hero cult on Aigina,[11] but Aiakos was the son of the

---

[6] Hdt. 5. 79–81, on which occasion they were much less effective.

[7] Herakles: Roscher, *Lex.* s.v. 'Telamon' 221–2, Gantz 1993: 442–4; Agamemnon: *LIMC* Aias I.

[8] Especially if the story was already current that the Persians were in some way related to Laomedon's grandson Memnon, who later has strong associations with Susa, Hdt. 5. 53–4, Aesch. F405 (Radt, *TrGF* iii) in Strabo 15. 3. 2, Paus. 1. 42. 1, Georges 1994: 48–9.

[9] Bowra 1964: 407.

[10] Pind. *Isthm.* 6. 24–7, trans. R. Lattimore 1947.

[11] Hdt. 5. 80, 8. 64, Paus. 2. 29. 6, cf. 1. 35. 2, Pind. *Nem.* 5. 53–4, schol. on Pind. *Ol.* 7. 156.

nymph Aigina and the first ruler of the island.[12] As the father of Peleus, grandfather of Achilles, and great-grandfather of Neoptolemos, Aiakos headed a good heroic dynasty. The Athenians, however, had already attempted to poach the Aiginetan hero some years earlier by setting up their own sanctuary of Aiakos.[13] Aias' position was more controversial; he received cult honours on Salamis rather than Aigina, but the Aiginetan version of the Aiakid family-tree made him Aiakos' grandson through his father Telamon. It is this version that Herodotos accepts.[14] Their Athenian rivals, however, could also lay claim to Aias; Salamis was now part of their state; Kleisthenes had named a tribe after Aias and the Athenians may already have begun honouring Aias as a hero.[15] The link between Aias and Aigina was completely severed by the fifth-century Athenian genealogist Pherekydes. For him Telamon's father was not Aiakos at all but a certain Aktaios, perhaps identical with the Aktaios who was the father-in-law of the mythical Athenian Kekrops and on occasion is said to have been the first king of Athens.[16] But such Athenian claims did not find their way into Herodotos.

The Trojan myth and the role of the Aiakids were central elements of the Aiginetan self-image at this time. They recur on the pediments of the temple of Aphaia on Aigina.[17] The sack of Troy by Herakles has been identified as the theme of the east pediment, while the sculptures on the west have been interpreted as a representation of Agamemnon's war against Troy. Both are events in which the Aiakids were important participants. With the exception of a single archer kneeling on the west pediment Greek and Trojan warriors are indistinguishable. The archer, on the other hand, dressed in trousers and wearing a high cap, looks ethnically distinct. This figure has sometimes been identified as Paris, but he

---

[12] On the Aiakids, Roscher, *Lex.* s.v. 'Aiakos', *RE* 1/1, s.v. 'Aiakos', 923–5, Gantz 1993: 219–32. For the development of the Aiginetan version of the Aiakid myth, F. Prinz 1979: 34–56.

[13] Hdt. 5. 89. 2.

[14] Cult: Hdt. 8. 121, Pind. *Nem.* 4. 44–8, Paus. 1. 35. 2–4, Farnell 1921: 304–10; ancestry: Gantz 1993: 221–2; Herodotos accepts: 8. 64. 2. The earliest evidence for Telamon as son of Aiakos is Pind. *Nem.* 5. 11–12, so Gantz 1993: 221, cf. *Isthm.* 6. 24–7, *Pyth.* 8. 100; for Pindar as a poet with a particular affection for Aiginetan myths, Bowra 1964: 297–8.

[15] Athens and Salamis: Nilsson 1972: 25–36; tribe: Hdt. 5. 66; hero cult: Deubner 1932: 228, Kearns 1989: 141.

[16] Pherekydes *FGrH* 3F60 (Apollod. *Bibl.* 3. 12. 6); on Athenian Aktaios, Paus. 1. 2. 6, Apollod. *Bibl.* 3. 14. 2, suggested by Williams 1987: 673, cf. Gantz 1993: 222 n. 25.

[17] Williams 1987: 669–74, Stewart 1990: 137–8, Ohly 1992: 65–94.

resembles the Skythians found in Trojan War scenes on roughly contemporary Attic vases and thus is as likely to be a Skythian as a Trojan.[18] If these sculptures dated from the time of Xerxes' invasion, they would be important early evidence for the development of parallels between the Trojan War and the Persian Wars. The date, however, is hard to determine, but here the archaeological evidence is puzzling and yet suggestive. The Trojan pediments were apparently not part of the original plan for the temple; the intention had been to decorate the temple with an abduction scene and amazonomachy. These pediments were completed and preparations were being made for their installation when there was a sudden and very late decision to abandon the original design in favour of a new concept based on the Trojan myth. The rejected pediments were put on one side and work began on a new set.

The explanation for this radical change of plan may lie in the battle of Salamis. The Aiginetans may have sought to celebrate their own success in the battle and the Aiakid assistance.[19] On the other hand, the decision could have been taken before the battle; the Aiginetans may have promised to honour the achievements of the Aiakid dynasty on the temple of Aphaia, and in return the Aiakids were expected to provide support in the approaching confrontation. Certainty is not possible, but it is plausible to think that the appearance of the Trojan myth on the pediments of the temple of Aphaia reflects the conflict with Persia. There is, however, no consensus about the date of these new pediments; one scholar proposes a date in the 490s, another accepts a range of *c.*490 to *c.*475, and yet another would place the construction of the whole temple after the Persian Wars.[20]

The implications of the earlier date for the pediments should, therefore, be considered here. If they were earlier, then the relationship between the sculptures and the Persian Wars may have been rather more oblique. An alternative explanation for the change has been found in the war fought between Athens and

---

[18] Paris: Ohly 1992: 84, *LIMC* Alexandros 75; simply an archer in Stewart 1990: pl. 243; for Skythian costume: Vos 1963: 40–51, Raeck 1981: 10–41; Skythians appear in Trojan War scenes on 6th-cent. Attic vases accompanying both Greeks and Trojans, Vos 1963: 35–9.

[19] Stewart 1990: 138, Francis 1990: 26–30.

[20] 490s: Williams 1987: 669–71, slightly later than Ohly 1992: 65, 74; 490–475: Stewart 1990: 138 with pl. 240. After Persian Wars: Gill 1993, also preferred by Francis 1990: 28–30. Both Williams and Gill argue on the basis of pottery finds.

Aigina during the first two decades of the century.[21] This may have been a suitable context for sculpture that highlighted famous victories of the Aiginetan Aiakids. The Athens–Aigina war also had a religious dimension that could have influenced the decoration of the temple. At the commencement of the war the Athenians had appropriated the Aiginetan hero Aiakos by establishing a sanctuary in the agora.[22] The very noticeable presence of Athena at the centre of both the Aphaia pediments may, therefore, have been a retaliatory response and the whole theme a reaffirmation of Aiakos' Aiginetan roots. On this dating the conflict with Persia would have had no bearing on the choice of subject matter, but it may, nonetheless, have led to a subsequent reinterpretation of the meaning of the sculptures, as Greeks came to see the Trojan Wars as a mythological model for the Persian Wars.

Certainly, the possibilities for reinterpretation would soon have been evident. In Pindar's *Fifth Isthmian* the analogy between myth and recent events is clearly stated. The ode was commissioned to celebrate the success of the Aiginetan athlete, Phylakidas; it was written after the battle of Salamis, probably in the early 470s, although perhaps even as early as 480.[23] After listing some of the heroes praised in verse, such as Iolaos at Thebes and Perseus at Argos, Pindar turns to Aigina:

Here at Aigina it is the great hearts
of Aiakos and his sons. Embattled
twice, they sacked the city of the Trojans, following
Herakles that first time,
thereafter with the Atreidai. Take flight now from earth.
Say, who slew Kyknos, Hektor,
the fearless marshal of Aithiopian men,
Memnon armored in bronze? Who wounded
brave Telephos with the spear, at the Kaïkos banks?

Therefore, my lips give them to their land, Aigina,
the glorious island, a tower builded from time
primeval, for the highest valors to storm.

---

[21] Williams 1987: 672–4, also discussed by Stewart 1990: 138 who inclines towards a Persian Wars context.

[22] Hdt. 5. 89. 2, Wycherley 1957: 132, Kearns 1989: 141.

[23] On date, Bowra 1964: 407; 480 has been suggested because the poem does not mention the battle of Plataia, though it is hard to see why a poem in praise of an Aiginetan should mention Plataia even if it had taken place. Pindar and the Persian Wars, Finley 1958, Bowra 1964: 111–17.

There are many arrows of song
my speech has skill to sound forth in their honor.
Today the city of Aias, defended in battle by sailors, will speak for them,

Salamis, in God's rain and the bloody death-sleet,
where numberless men went down.[24]

The ode thus moves from the role of the Aiakids in the two successive wars against Troy to the recent battle of Salamis. The link between past and present is made explicit by the reference to Salamis as 'the city of Aias'. Pindar's double sack can hardly fail to have recalled the temple sculpture, perhaps only recently completed.[25] Whether or not Pindar intended an allusion to the sculptures, the verses show how a viewer in the 470s could have interpreted them.

Together, the invocation at the battle, the sculpture of the temple of Aphaia, and Pindar's *Fifth Isthmian* form an impressive series of parallels. Through their mythical past the Aiginetans could emphasize and glorify their role in the Persian Wars. This would be partly a consequence of their elation at their own success in such a critical battle so close to home, but two other interrelated factors may also be relevant, their poor record in earlier dealings with the Persians and their rivalry with Athens. They may have wished to draw attention away from their rather shameful behaviour at the time of Darius' invasion. On that occasion they submitted to Persian demands for earth and water.[26] Athens, on the other hand, had resisted the Persians at Marathon with help from no one but the Plataians. The Trojan War made up for Aigina's more recent failures by offering an analogy that favoured Aigina over its rival, Athens. The Athenians may have been at Marathon but they had made little impact on the Trojan War.[27] The Aiginetans could emphasize their important contribution to both wars; they had excelled at Salamis in the tradition of their illustrious and heroic ancestors at Troy.

It would, of course, be wrong to explain the development of the analogy solely by reference to factors peculiar to Aigina. The Trojan War was *the* great war of the past and so it provided an effective means of elevating the present. Others too might be

---

[24] Pind. *Isthm.* 5. 34–50, trans., R. Lattimore 1947.
[25] Unless of course the poem came first; on date of sculptures, n. 20 above.
[26] Hdt. 6. 49–50, 8. 92. 1, cf. 6. 73, 6. 85.
[27] See n. 34 below on Menestheus.

expected to have used the analogy. One such writer is Simonides, who composed a poem on the battle of Plataia, which most likely dates from the first half of the 470s.[28] It is known only from papyrus fragments, the incompleteness of which leaves considerable scope for debate, not only about the content but also about the date and circumstances of composition.[29] The main narrative of the Plataia campaign appears to have been preceded by a hymn addressed to Achilles, which celebrates both the achievement of the Greeks at Troy and Homer's role in securing them immortal fame. The analogy between the two wars (and the poets) is thus clear.[30] It is hard to know how common it was in the literature of the 470s. The example of Simonides, for instance, can be balanced by the absence of any overt Trojan analogy in Aischylos' *Persians* of 472.[31] Aigina, however, is rather different. The range of material, that is to say Pindar, the sculpture, the invocations, the wartime stories, all help to establish that the analogy had a special significance for Aigina and at an early date.

2. ATHENS AND THE DELIAN LEAGUE

Nevertheless, the analogy between Troy and Persia is most evident in Athens, where it came to be promoted in art, drama, and oratory. There is a certain paradox here; Athens may have been one of the most important states in the expulsion of the Persians, but its contribution to the war effort against Troy had hardly been noteworthy. Some explanation for this Athenian perversity is, however, possible. In part it may have begun as a consequence of their rivalry with Aigina;[32] the Athenians could have resented the way Aigina was taking the credit for victory and glamorizing it with mythological parallels. But the analogy with the Trojan War had a continuing importance for Athens because of its leadership of a Panhellenic alliance, the Delian League. When the unity of

[28] M. L. West 1992: frags. 10–18 (trans. in M. L. West 1993*b*: 168–72), also published with photographs and discussed in Boedeker and Sider 1996.

[29] Date: immediately after Plataia (Aloni 1994, Boedeker 1996: 232), or after the foundation of the Delian League (M. L. West 1993*a*). Rutherford 1996: 174–6 sums up the debate on circumstances of composition. The surviving evidence places most emphasis on Sparta, but it would be unwise to assume that the poem was pro-Spartan; the picture may be very different if we had the complete poem.

[30] Boedeker 1998.

[31] Boedeker 1996: 232.

[32] On rivalry: Podlecki 1976, Osborne 1996: 325–8.

the Greek world against Persia was the object, the Trojan War was the myth that best encompassed and symbolized this goal. It was a myth that emphasized aggression rather than defence; in imitation of Agamemnon the Greeks would take the war to Asia. The high point of this campaign was Kimon's victory over Persian land and sea forces at Eurymedon in the early 460s.[33] So, although the myth in Athens was celebratory, it was also part of an active, anti-Persian rhetoric. It was not only about what had happened, it was also about the present and what would happen. Athens' willingness to embrace such a myth is a valuable indicator of its confidence in the post-war years.

The first sign that the Athenians are prepared to exploit the analogy between the two wars, the one mythical, the other recent, comes after Kimon's successful siege of the northern town of Eion and its Persian garrison. Kimon was honoured by being allowed to dedicate three Herms in the Stoa of the Herms. On each was a verse, one of which commemorates the victory at Eion, while another celebrates Menestheus, commander of the Athenian forces in the Trojan War:

Menestheus once commanded this city's forces on the sacred plain of Troy as part of the expedition of the Atreidai. He surpassed, said Homer, all the bronze-clad Danaans in his skill at marshalling the troops in battle. So it is not inappropriate for the Athenians to be called marshallers of war and courage.

This verse in the context of the victory at Eion draws a clear parallel between the Trojan War and the more recent war against the Persians. The capture of Eion occurred in about 477, and so these Herms are likely to have been set up in the later 470s.[34] Perhaps this is simply a continuation of themes already developed around the time of Salamis but perhaps it is somewhat more competitive, as the Athenians try to claim the Trojan War analogy for themselves. The absence of any known cult of Menestheus in Athens suggests that Menestheus had not previously been especially important in Athens.[35]

---

[33] Thuc. 1. 100. 1, Plut. *Cim.* 12–13.

[34] Verse quoted in both Aeschin. *In Ctes.* 183–5, Plut. *Cim.* 7. 5; for Menestheus, Hom. *Il.* 2. 546–56, 4. 327–48, 12. 331–76, 13. 689–90, *LIMC* Menestheus, Kearns 1989: 185; Herms: Wycherley 1978: 38, Osborne 1985: 58–64, Camp 1986: 74–7, Hölscher 1998: 165–6. Siege of Eion: Thuc. 1. 98, Hdt. 7. 107.

[35] Kearns 1989: 185. Menestheus is not found as an Athenian name until the 4th cent., see below, n. 84.

Athenian artistic celebration of the Greek victory in the Persian Wars involves a similar parallelism, identifying Persians and Trojans. The Painted Stoa was erected in about 460, perhaps sponsored by Peisianax, the brother-in-law of Kimon. It was located in the agora at the heart of Athens and decorated with paintings of well-known conflicts, mythical and historical. These included a famous work of Polygnotos, a Thasian painter who later became an Athenian citizen.[36] Set immediately after the fall of Troy, it is described by Pausanias: 'Next to [the painting of] the Amazons, are the Greeks after the capture of Troy and the kings are gathered together on account of the crimes of Aias [son of Oileus] against Kassandra. The painting shows Aias himself, Kassandra, and other captive women.'[37] The choice of theme, if Pausanias' description is an accurate reflection of the painting, is a little curious; perhaps it was intended to emphasize the moral superiority of the Greeks, concerned for justice even when sacking a city.[38] It is the context, however, that is especially significant. The Trojan scene was placed between two other paintings; one was a depiction of Theseus and the Athenians fighting against the Amazons, the other showed the Athenians and Plataians victorious over the Persians at Marathon. The Trojans are thus grouped with their Asiatic partners, the Persians and the Amazons. It is Greek versus non-Greek, winners versus losers, good versus bad.

Pausanias also tells of another painting, the first one that comes across when approaching the Stoa; this was a representation of an Athenian victory over the Spartans at the obscure battle of Oinoe in the Argolid.[39] The presence of the Spartans may seem to detract from parallels between the other groups, but the spatial

[36] Literary and epigraphic evidence for the Painted Stoa: Wycherley 1957: 31–45. On the excavations: Camp 1986: 66–72. On the paintings: Hölscher 1973: 50–73, Robertson 1975: 242–5, Francis and Vickers 1985, Francis 1990: 85–90, Castriota 1992: 76–89, 127–33. On Peisianax: Boersma 1970: 55–7. On Polygnotos and Kimon: Kebric 1983: 33–6.

[37] Paus. 1. 15. 2.

[38] So Castriota 1992: 127–33.

[39] The obscurity of the battle has led to much debate. J. G. Taylor 1998 argues that the painting was not placed in the Stoa until much later and depicted not a battle in the Argolid but the defence of Attika against the Spartans at the beginning of the Peloponnesian War. Francis and Vickers 1985 remove the Spartans from the picture altogether; for them it is the meeting of the Athenian and Plataian forces before the battle of Marathon, Oinoe being a village near Marathon. This creates a neat, if speculative, balance, two scenes of conflict with mythical barbarians paired with two Persian War scenes. For earlier arguments on the Oinoe painting, Meiggs 1972: 469–72.

relationship between this painting and the rest is unclear.[40] Even so the Spartans become damned through their association with these barbarian adversaries, Persians, Amazons, and Trojans. If one is not a friend of Athens, one might as well be a Persian. It is possible that the Oinoe painting was not added until later, perhaps during the Peloponnesian War, a time when it was more common to compare Spartans with barbarians.[41]

The choice of Marathon, too, is significant. Here the Athenians fought with only the assistance of the Plataians. There was no need to share the glory with the Aiginetans as celebration of Salamis would force them to do, nor with the Spartans who had been so important at the battle of Plataia. By focusing on the first war against Persia, the Athenians could promote themselves as heroic defenders of the Greeks, while excluding the Aiginetans and the Spartans. It is no coincidence that the late 460s were a time of worsening Athenian relations with these two states. Distrust of Sparta reached the point where the leading pro-Spartan politician Kimon was ostracized from Athens and a series of anti-Spartan alliances was established.[42] Aigina would soon find itself besieged by Athenian forces; by *c.*457 its fortifications were being torn down and it had agreed to pay tribute to the Athenians.[43]

The Trojans of the Painted Stoa are tainted by their context. They are grouped together with enemies and barbarians and would be seen as belonging with them. But this was not the only painting of Trojans produced by Polygnotos. He also decorated the inside of the Hall of the Knidians at Delphi with an elaborate depiction of the aftermath of the sack of Troy. Again, it is Pausanias who provides our evidence for the painting and its companion, Odysseus in the Underworld, giving a vivid description in his chapters on Delphi, but in contrast to the Painted Stoa

[40] Wycherley 1978: 40 suggests the Amazons, Troy, and Marathon may have been on the rear wall while Oinoe was on an end wall with captured Spartan shields at the other end, though as he says this is 'purely conjectural'.

[41] J. G. Taylor 1998 for a Peloponnesian War date; E. Hall 1989: 213–15 on Spartans as barbarians.

[42] Thuc. 1. 101–3. Possible sponsorship of the Painted Stoa by the pro-Spartan Kimon need not undermine this interpretation; the Spartan painting could have been added after his ostracism and could even be a way of redefining the building and Athenian policy.

[43] Thuc. 1. 105, 108; MacDowell 1960 argues that Aigina was a founder member of the Delian League and revolted in the late 460s; this argument is rejected by Meiggs 1972: 51–2; debate centres on Diod. Sic. 11. 70. 2–3 and 11. 78. 3–4.

there are in this instance no parallels to guide interpretation.[44] Scholars have argued over the significance of these lost paintings. Although some have detected an anti-Athenian undertone, more recent scholarship has suggested that they should be seen in the context of Knidian membership of the Delian League. According to this view Knidos, a city in Asia Minor vulnerable to Persian rule, may have commissioned the paintings in gratitude for the League's victory over the Persians at Eurymedon.[45] By focusing on Troy after it has been sacked Polygnotos could celebrate Eurymedon as a battle that marked some form of conclusion.[46] The siege of Eion, an earlier stage in the overall Athenian campaign against Persia, is recalled by the sight of a dead Trojan whom the painter identifies as 'Eioneus', surely an eponym.[47] On this interpretation, then, the Knidian painting is a further manifestation of the exploitation of the Trojan myth in the ideology of Athens and the Delian League.

Parallels continue in Athens, where the Trojans are to be found adorning the metopes of the Parthenon. The north metopes, now in very poor condition, are best interpreted as depicting the sack of Troy and appear to include a scene in which Aineias is escaping from Troy with his son and father.[48] On the east metopes gods are fighting giants, on the west it is Greeks versus Amazons and, finally, the south side is illustrated for the most part with the Greek Lapiths fighting semi-bestial centaurs.[49] There is no explicit reference to the Persians here, but it is implicit in the cumulative effect of the metopes. Indeed the whole edifice can be viewed as a thank-offering for victory over the Persians and a celebration of Athenian identity.[50] Just as with the paintings of the Painted Stoa

[44] Paus. 10. 25–7 (sack of Troy), 10. 28–32 (Odysseus in the Underworld); for an acute discussion of these paintings, Anderson 1997: 247–55. The hall is often known as the *Lesche* of the Knidians.

[45] Anti-Athenian: Dugas 1938; celebrating Eurymedon: Kebric 1983: 14–32, followed by Castriota 1992: 89–95. Knidos and Eurymedon: Plut. *Cim.* 12, though Meiggs 1972: 74 has doubts about Plutarch's accuracy.

[46] Kebric 1983: 15–16.

[47] Paus. 10. 27. 1, Castriota 1992: 90–1.

[48] Brommer 1967: 212–16 with plates 85–144 giving a good idea how tentative any identification must be. Berger 1986: 14–17 summarizes possible interpretations. Aineias is north metope no. 28 (*LIMC* Aineias 156).

[49] Brommer 1967, Berger 1986, Stewart 1990: 150–5, Castriota 1992: 134–83 with 165–74 on the Trojan metopes.

[50] Stewart 1990: 150, 152, Castriota 1992: 134–8, but note the cautionary remarks of B. S. Ridgway 1981: 18–19. Hölscher 1998: 166–8, while acknowledging the relevance of the Persian Wars, argues also for a broader meaning.

each group of metopes sets up a parallel conflict in which the Greeks versus barbarians motif is foremost. Even the Gods versus Giants battle can carry this interpretation, since the Gods, like the Greeks, embody law and order as opposed to the disorder and lawlessness of the Giants.[51] The analogy between Amazons and Persians has already been observed in the Painted Stoa. On the Parthenon metopes, however, these mythical and contemporary barbarians are brought rather closer together due to the poor state of preservation, which has led to some uncertainty over whether the figures are Amazons or Persians.[52] Thus by the 430s the Trojans have sunk from Homeric heroes to join the ranks of the more monstrous apparitions of Greek myths, Centaurs, Giants, and Amazons.

3. Drama and Characterization

The parallel between the two wars by itself makes no explicit statement about ethnicity, that is to say about whether or not the Trojans are barbarians. Nonetheless, the continuing anti-Persian sentiment which was so integral to the Delian League did gradually change the way that Trojans were represented and perceived. This finds its clearest expression in Athenian drama, where the Trojans seem almost to have become Persians.[53]

This portrayal of the Trojans as a barbarian people is evident in many of the tragedies that survive from fifth-century Athens. The Trojan, for instance, can be called a 'barbarian'; thus Hermione addresses Euripides' Andromache as 'you barbarian creature'.[54] 'Barbarian' can also be used as an epithet for any aspect of Trojan culture; Paris is clothed in 'barbarian luxury', Troy has 'barbarian laws', the myrrh on the altar in Sophokles' *Laokoon* is described as 'barbarian scent'.[55] The Trojans were even given a new name, one that reinforced this non-Greek identity; as an alternative to 'Trojans' they were sometimes called 'Phrygians', a people who had been allies of the Trojans in the *Iliad*.[56] Strabo

---

[51] Cf. E. Hall 1989: 51–3.

[52] Brommer 1967: 191–5 raises the possibility that it is Greeks v. Persians; on representation of Amazons, *LIMC* Amazones.

[53] On Trojans and barbarians in tragedy, Bacon 1961, E. Hall 1989.

[54] Eur. *Andr.* 261 (ὦ βάρβαρον σὺ θρέμμα), cf. *Andr.* 173, *Tro.* 1021.

[55] Eur. *IA* 74 (βαρβάρῳ χλιδήματι), *Andr.* 243 (βάρβαροι νόμοι), Soph. *Laokoon* frag. 370 (Radt, *TrGF* iv).

[56] Phrygians as allies, Hom. *Il.* 2. 862; examples in tragedy, Soph. *Aj.* 1054, *Lakainai*

73

comments that this is a distinctive feature of the tragedians and a scholiast to the *Iliad* singles out Aischylos.[57]

The presentation of these barbarian Trojans in tragedy is in keeping with the Greek image of contemporary Persians. Numerous passing references show how the tragic Trojan was modelled on the Persian, reflecting a conception of the Trojan as non-Greek and barbarian. Aischylos' *Persians* had depicted Xerxes' court as a place awash with wealth and luxury, a common Greek perception of the Persians.[58] The mythical Trojan court was no different. Paris dressed in gold raiment, the Trojan Ganymede walks among golden wine cups, Hekabe is queen of 'the golden Phrygians', gold is everywhere.[59] Troy on the Athenian stage was a place where the king was surrounded by eunuchs, a place where you could find the abasement of *proskynesis*, that servile act of prostration.[60] In Aischylos' *Agamemnon* Greek is not Kassandra's first language.[61] Sophokles in particular added touches of Persian authenticity to his Trojans by his use of Persian terminology, titles, and clothes; even their exclamations and laments have Persian echoes.[62] The audience, moreover, is likely to have seen the Trojan characters appear on stage in Persian-style costumes, further enhancing the oriental effect.[63] Although both Greeks and Trojans in tragedy have kings, the Trojan ruler tends to be depicted in a manner that reflects the absolute power of the Persian

frag. 368 (Radt *TrGF* iv), *Laokoon* frag. 373 (Radt *TrGF* iv), Eur. *Cyc.* 284, *Andr.* 194, 291, 363, 455, *Hec.* 4, 492, 1141, *Tro.* 7, 994, *IA* 773, 1197, 1290, 1525, on which Bacon 1961: 156, cf. 101 n. 44.

[57] Strabo 12. 8. 7, schol. on Hom. *Il.* 2. 862 (=Aesch. frag. 446 (Radt *TrGF* iii)) on which E. Hall 1989: 38–9. Dion. Hal. *Ant. Rom.* 1. 29. 1 complains about the confusion between Trojans and Phrygians.

[58] E. Hall 1989: 80–1 on *Persians*, M. C. Miller 1997: 109–33 for Greek impressions of the Persian court.

[59] E. Hall 1989: 127–8 on gold; Paris: Eur. *Tro.* 992, *IA* 74; Ganymede: *Tro.* 819–22; Hekabe: *Hec.* 492; cf. also Aesch. *Phrygians* in schol. on Hom. *Il.* 22. 351 (Radt *TrGF* iii. 365), Eur. *Hec.* 923–5, *Tro.* 995, 1074; on Trojan luxury (τρυφὰι Τρωικάι), Eur. *Or.* 1113.

[60] Eunuchs: Soph. *Troilos* frag. 620 (Radt *TrGF* iv), Eur. *Or.* 1110–14, 1426–30, 1528, on which E. Hall 1989: 157–8; among Persians: Hdt. 3. 48, 8. 104–6; *proskynesis*: Eur. *Tro.* 1021; among Persians: Hdt. 7. 136.

[61] Aesch. *Ag.* 1050–2, 1060–1, 1200, 1254, Bacon 1961: 16–17. For the sophist Gorgias too Trojans are barbarians and speak a foreign language, Palamedes 82 B 11a 7 DK.

[62] Bacon 1961: 101–4, E. Hall 1989: 120–1, Soph. frags (Radt *TrGF* iv). *Laokoon* 373. 3, *Poimenes* 515, 519, 520, *Troilos* 634 (cf. Hdt. 8. 85); exclamations and laments: *Poimenes* frag. 521, *Troilos* frag. 631; note also Persian footwear, *eumarides*, in Eur. *Or.* 1370, as worn by Darius at Aesch. *Pers.* 660.

[63] E. Hall 1989: 84–5, 136–7, Castriota 1992: 106–8; on stage costume in Athenian tragedy, Webster 1970: 35–55.

monarch. Troy is repeatedly characterized as a tyranny; Hektor's son, Astyanax, for example, is said to have died before he attained 'a tyranny equal to that of a god'.[64] The contrast between Greek and Trojan leaders is evident in Aischylos' *Agamemnon*, where the reluctant Agamemnon has to be persuaded to step onto the path of purple cloth. Priam, it is observed, would have been untroubled by such an act, one more appropriate to gods than to men.[65]

These examples have tended to focus on wealth, dress, political organization, and the court; in other words, the Trojans display the outward signs of Persian barbarism. What are less obvious in the evidence for fifth-century tragedy are the moral failings associated with barbarians. Typical barbarian characteristics include cowardice, cruelty, injustice, greed, lack of self-control, effeminacy, servility and mendacity, but these do not occur in any abundance in representations of Trojans, although they are displayed by other barbarians in tragedy.[66] Such accusations are found in Euripides' *Andromache*, where the Spartan Hermione delivers her bitter denunciation of Andromache as a typical barbarian; yet, the charges are contradicted by Andromache's noble stance, both in her reply and in the play as a whole.[67] Where Trojans do exhibit the extreme behaviour characteristic of barbarians is in their overwrought and excessive displays of grief.[68] Two factors mitigate this, however; first, the grief-stricken Trojans tend to be women rather than men, and women were considered to have less self-restraint anyway; secondly, the Trojans had much to grieve about, the death of Hektor and other Trojan heroes, and of course the sack of their city.

Two explanations can be suggested for the absence of these barbarian character faults. First, it could be a consequence of a certain ambivalence about the idea of the Trojans as barbarians. On this view the strength of earlier traditions of heroic Trojans would have made the Athenian tragedians reluctant to take the orientalization of the Trojan to its logical conclusion. A second

[64] Eur. *Tro.* 1168–9 (ἰσόθεος τυραννίς), cf. Aesch. *Ag.* 828, Eur. *Andr.* 3, *Hec.* 55–6, 365–6, 809, *Tro.* 474, 748, 933–4; on these and the meaning of τύραννος in the context of Athenian drama, E. Hall 1989: 154–6. Cf. also μέγας ἀνάκτωρ of Hektor at Eur. *Tro.* 1217, which recalls the Persian 'Great King'.

[65] Aesch. *Ag.* 914–38, on which Denniston and Page 1957: 151–3, Dover 1987: 151–80. Note the 'tyrant's blood' at 828 with Denniston and Page's comments.

[66] E. Hall 1989: 121–7.

[67] Eur. *Andr.* 155–80, cf. E. Hall 1989: 213–14, M. Lloyd 1994.

[68] E. Hall 1989: 131–2.

explanation lies in the nature of the evidence. Much of the evidence for the dramatic representation of Trojans comes from the plays of Euripides, particularly the *Andromache*, the *Trojan Women*, and the *Hekabe*. Here historical context is important; these plays were performed during the Peloponnesian War.[69] The Spartans who had been at the forefront of the war against Troy were now the enemies of the Athenians and the Trojans were due for rehabilitation. Euripides demonstrates that it is the Spartans who are the real barbarians, not the Trojans, because the Spartans behave like barbarians. In the *Andromache* the Spartans have many of the barbarians' vices, mendacity, greed, treachery, cowardice, lack of control over women, hunger for power.[70] In the *Trojan Women*, a play in which the only Greek warrior to appear on stage is the Spartan Menelaos, the confusion of the traditional antithesis is explicit when Andromache laments, 'O Greeks, who have invented barbarian crimes'.[71] Because Euripides is subverting expectations in this way, it makes sense that his Trojans have the external attributes of barbarism but not the character. Is it possible that before the Peloponnesian War Trojans on stage were more fully barbarized?

Unfortunately the plays of Aischylos and Sophokles can offer very little help on the moral character of Trojans before the war, because so few of their Trojan plays survive. Aischylos wrote fourteen plays on Trojan themes, of which only the *Oresteia* trilogy remains. The subject must have fascinated Sophokles; he wrote thirty-three plays on it, only three of which survive, *Aias*, *Philoktetes*, and *Elektra*. In contrast, there are eight Trojan plays of Euripides to survive out of fourteen credited to him, hence a disproportionate amount of the evidence comes from Euripides.[72] What remains of Aischylos' and Sophokles' Trojan output re-

---

[69] *OCD*³ s.v. 'Euripides' gives accepted production dates. For more on the significance of this context see section 6 below.

[70] See especially Eur. *Andr.* 445–62, 590–641, on which E. Hall 1989: 213–14, M. Lloyd 1994, Schmal 1995: 224–30.

[71] Eur. *Tro.* 764, the only other Greek in the play is the herald, Talthybios. In this play (line 477) a distinction is drawn between Greeks, Trojans, and barbarians, but as it is uttered by the Trojan Hekabe it is unlikely to represent anything more than an imagined Trojan viewpoint.

[72] The statistics come from Bacon 1961: 103 n. 47, cf. also Anderson 1997: 105. The 8 plays of Euripides are *Andromache*, *Helen*, *The Trojan Women*, *Iphigeneia in Aulis*, *Iphigeneia in Tauris*, *Hekabe*, *Elektra*, and *Orestes*. The Trojan War and its ramifications were the subject of approximately a quarter of the 293 known 5th-cent. plays, Knox 1979: 8–9.

volves around Greeks rather than Trojans; in all six plays there are only two Trojan characters, both women, Kassandra in Aischylos' *Agamemnon* and Tekmessa in Sophokles' *Aias*.[73] The plays in which Trojans are likely to have figured more prominently are lost, for instance Sophokles' *Laokoon* and *Troilos*. From the echoes of Persian society, costume, and language in the surviving fragments it is apparent that Sophokles at least presented Trojans after the manner of Persians.[74] The moral failings of barbarians, however, are unlikely to surface in such fragments; they require extended passages, even complete plays, in order to be observed, and that is what is lacking.

Tradition may have played a part in preserving the heroic identity of the tragic Trojan, but the problem of evidence must be remembered. Andromache, a Trojan with a Greek heart, was appropriate for the Peloponnesian War, but perhaps more typical of the mid-fifth century was the arrogant Priam of the *Agamemnon*, a man who could be imagined as hubristically striding on purple cloth.

4. ATHENIAN AMBIVALENCE

This Chapter has so far concentrated on the use of the Trojan myth in the public sphere. Here it became part of anti-Persian rhetoric, symbolizing the victory of Greek over non-Greek. Athenians could hear it invoked in speeches, look at the depiction of the sack of Troy in the Painted Stoa, read the verses on Kimon's Herms in the agora, watch barbarian Trojans on the stage.

Consequently it is somewhat disconcerting to learn that sitting in the audience watching these plays would be men with names such as Aineas, Anchises, Antenor, Polydamas, all good Trojan names. These men were not visitors to Athens, but Athenian citizens with no doubt about their Greek cultural identity. They certainly did not think themselves to be barbarians. Their names appear as members of the council, nauarchs, treasurers. Anchises was the eponymous archon of 488–7, Aineas presided as *epistates* when a sacred law about the Dioskouroi was passed in the 430s or

---

[73] Tekmessa is Phrygian rather than Trojan, daughter of the Phrygian king Teleutas, Roscher, *Lex.* s.v. 'Tekmessa (1)'; Sophokles does call her a Phrygian (lines 210, 488), but given the haziness of Trojan/Phrygian distinctions in tragedy this does not mean much; in the same play 'Phrygian' is also used for 'Trojan', line 1054.

[74] Bacon 1961: 101–4.

420s, Polydamas, whose namesake was dispenser of sound advice in the *Iliad*, was one of the treasurers of the other gods (as opposed to a treasurer of Athena) in 375–4.[75]

So, however much the Athenian state denigrated the Trojans as proto-barbarians, there was a sense in which the Trojans were not alien, because their names were familiar Greek names. Whatever the roots of these names, these were names that could and did belong to Athenian citizens, whereas Persian names did not.[76] It is possible that Trojan names became less popular in the mid-fifth century as the Trojan image acquired negative connotations, but the sketchy nature of the evidence is insufficient for establishing trends. If there was any such lull in popularity, it was only temporary. 'Aineas' and its variation 'Aineias' in particular are well recorded in subsequent centuries.[77] 'Antenor', however, makes no appearance in our Athenian evidence between the end of the fifth century and the beginning of the first century BC, perhaps the result of Antenor's developing reputation as a traitor.[78] Some Trojan names were more acceptable than others. Names reflect the family's aspirations for the children, so the characteristics of the Trojan hero himself would have been relevant.[79] Aineias, Anchises, and Antenor were all survivors; parents, anxious about the prospect of old age, may have been impressed by the care Aineias took of his father; Antenor was considered to be well disposed to the Greeks, and a similar philhellenic reputation is later attributed to Aineias; Polydamas was constantly approaching Hektor with sensible advice.[80] The name of an ill-fated Trojan,

---

[75] Anchises as archon: Develin 1989: 57 (*PA* 182); Aineas as *epistates*: *IG* i³ 133. 2 (*PA* 296); Polydamas as treasurer: *IG* 2² 1446. 2, 1445. 7. *LGPN* 2 (Athens) gives Ἀντήνωρ (3 or 4 from 7th–5th cent. BC), Πολυδάμας (6 from 4th cent. BC, 2 probably 3rd cent. BC; none earlier, and the variant Πουλυδάμας once in 4th cent.), Τρωίλος (1 from 4th cent. BC), Αἰνέας (5 or 6 from 6th–4th cent. BC).

[76] On the varied roots of Homeric names, von Kamptz 1982, cf. Kirk 1985: 257.

[77] *LGPN* 2 s.v. 'Αἰνέας' (6 from 4th cent. BC or later), Αἰνείας (10, all 2nd cent. BC or later). The name is generally spelt Αἰνέας in the classical period, cf. *LIMC* 'Aineias' 24, 33, 57, *RE* 1 'Aineias' col. 1010, but this spelling becomes less common after the 2nd cent. BC when it is replaced by Αἰνείας. This shift is discernible in *LGPN* 1 and 2, although the extra iota never seems to have been common in the Peloponnese and the West (*LGPN* 3/1).

[78] First found in Lycoph. 340, cf. Dion. Hal. *Ant. Rom.* 1. 46. 1, perhaps already present in Sophokles, Strabo 13. 1. 53 (Radt *TrGF* iv. 160–1). The name does not disappear altogether; it is found throughout the Greek world in the Hellenistic period, *LGPN* 1 and 3/1, s.v. 'Ἀντήνωρ'.

[79] Golden 1986, A. Erskine 1995a: 371.

[80] Antenor: Hom. *Il.* 3. 203–8, 7. 344–54, cf. Strabo 13. 1. 53, Paus. 10. 26. 7–8, 27. 3–4, Livy 1. 1. 1; Aineias: Livy 1. 1. 1, Dion. Hal. *Ant. Rom.* 1. 48. 3, perhaps stemming from the

on the other hand, would have been considered unlucky. The cowardly Dolon would hardly have been an attractive role model for a son.[81] Yet there are exceptions even here; Troilos, decapitated by Achilles, is found occasionally in Athens, but perhaps the young Trojan's much-celebrated death was considered inspiring in some way.[82] Athenians were also named after warriors on the Achaian side; 'Achilles', 'Aias', 'Diomedes', and 'Nestor' were all used in fifth-century Athens.[83] 'Menestheus', the name of the Athenian leader, is not found until the fourth century, after which it is common;[84] its emergence at this point may have been a response to the fifth-century emphasis on the myth. This use of both Achaian and Trojan names suggests that no sharp difference was perceived between them; for much of the time their common heroic past was more important than their ethnic significance.

The giving of Trojan names to children highlights the complexity of Athenian attitudes to the Trojan. The ambivalence that this implies is also evident in fifth-century vase-painting. In contrast to the very public nature of the art and drama which have been considered above, vase-painting is on the border between the public and private spheres. It is used domestically, but it is bought in the market; the subject matter may be limited by the repertoire of the producer, yet it may also reflect the tastes of the purchaser; when used in the gymnasium or symposium it is moving into the public arena of the male citizen.[85] Public art uses and adapts myth as a way of addressing and formulating contemporary problems and objectives; vase-painting, operating in a semi-private context, will not share these concerns in the same way, although it may echo them. The clash between the barbarized Trojan of the public anti-Persian rhetoric and the heroic Trojan of the archaic period brings about an interesting ambivalence in

hints in Homer that relations between Aineias and Priam were not good, Hom. *Il.* 13. 460, 20. 215–60; Aineias as family man, Anderson 1997: 62–3, Aineias appears as pious, father-saving, and an object of Greek goodwill in Xen. *Cyn.* 1. 15, although this opening chapter may date to the imperial period; Polydamas: Hom. *Il.* 12. 60–81, 13. 723–50, 18. 249–315. See further Ch. 5.2.

[81] Hom. *Il.* 10. 312–456.
[82] Gantz 1993: 597–603.
[83] *LGPN* 2, contrary to Nilsson 1972: 108, who claims that 'heroic names were not given to living men'.
[84] *LGPN* 2; 6 or 7 in 4th cent., 27 altogether.
[85] On use and producer, Sparkes 1996: 64–89. On sculpture as public art and vase-painting as private, Burn 1989, Buxton 1994: 53–63.

the private or semi-private sphere. This ambivalence shows itself in vase-painting both in the external appearance of the Trojans and in the choice of scenes.

If attention is focused on the appearance of the Trojan, then change is limited. The oriental image which is familiar from the theatrical Trojans occurs only occasionally on fifth-century vases.[86] Here the Attic vase-painters showed little inclination to imitate drama.[87] Thus, most Trojans are depicted as they were before the Persian Wars, for instance Priam, Hektor, and Aineias. The dress of Priam is unchanged as he continues to be murdered by Neoptolemos wielding either a spear or the unfortunate Astyanax; this Priam is far from the oriental tyrant of tragedy.[88] When a weeping Priam bids farewell to Hektor on a mid-fifth-century amphora, the pair could easily be interpreted as Greeks, if it were not for the inscriptions identifying them.[89] Like Hektor Aineias is still wearing his hoplite gear when he carries Anchises off on a crater of 470/460.[90] Although these traditionally respected figures of the Trojan side are little changed, Paris, who even in Homer comes in for criticism, does not fare well. From the mid-fifth century Paris is sometimes represented as an oriental, especially in non-battle scenes, for instance when performing his judgement.[91] Individual character, therefore, is more important than ethnicity.

It is in the choice of scenes that change is most evident.[92] Thus Priam, Hektor and Aineias may be very much the same, but they are depicted less often. Familiar scenes from the archaic period, such as the death of Priam, the flight of Aineias, the rape of Kassandra, and the pursuit of Troilos, become less common as

---

[86] Amazons, on the other hand, do appear in oriental costume (e.g. *LIMC* Amazones nos. 303, 306, 324), as not surprisingly do Persians, Bovon 1963, Raeck 1981: 101–63.

[87] The influence of drama on vase-painting in 5th-cent. Athens can be overemphasized; it is important to recognize the separateness of the two artistic traditions; Boardman 1989: 222–4, Shapiro 1994: 1–10, 124–82, Sparkes 1996: 123–4 , tend towards caution, J. R. Green 1994: 22–9 would see greater influence.

[88] Wiencke 1954, M. C. Miller 1995, *LIMC* Priamos 95–6, 126–30; Priamos 97 dated to 400–390 does show Priam in an oriental outfit, but the vase may be Italian rather than Attic; on Italian vases see last section of this Ch.

[89] *LIMC* Hektor 19, a neck amphora of *c*.450–40, cf. Hektor 18–20.

[90] *LIMC* Aineias 90, illustrated Galinsky 1969: fig. 39.

[91] Oriental: *LIMC* Paridis Iudicium nos. 40, 48, 50; Greek manner: nos. 38–9, also Boardman 1989: fig. 308 from late 5th cent. and fig. 11, Paris killing Achilles. On Paris' appearance, Clairmont 1951: 104–6, also 54 with pl. 35. Paris in Hom. *Il.*: 3. 30–7 (fearful), 3. 38–57, 6. 325–331, 6. 520–9 (criticized by Hektor), 3. 437–50 (in bed with Helen during battle).

[92] Boardman 1989: 229 with 1975: 230–3 succinctly sums up the changes.

the middle of the fifth century approaches.[93] General panoramic scenes of the sack of Troy, however, did enjoy something of a boom in the first half of the century, but then they too virtually stop. These have been explained not as a celebration of the sack of Troy but as a means of using myth to evoke the recent sacks of Miletos in 494 or Athens itself in 480, a valuable indication of the flexibility of the Trojan motif.[94] The most noticeable change of all is the almost complete disappearance of combat scenes between Greeks and Trojans; duels such as those between Achilles and Hektor, Aias and Aineias, Diomedes and Aineias, had been particularly popular in archaic art.[95] Instead of combat the vase-painters show the preparations for battle, such as the arming of Achilles or the departure of Hektor.[96] The judgement of Paris, on the other hand, becomes if anything more popular, perhaps because it highlighted Trojan responsibility; the use here of an oriental costume confirms the negative impression of him that can be found in Herodotos.[97]

The shifts in representations of the Trojan myth in vase-painting may reflect indirectly Athenian public rhetoric. Vase-painters, however, were not duplicating the myth as projected in the public sphere, but responding to the way in which it was presented there. The emergence of the barbarian Trojan was causing a tension between the old and the new in the semi-private sphere of vase-painting. Familiar scenes were not barbarized, for instance by putting Trojan warriors into oriental battle-dress; instead they were dropped. This could be explained by reference to the conservative nature of vase-painters, who will have learnt a set repertoire and been reluctant, therefore, to make changes in costume. But conservatism seems inadequate as an explanation. New scenes were introduced, and Paris could be dressed up in what passed in Athens for an eastern outfit. The reluctance to orientalize the

---

[93] *LIMC* Priamos, Aias II (for Kassandra), and Achilleus 206–370 (for Troilos) give very few examples dated after *c*.450, and *LIMC* Aineias has only 3 after *c*.480.

[94] *LIMC* (vol. 8 Suppl.) Ilioupersis 1–15, all dated *c*.450 or earlier, nos. 16–17 are 4th cent. For the Miletos and Athens explanation: M. Pipli, *LIMC* Ilioupersis p. 657. For a study of the scenes themselves, Anderson 1997, esp. 192–245.

[95] Boardman 1989: 229 with 1975: 231–2; they have ceased by 480/470, Knittlmayer 1997: 54–7. An exception is Achilles v. Memnon, *LIMC* Memnon on which see below.

[96] Achilles: *LIMC* Achilleus 510–23; Hektor: 18–20. These themes were not, however, new.

[97] *LIMC* Paridis Iudicium; Hdt. 2. 112–20, though Isoc. *Helen* 42–8 can find something to say in Paris' favour.

Trojans in fifth-century vase-painting is a sign of Athenian respect for Trojan heroes; after all there were Athenians called 'Aineas'. But at the same time the public image of the Trojans made the Athenians less comfortable with these epic heroes. This discomfort is reflected in the replacement of traditional scenes with new ones, or at least a change in the proportions. Such new scenes perhaps were less problematic in that they were free of old associations. This also meant that with the exception of Paris there was less need to orientalize the Trojans.

The disappearance of combat scenes provides a good example. In the archaic period these were evenly matched scenes, in which one side mirrored the other; both were in hoplite dress, both had equal heroic status, although, if one side did have the advantage in a contest, it was generally the Achaian. In the fifth century the focus turns instead to the preparation for battle on both the Greek and the Trojan side.[98] The effect of this change is that the Greeks and the Trojans are separated. Hektor remains in his hoplite dress, but he no longer shares the scene with his Greek opponent; the suggestion of equal heroic status is thus avoided. It is not, however, denied, as it would be if the Trojans were clothed in oriental manner. Given the use of the Trojan War as a parallel for the Persian Wars, the disappearance of these combat scenes is significant. The Athenians did not seek to avoid other combat scenes that could be interpreted as paralleling the Persian Wars. Battles with Amazons in oriental outfits, for instance, are especially common in the fifth century, more common than they were in the archaic period.[99] One Trojan War combat scene that does continue is Achilles versus Memnon, an Ethiopian on the Trojan side who is later closely linked with the Persian capital Susa. Normally he wears hoplite dress, but on occasion he is found in oriental attire; nor is there any mirroring—instead he is usually depicted as the losing party in the confrontation.[100] So combat with barbarian types is a suitable subject for vase-painting, but there is a reluctance to treat Trojans as barbarian types, or at least as typical barbarians.

In Athens, therefore, public anti-Persian rhetoric conceals, and

---

[98] Achilles: *LIMC* Achilleus 510–23; Hektor: 18–20.

[99] P. Devambez in *LIMC* Amazones p. 640.

[100] *LIMC* Achilleus 831, 833 (hoplite), 839 (oriental); Memnon and Susa: Hdt. 5. 54. 2, cf. 5. 53, Georges 1994: 48–9; this battle occurred in the *Aithiopis* but not the *Iliad*, cf. Pind. *Nem.* 6. 48–53, *Ol.* 2. 83.

may even have generated, an ambivalence about the Trojans among the people of Athens. The new image and the old one sat uncomfortably together. The pre-Persian War attitude could not just be abandoned. Men born before the war had been named after Trojan heroes, their houses contained pre-war vases that emphasized the heroic qualities of the Trojans. So within the house Athenians may be surrounded by a different set of signs from those apparent in the public sphere. Such vase-paintings may have been reinterpreted in the light of the new ideological significance of the Trojans, but the disappearance of familiar scenes in the fifth century suggests that reinterpretation was no easy matter. The direct parallelism of the public sphere tends to be avoided rather than imitated.

5. HERODOTOS AND THE 'PERSIAN' VERSION

The Trojan–Persian analogy appears to have taken shape in Aigina around the time of Salamis before being adopted by the Athenians. As part of the public rhetoric of the Athenian state and the Delian League it provided a mythical basis for the campaign against Persia. But another possibility for the origins of the analogy does exist, that it began even earlier than Salamis, and that the Persians themselves were responsible.

Herodotos, from Halikarnassos in Karia, writing in the latter half of the fifth century, begins his history of the Persian Wars with what he calls the Persian account of the origins of the conflict between Greeks and Persians; it all went back to the Trojan War. As in the work of his contemporaries, the 'Achaians' of the *Iliad* have been replaced by the 'Greeks'.[101] After describing the tit-for-tat kidnapping of young women, including Helen, by Greeks and Asiatics, he then considers the repercussions, still from the Persian point of view:

The Asiatics, say the Persians, looked upon the kidnapping of the women as something of no importance, but the Greeks, for the sake of a Spartan woman, gathered together a great army, invaded Asia, and destroyed the empire of Priam; from that time on they have always considered the Greek world to be hostile to them. For the Persians treat Asia and the barbarian peoples who live there as their own, while they consider Europe and the Greek world to be separate. This is the Persian

[101] For consciousness of this change, see Thuc. i. 3.

version of what happened. In their view the beginning of the hostility towards the Greeks was a consequence of the capture of Troy.[102]

There is much that is striking about this fascinating passage. First, rather than suggesting that the Trojans are analogous to the Persians or are their precursors in some way, Herodotos goes further than this: there is a causal link between the Trojan War and the Persian Wars. Instead of the mythological parallels of the Athenians or the Aiginetans, Herodotos is presenting a historical explanation. Secondly, and more surprisingly, this view is attributed to the Persians themselves, implying that the Persians used it as a justification in their war against the Greeks. Did the Persians really align themselves with the Trojans in this way? Or is this simply Greek interpretation of Persian actions? Herodotos can be somewhat fanciful when attributing views to the Persians, as his account of the constitutional debate at the time of Darius' accession demonstrates.[103] This explanation of the war is more likely to have developed out of the Greek parallels discussed earlier than out of a Persian knowledge of Greek poetry and stories.

In spite of their alleged resentment over the fate of Troy the Persians show little interest in the Trojan War. Herodotos explicitly refrains from commenting on the truth or falsity of the story and it does not affect his interpretation of Persian actions in the rest of the *Histories*. When Darius and his wife Atossa have their bedtime conversation about the advantages of expanding the empire, Greece is Atossa's desired objective but there is no mention of Troy. Nor does Troy feature among the many reasons put forward by Xerxes and the leading Persians when the launching of his expedition is being proposed.[104] Persian interest can be observed on only two occasions in the *Histories*.

The first is when Xerxes stops at the site of Troy while on his way with the army to the Hellespont. The visit is described very briefly by Herodotos: 'When Xerxes reached the Skamander, he went up into the citadel of Priam, because he wanted to see it.

[102] Hdt. 1. 4. 3–5. 1.

[103] Scepticism about some of Herodotos' citations need not entail acceptance of Fehling's 1989 extremist thesis that they are almost all fabrications, cf. the more judicious and restrained positions of Fowler 1996 (esp. 80–6) and Moles 1993, both of whom discuss Hdt. 1. 1–5; for a point by point rebuttal of Fehling, Pritchett 1993: 10–143. Tom Harrison has kindly guided me through this and other Herodotean problems in person and via a preview of Harrison 2000. For the Persian debate, Hdt. 3. 80–3, cf. 6. 43. 3.

[104] Darius: Hdt. 3. 134, cf. 6. 43. 4, 6. 94, 7. 4; Xerxes: 7. 8–11.

After he had seen it and had learnt all the details of the events there, he sacrificed one thousand oxen to Athena Ilias, and the Magi poured libations to the heroes.'[105] Various explanations have been proposed for this visit. Perhaps Xerxes was intending to signal to his Greek enemies the Persian desire to avenge Troy. This, however, requires both the Greeks and the Persians to have already made the identification of Persians and Trojans. Alternatively Xerxes may have been deliberately exploiting Greek myths in order to win over the Greeks of Asia Minor who felt a strong affinity with their Trojan predecessors; if he showed himself as successor of the Trojan kings, he could be more sure of their support.[106] Nevertheless, Herodotos' presentation of the visit is sketchy and low-key; there is no mention of any connection between Troy and Persia and no indication whether the libations are to Greek or Trojan heroes or to both. Herodotos may have expected his readers, some of them at least, to see the Trojan–Persian parallel, but this does not mean that Xerxes himself was aware of it too. The visit can be explained without assuming that the Persians were conscious that they were heirs of the Trojans. It was, after all, a famous city. Furthermore a lavish sacrifice and feast at an important local religious centre would help to integrate local Greeks into his army.[107] Once the parallel between the Persian Wars and the Trojan War had developed, however, Xerxes' visit to Troy and Athena Ilias would take on a new significance.

For the second occasion the reader must wait until the end of the final book. Herodotos tells how the Persian Artaÿctes had gone to Elaious in the Chersonese and plundered the rich tomb of the hero Protesilaos, the first Greek to be killed during the campaign against Troy. No respecter of heroic dignity, Artaÿctes turned the sacred ground into farmland and used the sanctuary for his harem. Such conduct is not unusual in wartime but Herodotos adds an extra dimension to it, an element of Greek interpretation which turns it into a story worth telling. Before

---

[105] Hdt. 7. 43.

[106] So Georges 1994: 59–63, cf. Hauvette 1894: 303.

[107] Cf. also Datis' offering at Delos, a sign of Persian respect for the deities of friendly states, Hdt. 6. 97, contrast Naxos, Phokis, and Athens for treatment of temples of unfriendly states, Hdt. 6. 96, 8. 30–9, 8. 51–3. Georges 1994: 60 also suggests that respect for Athena may have been intended to send a conciliatory message to Athens. On significance of Ilion, see further Ch. 9.

seizing this sacred site Artaÿctes approaches Xerxes to ask his permission, 'Master, there is a house of a Greek hero who fought against your land and met a just death. Give his house to me, so that others too may learn not to make war on your land'.[108] An attack on Troy, therefore, is an attack on Persia. But here this devious argument is being used to justify the action not of the Persian state but rather of one thoroughly unscrupulous Persian; whether the Persian king would accept the underlying premise is not made clear. The source for this story may be Athenian; when Elaious was eventually liberated from the Persians, it was the Athenian Xanthippos who commanded the fleet and who super-vised the savage punishment of Artaÿctes.[109]

Herodotos adds a very revealing note of explanation to the Protesilaos story: 'Artaÿctes said that Protesilaos made war on the land of the Persian king with the following idea in mind: the Persians think that the whole of Asia belongs to them and the reigning king.' If all Herodotos' readership were well aware of parallels between the Trojan War and the Persian Wars, then an explanation of Artaÿctes' remark would appear to be unnecessary. This suggests that, although these parallels were common in Athens where they had immediate political significance, they were not well known throughout the Greek world. Yet, even so, the explanation is one that does not in fact need the parallel for it to make sense. When Artaÿctes describes the campaign against Troy as an attack on 'your land', he could be interpreted as being deliberately ambiguous in order to deceive Xerxes but still speak the truth. It is the king's land now, even if it was not then.

Herodotos may have included his 'Persian' version as merely an entertaining prelude to his history proper, but it is a valuable sign of the extent to which the Persians could now be identified with the Trojans. Once the analogy between the two wars had been established, it was a small step to imagine that the Persians felt resentment over the Greek treatment of their Asiatic pre-decessors. Xerxes' presence at Troy, if he ever was there,[110] would have been an additional factor in forming this view. The implica-tion of the Protesilaos story, that the analogy was not as well known as our Athenian evidence might lead us to believe, strong-

---

[108] Hdt. 9. 116, cf. 7. 33, 9. 120.   [109] Hdt. 9. 120–1, on which Derow 1995.

[110] Hdt.'s information about Xerxes' route across the Troad is a puzzle, J. M. Cook 1973: 392–3.

ly suggests that on this point at least Herodotos is reflecting an Athenian interpretation of the Persian Wars.

6. Change and Context

Art, drama, and history demonstrate how the Trojan War was used as a political symbol, a mythical precursor to the Greek victory in the Persian Wars, rooting the barbarian–Greek conflict of the recent war in an earlier age. It was in Athens that its symbolism was particularly potent. Whereas Sparta withdrew from the struggle with Persia soon after the failure of Xerxes' invasion, Athens persisted with its opposition to Persia.[111] Athens' hegemonial position within the Delian League and subsequently the Athenian Empire was grounded in its conflict with Persia. The Trojan War supplied a positive image for this contemporary conflict and a mythical authority for the continuing struggle against the barbarian. The myth with Trojans cast as barbarians was, therefore, particularly appropriate to Athenian circumstances. It gave a Panhellenic cloak to Athenian imperial aspirations.

Context, however, is important. The unfavourable depiction of the Trojans tends to occur primarily in the context of conflict with the Persians. Thus a negative view of the Trojans is a feature of Athenian public rhetoric for much of the fifth century. When Athenian attention turns from Persia to Sparta as it does with the onset of the Peloponnesian War, then the public representation of the Trojans changes to accommodate the new circumstances. On stage Euripides takes the by now accepted stereotype of the Trojan as barbarian and subverts it by transferring the barbarian characteristics to the Greeks, or more particularly to the Spartans.[112]

Soon the Spartans themselves would be using the Trojan myth to promote their own Panhellenic campaign against the Persian Empire. When Agesilaos took command of the Spartan expedition in 396, the Trojan resonances were unmistakable. Imitating Agamemnon he attempted to sacrifice at Aulis in Boiotia before his departure for Asia, an event which was described by his friend Xenophon.[113] According to Plutarch Agesilaos was inspired to do this by a voice in a dream,

---

[111] Cf. Thuc. 1. 95–6.   [112] E. Hall 1989: 201–23.

[113] Xen. *Hell.* 3. 4. 3, cf. 3. 5. 5, 7. 5. 35; the sacrifice was never completed due to an inter

[*n. cont. on p. 88.*]

King of the Lakedaimonians, you are no doubt aware that no one has been appointed general of all Greece together except Agamemnon in earlier times, and now after him yourself. Since you are commanding the same peoples as he did, are making war against the same enemy and setting out for war from the same place, it is fitting that you should sacrifice to the goddess the same sacrifice that Agamemnon offered there before he set sail.[114]

The parallels could not be more clearly stated. Unhappy about sacrificing his daughter, Agesilaos opted instead for an animal sacrifice. Another story helps to confirm the impression that Agesilaos deliberately sought to identify himself with Agamemnon and his campaign with the expedition against Troy. When he was raising a cavalry force in Ephesos, the rich were allowed to provide a horse and rider instead of serving in the cavalry themselves; in doing this he was, it was said, copying Agamemnon, who had accepted a horse from Echepolos of Sikyon and exempted the donor from service in return.[115]

Agesilaos was not only imitating Agamemnon he was also imitating the Athenians. By appropriating the Trojan myth with all the connotations it had acquired in the previous century, Agesilaos was declaring Sparta to be the new anti-Persian power. Recent events meant that some dramatic step was necessary. Spartan victory in the Peloponnesian War had been secured, rather embarrassingly, by assistance and subsidies from the Persians; in exchange the Spartans had recognized Persian claims to rule the Asiatic Greeks.[116] By exploiting the Trojan War analogy Agesilaos could emphasize and publicize the long-standing Spartan tradition of hostility to the rulers of Asia, a tradition which could be traced back as far as Agamemnon himself.[117] Recent behaviour could be passed over as an aberration.

The Athenians themselves became less concerned about war with Persia. So in fourth-century Athens the very negative barbarian image of the Trojan is most noticeable in the work of the persistent anti-Persian campaigner, Isokrates. He repeatedly

ruption by the Boiotians. Agamemnon may not impress in the *Iliad*, but for a 4th-cent. view see the praise of him in Isoc. *Panath.* 74–83. Cartledge 1987: 180–202 discusses Agesilaos' Persian policy, though he has little to say on his impersonation of Agamemnon.

[114] Plut. *Ages.* 6. 6–11.
[115] Plut. *Ages.* 9. 5–7, Hom. *Il.* 23. 296–300.
[116] Thuc. 8. 18, 37, 58.
[117] For Agesilaos as μισοπέρσης (Persian-hater), Xen. *Ages.* 7. 7.

makes comparisons between the Trojans and the Persians and labels the Trojans 'barbarians'.[118] This attitude is most pronounced in the *Panegyrikos* of *c.*380, which argues for unity among the Greeks and war against the Persians. Isokrates here uses Greek successes in the Trojan and Persian wars to inspire his contemporaries to embark on a panhellenic campaign against Persia, as is evident for instance in the passage in praise of Homer quoted in the last Chapter. If the Greeks of the past could destroy Troy over the kidnapping of a single woman, surely the Athenians should act to stop the enslavement of their allies by the Persians.[119] Almost forty years later Isokrates continues this theme, this time addressing the Macedonian king Philip II. He recommends that Philip should fight against the barbarians in emulation of his ancestor Herakles who fought against Troy.[120]

Elsewhere in Athens it is not so apparent. The representation of the Trojan as a traditional barbarian enemy was heavily dependent on the anti-Persian context. Demosthenes, for instance, in all his many attacks on Philip of Macedon made no reference to any Trojan parallels even though he did regard Philip as a barbarian.[121] He seems almost completely uninterested in the Trojan War.[122] Even Isokrates could speak well of the Trojans when he was not immersed in anti-Persian rhetoric; a favourable depiction of Paris spans several chapters of his *Helen*, but an encomium is not a place for criticism.[123]

The importance of changing historical circumstances is suggested also by the evidence of Athenian funeral speeches. A speech for the dead in war was an annual event in the city's political and religious calendar, a tradition that probably began in the 460s.[124] An element of the speech was the catalogue of great achievements from the Athenian past, both mythological and historical. Very few examples of these speeches survive, but it is

---

[118] Comparison: Isoc. *Paneg.* 82–4, 157–9, 181, 185–6; *Phil.* 111–14; *Evag.* 65; and it underlies the praise of Agamemnon in *Panath.* 74–83. Labelled 'barbarians': *Evag.* 17–18; *Paneg.* 159; *Panath.* 77, 80, 83; *Helen* 52, 67. For Isokrates' attitude to barbarians, Schmal 1995: 163–5.

[119] Isoc. *Paneg.* 181.

[120] Isoc. *Phil.* 111–14.

[121] Dem. 3. 16, 3. 24, 9. 30.

[122] At 19.337 Dem. criticises Aischines' performances in Trojan dramas.

[123] Isoc. *Helen* 42–8, on which Papillon 1998.

[124] Loraux 1981, K. Prinz 1997. The details of surviving speeches are given in Loraux, 1981: 478–9.

still noticeable that the Trojan War does not feature among the achievements.[125] While this war was a valuable myth to exploit during the conflict with Persia, it was not one in which the Athenians played an especially large part. So, if circumstances did not demand it, then there would have been little reason to include the war in the list of achievements, the focus of which was very much on Athenian war efforts rather than Greek. When there was no conflict with Persia, the Trojan War could be omitted. The absence of a Trojan War example is thus likely to be because the surviving speeches largely date from the fourth century, when Athens had lost its anti-Persian fervour. The fifth century can offer only the highly stylized Thucydidean version of Perikles' funeral speech, the latter explicitly rejecting the conventional practice of listing achievements.[126] It is thus very hard to know what a fifth-century funeral speech would have been like.[127] More typical might be the arguments Herodotos gives to the Athenians in their debate with the Tegeans before the battle of Plataia. This is not a funeral speech but similarities have long been noted.[128] In the manner of a funeral speech it lists past Athenian successes, among which is their contribution to the Trojan War. Here the war is very appropriate to the anti-Persian context and its inclusion may reflect the catalogue of achievements that would have been heard by the Athenian public in the mid-fifth century.[129]

7. Consequences

The enormous influence of Athens on both the artistic and literary tradition meant that the image of the barbarian Trojan had

---

[125] This is not to say that the Trojan War is not mentioned at all, but it is not included in the list of achievements, e.g. [Dem.] 60. 10–11.

[126] Thuc. 2. 36. 4 for the rejection, 2. 35–46 for the speech.

[127] On inadequate 5th-cent. evidence, S. Hornblower 1991: 295; there is also a fragmentary speech of Gorgias, 82 B 5–6 DK.

[128] Hdt. 9. 27, cf. Jacoby *RE* Suppl. 2 col. 464, s.v. 'Herodotos'.

[129] Loraux 1981: 69–72 argues that Herodotos added the example and that the Trojan War was not a feature of the funeral speech in either the 5th or 4th cent.; that the Trojan myth as part of the Kimonian ideology had little part in the extreme democratic ideology of the later 5th cent., of which the funeral speech is a manifestation. Given the lack of 5th-cent. funeral speeches such an argument is as speculative as my own, more so perhaps; 4th-cent. Athens was very different from its 5th-cent. predecessor. As an analogue for the conflict with Persia the myth was anyway not a monopoly of Kimon; Xanthippos, Kimon's political enemy, may have exploited it at Elaious, Hdt. 9. 120; it later appears on the Parthenon and in Athenian drama.

repercussions that extended long after the overthrow of the Persian Empire took away the fundamental cause. Athens had established a model for the way in which Trojans were to be portrayed in subsequent art and literature.

Costume provides a useful example. Eastern dress appears to have been worn by Trojans on the Athenian stage, and even in the less public medium of Attic vase-painting a creeping oriental-ization is evident in the changing depictions of Paris. The oriental appearance of the Trojans comes to be increasingly common throughout the Greek world, but as it becomes further removed from its original anti-Persian context, so the meaning imposed on it by the observer changes. At the very minimum the eastern dress conveniently designates a Trojan.

South Italian and Sicilian vases, in contrast to the more restrained Attic vases, frequently present Trojans in some form of eastern outfit. Representations of the sack of Troy are often crowded with figures in oriental costume, while Priam himself is now an overdressed eastern monarch, killed by a nude Neoptole-mos.[130] The heyday of these vases was the fourth century, slightly later than the Attic vases discussed earlier in this Chapter. The tendency of Italian and Sicilian vases to depict Trojans in this manner could be explained simply as a result of the increasing diffusion of the oriental costume, but these vases also display a much stronger relationship with the theatre than Attic vases do. The artists seem to have deliberately copied theatrical pro-ductions.[131] Whereas the Athenians were very conscious of the Trojan–Persian parallel implicit in the costume and appear to have been uncomfortable with it, the response among the western Greeks is likely to have been rather different. The Italian artists may have painted Trojans in the same way that they painted Persians,[132] but since the Persians were no threat to the West the costume would not have had the same significance as it had for the Athenians who had spent so long fighting the Persians.

For the Greeks of South Italy the costume did not necessarily mark the Trojans out as enemies or as dangerous, but it did mark them out as non-Greeks. These Greeks had different needs from the Athenians. They were anxious about being culturally sub-

---

[130] Moret 1975: 151–9 on Ilioupersis, 45–50 on Priam.
[131] Trendall 1991. Taplin 1993: 21–9 (tragedy), 6–11 (Attic vases), J. R. Green 1994: 56.
[132] Cf. the representation of Persians on Darius vase in Trendall 1989: pl. 203.

merged by the non-Greeks who surrounded them, many of whom they believed to have Trojan ancestry.[133] In this fresh context the sharp Greek/non-Greek distinction which is evident on their vases may have appealed to them.

Classical literature, in the form of tragedy, Herodotos, and Isokrates, represented the Trojans as barbarians and enemies of the Greeks. This, too, could persist, because of the importance placed later on the literature of this period. Separated from its original context the idea of the barbarian Trojan could continue in the literary and intellectual tradition. It could be carried through Alexandria, picked up by Vergil, exploited by Homeric scholiasts oppressed by their own eastern problems, such as affected the later Roman Empire and the Byzantines. But the rarefied environment of the intellectual is far from the world inhabited by most Greeks.

[133] Lomas 1995: 349–53 on cultural pressure; on ancestry, see Ch. 5 below.

4

Trojan Past and Present

Many Greek cities absorbed the Trojan myth into their own traditions; they may have claimed Trojan descent or a Trojan founder; they may have had a cult of a Trojan hero or other ties with the mythical city. Often these are obscure cities which left little or no artistic or literary record, virtually ignored by historians such as Herodotos, Polybios, and Livy, salvaged only by the comprehensive scrutiny of a geographer such as Strabo or a travel writer such as Pausanias. Then there are the many Greeks who gave their children the names of Trojan heroes. All this combines to produce a world in which Trojans are by no means anathema. It is not, however, monolithic and uniform, but full of variety as different cities approach the Trojan past in different ways. Some areas such as the Troad itself seem to have valued it particularly highly. Nonetheless, it is not the Troad that opens the present Chapter's exploration of these numerous local traditions but rather the northern city of Aineia. This city is especially illuminating both because it provides the earliest evidence for the celebration of a Trojan past and because it helps to highlight the problems of approach.

I. AINEIA

Aineia was a Greek city on the Chalkidic peninsula overlooking the Thermaic Gulf. It was a city of little significance, only occasionally impinging on the historical record.[1] Its coins testify to its existence by the end of the sixth century BC, but when and how it was founded are obscure.[2] Less problematic is its mythical foundation, described by Dionysios as follows:

They [Aineias and his followers] came first to Thrace where they landed on the peninsula known as Pallene. This area was, as I said earlier,

[1] Zahrnt 1971: 142–4, Hammond 1972: 186–7.
[2] Meritt, Wade-Gery, and McGregor 1939: 464–5, largely under the influence of the enigmatic Lycoph. 1236 and the scholia for 1232 and 1236, suggest identifying Aineia with the Peisistratid foundation Rhaikelos ([Arist.] *Ath. Pol.* 15. 2), but Momigliano 1945*a*: 102 is

occupied by barbarians called Krousaians, who now gave the Trojans a safe place to stop. Staying there for the winter months, they built a temple to Aphrodite on one of the promontories, and founded the city of Aineia, where they left behind those who were too exhausted to continue the voyage and all those who wished to stay there with a view to making this land their own.[3]

Dionysios does not name a source for this account, although it may ultimately derive from the *Troika* of the fifth-century writer Hellanikos of Lesbos.[4] Such stories are often rejected by modern scholars as late developments, fabrications even, responding to the rise of Rome. Writers under pressure to supply Aineias with a route to Italy landed him at any suitable city, or cities eager to ingratiate themselves with the Romans devised their own Trojan connection, or even a combination of the two.[5]

Perhaps Dionysios' story of Aineia would have fared the same way, even with the possible backing of Hellanikos, were it not for a remarkable series of coins. These coins demonstrate that Aineias had been celebrated by the people of Aineia since the sixth century BC, presumably as the eponymous founder of Dionysios' account. Most remarkable of all are the silver tetradrachms from the sixth century. These are decorated with a scene which is best interpreted as the flight of Aineias and his family from Troy; Aineias is carrying an adult on his shoulders, while the woman who accompanies him carries a child. This is the earliest representation of a Trojan myth on a coin.[6] Fifth- and fourth-century coins of the city are adorned with a helmeted head which has been taken to be the head of Aineias.[7] It is not certain that this is Aineias, but the Trojan theme continues in the city's coinage with the minting of a coin in the late fifth or first half of the fourth

wisely sceptical; Hammond in Hammond and Griffith 1979: 68 considers the two cities to be distinct. The number of Chalkidian colonies in the area of Thrace might suggest that Aineia is a Euboian colony, but Bradeen 1952: 369–70 with n. 2 is doubtful on the grounds that Aineia is probably non-Ionic.

[3] Dion. Hal. *Ant. Rom.* 1. 49. 4 , cf. 1. 47. 6, 1. 54. 2. Although Pallene is usually used only of the western peninsula of Chalkidike, Dionysios seems to have a much broader area in mind, see his use of Pallene at 1. 47. 6, on which E. Cary in the Loeb edn. Similarly in this part of his history Thrace seems to include Chalkidike, cf. also 1. 49. 1.

[4] Cf. 1. 47. 6–48 (*FGrH* 4F31), which is clearly attributed to Hellanikos.

[5] Cf. Perret 1942 who ruthlessly rejects as many stories as he can, on which Momigliano 1945.

[6] Head 1911: 214, *LIMC* Aineias 92, Fuchs 1973: 617–18. Whether the child is a boy or a girl is unclear: boy (Head), girl (*LIMC*), child (Fuchs, P. M. Smith 1981: 30 n. 26).

[7] Cf. Head 1911: 214, *LIMC* Aineias 4.

century which depicts a head wearing a Phrygian cap. Whether this is Aineias or Askanios is less important here than the coin as evidence for a continuing Aineian interest in the Trojan myth into the fourth century.[8]

The people of Aineia alluded to the Trojan myth not only by their coin types, but also by the inscription on the coin. Several of the coins, including the family in flight, are inscribed *ΑΙΝΕΑΣ*. This is the city's name in the genitive, but it can hardly have escaped the attention of the observer that this is also the nominative of Aineias the man. The genitive is the standard way of marking out the issuing authority, but what is unusual here is the use of the name of the city rather than the ethnic, *ΑΙΝΕΑΣ* rather than *ΑΙΝΕΙΑΤΩΝ*. The ethnic was a far more common means of signalling the issuing authority than the name of the city.[9] The Aineians did sometimes use the genitive of the ethnic but what is significant here is their decision to employ the city name. Surely the resulting ambiguity is a deliberate allusion to the famous Trojan.

Aineias was special to the people of Aineia not simply because of the extraordinary similarity in their names, but because he was, they believed, the eponymous founder of the city.[10] As elsewhere in the Greek world the founder was a continuing presence, incorporated into the religious life of the city.[11] The coin evidence might lead us to suspect that Aineias was the object of hero cult in Aineia, and this supposition is confirmed by a chance reference in Livy to an incident that took place in the late 180s BC. The story that Livy tells is illuminating. The family of Poris, a citizen of Aineia, who appears to live in Thessalonika, is intending to flee from Philip V of Macedon to the safety of Euboia. They need an excuse to leave Thessalonika that will not arouse suspicions. Consequently they pretend that they are making a return trip to

---

[8] Askanios: Head 1911: 214 ; Aineias: *LIMC* Aineias 5.

[9] So Head 1911: p. lxv; Hammond in Hammond and Griffith 1979: 79 notes that it is a genitive of Aineia; on the spelling of Aineias, see Ch. 3 n. 77. Such ambiguity is not unique, cf. the coinage of Taras in S. Italy, on which the hero Taras appears riding a dolphin; here the issuing authority is specified in the less common nominative so the coins are inscribed *ΤΑΡΑΣ*, alluding to both the city and the local hero, on which Malkin 1994: 137–8 with n. 128.

[10] Dion. Hal. *Ant. Rom.* 1. 49. 4, Livy 40. 4. 9, Konon *FGrH* 26 F1.46, Steph. Byz. s.v. 'Αἴνεια'.

[11] Malkin 1987: 189–203; although this is concerned primarily with historical founders, he also considers Aineia (p. 196).

Aineia which providentially is about to hold its annual festival in honour of its founder Aineias. This, says Livy, is a festival involving sacrifice, great ceremony, and feasting. The local hero proves to be of little use; after being spotted by the king's forces while on their way from Aineia to Euboia, the ill-fated family commits suicide.[12] The festival was clearly an important, local event which attracted people from a fair distance. Part of the population of Aineia seems to have been transferred by Kassander to Thessalonika when he established that city in the late fourth century.[13] Many of these may have maintained their links with their former city, making Poris' visit to the festival all the more plausible.

Tombs of Aineias could be found scattered throughout the Greek world, the objects of civic pride, a link between the city and the heroic past.[14] Such tombs were a feature of hero cult, especially the cult of the founder, whether mythical or historical.[15] There is no direct evidence for a tomb of Aineias at Aineia. Dionysios, as we have seen above, presents Aineias as settling the weaker members of his party and then moving on, but it is Rome that is the focus of Dionysios' account, not Aineia. Nevertheless, Hegesippos from nearby Mekyberna apparently thought that Aineias was buried in the Chalkidic peninsula; an author of a history of Pallene, Hegesippos had a particular interest in the area and knowledge of it and its traditions.[16] So, perhaps the people of Aineia did indeed lay claim to the tomb of Aineias and point it out to strangers.[17] A tomb of his father Anchises was also said to be in the vicinity of Aineia.[18]

[12] Livy 40. 4 with sect. 9 on the festival: 'Profiscuntur ab Thessalonica Aeneam ad statum sacrificium, quod Aeneae conditori cum magna caerimonia quotannis faciunt. Ibi die per sollemnes epulas consumpto. . . .'

[13] Dion. Hal. *Ant. Rom.* 1. 49. 4, Strabo 7, frags. 21, 24, suggest that the whole city was moved, but in addition to the present passage of Livy and Livy 44. 10. 7 epigraphic evidence makes it clear that the city, at least in part, survived the foundation of Thessalonika, see Hammond 1972: 187, and Cohen 1995: 102–3.

[14] Dion. Hal. *Ant. Rom.* 1. 54, Pfister 1909: 137–46.

[15] Malkin 1987: 201–2, 1994: 127–33, Kearns 1989: 3–4.

[16] Dion. Hal. *Ant. Rom.* 1. 49. 1 (*FGrH* 391F5), on Thrace and Pallene in this passage see n. 3 above. Hegesianax (also known as Kephalon of Gergis) seems to have been of a similar view, Dion. Hal. *Ant. Rom.* 1. 49. 1 (*FGrH* 45F7). Hegesianax' claim is consistent with his belief in a Trojan foundation of Rome, because he held that Aineias' son Rhomos founded Rome, Dion. Hal. *Ant. Rom.* 1. 72. 1 (*FGrH* 45F9).

[17] It is perhaps significant that Aineia is mentioned in Dionysios' ch. on tombs and memorials, 1. 54. 2.

[18] Steph. Byz. s.v. 'Αἴνεια', Konon *FGrH* 26F1. 46, schol. on Lycoph. 1236; for other graves of Anchises, Pfister 1909: 158 n. 582.

The combination of the coins and the festival indicates that this close affinity with Aineias was a long-standing one, lasting from as early as the sixth century through to at least the second century BC. Given the coincidence of the names of the Trojan hero and of the city it might seem hardly surprising that Aineias should have been adopted as their founder. Nevertheless, if we accept that Aineias is unlikely to have founded the city, then there must have been a real founder. So why was a mythical founder allowed to overshadow the real one, whoever he may have been? Perhaps the answer lies in the exposed position of Aineia at the top of the Chalkidic peninsula, open to attack from Thracian tribes. In a hostile environment the inhabitants may have needed to assert their claim to the land against such predators. They could deny the newness of the city by rooting it in a mythical past. This would conform with a picture found elsewhere in which cities with mythical, often eponymous, founders are colonies that are under pressure from outsiders.[19] The Trojan colouring is also affirmed by the story that it was in this area that the Trojan women burnt their boats.[20]

Aineia and its coins provide valuable evidence for the changing ethnic identity of Aineias. On the earliest coin, which shows the flight of Aineias, there is nothing to suggest that Aineias and his family are not Greek. Later coins are particularly interesting. Some fifth-century coins showed a head with a Corinthian helmet; it is likely that this is Aineias, but because there is nothing obviously Trojan about him it is not certain.[21] But later when a head appears wearing a Phrygian cap the ethnic identity of the figure is clear.[22] Thus by the late fifth or early fourth century the notion that the Trojans wore Phrygian dress has spread to Aineia and northern Greece. In the context of Athenian tragedy this would all be interpreted as part of the barbarization of the Trojan, a sign of a growing negative attitude towards these mythical figures. The change in representation would associate the Trojans with the Persian Empire and the east. Yet, here in Aineia a 'barbarian' Aineias can coexist with cult worship, a practice that would last for several more centuries. The Aineians are so unembarrassed

---

[19] Cf. Malkin 1994: 133–9, esp. 136–7.
[20] Strabo 7, frag. 25.
[21] *LIMC* Aineias 4, with inscription *ΑΙΝΕΑΣ*, Head 1911: 214.
[22] *LIMC* Aineias 5.

by this Trojan, ostensibly barbarian, past that not only do they continue to celebrate it on their coins but they actually add the prevailing Phrygian outfit. Perhaps for the Aineians the Trojans, even with their apparently barbarian clothes, were not barbarians. It is hard to imagine that the Aineians would wish to publicize to the rest of the world that they were descended from a bunch of barbarians. Yet, by adopting the Phrygian costume on their coins themselves, the Aineians are to some extent defusing the negative connotations of the image. The acceptability of Troy, even in its barbarian guise, is something which should be kept in mind in the rest of this Chapter.

Aineia was a city that revered the Trojan hero Aineias, but, if this had not been alluded to on their coins, it is likely that historians would have been very wary of believing that such reverence developed any earlier than the date of the Roman appearance in the East. It would be easier to assume that cunning Aineians exploited the Trojan implications of their name to win the favour of the Romans. Yet, this is not the case. Local tradition here is of far greater importance than Roman power. Similarly it is local tradition and its regional variations which will be the focus of this Chapter. The evidence may often be late, but there is good reason to think that it reflects traditions as strong and long-standing as those of Aineia.

2. The Troad and Neighbouring Regions

The Troad is a mountainous region, occupying the north-western corner of Asia Minor. Reputed to have been the home of Troy and Priam's empire, it was probably first settled by Greeks in the late eighth century BC.[23] For the Greeks living there the landscape would have presented a vivid and constant reminder of the epic stories of the Trojan War. They could see Mt. Ida, the cairn of Aisyetes, the tomb of Ilos, the place where Paris performed his judgement and other such landmarks.[24] That they should plot the Homeric landscape onto their own environment is not surprising. They had the good fortune to live in one of the most celebrated

[23] On the region, J. M. Cook 1973, Tenger 1999; the fundamental ancient account is Strabo, bk. 13; a new edn. of 13. 1. 26–42 is published in Radt and Drijvers 1993 in advance of the forthcoming Groningen edition of Strabo.

[24] Strabo 13. 1. 34, 37, 51, cf. also Pliny *HN* 16. 238 for the oak on the tomb of Ilos; in the *Iliad*, Aisyetes, 2. 793, Ilos, 10. 415, 11. 166, 371–2; Leaf 1923: 184–6.

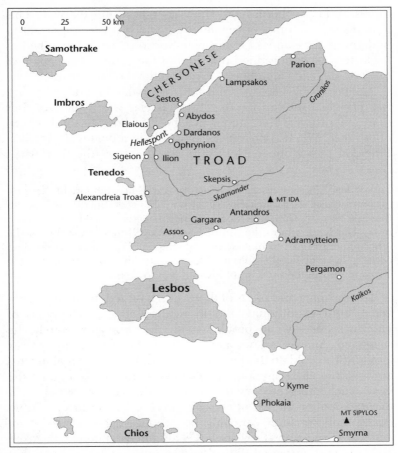

Map 1. The Troad and N. W. Asia Minor

regions of the Greek world.[25] But they went further than this
mixture of civic pride and antiquarianism. Although Greek, they
sought to identify themselves in some respects with their Trojan
predecessors. Rather than glorifying the Achaian victory, they
looked to a *Trojan* past. The focus was the Greek city of Ilion, said
to be on the site of Troy itself, but other cities throughout the
region found ways of claiming and publicizing their own Trojan
roots. They could stress continuity of location, point out the

---

[25] Cf. Strabo 13. 1. 1.

99

tombs of Trojan heroes and show off relics from the war. This took place in a competitive context in which it was important to undermine the claims of rival cities. Nor were the Achaian heroes neglected; by celebrating both sides of the conflict the people of the Troad could claim both a Greek and a Trojan heritage.

Aineias and his family loom large over the Troad. There are two principal reasons for this; first, Aineias was a survivor, but more important is the famous prophecy of Poseidon in book 20 of the *Iliad*. When Aineias is faring badly in a duel with Achilles, Poseidon points out to Hera that this is not yet the time when Aineias is fated to die:

> Let us lead Aineias away from death, lest Zeus the son of Kronos, becomes angry if Achilles should kill him. He is destined to escape, so that the race of Dardanos does not perish without seed and without trace, Dardanos whom the son of Kronos loved more than any of the other children born to him by mortal women. The son of Kronos has come to hate the family of Priam. Now mighty Aineias will rule over the Trojans, and so too the sons of his sons, yet to be born.[26]

The meaning and status of these lines have led to much controversy, both in antiquity and in modern times.[27] Dionysios of Halikarnassos saw no problem with the prophecy. Surely, he suggested, Aineias did not have to stay in the Troad to rule over Trojans; he could do this just as easily in Italy.[28] But in making this argument at all Dionysios was acknowledging the strength of the view which interpreted the lines to mean that Aineias remained in the region after the fall of the city. Strabo, for instance, is in no doubt that Poseidon can only be prophesying the rule of an Aineiad dynasty in Troy itself.[29] This interpretation was taken seriously and presented difficulties for anyone who believed that Aineias had travelled west, whether to Aineia or to Italy. One solution was to suggest that after reaching Italy he returned to Asia, where he ruled over Troy until succeeded by his son Askanios; the family then continued to hold the kingship for many generations.[30] Such an explanation would appear to be an attempt to make Aineias' westward travels compatible not only with

---

[26] Hom. *Il.* 20. 301–8, cf. *Hymn to Aphrodite* 196–7.

[27] P. M. Smith 1981 surveys ancient and modern arguments, cf. Edwards 1991: 298–301, 322–7.

[28] Dion. Hal. *Ant. Rom.* 1. 53. 4–5.

[29] Strabo 13. 1. 53.

[30] Reported in Dion. Hal. *Ant. Rom.* 1. 53. 4–5.

Homer but also with a local tradition in the Troad. Others, however, chose to resolve the problem by emendation. If 'rule over Trojans' were to be replaced by 'rule over all', then Poseidon may even have prophesied the world dominion of the Romans.[31] At some point in the late third or early second century BC the Alexandrian scholar Aristophanes of Byzantion proposed to delete the troublesome lines altogether.[32] It is the authority of Homer that makes these verses problematic, but the prophecy is not found only in the *Iliad*. The *Hymn to Aphrodite*, which was probably composed in the seventh century BC, uses very similar words for Aphrodite's prophecy that the descendants of Anchises will rule over Trojans.[33] There is also a story attributed to the pre-Persian Wars writer Akousilaos of Argos that when Aphrodite heard a prophecy that the descendants of Anchises would replace Priam's family as rulers of the Trojans she seduced Anchises to ensure that they would be her descendants too.[34]

Modern scholars have had different anxieties about the Achilles versus Aineias episode. Were the duel and the accompanying prophecy included in the *Iliad* in order to glorify a noble family in the Troad who claimed descent from Aineias? And, if so, was it an addition to the *Iliad*? It is, however, most likely that the episode was an integral part of the *Iliad*, but, even if it were added at a later date, this can hardly be later than the sixth century BC.[35] Thus already, at this early stage, Poseidon's prophecy together with the *Hymn to Aphrodite* would have contributed to the promotion of a Trojan self-image for the Greeks of the Troad. Aineias as a survivor could provide a link between Trojan past and Greek present.

The people of Ilion were proud of the connection with their epic forerunners, even if the Trojans had been defeated by the Achaians. Whereas a sharp Greek–Trojan polarity was evident in Athens, Ilion was a city that drew on both a Greek and a Trojan

---

[31] Schol. on Hom. *Il.* 20. 307, Strabo 13. 1. 53, Edwards 1991: 326, cf. Verg. *Aen.* 3. 97–8.

[32] Schol. on Eur. *Tro.* 44; see also Erbse's notes to schol. on Hom. *Il.* 20. 307–8, the controversial lines.

[33] Lines 196–7; Janko 1982: 151–80 dates the hymn to the 7th cent BC, though some would go much later.

[34] Akousilaos *FGrH* 2F39 (=schol. on Hom. *Il.* 20. 307); pre-Persian Wars: Jos. *Ap.* 1. 13.

[35] P. M. Smith 1981 and Edwards 1991 argue for integrity against, e.g., Heitsch 1965: 112, who considers this section to have been composed by a different poet working in the 2nd half of the 7th cent. BC. Jacoby 1933: 42–4 thought the whole work was written for a family in the Troad.

past. Already in the fifth century BC the Ilians appear to have been claiming Trojan founders. Dionysios of Halikarnassos in an account that is probably based on the fifth-century writer Hellanikos of Lesbos tells of Aineias and his family after the sack of Troy:

Aineias . . . sent Askanios, the eldest of his sons, with some of the allies, mainly Phrygians, to the land called Daskylitis, where the Askanian lake is, since his son had been invited by the inhabitants to rule over them. Askanios did not dwell there for long. When Skamandrios and the other descendants of Hektor approached him after Neoptolemos had released them from Greece, he went to Troy and restored them to their ancestral kingdom.[36]

This account envisages a joint re-foundation of Troy by Askanios, son of Aineias, and Skamandrios, son of Hektor, although, unlike the *Iliad* and the *Hymn to Aphrodite*, there is no suggestion here that Askanios and his family continue to rule. According to *Iliad* 6. 402–3 'Skamandrios' was Hektor's name for his son, who was known by everyone else as 'Astyanax'. This use of 'Skamandrios' rather than 'Astyanax' reflects the local nature of the tradition and also implies the adoption of a Trojan perspective. It is most likely that the promoters of the joint foundation were the people of Ilion themselves, seeking to emphasize the continuity between themselves and Troy.[37] The story conflicts directly with more familiar accounts of the Trojan War, in which Astyanax is killed by Neoptolemos when Troy is captured, a tradition vividly represented on Attic vases.[38] It is not even consistent with Poseidon's prophecy that one day the family of Aineias will rule over the Trojans, because an important part of that prophecy was the end of Priam's dynasty. But in the murky and ever-changing world of local myths it is too much to expect the consistency and accuracy which might be demanded by a rigorous philologist. What is important is a sense of the type of stories that were circulating.

[36] Dion. Hal. *Ant. Rom.* 1. 47. 5–6 (Hellanikos *FGrH* 4 F31); P. M. Smith 1981: 28–31; at 1. 48. 1, Dionysios appears to give Hellanikos as his authority for this passage.

[37] Cf. P. M. Smith 1981: 30–1 who stresses local traditions.

[38] Wiencke 1954, Gantz 1993: 650–7, *Ilias Parva* F21 (M. Davies 1988), Eur. *Andr.* 10, *Tro.* 719–98, 1118–255, Paus. 10. 25. 9, though in *Iliou Persis*, line 30 (M. Davies 1988: 62) the killing is done by Odysseus; P. M. Smith 1981: 53–8 is valuable on Skamandrios; he suggests (p. 57) that there may have been an earlier tradition that Hektor had two sons, Astyanax and Skamandrios, only one of whom survived; Homer may have merged them into one, because there was more poetic power in one doomed son.

Variations on the re-foundation story do occur elsewhere, attributed to lost and obscure writers, sometimes specifying Skamandrios, sometimes his alter ego Astyanax. One of these is Abas, author of an otherwise unknown and undated *Troika*. In this account Astyanax takes over Troy after the departure of the Greeks, but is then expelled by Antenor and finally restored by Aineias.[39] Konon, who dedicated his mythological tales to the Kappadocian king Archelaos in the late first century BC or early first century AD, tells a different story. Two of Hektor's sons, Skamandrios and Oxynios, who had been sent to Lydia for safety during the war, returned to Troy to reclaim their ancestral inheritance. Good relations between the family of Priam and that of Aineias are less in evidence here; there is even some suggestion that Aineias who had retreated to Mt. Ida after the war was forced to leave their territory.[40] Aineias is absent altogether from a scholiast's brief comment on *Iliad* 24. 735, that some writers say that Astyanax was founder of Troy and other cities.

A corollary of such foundation stories would be cult worship of the founder,[41] but, although this is a reasonable conjecture, direct evidence is lacking until the imperial period, when both Aineias and Hektor are known to have been honoured in this way. A statue of Aineias was erected on a base that describes Aineias as 'the ancestral god'.[42] Aineias accompanied by Anchises was also celebrated on the coins of the city.[43] Writing in the late second century AD Athenagoras pleads the Christian cause with Marcus Aurelius and Commodus. He notes that in the Roman Empire everyone is allowed to follow ancestral custom in religion, and the very first example he gives is the people of Ilion who call Hektor a god. The cult status of Hektor in this period is confirmed by Philostratos and Lucian.[44] This reverence for Aineias and Hektor in imperial Ilion may be the result of a continuous tradition, but it is a tradition that may also have been moulded and reinforced by the importance of Troy in the Augustan Empire. The absence

[39] Abas *FGrH* 46F1 (Serv. Auct. on Verg. *Aen.* 9. 262).

[40] Konon *FGrH* 26F1.46, but P. M. Smith 1981: 55, influenced by the Dion. Hal. version, interprets the passage to imply cooperation between the sons and Aineias.

[41] See n. 15 above.

[42] *I.Ilion* 143: Ἰλιεῖς τὸ[ν] πάτριον θε[ὸν] Ἀινείαν.

[43] Bellinger 1961: 41–2, T 115, 129, 134, 140, 148, 208, 210.

[44] Athenagoras *Leg.* 1, Philostr. *Her.* 683, Lucian *Deorum concilium* 12, cf. Julian *Epist.* 79, Synesius *Calv. Enc.* 19. 82C, *I.Ilion* 142 (statue); on coins, Bellinger 1961: T 135, 147, 150, 158, 160–4, Voegtli 1977: 113–15. Cf. *I.Ilion* 141 for a statue of Priam.

of any sign of a cult of the descendants of Hektor and Aineias is noteworthy. It was, after all, Skamandrios and Askanios who were earlier credited with the re-foundation of Troy. The disappearance of these more idiosyncratic features of the Ilian foundation myth may have been a consequence of the growing authority of the Roman myth as propounded by the Iulii.

Reverence for old Trojan heroes manifested itself in different ways at different times, but, throughout, the people of Ilion seem to have had a strong sense that their city was a direct descendant of old Troy. The foundation stories were a reflection of this conviction; Aineias and his family were well known as survivors of the sack, while Skamandrios provided a link not merely with Troy but with the ruling dynasty itself. This close identification with old Troy is evident in the refusal of the Ilians to worship Herakles because of his sack of their city, whereas Dardanos, ancestor of the Trojan royal family, does appear to have been the object of cult.[45] Trojan heroes may even have been recalled in the names of the tribes of Ilion. The Trojan elder Panthoös can be identified in the tribe of Panthoïs, while another tribe may have been named after Priam's son Deiphobos. The nicely ambiguous Alexandris could have recalled both Paris and Alexander the Great, the heroic past and the contemporary benefactor.[46]

Objectors argued that Priam's city had been completely destroyed, it was located on a different site and anyway the new Ilion was established on its present site only in the reign of Kroisos.[47] The people of Ilion rejected all these slanders against their integrity. They denied that their city was ever completely abandoned and pointed to the tradition of the Lokrian maidens. In expiation for Aias' rape of Kassandra two Lokrian girls had to be sent regularly to the temple of Athena Ilias.[48] From this the Ilians concluded that the city and the temple must have been in existence since the war. They may also have produced relics that had survived from old Troy; the cult statue, weapons, and the lyre of

[45] Herakles: Strabo 13. 1. 32; Dardanos: Rose 1993: 104–5.

[46] The tribes (*phylai*) of Panthoïs, Alexandris, and Attalis are mentioned in *I.Ilion* 121–3, which date from the late 1st cent. AD, but Attalis at least must date to before 133 BC; the early Hellenistic period would be the most likely date for a tribe called Alexandris; on these in addition to Frisch's commentary in *I.Ilion*, N. Jones 1987: 300, Cohen 1995: 152–3; for Deiphobos, Rose 1993: 105, *SEG* 44. 982. For tribes Troas and Ioulias, *BÉ* 2000, no. 32.

[47] Strabo 13. 1. 25, 13. 1. 40–2.

[48] Strabo 13. 1. 40, Polyb. 12. 5, on which Walbank 1967: 333–6, Bonnechere 1994: 150–63.

Paris are all mentioned in the sources.[49] Further support for their case came from Hellanikos who placed new Ilion on the same site as old Troy. Strabo doubts the reliability of Hellanikos' testimony on this point, dismissing it as an attempt to humour the Ilians.[50]

The truth of these claims for continuity is of no significance here, but what is important is the fact that they were made at all. Instead of seeing themselves as Greeks who had supplanted the Trojans, the Ilians felt it added to their own glory to place themselves in a direct line from the Trojans.[51] Yet, respect for Trojans was balanced by respect for the Achaians. Offerings were made by the Ilians to Achilles, Patroklos, Aias, and Antilochos.[52]

When Alexander the Great visited Ilion, he was visiting a place where a guided tour of Trojan Ilion was possible.[53] Arrian describes the occasion. Alexander went to the temple of Athena Ilias, where relics from the Trojan war were said to be kept; perhaps these included the lyre of Paris, reported by Plutarch. Here he exchanged his full armour for some of these ancient weapons, including a shield which was later to be carried before Alexander into battle.[54] He sacrificed to Priam at the altar of Zeus Herkeios, the very place where the Trojan king had been killed by Neoptolemos;[55] whether the sacrifice is an isolated instance or a reflection of a continuing cult of Priam in Ilion is unclear. Finally, he paid homage at the tomb of Achilles, while Hephaistion did the same at that of Patroklos. The rather too neat parallelism of this last visit suggests the influence of literary artifice.[56] It may be that much of Alexander's excursion to Ilion is later elaboration; all the above examples appear to have the suspect authority of the vulgate behind them.[57] Nevertheless, the people of Ilion

[49] Statue: Strabo 13. 1. 41; weapons: Arr. *Anab.* 1. 11. 7–8; lyre: Plut. *Alex.* 15. 9.

[50] Strabo 13. 1. 42.

[51] Strabo 13. 1. 25 comments that the Ilians are motivated by love of glory, φιλο-δοξοῦντες.

[52] Strabo 13. 1. 32; ἐναγίζουσιν implies that these offerings are made to the Achaians as heroes, cf. Kearns 1989: 3–4.

[53] Arr. *Anab.* 1. 11–12, on which Bosworth 1980, cf. Plut. *Alex.* 15. 7–9, see also Ch. 9. 1 below; Xerxes' earlier visit, Hdt. 7. 43, and Ch. 3. 5 above.

[54] Arr. *Anab.* 1. 11. 7–8, cf. 6. 9. 3, 10. 2 with Plut. *Alex.* 15. 9 on the lyre.

[55] Arr. *Anab.* 1. 11. 8; for respect for Zeus Herkeios in the Late Empire, *I.Ilion* 144.

[56] Arr. *Anab.* 1. 12. 1, Aelian *VH* 12. 7, on which Bosworth 1980: 103; on Hephaistion and Alexander, Arr. *Anab.* 7. 14, 7. 16. 8, Plut. *Alex.* 72; the story of Hephaistion is rejected by Stewart 1993: 83, 249 n. 62.

[57] On vulgate, Bosworth 1980: 20–1; although the mention of the shield from Ilion in the account of the siege of the Mallians seems to be integrated into the narrative, Arr. *Anab.* 6. 9. 3, 10. 2.

would have appreciated the sense of continuity implicit in the account.

Demetrios from neighbouring Skepsis, on the other hand, would have been less pleased. In the first half of the second century BC he wrote a now lost commentary on Homer's catalogue of Trojan forces which was used extensively by Strabo in his account of the Troad.[58] Demetrios glorified his home town of Skepsis at the expense of Ilion and may have been one of those who dismissed Ilian claims to be the direct successor of Troy.[59] What is significant, however, is that Demetrios shared the attitude of the Ilians towards the Trojans. Like them he considered the Trojan past to be important but he wanted to claim it for Skepsis instead. His work reflected the spirit of competition that existed between the cities of the Troad as each vied for a creditable Trojan past. In Demetrios' account Skepsis had been the site of the palace of Aineias.[60] The present city was founded by Askanios and Skamandrios. The descendants of these two families ruled the city as kings and kept the title when the constitution turned into an oligarchy and even when it made the transition to democracy.[61] Such claims were not easily compatible with the rather similar ones made by nearby Ilion, where Skamandrios at least seems to have been involved not merely as founder but also as ruler. When Demetrios was not extolling Skepsis, he was critical of its rivals and of Ilion in particular. He had visited the place, he said, and could report that it was now a shambles with roofs bare of tiles, a statement which has often mistakenly been interpreted as an impartial observation.[62] Strabo's reliance on Demetrios allows us a valuable insight into the importance of Troy in the civic self-image of the cities of the Troad.

Demetrios has often been held up as a prime example of a writer who used the Trojan myth as a means of expressing anti-Roman feeling. By presenting an Aineiad dynasty in Skepsis, it is argued, Demetrios was deliberately rejecting Rome's own version

[58] Strabo 13. 1. 45, 55; on Demetrios of Skepsis, Leaf 1923: pp. xxvii–xlvii, Pfeiffer 1968: 249–51, Gruen 1992: 40–2.

[59] Pro-Skepsis: Gruen 1992: 40–1; dismissed claims: Walbank 1967: 335.

[60] Strabo 13. 1. 53.

[61] Strabo 13. 1. 52–3; Strabo does not explicitly attribute the foundation story to Demetrios but there is little doubt that it should be so attributed.

[62] Strabo 13. 1. 27, even accepted by Gruen 1992: 40–1 who rightly notes the importance of civic competition.

of its origins and denying the Romans a creditable place in the Greek past.[63] Demetrios' thirty-volume commentary naturally dealt with the early history of Skepsis but to imagine that his Aineiad dynasty was implied criticism of Rome is surely a case of overinterpretation. More importantly the argument takes insufficient account of the Hellenistic context and thus ignores the vitality of competing local traditions. Once Demetrios is placed within the Troad, it becomes clear he was far more interested in these local traditions than in Rome; they after all were the subject of his commentary. What bothered him was not Rome but the claims of nearby cities such as Ilion. If Demetrios did indeed say that Aineias never left the Troad (and this is far from certain), it would have been implied criticism of all those many cities whose local history included Aineias, not merely Rome.[64] Indeed quite often Aineias had died while visiting those cities.[65] Was every tomb of Aineias an anti-Roman gesture?

Skepsis and Ilion, however, were not the only cities in the Troad to claim Askanios and Skamandrios as their founders. A scholiast on Euripides' *Andromache* reports a curious tale about Akamas, the son of the mythical Athenian king Theseus. Shortly after the Trojan War Akamas planned to help Askanios and Skamandrios re-found Troy and Dardanos, but his plan was opposed by the Athenians. Instead Akamas founded or re-founded other settlements in the area and he permitted Askanios and Skamandrios to be proclaimed as founders of the cities. In total there were twelve cities that benefited in this way, Gergis, Perkote, Kolonai, Chryse, Ophrynion, Sidene, Astyra, Skepsis, Polichna, Daskyleion, Iliou Kolone, and Arisbe. This story is attributed to Dionysios of Chalkis, the author of a lost work on the founding of cities, about whom little is known.[66] Some have dated him to the

[63] 'The theory denying the emigration of Aeneas and the Trojans, held by the Greek historians and antiquarians of the second century BC, served to refute the thesis of a Trojan origin for the Romans', Gabba 1991: 197, argued more fully in Gabba 1974 and 1976; or Cornell 1975: 26: 'It would be difficult to imagine that Demetrius was unaware of the grave political implications of his theory.' Gabba is followed also by Momigliano 1984: 451–2, Horsfall 1987: 12, with reservations by Ferrary 1988: 223–9, and rejected forcefully by Gruen 1992: 40–2.

[64] That Demetrios held that Aineias never left the Troad seems to be derived from the fact that he said that Aineias' family ruled at Skepsis. It is possible that he somehow used the famous prophecy of Poseidon, but Strabo himself only uses that to disprove Demetrios' contention of Aineiad dynasty at Skepsis, Strabo 13. 1. 53.

[65] See n. 14 above.

[66] Schol. on Eur. *Andr.* 10, who quotes Lysimachos of Alexandria, citing Dionysios of

fourth century BC but he has also been placed as late as the early second century BC.[67]

Akamas' role in the foundation of these cities is likely to have developed in conjunction with Athenian territorial ambitions in the Troad. Several occasions might have seemed suitable for the promulgation of such a myth: the time of the first Athenian settlement at Sigeion in about 600 BC, or the recolonization under the Peisistratids when, according to Herodotos, arguments from myth were flung back and forth between the Athenians and Mytilenians, or in the mid-fifth century when Aischylos' *Eumenides* appears to be offering a justification for an Athenian claim to the Troad.[68] The strange altruism of Akamas in allowing others to get the credit for the foundation of these cities is most easily explained if he is being incorporated into earlier stories that held the two Trojans to be the founders and that were probably current locally well before the fifth century BC. The whole myth presented by Dionysios strongly suggests that the cities in the Troad had a keen sense of affinity with their Trojan precursors and that this feeling was widespread and long-standing.

This feeling of affinity, even identity, with the Trojans continued to be found throughout the Troad. Cities vied with one another to have an important Trojan shrine or at least some Trojan associations. According to Demetrios of Skepsis those living in the area of Kebrenia, roughly east of Ilion, would point out the tombs of Alexander (Paris) and Oinone, who was his wife before Helen. Kebrenia was the locality in which the city of Kebren had stood before the population was moved to the new city of Antigoneia (later Alexandreia Troas) towards the end of the third century BC. Again, there is a Trojan echo, because the name recalled Priam's son Kebriones. Nor was this the only tomb of Paris to be found in the Troad. Parion on the north coast, perhaps not surprisingly, claimed Paris as its founder. In the second century AD the tomb of Paris together with a statue could be seen

Chalkis (Lysimachos *FGrH* 382F9), on which P. M. Smith 1981: 36 n. 32, 54–5. The joint foundation of Arisbe is also noted by Steph. Byz. s.v. 'Ἀρίσβη'. Cf. also Antandros as a foundation of Askanios, Pomponius Mela 1. 92.

[67] Fourth cent.: Schwartz *RE* 5. 929, P. M. Smith 1981: 36 n. 32; early second cent.: Perret 1942: 387–8. Fragments of Dionysios are in C. Müller, *FHG* iv 393–6.

[68] Hdt. 5. 94–5 (with 94. 2 on myth arguments), Strabo 13. 1. 38, Aesch. *Eum.* 397–402 (on which Podlecki 1989, Sommerstein 1989); Graham 1964: 32–4, 192–6, Boardman 1980: 264–6 on Athenian interests in the Hellespont region.

in the agora; festivals were held and sacrifices performed.[69] One of the prizes of the Troad could be found at Ophrynion, a city on the coast just north of Ilion. Lykophron in his *Alexandra* speaks of the tomb of Hektor here, which seems to have been clearly marked by a sacred grove.[70] This tomb may have been celebrated on the coins of Ophrynion in the fourth century BC: these depict the head of a warrior which some have suggested is Hektor.[71]

Further up the coast not far from the mouth of the river Aisepos and near the village of Memnon was the tomb of Memnon, brother of Priam. This tomb was famous not only for its alleged occupant but also for the flocks of birds that visited it annually. The locals would proudly show off the tomb and even point out the road which Memnon took on his one-way trip from Susa to Troy.[72] It was near here at Harpagia, which lay between Kyzikos and Priapos, that Ganymede was supposedly kidnapped, although others located the crime near Dardanos. He was subsequently buried on Mysian Olympos.[73] Also buried in the mountains was Anchises; his tomb was said to be on Mt. Ida, where every autumn the shepherds and cowherds of the area would hold a festival and garland the tomb.[74]

Other places in the vicinity of the Troad also made claims. Across the Hellespont in the Chersonese was the tomb of Priam's

---

[69] Kebrenia: Strabo 13. 1. 33, with Hom. *Il.* 16. 738; Parion: Athenagoras *Leg.* 26. On tombs of heroes in several different places, Pfister 1909: 218–38. An enigmatic inscription from Parion tells how a 6-year-old boy was killed by a horse, said to have been the responsibility of 'Aineadai'. Who these Aineadai were is a puzzle. Some local tradition may lie behind it. Perhaps the accident happened during a festival in which certain townspeople took the part of Aineadai. L. Robert's suggestion (1955: 276–82 with text) that it reflects tensions within the Roman colony of Parion is unsatisfactory and fails to take account of the way the Trojan past pervaded the whole Troad.

[70] On the tomb: Lycoph. 1208 with schol. 1194 and 1208 (ed. Scheer); Strabo 13. 1. 29 mentions only a conspicuous grove of Hektor (τὸ τοῦ Ἕκτορος ἄλσος), cf. *Anth. Pal.* 7. 136–7, 140. Pfister 1909: 193–4. On sacred groves, Birge 1994. Hektor was also claimed by Thebes, Paus. 9. 18. 5, Schachter 1981: 233–4, see n. 142 below with accompanying text. On Ophrynion, J. M. Cook 1973: 72–7.

[71] *LIMC* Hektor 1, Head 1911: 547–8, who also notes a coin with 'Hektor advancing: also crouching behind shield'.

[72] Strabo 13. 1. 11, Paus. 10. 31. 6, Aelian *NA* 5. 1; the birds were known as Memnonides, cf. Pollard 1977: 101–2, 163.

[73] Strabo 13. 1. 11, Harpagia could be linked to ἁρπάζω, 'to snatch away'. The story was also claimed by the Chalkidians of Euboia, Athen. 13. 601ef. Burial: schol. on Hom. *Il.* 20. 234 ; another version places his grave on Crete, *Suda*, s.v. 'Μίνως'.

[74] Eustath. on Hom. (*Il.*) 894. 35; for other tombs of Anchises, Pfister 1909: 158 n. 582. It was on Mt. Ida that Anchises had his encounter with Aphrodite Hom. *Il.* 2. 819–21, Hes. *Theog.* 1008–10.

wife Hekabe; Strabo says that this tomb is pointed out after one has sailed round the headland of Kynos-Sema, literally the Dog's Tomb.[75] This story was current as early as Euripides' *Hekabe*, where it is prophesied that Hekabe will be turned into a dog and her burial place will become a landmark for sailors known as 'the tomb of the suffering dog'.[76] The Lykians, however, thought that she had come their way.[77] Pergamon was said to have been named after Pergamos, son of Andromache and Neoptolemos, a combination that enabled Pergamon to claim both a Greek and a Trojan heritage and was perhaps related to Pergamene territorial aspirations in the Troad. It is not known whether the citizens of Pergamon could point to his tomb, but they did have a shrine of Andromache.[78] Many burial places are known for Aineias, but none in the Troad itself. The closest comes in Festus' report of Agathokles of Kyzikos, a historian who has been dated to the mid-third century BC. According to Agathokles several writers said that Aineias was buried at Berekynthia near the river Nolon; the location of this city is uncertain, but it is most likely to have been in Phrygia.[79] Further afield but linked closely in myth with Troy is the island of Samothrake, where Aineias dedicated his shield in a temple.[80]

All the examples in this section reflect a long-standing veneration of the Trojan past in the Troad. Although much of the evidence is fairly late, it would be wrong to explain these stories as a calculated response to Rome's Trojan ancestry. More important is the very vitality of the local traditions recorded, whether they are those of the shepherds of Mt. Ida, the villagers of Memnon or the citizens of Ilion. This was an oral culture in which stories and

---

[75] Strabo 7, frag. 55, 13. 1. 28, Pliny *HN* 4. 49, Amm. Marc. 22. 8. 4.

[76] κυνὸς ταλαίνης σῆμα, Eur. *Hec.* 1270–5, on which Mossman 1995: 35–6, who considers Euripides to be adopting a local myth of the Chersonese.

[77] Paus. 10. 27; other heroes from the Trojan side revered in Lykia are Pandaros, Sarpedon, and Glaukos, see Ch. 7.2 below.

[78] Paus. 1.11.2 (ἡρῷον), *I.Perg.* pp. 219–20; Scheer 1993: 123–5, 130, Kosmetatou 1995. In imperial period Pergamos appears on coins of the city, Head 1911: 536. See further Ch. 8. 3 below.

[79] Festus 328L (Agathokles *FGrH* 472F5). Steph. Byz. gives a Berekyntos in Phrygia. On location, Jacoby commentary to Agathokles F5, cf. also the μνῆμα of Koroibos, son of Mygdon, Phrygian ally of the Trojans, at Stektorion in Phrygia, Paus. 10. 27. 1.

[80] Serv. on *Aen.* 3. 287, a story that should be dated earlier than the mid-2nd cent. BC, Cole 1984: 101; how much earlier is disputed; Wissowa 1887: 39 n. 2 goes back to 5th cent., but Perret 1942: 30–1 stays in 2nd cent.; for Troy and Samothrake, Dion. Hal. *Ant. Rom.* 1. 61. 3, 1. 68–9, 2. 66. 5, Strabo 7, frag. 49, Rose 1998: 73–90.

customs were passed down from generation to generation, only occasionally to be pinned down in writing. These were local traditions that developed independently of Rome. The sources repeatedly allude to the local and oral nature of what they report: 'Demetrios says that the tomb of Alexander is *pointed out* (δείκνυσ-θαι) there', 'Hekabe's tomb is *pointed out* (δείκνυται)', 'It is the belief of the local inhabitants', 'the tomb of Anchises was *pointed out* (ἐδείκνυτο)', 'the people of Ilion are fond of glory and want their city to be the ancient city'.[81] Such remarks enable the writer to distance himself from the information reported and thus to cite it without endorsing it. In considering these traditions it is important to look back at the model of Aineia discussed in the last section. It was only the accident of its coinage that allowed us to see the importance of Aineias in the city over centuries. The traditions of the Troad should be seen as equally long-standing, unless there is explicit evidence to the contrary. The form they took no doubt changed over time in ways that are difficult for us now to detect, but the value that was placed on the Trojan past should not be underestimated.

It is not only the *Trojan* past that was celebrated. The graves of Achaian heroes who fell in battle could be found around the Troad. According to Strabo there was a *mnema* and a sanctuary of Achilles near Sigeion, along with *mnemata* of Patroklos and Antilochos; these are most likely to have been tombs, although Achilles was also reported to be buried at Ilion and Achilleion.[82] At Rhoiteion on the coast there was a tomb, sanctuary, and statue of Aias, while nearby Aianteion also possessed the tomb.[83] This confusing multiplicity of tombs could be a consequence of local competition or it could result from alternative descriptions of the same monument.[84] Whichever is the case, a dead Achaian seems to

---

[81] Alexander: Strabo, 13. 1. 33; Hekabe: Strabo 7. 55; belief: Aelian *VH* 5. 1; Anchises: Eustath. on Hom. (*Il.*) 894. 35; Ilion: Strabo 13. 1. 25.

[82] Sigeion: Strabo 13. 1. 32; Ilion: Plut. *Alex.* 15. 9, Arr. *Anab.* 1. 12. 1; Achilleion: Strabo 13. 1. 39, Pliny, *HN* 5. 125, cf. also Amm. Marc. 22. 8. 4 for tombs of Achilles and Aias in the area; Ampelius 8. 11 gives Rhoioteion as the location of tombs of Achilles and Patroklos. For cults of Achilles in the Black Sea area, Hedreen 1991. A good distance south of the Troad there is the curious foundation story of Pygela whose first inhabitants were some of Agamemnon's veterans who suffered from a disease of the buttocks, *pygalgeia*, hence the name of the town, Strabo 14. 1. 20.

[83] Rhoiteion: Strabo 13. 1. 30; Aianteion: Pliny, *HN* 5. 125; note also Paus. 1. 35. 4–5, Philostr. *Her.* 668, Pomponius Mela 1. 96. On the tomb, J. M. Cook 1973: 88–9.

[84] J. M. Cook 1973: 86–8, for instance, thinks that Aianteion was not a city but a harbour town in the territory of Rhoiteion.

have been worth having. The evidence of tragedy suggests that
tombs of both Achilles and Aias in the Troad had already been
identified by the fifth century BC.[85] Nor were these the only
Achaian heroes. Over in Elaious in the Chersonese there was the
shrine and tomb of Protesilaos, despoiled by the Persian Artaÿctes
and venerated by Alexander.[86]

The Greeks of the Troad could look back to both a Greek and
a Trojan past. Memorials of the Greek heritage linked them with
the wider Greek world while the Trojan past gave them roots in
the land in which they lived.

3. THE MAINLAND

The perspective of mainland Greece is rather different. This was
Agamemnon's recruiting ground for the expedition *against* Troy.
Cities of the region could look to the *Iliad*'s catalogue of ships to
confirm their participation in the war. Here, if anywhere, we
might expect the Trojans to be anathematized, yet this does not
appear to have happened. Instead Trojans are found incorporated
into local traditions and civic ideology as important and revered
figures who shared the heroic past with their Achaian counterparts. Survivors of the fall of Troy left their mark throughout
Greece with a particular fondness for the Peloponnese where
tombs of Anchises, Kassandra, and Helenos could be found.

This emphasis on the Peloponnese is partly a consequence of
the evidence. Whereas Strabo provided much of the material for
the Troad, it is the traveller Pausanias who performs this service
for the mainland. His guide to the antiquities of ancient Greece,
written in the second century AD, embraces the Peloponnese and
Attika but extends no further north than Boiotia and Phokis, and
does not include Euboia or the islands.[87] The area which he does
cover, however, is described with great thoroughness. He visited
these places in person and is a valuable, if at times sceptical,

---

[85] In Eur. *Hec.* 40–1, 304–31, and *passim* (cf. Proklos' summary of *Iliou Persis* in M. Davies
1988: 62), sacrifice was to be offered at the tomb of Achilles, perhaps a reference to a contemporary Achilles cult in the Troad, cf. Mossman 1995: 48 n. 2 on 'local legend'. Achilles
is also invoked as a hero of cult in Simonides' Plataia elegy, Boedeker 1998: 236–8, and Ch.
3. 1; Soph. *Aj.* 1163–7 speaks of τὸν ἀείμνηστον τάφον of Aias in the Troad.

[86] Artaÿctes: Hdt. 9. 116, cf. 7. 33, 9. 120; Alexander: Arr. *Anab.* 1. 11. 5, cf. also Thuc.
8. 102, Pliny *HN* 16. 238, Strabo 7, frag. 51, 13. 1. 31, Philostr. *Her.* 672, Lucian *Deorum concilium* 8.

[87] Habicht 1985: 4–7 on area covered.

reporter of local traditions.[88] Nevertheless, Pausanias is not the only source of information. Other evidence may be more disparate but it is often considerably earlier and thus provides confirmation that traditions of the type recorded by Pausanias are not themselves products of the second century AD.

Some of the features observed in the previous two sections are also apparent on the mainland. Again, there is competition between cities, each claiming to be the sole possessor of the burial place of a famous Trojan such as Kassandra. The existence of such rivalry is an important indicator of the value attached to the Trojan past. In the Troad Trojan ancestors or founders helped to give Greek cities a justification for their presence in the area. Yet, it may seem surprising to find Trojan ancestors or founders on the mainland, particularly in the Peloponnese, the source of the expedition against Troy. The examination that follows will begin with the Peloponnese, the regions of Lakonia, the Argolid, and Arkadia, before turning to the island of Zakynthos off the Peloponnesian coast, Epiros, and Boiotia.

Lakonia

Prominent among the many cults of Lakonia was that of Kassandra, the prophetic daughter of Priam, who was brought back by Agamemnon to the Peloponnese. At least three places in Lakonia were said to have been associated with her cult, Amyklai, Leuktra, and Thalamai.[89] It is Amyklai, south of Sparta, for which there is the best evidence. Pausanias records that at Amyklai there is 'a noteworthy sanctuary (*hieron*) of Alexandra and a statue. The Amyklaians say that Alexandra is Kassandra, daughter of Priam. Here there is also an image of Klytaimnestra and what they believe is the tomb (*mnema*) of Agamemnon'.[90] Amyklai, then, possessed a sanctuary of Kassandra that seems to have contained an image of Klytaimnestra and the tomb of Agamemnon. Pausanias tells us elsewhere that the people of Amyklai claimed to have the tomb of Kassandra, so it is very likely that the tomb was part of the sanctuary.[91]

---

[88] Frazer 1898: i, pp. lxxvi–lxxix, Habicht 1985: 142–7, Arafat 1996: 8–12.
[89] On cults of Kassandra, Wide 1893: 333–9, Farnell 1921: 329–32, Davreux 1942: 88–96, Stiglitz 1953, Larson 1995: 83–4.
[90] Paus. 3. 19. 6, accepting Schubart's reading which omits ἄγαλμα before Ἀγαμέμνονος.
[91] Paus. 2. 16. 6–7; Davreux 1942: 92 n. 2.

The literary evidence of Pausanias is supplemented by archaeological and epigraphic evidence. Votive deposits from as early as the seventh century BC demonstrate the existence of a long-standing cult centre at Amyklai. The epigraphic evidence confirms that this cult centre was associated with Alexandra, which according to Pausanias was the local name for Kassandra. Pottery, inscribed with the names of Alexandra and Agamemnon (albeit restored), has been recovered.[92] An honorific decree from the second or first century BC gives instructions for its inscription on a stele and erection in the sanctuary of Alexandra. The decree was passed by the Amyklaians in honour of three ephors and so offers a useful insight into the role of the cult in civic life.[93] Further evidence for the vitality of the cult over a long period of time is given by an inscribed marble throne dedicated to Alexandra that dates from the first century BC or first century AD.[94]

The identification of Kassandra with Alexandra which Pausanias attributes to the inhabitants of Amyklai is not unique to the travel writer. The lexicographer Hesychios in his entry for 'Kassandra' notes that Kassandra is 'Alexandra in Lakedaimonia'. More important is the *Alexandra* of the poet Lykophron, written as if it were a prophecy of Kassandra. The identification is made in the title, but the use of 'Alexandra' at line 30 confirms that Lykophron himself was exploiting this dual persona. Whether Kassandra's alternative name was well known outside Lakonia is difficult to determine. Lykophron, whose work was notoriously enigmatic, may have been deliberately using a tradition current only in Lakonia in order to puzzle his readers. The poem, probably written in the early third century, is the earliest recorded use of the name Alexandra for Kassandra.[95] When and how Kassandra came to be identified with Alexandra is unclear.[96] Her association with Amyklai can be traced back as far as Pindar's eleventh *Pythian*, which places the murder of Kassandra and Agamemnon there.[97] This strongly suggests that the cult of Alexandra as

[92] Votive deposits: Salapata 1993, Hibler 1993; for the details of C. Christou's excavation reports, Salapata 1993: 195 n. 13 with summary of finds (189–90).

[93] *SIG*³ 932 (*IG* 5. 26), Stiglitz 1953 (with photo), Davreux 1942: 88 on civic life.

[94] *BÉ* 1968: no. 264, *BCH* 92 (1968), 816–17 and figs. 10–11, Delivorrias 1968.

[95] On the problem of the date of this poem, see Ch. 5. 5. Lycoph. 1123–40 also refers to a cult of Kassandra among the Daunians of Apulia, Farnell 1921: 330, Davreux 1942: 93–5.

[96] Davreux 1942: 90–3 sums up alternative explanations; it is perhaps significant that Homer's preferred name for her brother Paris was 'Alexandros', cf. Kirk 1985: 266–7.

[97] Pind. *Pyth.* 11. 17–34, Stiglitz 1953: 77, dated to either 474 or 454, Bowra 1964: 402–5.

Kassandra was already a feature of the Lakonian religious land-scape in the early fifth century BC.

In myth Kassandra, and her brother Helenos, had acquired their unfortunate prophetic powers from Apollo. The importance of Kassandra in Amyklai may, therefore, be connected in part at least with the nearby sanctuary of Apollo, the Amyklaion, the most famous sanctuary in Lakonia according to Polybios.[98] There does, however, seem to be a predilection for Kassandra in Lakonia as a whole which cannot be explained by the Amyklaion alone. The two southern cities of Leuktra and Thalamai both appear to have laid claim to her. At Leuktra, wrote Pausanias, there was 'a shrine (*naos*) and statue of Kassandra, daughter of Priam, called Alexandra by the locals'.[99] Here, however, there is no word of a tomb. Not far from Leuktra was the city of Thalamai, which may have claimed Kassandra's tomb. Plutarch records that there was a sanctuary and oracle of Pasiphae. The identity of Pasiphae was obscure and the subject of various conflicting stories. According to some, 'Kassandra, the daughter of Priam, died there and on account of declaring her oracles to all (διὰ τὸ πᾶσι φαίνειν τὰ μαντεῖα) was called Pasiphae'.[100] The reference to death at Thalamai suggests a tomb, which may have rivalled the one at Amyklai, but Plutarch reports several accounts of the identity of Pasiphae, none of which clearly reflects local tradition.

The cult of Alexandra/Kassandra should not, however, be viewed in isolation. The Lakonian landscape was full of memorials that enforced a sense of continuity with the heroic past of the Trojan War. On a single four-mile stretch of road leading north out of Sparta a traveller could see at least three such landmarks: a sanctuary of Achilles, the Horse's Grave where Helen's suitors swore an oath to defend Helen and her future husband against any injury, and finally the statue of Aidos, Shame, which was said to have been erected by Ikarios after his daughter Penelope chose to follow Odysseus to Ithaka.[101] The Spartan fascination with the

Both Stesichoros (Davies *PMGF* F216) and Simonides (Page *PMG* F549) located Agamemnon's palace in Lakonia, schol. on Eur. *Or.* 46.

[98] Polyb. 5. 19. 2, Paus. 3. 19. 6, cf. Pettersson 1992 on Apollo cults.

[99] Paus. 3. 26. 5.

[100] Plut. *Agis* 9, but Paus. 3. 26. 1 seems to be consciously contradicting this version; he says that it is a sanctuary and oracle of Ino and that there is a statue of Pasiphae there but it represents the moon not a local *daimon*. On Pasiphae, Wide 1893: 246–50.

[101] Paus. 3. 20. 8–11; Paus. 3, esp. 12–19, names over 20 *heroa* in Sparta and the surrounding area, Hibler 1993: 203 n. 6.

genealogies of both heroes and men is another feature of this sense of continuity.[102] Central to the evocation of the heroic past was the Menelaion, a shrine and tomb of Menelaos and Helen, at Therapne south-east of Sparta. Archaeological evidence suggests that the sanctuary was active from the seventh to the first century BC, and it appears in the literary evidence from Herodotos through to Pausanias.[103] The emphasis in Lakonia is, as might be expected, on the Achaians, but it is significant that the Trojan Kassandra should have become the object of cult rather than of neglect.

The Argolid

Lakonian claims to be heirs to this heroic past of the Peloponnese were not uncontested. Over in the Argolid amid the ruins of Mykenai was another group of tombs from the heroic era. Here, Pausanias tells us, were tombs not only of Agamemnon and Kassandra but also of Elektra, the charioteer Eurymedon, and Kassandra's twin sons.[104] Mykenai as the home of Agamemnon in Homer's poems was bound to attract such claims,[105] but it was occupied only intermittently after the mid-fifth century BC and then as a dependency of Argos.[106] No doubt local guides were always ready to identify tombs for visitors such as Pausanias, but to what extent the tombs were a focus of cult is unknown. For much of the time Argos was the dominant city of the region in which Mykenai lay; as such the Argives may have sought to promote the heroic associations of Mykenai, at least in so far as that was possible without undermining their own claims.[107]

Competition for the heroic past was part of the wider political and territorial rivalry that existed between Argos and Sparta.[108]

[102] Plato *Hipp. Mai.* 285d.

[103] Catling 1976–7; Hdt. 6. 61, Isoc. 10. 63, Polyb. 5. 18. 21, Paus. 3. 19. 9. Wide 1893: 340–6 collects the literary evidence.

[104] Paus. 2. 16. 6–7, cf. also [Arist.] *Pepl.* 1, 2 for Agamemnon's tomb at Mykenai; Pausanias is vaguer on the disreputable Klytaimnestra and Aigisthos who he says were buried beyond the walls.

[105] Hom. *Il.* 4. 376, 9. 40, 11. 45, *Od.* 3. 305, cf. also Hdt. 1. 67, 4. 103, 7. 159.

[106] Argive acquisition of Mykenai, Diod. Sic. 11. 65, Strabo 8. 6. 10, 8. 6. 19, and usurpation of its cults, J. M. Hall 1995*b*: 611–13.

[107] In Homer Diomedes is the ruler of Argos, *Il.* 2. 559–68, cf. 6. 224, 14. 119–20, *Od.* 3. 180–1, but 'Argos' in a broader sense is also used for the empire of Agamemnon, 1. 25, 4. 170, 6. 455, 9. 20, 140. On the other hand, in Aischylos' *Oresteia* it is Agamemnon who is king of Argos with no mention of Mykenai. For possible Argive promotion of Mykenai in 3rd cent. BC, Alcock 1997: 23–5.

[108] Rivalry stretched from archaic (Forrest 1980: 35–6) to Hellenistic times (Cartledge and Spawforth 1989: 25, 49–50).

This is best exemplified by the story of the Argive Palladion. Like many cities the Argives said that they possessed the famous guardian statue, the disappearance of which had precipitated the fall of Troy. Diomedes, leader of the Argive troops, had joined with Odysseus to steal it from the Trojans and brought it to Argos.[109] The Spartans cast doubt on the authenticity of the Argive statue and pointed to the real one in the hero-sanctuary, or heroon, of Odysseus at Sparta. The importance of Spartan–Argive rivalry is evident in the explanation for the statue's presence in Sparta: it was stolen from the Argives.[110] Nevertheless, this did nothing to end the Argive belief that they still possessed the real Palladion, as Pausanias discovered when he visited Argos. Pausanias was sceptical, however, not because the true Palladion was in Sparta but because it was well known that Aineias had taken it to Italy. Yet, the Palladion was so much part of Argive self-identity that it was represented on their coinage. Coins dating from the first half of the fourth century BC show Diomedes carrying the Palladion, and even in the Roman imperial period representations are to be found either in the hands of Diomedes or in a temple.[111] The Argives were prepared to affirm their own version in the face of the competing claims of Sparta and even of Rome.

The Argives could display numerous physical reminders of the Trojan past. Not only could they show off the Palladion and recount tales of its arrival in Argos, they could also boast a combined Mykenaian and Argive heritage. In Argos itself there was a cenotaph for all the Argives who died on the Trojan expedition.[112] To the tomb of Kassandra at Mykenai could be added that of her twin brother Helenos which was in Argos itself, thus trumping Sparta with a full set of prophetic Trojans. Pausanias, who knows of the story that Helenos went to Epiros, is very sceptical and

---

[109] In Argos: Plut. *Mor.* 302d (*Greek Questions*), Paus. 2. 23. 5; theft by Diomedes and Odysseus: Proklos' summary of the *Ilias Parva*, lines 19–24 (M. Davies 1988: 52), Dion. Hal. *Ant. Rom.* 1. 69, Apollod. *Epit.* 5. 13, Gantz 1993: 642–6; on the Palladion, *RE* 18.2 s.v. 'Palladion' 171–201, Austin 1964: 83–5, Burkert 1977: 221, Dubourdieu 1989: 460–7, Faraone 1992: 6–7. For a list of the cities claiming the Palladion, *RE* 18.2, col. 172–85.

[110] Plut. *Mor.* 302d, on which Halliday 1928: 192–4.

[111] 4th cent.: Head 1911: 438–9, *LIMC* Diomedes I 37, *BMC Peloponnese* pp. 139–40; imperial: Head 1911: 440, Voegtli 1977: 120–3, pl. 24a–b, *LIMC* Athena 109, *LIMC* Diomedes I 55.

[112] Paus. 2. 20. 6.

doubts whether even his Argive guides can believe it.[113] Mykenai was the major heroic landmark in their territory, but there were other lesser points of contact with this past. Not far from Mykenai was the Heraion, an important sanctuary of Hera; Menelaos, they said, had visited the sanctuary on his return from Troy and dedicated the shield of the Trojan Euphorbos; this shield, still on display in Pausanias' time, established another valuable and tangible link with the heroic past.[114] Since Homer's Menelaos failed to strip Euphorbos of his arms, this shield represents a distinctly Argive version of the encounter between Menelaos and Euphorbos, a tradition that may date back as far as the seventh century BC.[115]

Tenea

Sparta and Argos were reconstructing a past in which they were the major forces in the war against Troy, but outside Lakonia and the Argolid Trojans could play a more central role in civic self-image. Even in the Peloponnese they are occasionally invoked as ancestors and founders. Across the mountains from Argos, about seven or eight miles from Corinth was the town of Tenea, which made what was perhaps the oddest Trojan claim in the Peloponnese. These people said that they were Trojans who had been brought to the mainland as prisoners from Tenedos, an island off the coast of the Troad; Agamemnon had then given them land. This genealogical story is reported by Pausanias but it would appear to have been around in some form since at least the time of Aristotle. According to Strabo Aristotle had said that there was kinship between the people of Tenea and Tenedos through Tennes, son of Kyknos.[116] The claim may have been given some plausibility by the similarity of their names and by the presence of a temple of Apollo in each. The temple at Tenea would then be a descendant of the more famous one at Tenedos, celebrated in the

---

[113] Paus. 2. 23. 5–6; for Helenos in Epiros see nn. 131–4 below with accompanying text. Paus. 2. 21. 1 also notes a bronze statue of Aineias in Argos; its proximity to the altar of Zeus Phuxios, Zeus of Escape, may allude to the survivor aspect of his story.

[114] Paus. 2. 17. 3, J. M. Hall 1995*b*; the story is also told of the Branchidai at Didyma, Diog. Laert. 8. 5. For relics, cf. the temple of Apollo at Sikyon which contained belongings of, among others, Agamemnon, Odysseus, Teukros, Ampelius 8. 5, Scheer 1996.

[115] Hom. *Il.* 17. 1–105; on the date R. M. Cook 1983: 2–3, Snodgrass 1998: 105–8, arguing from a 7th cent. Rhodian plate depicting Menelaos and Hektor fighting over the body of Euphorbos.

[116] Paus. 2. 5. 4, Strabo 8. 6. 22 (=Arist. frag. 611. 1 Gigon); Tennes and Kyknos: Gantz 1993: 591–2; Tenedos and Troad: Leaf 1923: 214–22, J. M. Cook 1973: 189–90.

Iliad.[117] In both Strabo and Pausanias the temple is adduced as evidence for kinship.

Aristotle spoke of kinship but whether or not he also said that the Teneans were therefore Trojans Strabo does not say. The Tenedians were certainly on the Trojan side in the war, but the implication of Trojan rather than simply Tenedian ancestry may not have been drawn out until later.[118] Possibly the Teneans highlighted this aspect of their mythical past in order to win the favour of the Romans. In the 140s BC they revolted from Corinth to join the Romans and thus avoided the destruction suffered by Corinth after the Achaian War.[119] Trojan kinship may have been useful in an appeal to the Romans. On the other hand, their actions at the time of the Achaian War suggest a long-term lack of sympathy with Corinth. Consequently they may have exploited their Trojan ancestry for many years in order to distance themselves from their powerful neighbours. The evidence of Aristotle, therefore, makes it plausible but not certain that the Teneans claimed Trojan ancestry in the fourth century BC.

Arkadia

Arkadia, too, had a strong local tradition that Trojans had visited the area after the war. Dionysios of Halikarnassos reports two Arkadian writers, Ariaithos of Tegea and Agathyllos, both of whom wrote about a visit by Aineias to Arkadia. Dionysios attributes to Ariaithos and other writers the story that Aineias lived at a place called Nesos in the vicinity of Arkadian Orchomenos; while he was in Arkadia he founded Kaphyai which was named after the Trojan Kapys, a story also recorded by Strabo and by Stephanos of Byzantion who identifies Kapys as the father of Anchises.[120] Dionysios alludes to a tradition that Aineias died in Arkadia, perhaps contained in the writings of Ariaithos, but adds that Agathyllos and others take Aineias off from Arkadia to die in Italy. In Agathyllos' verses Aineias leaves two daughters at Nesos and heads westward to father Romulus.[121] Dionysios makes clear

---

[117] Hom. *Il.* 1. 35–42, 450.

[118] Hom. *Il.* 11. 625, Tenedos sacked by Achilles; Paus. 10. 14. 4, Diod. Sic. 5. 83, Plut. *Mor.* 297d–f, Tennes killed by Achilles. [119] Strabo 8. 6. 22.

[120] Dion. Hal. *Ant. Rom.* 1. 49. 1, Strabo 13. 1. 53, Steph. Byz. s.v. 'Καφύαι'. Paus. 8. 23. 2–3 gives an alternative, Kepheus, son of Aleos, a story known to Stephanos; cf. also Capua in Italy, Steph. Byz. s.v. 'Καπύα' (Hekataios *FGrH* 1F62), Dion. Hal. *Ant. Rom.* 1. 73. 3.

[121] Dion. Hal. *Ant. Rom.* 1. 49. 1–2, cf. Strabo 5. 3. 3, where Rome is an Arkadian colony

that this Trojan visitation is a local Arkadian tradition, although little is known about the two Arkadian writers that he cites. Ariaithos was from Tegea and wrote an *Arkadika*, presumably a local history; speculation about his dates ranges from the fourth century to the first half of the second century BC.[122] Agathyllos was an Arkadian poet but nothing more is known of him.[123]

Some confirmation of this Arkadian tradition can be found in Pausanias, who records a tomb of Anchises on the road between Mantinea and Orchomenos at the foot of Mt. Anchisia which he says was named after the famous Trojan. Alongside the tomb was what Pausanias believed to be a sanctuary of Aphrodite. Since Pausanias knew of no tomb of Anchises in the Troad, he was prepared to accept that this could indeed be his tomb. Nevertheless, what Anchises was doing in the middle of Arkadia puzzled Pausanias. It was not obvious why a voyage round the Peloponnese to Sicily and Italy should take someone to the most landlocked part of the peninsula. Pausanias half-heartedly explains that when Aineias landed his ships on the Lakonian coast and founded the cities of Aphrodisias and Etis, Anchises went to Arkadia 'for some reason'. When Anchises died during the visit, Aineias buried him there. This mysterious detour suggests an attempt to incorporate a long-standing Arkadian tradition into the by-then-dominant story of Aineias' voyage to Italy.[124] How long-standing the tradition was must remain uncertain. The use of Trojan personal names in Arkadia may reflect such a tradition. At Stymphalos in the fifth and fourth centuries there was a series of important men called either 'Aineas' or 'Aineias', presumably all of the same family.[125] The name recurs attached to a boxer from Kynaitha and is also found on an early-fifth-century BC bronze dedication.[126] At the very least such names show no aver-

founded by Evander, or Polemon in Festus 439L, where the Roman priesthood of the Salii is said to take its name from Salius, a man from Mantinea, brought by Aineias to Italy (cf. Plut. *Num.* 13. 7).

[122] Ariaithos *FGrH* 316; Schwartz *RE* 2 s.v. 'Araithos', col. 374 , with alternative spelling, argues for 4th cent. BC while Perret 1942: 46–7 prefers the first half of the 2nd.

[123] *FGrH* 321F2.

[124] Paus. 8. 12. 8–9, though Perret 1942: 43–5 dismisses it as a Hadrianic invention, and Jost 1985: 508–10, influenced by Perret, dates it to Augustan period.

[125] *RE* 1 s.v. 'Aineas (nos. 4–6)'. A. Griffin 1982: 72–4.

[126] Kynaitha: *RE* 1 s.v. 'Aineas (no. 3)'; note that the name 'Kynaitha' itself could have Trojan connotations, cf. Dion. Hal. *Ant. Rom.* 1. 50. 2; dedication: Jeffery 1990: 210. In general 'Aineas' was quite a popular name in the Peloponnese, *LGPN* 3.1.

sion to things Trojan. Dionysios of Halikarnassos even records a mythic genealogy that gives the Arkadians and the Trojans a common ancestry.[127]

Zakynthos and Epiros

Zakynthos, an island off the north-west coast of the Peloponnese, could also offer tales of a Trojan past. The main evidence comes not from Zakynthos itself but from a Zakynthian dedication to the oracle of Zeus at Dodona in Epiros. This dedication not only illuminates the traditions of each community but also the interplay of such traditions in the diplomacy of the Greek world. The dedicator was Agathon, son of Echephylos, a man whose family had long been *proxenoi* of the Molossians and their allies in Zakynthos. Since the Molossians controlled Dodona, a dedication there was a means of affirming Agathon's relationship with them. The dedication, which dates from the late fourth or early third century BC, is a short text, inscribed on bronze. In it Agathon makes a striking claim: he and his family are descended from 'Trojan Kassandra'. Since the Greek is not without ambiguity, Agathon may even be interpreted as saying that the descendants of Kassandra include not only his family but also all Zakynthians.[128] Various proposals have been made for Kassandra's partner in this family tree, Apollo, Agamemnon, and Aias,[129] but perhaps such genealogical speculation is misconceived. Instead we should ask why the claim was made at all. Part of the answer may lie with Zakynthos. The city prided itself on its temple of Apollo and in the fifth and fourth centuries BC regularly used the head of the god as an emblem on its coinage.[130] As it was Apollo who had given Kassandra her prophetic powers, the two may have played some, no longer recoverable, part in the mythology of early Zakynthos. There may be a similarity with Lakonia where, it was observed above, the sanctuary of Alexandra and the Amyklaion of Apollo were close to each other. But more interesting here is the role of Kassandra

---

[127] Dion. Hal. *Ant. Rom.* 1. 61.

[128] Θεός. Τύχα. Ζεῦ Δωδώνης μεδέων, τόδε σοι δῶρον πέμπω παρ' ἐμοῦ Ἀγάθων Ἐχεφύλου καὶ γενεὰ πρόξενοι Μολόσσων καὶ συμμάχων ἐν τριάκοντα γενεαῖς ἐκ Τρωΐας Κασσάνδρας (image of phallus) γενεᾶ Ζακύνθιοι. Text as printed by Egger in Carapanos 1878: 196–9 (*BCH* 1 (1877), 254–8); Carapanos' own text is on p. 39; see also discussion of Davreux in Dakaris 1964: pl. 4; date: Davreux p. 85 (first half of 3rd cent. BC), Franke 1955: 38, Hammond 1967: 534 (soon after 334 BC).

[129] Davreux 1942: 85–7 surveys the suggestions.

[130] Head 1911: 429–31.

in Zakynthos' relationship with the outside world. The inscription was found at Dodona, where Agathon, Zakynthian *proxenos* of the Molossians, made a dedication. In this context it is Kassandra who represents the common ground between the parties involved.

Through Kassandra a web of kinship is established that bonds Agathon and Zakynthos with the Molossians and Dodona. A Trojan presence in Epiros was well established by the fifth century BC and finds clear expression in the prophecy at the end of Euripides' *Andromache*, written in the mid-420s BC. Andromache had been brought to Greece as part of the spoils of war by Achilles' son, Neoptolemos (also known as Pyrrhos). On the death of Neoptolemos, Thetis prophesies that Andromache will move to the land of Molossia where she will marry Helenos; here Andromache's son by Neoptolemos will succeed to the throne and his descendants will continue as kings of the Molossians (according to Pausanias this son was called Molossos).[131] There are signs of this story already in the remains of the earlier epic cycle; in the *Nostoi* Neoptolemos has returned when he reaches the Molossians, in the *Iliou Persis* he is awarded Andromache as his prize and in the *Little Iliad* he returns to Greece with Andromache and Aineias.[132] Hellanikos in the fifth century is said to have recorded a variant of this in which Aineias stops over among the Molossians before continuing to Italy.[133] After his appearance in Euripides' *Andromache* Helenos is frequently associated with Epiros. He is reported to have been the founder of the coastal city of Bouthroton. He is at Dodona when Aineias arrives there; according to Dionysios some of the inscribed bronze kraters and other offerings dedicated by Aineias are still to be seen in the sanctuary, sure evidence of the truth of these stories. From Pausanias we learn that Kestrine, a region of Epiros, was named after Kestrinos, the son of Helenos and Andromache, and that Helenos died in Epiros, whatever the Argives said.[134]

---

[131] Eur. *Andr.* 1238–52; M. Lloyd 1994: 12 on date. Plut. *Pyrrh.* 1, for Neoptolemos as Pyrrhos; Molossos: Paus. 1. 11. 1.

[132] Proklos' summary of the *Nostoi*, lines 20–4, (M. Davies 1988: 67) summary of the *Iliou Persis*, line 32 (Davies 1988: 62), *Ilias Parva* F20 (M. Davies 1988); Neoptolemos himself is firmly associated with the Molossians by the time of Pindar, cf. *Nem.* 4. 51–3, 7. 36–40, *Paean* 6. 109–10, Hammond 1967: 383–6. On Trojan legend in Epiros, L. Robert 1940: 95–105.

[133] Dion. Hal. *Ant. Rom.* 1. 72. 2 (Hellanikos *FGrH* 4F184).

[134] Bouthroton: Steph. Byz. (Teukros of Kyzikos *FGrH* 274F1); and Aineias: Dion. Hal. *Ant. Rom.* 1. 51. 1, cf. Verg. *Aen.* 3. 294–505; Kestrinos: Paus. 1. 11. 1–2, 2. 23. 6; Argives: Paus. 2. 23. 6. Cf. also Apollod. *Epit.* 6. 12–13 (Helenos with Neoptolemos to Molossia),

The Epirote royal families were proud of this heroic ancestry and often used names that drew attention to their illustrious forebears. Alexander's mother, Olympias, was said to be descended from Pyrrhos, son of Achilles, and from Helenos, son of Priam; her own father was a Neoptolemos and her sister was called Troas.[135] The great Molossian king Pyrrhos of the early third century BC had a sister Troas and named his son Helenos, while at the same time highlighting his descent from Achilles which was already signalled by his own name.[136] Andromache too is found as a name among Molossian royalty.[137] So the Epirote royal families looked to both Achilles and Priam, to both Greeks and Trojans, as ancestors.

Agathon and the Zakynthians could have justified and affirmed their close relationship with the Molossians without resorting to Trojan kinship but Kassandra offered something special to the standard kinship claims of Greek diplomacy.[138] Her prophetic powers made her peculiarly appropriate for a dedication at the oracle of Zeus. More than this, the importance of Helenos among the Molossians made his sister Kassandra an ideal ancestor to publicize there. The Zakynthian–Molossian friendship could be interpreted as a reunion of twins. This is not to suggest that the Zakynthians or Agathon and his family invented their relationship with Kassandra for the occasion. It is more likely that they highlighted and developed one aspect of a multitude of now lost local traditions. What is important for this account is that both the Zakynthians and the Molossians show the acceptability of a Trojan past. Both publicized it and both had a choice not to do so.

There is another, quite different, story about Zakynthian kinship with the Trojans, recorded about three centuries later by Dionysios of Halikarnassos.[139] Aineias stopped at Zakynthos on his

Serv. on Verg. *Aen.* 3. 297 (Helenos' marriage to Andromache). Local traditions may have featured on a 5th cent. BC Apollonian dedication at Olympia which was decorated with figures from the Trojan War including Helenos and Aineias, Paus. 5. 22. 2–3, Hammond 1967: 384–5. Helenos may also have been the founder of Epirote Ilion, Steph. Byz. s.v. 'Ilion', although Stephanus refers to 'Ilion in Macedonia', but see Hammond 1967: 697 n. 2 with 1972: 301 n. 4.

[135] Schol. on Lycoph. 1439 (Theopompos *FGrH* 115F355), Just. *Epit.* 7. 6. 10–11; Hammond 1967: 412, Nilsson 1972: 105–8.

[136] Plut. *Pyrrh.* 1, 9, Just. *Epit.* 17. 3; on Pyrrhos and Achilles, Ch. 6.

[137] Hammond 1967: 563.

[138] On kinship in Greek diplomacy, Ch. 7.1 below.

[139] Dion. Hal. *Ant. Rom.* 1. 50.3–4.

westward journey, where he was well treated because of his kinship with the Zakynthians. The eponymous founder of Zakynthos was the son of Dardanos from whom Aineias and the Trojan royal family were also descended.[140] Partly because of this kinship Aineias and the Trojans built a temple of Aphrodite on Zakynthos, where they offered sacrifices which were still being performed in Dionysios' day; they also set up games, including a foot race to the temple, which is known as the race of Aineias and Aphrodite; there are also, says Dionysios, wooden statues (*xoana*) of Aineias and Aphrodite. Zakynthos is on the coastal route to Italy, so a story about Aineias might be considered fairly predictable, but the existence of Agathon's earlier kinship story suggests that there is more to it than a convenient stopping point for tidy-minded mythographers trying to get Aineias to Italy. Together the stories suggest that the Zakynthians had a sense of a Trojan past on which they could draw in different ways at different times. It was a past, moreover, that was already well established before the Romans became important in the area.[141] The constant factor might have been a belief that Zakynthos was a son of Dardanos. In the Zakynthian relations with the Molossians and Dodona, Kassandra could embody that past; in relations with the Romans, perhaps, it was Aineias.

Boiotia

A final example comes from Boiotia, where there was a tomb cult of Hektor. Our main accounts, beginning with Lykophron, agree that Hektor's bones were in the possession of the Thebans and they had been transferred to Thebes on the instructions of an oracle, but there is disagreement on details. Pausanias reports that the tomb was to be found a few miles out of Thebes on the road to Chalkis at a place called the Springs of Oedipus, but a certain Aristodemos who himself may have been a Theban locates it at Dios Gonai, that is to say the birthplace of Zeus.[142] It is possible

[140] For the relationship of Aineias and Hektor to Dardanos, Hom. *Il.* 20. 215–41; Paus. 8. 24. 3 also knows of Zakynthos as the son of Dardanos.

[141] Cf. Vanotti 1995: 156.

[142] Lycoph. 1189–213 with schol. on 1194, 1204, 1208, Paus. 9. 18. 5, Aristodemos cited in schol. on Hom. *Il.* 13. 1 (*FGrH* 383F7), [Arist.] *Pepl.* 46; L. Ziehen, *RE* 5A, 'Thebai, Kulte', 1514–15, Jacoby on *FGrH* 383F7 (also quoting the main passages), Pfister 1909: 193–4, Schachter 1981: 233–4, Symeonoglou 1985: 193–4. Lykophron may have added further confusion for his struggling scholiasts with a reference to islands of blessed, νῆσοι μακάρων, line 1204.

that these were simply two ways of referring to the same place. The reasons given for the transfer vary from writer to writer; it was to avert famine or invasion; it was on behalf of all Greeks or just the Thebans; if the Thebans did it, they would prosper. Such variety need not cast doubt on the existence of the tomb but on the contrary it is a revealing sign of the vitality of the cult over the centuries as different generations accounted for it in different ways.

It is, nonetheless, unclear why the Thebans should have celebrated a Trojan hero, and in particular Hektor. Achilles had made sure that there could be no stories of a wandering Hektor in the manner of Aineias or Antenor. Elsewhere in Boiotia the leaders of the Boiotian forces at Troy could be found remembered. The tomb of Leitos, the sole survivor, was at Plataia, Arkesilaos at Lebedeia, Peneleos at Kephissa.[143] Perhaps an important Trojan was better than a minor Boiotian warrior. Or perhaps the cult of Hektor could be interpreted as an example of the worship of an enemy, a means of restraining his hostile power when the city is faced with some calamity such as plague. Hektor, however, was no especial enemy of Thebes and even if this is considered a satisfactory explanation of the cult's origins it does little to explain its longevity.[144] More probably the tomb allowed Thebes to mark itself as distinct from the rest of Boiotia. Hektor had been one of the great warriors of the Trojan War and was no respecter of Boiotians; he had killed Arkesilaos and had wounded Leitos. His presence could thus assert Theban authority over Boiotia.[145]

The mainland, therefore, offers Trojans in many guises, ancestors, founders, visitors, a continuing presence in tombs, cults, and local and personal names. Of course Trojans form only a fraction of the many heroes who are celebrated in these ways,[146] but what is significant is that they are celebrated at all. There is no single explanation. The importance of Trojans in Arkadian tradition

[143] Leitos: Paus. 9. 4. 3; Arkesilaos: Paus. 9. 39. 3; Peneleos: [Arist.] *Pepl.* 21; Hom. *Il.* 2. 494–5 gives 5 Boiotian leaders; the later whereabouts of Prothoenor and Klonios are unknown.

[144] Cults of enemies are discussed in Visser 1982.

[145] Arkesilaos: Hom. *Il.* 15. 329–30; Leitos: *Il.* 17. 601–6. Some suggested that Hektor was originally a Boiotian hero whose story was transferred to the Troad, hence his predilection for attacking Boiotians, details in Pfister 1909: 194, and Schachter 1981: 233, who also lists other theories explaining Hektor's presence.

[146] Pfister 1912: 627–43 and Farnell 1921: 403–26 provide catalogues.

may be a reflection of the relative isolation of Arkadia. The Trojan ancestry of the Teneans may result from a need to distance themselves from powerful neighbours such as Corinth or even Argos.[147] In Lakonia and the Argolid competition to appropriate the mythical past of the Trojan expedition brought with it not only prominent Achaians but also Trojans such as Kassandra and Helenos. Perhaps some cults of local non-Trojan heroes came to be identified later with famous Trojans, such as Alexandra/ Kassandra in Lakonia. The transformation itself, however, is revealing for what it says about the acceptability of Trojans, even in places which might most naturally be considered enemies of the Trojans by tradition.

There is a temptation often to explain any emphasis on a Trojan past by reference to Rome,[148] but many of the traditions discussed here are clearly independent of Roman influence. The Trojan descent of the Zakynthian Agathon is directed not at Rome but at the Molossians whose connection with Andromache and Helenos is already vouched for by Euripides in the fifth century BC. The sanctuary of Alexandra at Amyklai had been active for many centuries and associated with Kassandra since at least the fifth century. If international relations had any bearing on the cult of Kassandra, then it was Spartan–Argive rivalry. The Aineias material is more directly relevant to Rome and thus more problematic, but it is important to remember the case of Aineia and be wary of too much scepticism. Even if Aineias was a recent, politically sensible arrival in a city's mythology, that may have been the development of an earlier Trojan tradition rather than an abrupt and arbitrary addition.

4. CONCLUSION

Far from rejecting the Trojans as enemies, many communities in the Greek world incorporated them into their own traditions and self-image; many others would probably have had no special interest at all. No doubt perceptions of the Trojans changed from place to place, from region to region. When Dionysios of Halikar-

---

[147] Cf. also Boiai in Lakonia which claimed to be a partial Trojan foundation and may have wished to mark itself out from the rest of Lakonia or at least Sparta; it was a synoecism of Etis, Aphrodisias, and Side, the first two of which were said to have been found by Aineias, Paus. 3. 22. 11, 8. 12. 8, cf. Malkin 1994: 85.

[148] Perret 1942 too readily succumbed.

nassos argues that the Trojans were Greeks, he may not have
been uttering an eccentric opinion but rather a belief common in
Asia Minor where there was a much stronger affinity with Troy.[149]
There will also have been change over time as communities
remodelled their past to suit the present, but such details are often
beyond recovery. Our evidence can allow only glimpses at the
traditions of cities and peoples about which too little is known,
leaving the way in which the Trojan past is used in a particular
city at a particular time hard to determine. Some of our evidence
for Trojan traditions, whether cults, founders, or names, is early
while some is as late as Pausanias or later still. Even where the
traditions are only recorded in late authorities, they may have
existed in some form for a considerable length of time. Nevertheless, regardless of such arguable individual cases, collectively the
evidence reveals the vitality and variety of these traditions over
centuries.

In the rhetoric of Athenian politics the Trojans had been
barbarians, but even in Athens there was ambivalence. Outside
Athens the Trojan barbarian is less evident. Cities and peoples
could proclaim Trojan founders or ancestors without calling into
question their own Greekness. When anti-barbarian rhetoric was
flourishing in Athens, the people of Aineia could put a figure in a
Phrygian cap on their coinage. The Teneans may have had many
reasons for wanting to claim Trojan descent but they can hardly
have intended to present themselves as barbarians. It may well be
that in general the Trojans remained less vulnerable to the charge
of barbarism because they were a people from the heroic age,
the equals of the Achaian heroes. In that sense they were pre-
barbarian.[150] It is only by analogy with the Persians that they are
barbarized, and this is largely in Athens, although the barbarian
Trojan does develop a momentum of its own, especially in the
intellectual tradition.[151] Nevertheless, Alexander's conquest of the
Persians in the latter half of the fourth century BC takes away
the important political and rhetorical context. It was into this
world of local myths and traditions that the Romans came as the
descendants of the Trojans.

[149] Dion. Hal. *Ant. Rom.* 1. 61–2; many cities in the Troad claimed Trojan founders and
much of Asia had supported the Trojan cause.
[150] Cf. E. Hall 1989: 21 on Eur. *Phoen.* 1509–13.
[151] See Ch. 3 above and Epilogue.

Part III

Between Greece and Rome

5

Troy and the Western Greeks

The beginnings of Rome's Trojan ancestry should be sought not in Rome, nor among Greek intellectuals and antiquarians, but rather in the relationship between the Greeks and non-Greeks who together inhabited Italy and Sicily. From the outset it was a myth of interaction, a collaboration between the Greeks and their neighbours. It is easy to imagine that Rome was unique or exceptional. In many ways, of course, it was, but in acquiring a mythological past that led directly into the mythological past of the Greeks, Rome was like so many other non-Greek states. Lost or homeless warriors from either side in the Trojan War had a tendency to turn up in the West, where they were incorporated into the traditions of both Greek and non-Greek communities. Any understanding of Rome's Trojan past, therefore, must start with this phenomenon.

1. THE WANDERER

The myth of the Trojan refugees may have become part of Rome's heritage, but it originated among the Greeks. The Trojans were one group among many wanderers who populated Greek myth. They were in competition with other famous wanderers such as Herakles, Jason and the Argonauts, and the Greeks returning from the Trojan War, warriors such as Odysseus, Menelaos, Philoktetes, and Epeios.[1] Herakles travelled throughout the Mediterranean;[2] Jason was associated particularly with the Black Sea region;[3] the returning Greeks with the West, although Menelaos also paid a visit to North Africa.[4] So the Trojan myth cannot be

---

[1] The theme of the wanderer was already recognized in antiquity, see Strabo 1. 2. 9, 1. 2. 39, 3. 2. 13, 3. 4. 5.

[2] Bayet 1926: 9–124, Bérard 1957: 402–17, Lacroix 1974, Hartog 1988: 22–7.

[3] Moreau 1994: 157–72, Braund 1994: 8–39.

[4] Bérard 1957: 303–83, de la Genière 1991, Malkin 1998; the *Nostoi*, tales of returning Greeks and homeless Trojans, were the subject of a 3-vol. work by Lysimachos of Alexandria, *FGrH* 382F6–16 with Jacoby's notes. Menelaos in Africa: Malkin 1994: 46–66.

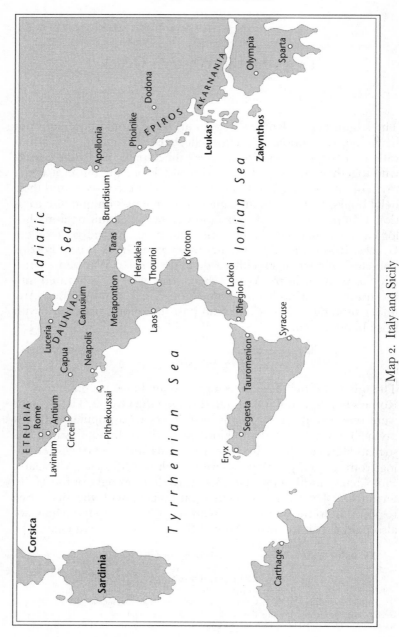

Map 2. Italy and Sicily

interpreted separately from other myths of a similar sort. The nature and use of the myth will have changed over time, but it is the common theme of the wanderer which is of interest here.

These wandering stories reflect a Hellenocentric view of the world.[5] They snake out of a Greek core, linking the whole Mediterranean with Greece's heroic past. They do not function solely as entertainment, but are part of the Greek engagement with the non-Greek world that surrounded them. They are important for the Greek understanding of and relationship with this alien environment into which the Greeks moved as they colonized.[6] These mythological travelling stories are a form of colonization with the mind, overlapping with the process of colonization itself. Both wanderers and colonists tended to visit the same regions, the Black Sea, North Africa, Sicily, South Italy.

The myths are an attempt to comprehend and make safe an alien, potentially threatening environment. They are in a sense myths of exploration, mapping out the unknown by reference to the known, drawing it into the Greek world and incorporating it into the Greek conceptual framework. When Greeks do visit these peripheral areas, whether through colonization or trade, they can be reassured by the knowledge that they are not the first Greeks to have visited. The wanderers of myth have preceded them, leaving signs of their presence there. This may be simply the very fact that the tradition says that they went there or it may be more precise. They may have marked the land with a name or a building or some other memorial. According to Diodoros, Herakles' visit to Sicily left 'undying memorials of his presence' in the territory of Leontinoi, and elsewhere he excavated a lake bearing his name.[7] Libya had the port of Menelaos; Odysseus built a sanctuary of Athena on the Cape of Sorrento; Armenia is named after the Argonaut Armenos.[8]

This mythological interpretation of the land makes it less alien and less inhospitable, but the non-Greek peoples themselves are

[5] Bickerman 1952.

[6] Note especially Malkin 1994, Moreau 1994: 157–72, Braund 1994: 8–39, Dench 1995: 33–8.

[7] Diod. Sic. 4. 23. 4–24. 6, Malkin 1994: 208, cf. also Dion. Hal. *Ant. Rom.* 1. 38–44 on Herakles' travels.

[8] Menelaos: Hdt. 4. 169, Malkin 1994: 48–57; Odysseus: Strabo 5. 4. 8; Armenos: Strabo 11. 4. 8, 11. 14. 12. For other examples: Strabo 3. 2. 13, 3. 4. 3, 6. 3. 9, [Arist.] *Mir. ausc.* 105–10.

also woven into this mythical web with similar effect. Often they are the result of the wanderers' sexual relations with natives. Herakles left a good scattering of offspring around the Mediterranean, the ancestors of various peoples later to be encountered by Greek colonists. His liaison with Echidna, the half-woman, half-viper, produced Agathyrsos, Gelonos, and Skythes, progenitors of the Agathyrsoi, Gelonoi, and Skythians respectively. Such a monstrous mother helps to account for the particularly barbaric Skythians. In this case Herodotos specifically says that this is the story told by the Black Sea Greeks; the Skythians had their own account of their origins, one that did not include Herakles.[9] In Lydia Herakles sired the Heraklid dynasty of kings at Sardis, which lasted until Kandaules was overthrown by Gyges.[10] Odysseus and Kirke were the parents of a wide range of eponyms in central Italy, including Latinos, Auson, Rhomos, Anteias, and Ardeias.[11] Jason was said to have been the ancestor of people such as the Albanoi around Kolchis on the Black Sea.[12] Sometimes these Greeks from the mythical past founded cities, or groups of them were left by their leader, or they just drifted into unknown territory.[13]

The myths also perform a justificatory role. The earlier mythological presence could justify Greek occupation of this land, although such stories were more likely to convince the Greeks themselves than the native populations. Ancestral possession was always felt by the Greeks to be a powerful argument in territorial disputes, whether it be to defend existing territory or to legitimize any extension.[14] Thus, when territory lay outside the familiar

---

[9] Hdt. 4. 9–10, 4. 102, Hartog 1988: 22–7. Herodotos draws a link only between Skythes and the Skythians, although it is hard to imagine that the connection was not made in the case of the other two tribes. At 4. 108. 2 he suggests that the Gelonoi were originally Greeks, but this view is not attributed to the Black Sea Greeks. For Skythian version, Hdt. 4. 5–7. On Echidna: Hes. *Theog.* 295–305, *RE* 5. 2, s.v. 'Echidna'.

[10] Hdt. 1. 7. 4 (by a slave of Iardanos), Apollod. *Bibl.* 2. 7. 8, *Suda* s.v. Ἀλκαῖος' (by Omphale), Matthews 1974: 96–9, Georges 1994: 3, 22–3.

[11] Latinos: Hes. *Theog.* 1011–16; Auson: Serv. on *Aen.* 8. 838; Rhomos, Anteias, Ardeias, founders of Rome, Antium, and Ardea: Dion. Hal. *Ant. Rom.* 1. 72. 5, citing Xenagoras (*FGrH* 240F29); on all children of Odysseus and Kirke in this area, Wiseman 1995: 45–50. There was a cult of Kirke in Latium, Strabo 5. 3. 6. In mythology maternity could be as uncertain as paternity, thus Kalypso too was held responsible for Auson and Latinos, Serv. on *Aen.* 3. 171, Apollod. *Epit.* 7. 24.

[12] Pliny, *HN* 6. 38, though Just. *Epit.* 42. 3. 4 links them with Herakles (and Alba in Italy), cf. Braund 1994: 27–8.

[13] Founders: Epeios at Metapontion, Just. *Epit.* 20. 2. 1, Philoktetes at Petelia, Strabo 6. 1. 3; left behind: Dion Hal. *Ant. Rom.* 1. 34. 1 (followers of Herakles left on Capitoline); drifters: Strabo 3. 4. 3 (companions of Amphilochos).   [14] Cf. Tod 1913: 132–51.

Greek world, mythical ancestors could provide a convenient precedent. The Spartans could use the achievements of Herakles, ancestor of their kings, to justify the acquisition of land in Sicily. The Spartan Dorieus was advised to lead a colony there on the grounds that 'the whole country of Eryx belonged to the Heraklids, since it had originally been acquired by Herakles himself'.[15] Rarely is our evidence as explicit as this, although an analogous relationship is evident when the Minyan Argonaut, Euphemos, is given a 'clod of earth' as a sign that his descendants will later rule in Kyrene.[16]

2. THE TROJAN WANDERER

So there are many Greek myths about wanderers, and these are part of the Greek interaction with the non-Greek world. It is in this context that the stories of Trojan travels should be interpreted. Cityless, these survivors of the war had no choice but to wander. Aineias is the most famous of them, but there are many other stories of migrant Trojans and the evidence for them is extant from as early as the fifth century BC. Pindar's fifth Pythian ode reports the arrival of the sons of Antenor, the Antenoridai, in North African Kyrene, in the company of Helen and, presumably, Menelaos.[17] Later writers suggest that the Trojans settled there, thus becoming precursors of the non-Greek population of the Kyrene area.[18] According to Herodotos a Libyan tribe, the Maxyes, claimed that they were descendants of 'the men from Troy', by which they surely meant Trojans.[19] Then there was Helenos, son of Priam, who travelled to Epiros, where he eventually succeeded Neoptolemos as the husband of Andromache, his presence attested as early as Euripides.[20]

Others are found further west. Thucydides in his excursus on Sicilian prehistory says that the Elymians in western Sicily, whose main cities were Eryx and Segesta, were an amalgam of Sicanians

[15] Hdt. 5. 43, Malkin 1994: 203–18.

[16] Pind. *Pyth.* 4. 32–54, Chamoux 1953: 82–9, Malkin 1994: 174–80.

[17] Pind. *Pyth.* 5. 82–8, Chamoux 1953: 71–3, Malkin 1994: 52–6, 64–6.

[18] Strabo 7. 1. 34, Diod. Sic. 1. 56. 4, Lysimachos *FGrH* 382F6 (schol. on Pind. *Pyth.* 5. 110).

[19] Hdt. 4. 191; Perret 1942: 127–8, however, argues that the Greeks at Troy are meant here; they are also known as the Mazyes, Steph. Byz. s.v. '*Μάζυες*.'

[20] Eur. *Andr.* 1243–52 with schol. on 1245, Paus. 2. 23. 5–6, Verg. *Aen.* 3. 295, though Argives claimed that they had the tomb of Helenos, Paus. 2. 23. 5–6, see further Ch. 4. 3.

and Trojan refugees. Variations of this appear in later writers. The Trojan Aigestes is said to have been the founder of Segesta, coming directly from Troy in Dionysios, but sent from Italy by Philoktetes in Strabo.[21] Unspecified Trojans are reported to have settled on Sardinia, though against much opposition.[22] In Italy itself Antenor arrived overland from Troy with the Enetoi, stopping in the Po valley; their descendants later to be known to the Romans as the Veneti.[23] Capua in Campania was alleged to have been named after the Trojan Kapys, a claim supposedly made by Hekataios of Miletos in about 500 BC.[24] Elsewhere in Italy the Greek city of Siris near Metapontion on the Gulf of Tarentum was originally occupied by Trojans.[25] According to Strabo many places around the South Italian town of Kroton had Trojan names because it was here that the Trojan women stranded their Greek captors by burning their ships.[26] So, even without Aineias landing on the coast of Latium, there was a sizeable Trojan presence in the West, but it was Rome's political predominance that elevated the Trojans of Latium above all other Trojan migrants.

These wanderers are Trojan rather than Greek, and this raises a question: how do these Trojan myths fit with the explanatory hypothesis outlined earlier in this section? There I suggested two main roles for such myths, first, that they made an alien environment less intimidating and, secondly, that they provided a justification for Greek colonial presence. The Trojans, simply because they are Trojan, are less likely to have been used to provide a justification or precedent for later Greek occupation, although there were Greek cities in Italy and elsewhere that did choose to highlight Trojan aspects of their past. On the other hand, the Trojans can satisfactorily fulfil the first role, that is to say rendering

[21] Thuc. 6. 2. 3, Dion. Hal. *Ant. Rom.* 1. 52, Strabo 6. 1. 3, 6. 1. 14, Bérard 1957: 352–5. In Greek writers Segesta is also spelt 'Aigesta' and 'Egesta'. On Segesta, Ch. 7. 2 below.

[22] Paus. 10. 17. 6, Solin. 4, Serv. on *Aen.* 1. 601 (Sall. *Hist.* F2. 8, Maurenbrecher), Silius Italicus *Punica* 12. 344–5, 361–2; Perret 1942: 130–56, Bérard 1957: 417, Frazer 1898: 5. 323 on Ilienses.

[23] Livy 1. 1. 1–4 (on which Ogilvie 1965), Strabo 1. 3. 2, 3. 2. 13, 5. 1. 4, 12. 3. 8, 13. 1. 53, Just. *Epit.* 20. 1. 7–8; Perret 1942: 157–81, Bérard 1957: 366–8, Vanotti 1979: 103–12, Braccesi 1984, Capuis 1993: 23–35.

[24] Hekataios *FGrH* 1F62 (Steph. Byz.); Dion. Hal. *Ant. Rom.* 1. 73. 3 reports those who say that Rhomos named it after his great-grandfather Kapys, the father of Anchises, cf. also Serv. on *Aen.* 10. 145. For the various foundation stories of Capua, *RE* 3. 2, s.v. 'Capua'.

[25] Strabo 6. 1. 14, Athen. 12. 523c (Timaios *FGrH* 566F51, Arist. frag. 601 Gigon), Lycoph. 978–92; Bérard 1957: 350–2.

[26] Strabo 6. 1. 12.

the new world safe, both the land and its people. Trojan ancestry helps to bridge the gulf between Greek and non-Greek, tying the native population into the Greek world and giving both a heroic Greek past. The Elymians, the Enetoi, the Sardinians, the Latins, some of the people of Kyrene were all, in part at least, originally Trojans. Consequently these people are not being met for the first time but rather they are being rediscovered. The Greeks are transferring the known world to the unknown and defusing the terrors of the unknown.[27]

An alternative interpretation, however, has been suggested. Rather than stressing the familiarity of the Trojans this interpretation focuses on the role of the Trojans as celebrated enemies of the Greeks. Thus the attribution of Trojan ancestry to non-Greeks does not represent a need for reassurance in an alien world but, instead, it encapsulates the Greek hostility towards the barbarian.[28] Such an argument by itself is unsatisfactory. It underestimates not only the complexity of Greek attitudes to the Trojans, but also the complexity of the Greeks' relationship with their non-Greek neighbours. Furthermore, these myths are likely to have developed in conjunction with Greek colonial expansion and so precede the emergence of the barbarian Trojan that can be observed in Athens after the Persian Wars. Nevertheless, this interpretation does contribute something to our understanding of the problem of Trojan ancestry. The relationship between the Greek colonists and their non-Greek neighbours was by necessity one of interaction and even cooperation, but there was also a tension between the two parties that could on occasion degenerate into open conflict.[29] In one sense the choice of Trojan ancestry helped to provide a more reassuring and familiar environment, but at the same time it also reflected the ambiguous nature of the relationship.

Greeks could, nevertheless, recall that it was they, the Greeks, who had been victorious in the Trojan War and who had asserted their authority. The identification of native populations with Trojans, therefore, could also symbolize that superiority. Moreover,

---

[27] Cf. the discovery that the Etruscans were Lydian migrants, Hdt. 1. 94, Dion. Hal. *Ant. Rom.* 1. 27–8, Strabo 5. 2. 2.

[28] This position is surveyed by Galinsky 1969: 91–8 and rejected.

[29] For Greek colonists and neighbours, de la Genière 1979: 85–91, Boardman 1980: 189–92, Whitehouse and Wilkins 1989, Robinson 1990, Dench 1995: 46–50, cf. Momigliano 1975: 52–7 on Massalia.

whenever specific Trojans are named as ancestors, they are usually ones who were reported to have been well disposed to the Greeks, sometimes even treacherous to their own side. Often these stories of philhellenic Trojans are of a relatively late date, but Antenor had marked himself out as a friend of the Greeks as early as the *Iliad* by proposing that Helen should be returned to the Achaians and by playing host to Menelaos and Odysseus. Later, however, Antenor was to be represented as betraying Troy, signalling to the Greeks as they waited at Tenedos and letting the Greek soldiers out of the Wooden Horse. There is no sign in the *Iliad* that Aineias is well-disposed towards the Greeks, although his eventual survival is prophesied by Poseidon. But in later writers Aineias appears as a friend of the Greeks who recommends that the Trojans give up Helen, or even as a traitor to the Trojans. Antenor and Aineias, therefore, were not Trojans who were unrelentingly hostile to the Greeks, but, rather, they were men who favoured compromise and negotiation.[30] Helenos too was to become estranged from the Trojans and by his prophecies he revealed to the Greeks how Troy would be captured.[31] As the survivors of a defeated people, the descendants of the Trojans in places such as Italy and Sicily need not have been perceived either as threatening or as the objects of intense Greek hostility.

Not all non-Greeks, of course, were Trojans in disguise. In fact Trojans were probably in the minority. Nevertheless, Greeks always felt a need to understand the different peoples they encountered in terms of their own experience. As we have seen above, many of them were interpreted as the products of liaisons between Greek heroes, such as Herakles, and native females, some more human than others. Greek superiority is apparent here too.[32] The sexual subjugation of the non-Greek by the Greek hero can be compared to the defeat of the Trojans by the Greeks in the Trojan War. The result of both assertions of superiority are the 'barbarians' that populate the periphery of the Greek world. Both explanations are reassuring.

It is the west that seems to have the highest concentration of

[30] References for Aineias and Antenor, see Ch. 3 nn. 78, 80. Diktys 5. 8 and Dares 41 also develop this theme, but it is unclear to what extent they reflect existing traditions or indeed deliberately oppose them, cf. Farrow 1992: 342–51. On treachery of Antenor, Braccesi 1984: 123–44; of Aineias, Galinsky 1969: 46–9, Momigliano 1984: 450–1.

[31] Gantz 1993: 635–43; the story does not appear in Homer, but he has already revealed the prophecy in Soph. *Phil.* 603–21. [32] Cf. Dougherty 1993: 61–80.

Trojan migrants. This extensive Trojan activity is likely to have been a corollary of the many stories of Greek warriors returning from Troy who end up in Italy and Sicily. Odysseus, Menelaos, Epeios, Philoktetes, and Diomedes are all reported to have come this way. Odysseus left various memorials of his presence, as did his companions; there was a hero-sanctuary of Drakon near the Lucanian city of Laos, and another of Polites near neighbouring Temesa.[33] Menelaos made several landings in the Gulf of Tarentum before proceeding to western Sicily.[34] Epeios supposedly founded Lagaria, Metapontion, and Pisa, while Philoktetes was held responsible for a series of obscure cities in South Italy, Krimissa, Petelia and Makalla.[35] Diomedes reached Argos safely, but, finding that his wife was neither faithful nor well disposed to him, he fled to the kingdom of Daunos in Italy, where he is said to have founded several cities, including Arpi and Canusium.[36] It is perhaps no coincidence that the earliest evidence for Homer's *Iliad* comes not from mainland Greece but from the island of Ischia in the Bay of Naples, site of the early Greek settlement of Pithekoussai. Here an inscription on an eighth-century BC cup appears to allude to the cup used by Nestor in the *Iliad*: 'Nestor's cup was good to drink from, but anyone who drinks from this cup will soon be struck with desire for fair-crowned Aphrodite.'[37]

3. The Wanderer and Local Tradition

The mythical stories of Greek and Trojan wanderers are many and varied. They defy attempts to turn them into a single, seamless, coherent narrative and instead remain fragmented and

[33] Memorials of Odysseus: Strabo 3. 2. 13; heroon of Drakon: Strabo 6. 1. 1; Polites: Strabo 6. 1. 5, Paus. 6. 6 (where he is clearly not a benign presence), cf. Hom. *Od.* 10. 224–5; Phillips 1953, Bérard 1957: 303–22; cf. also Kalchas and Podaleirios in Daunia, Strabo 6. 3. 9.

[34] Malkin 1994: 57–64.

[35] Epeios: Strabo 6. 1. 14 (Lagaria), Just. *Epit.* 20. 2. 1, Vell. Pat. 1. 1 (Metapontion), Serv. on *Aen.* 10. 179 (Pisa); Philoktetes: Strabo 6. 1. 3, 6. 2. 5, Steph. Byz. s.v. 'Μάκαλλα', Lycoph. 911–29, [Arist.] *Mir. ausc.* 107; Bérard 1957: 334–9, 343–50, de la Genière 1991, A. Erskine 1998: 135–6.

[36] Domestic problems: Gantz 1993: 699–700; in Italy: Lycoph. 592–632 with scholia, Strabo 6. 3. 9, Bérard 1957: 368–76, *RE* 5 s.v. 'Diomedes' 820–3.

[37] D. Ridgway 1996, whose translation is used here, Hom. *Il.* 9. 628–43. The cup was imported from Rhodes, but it is not known whether it was inscribed before or after its arrival in Pithekoussai.

disjointed. This is not, I suspect, the fault of the Greek and Latin writers who preserve the myths, but rather an essential feature of their development. The inconsistencies and contradictions reflect the role of local, oral tradition in developing and moulding the myths in such a way that local variants could exist within a more widely accepted basic framework.[38]

The example of Epeios, builder of the Wooden Horse, may help to illustrate this. Justin in his epitome of Pompeius Trogus records: 'The people of Metapontum put on display in the temple of Minerva (Athena) the tools which Epeius their founder used to make the Trojan horse.' Yet, Lykophron and the author of the Pseudo-Aristotelian *De mirabilibus auscultationibus* believed that the tools were in the temple of Athena at the neighbouring Lagaria, a city which Strabo had noted as a foundation of Epeios.[39] Scholars can often be tempted to explain away differences: perhaps the proximity of Lagaria and Metapontion meant both stories are in fact referring to the same temple of Athena, or perhaps the story moved from one place to another.[40] But it is also very likely that two neighbouring towns could both lay claim in competition with each other to the Homeric hero and his toolkit, just as medieval churches and monasteries competed for relics.[41] Neither version fits very well with another tradition that Epeios was stranded in central Italy after the ubiquitous Trojan women burnt his boats and so he founded the city of Pisa there.[42] Rather than being the products of muddled and careless mythographers these stories reflect the different traditions of the cities in which they were current, Metapontion, Lagaria, and Pisa. The same phenomenon is attested on a larger scale with the multitude of burial places for Anchises and Aineias.[43]

The importance of local tradition in the development of these stories is apparent in a passage of Strabo:

Next [after Thurioi and Lagaria] there is the city of Herakleia, a little

---

[38] See the example of Menelaos in Malkin 1994: 57–64 .

[39] Just. *Epit.* 20. 2. 1, Lycoph. 930–50, [Arist.] *Mir. ausc.* 108, Strabo 6. 1. 14; A. Erskine 1998: 135–6.

[40] Some solutions are summarized by Dunbabin 1948: 35, Bérard 1957: 336–7, Giannelli 1963: 69–72 (who quotes the evidence).

[41] Geary 1990, esp. 3–27, Bentley 1985: 40–3 on analogy with mediaeval relics; 50, 91, 99, 106 on the many heads of John the Baptist.   [42] Serv. on *Aen.* 10. 179.

[43] Anchises: Pfister 1912: 629; Aineias: Pfister 1909: 142–3. Note the attempts to rationalize such stories, as in Dion. Hal. *Ant. Rom.* 1. 54 with 1. 49.

above the sea, and two navigable rivers, the Akiris and the Siris, on which a Trojan city of the same name was situated. In the course of time, after Herakleia had been founded by the Tarantines, it became the port of the Herakleotes. It is 24 stades distant from Herakleia and about 330 from Thurioi. The wooden image (*xoanon*) of Athena Ilias which is set up there is considered to be proof of the Trojan settlement. A story is told that this image closed its eyes when the suppliants were torn away by the Ionians who had captured the city. For these Ionians arrived as colonists in flight from the empire of the Lydians, and after seizing the city, which belonged to the Chones, they called it Poleion. Even now, it is said, the image is shown closing its eyes. It is certainly audacious to tell such a tale, saying not only that it closed its eyes just as the image in Ilion turned away during the assault on Kassandra, but also that it can still be seen closing its eyes. It is even more audacious to claim that as many wooden images were brought from Troy as writers say. For in Rome, Lavinium, Luceria, and in the territory of Siris Athena is called Ilias, as if brought from Troy. In addition, the exploit of the Trojan women is reported in many places and appears unbelievable, although it is possible.[44]

Strabo expresses a certain exasperation with this multiplicity of similar stories and claims, but the passage is indicative of the vitality of competing local traditions in the cities of Italy.

The cities found confirmation of these traditions in various objects that supposedly dated from the heroic period. The people of Herakleia could point to the wooden image of Athena Ilias in support of their claims to be situated on or near a Trojan settlement; this wooden image is surely meant to be identical with the famous Palladion of Troy.[45] The people of Lagaria and Metapontion both had proof of their foundation by Epeios in the form of his tools; Philoktetes' tomb provided incontrovertible proof of his presence, although it was said to be located at both Makalla and Thurioi.[46] Krimissa was not only founded by Philoktetes, it also had the temple of Apollo Alaios which he established. Like Epeios, Philoktetes had a particular object associated with him, that is to say Herakles' arrows, which gave him such extraordinary skill at archery. Something such as this would be a prize possession for any Greek city of south Italy. According to the author of the *De mirabilibus auscultationibus* Philoktetes had originally

---

[44] Strabo 6. 1. 14, following the text of Lasserre's Budé edn. For Siris as a Trojan settlement, also Athen. 12. 523c.

[45] The stories of doubles, copies, stolen Palladia gave tremendous potential for multiplication, Dion. Hal. *Ant. Rom.* 1. 68–9, 2. 66. 5 see further Ch. 4. 3 (Argolid).

[46] Lycoph. 927–9, Just. *Epit.* 20. 1. 16.

dedicated these arrows in the sanctuary of Apollo Alaios at Makalla, but the people of Kroton took them from there and offered them to their own temple of Apollo. But these were precious arrows, and Justin records that they were to be seen in the temple of Apollo at Thurioi.[47] These objects may have acted as material evidence to confirm and reinforce local tradition, but from our perspective they provide valuable evidence that these traditions were indeed local. Thus such traditions are likely to have been limited to South Italy and not widely known throughout the Greek world.

These myths were the property not only of the Greeks; many of the non-Greek peoples appear to have accepted and adapted the mythical origins provided for them by their Greek neighbours.[48] This is most well known in the case of Rome, but Roman acceptance is only part of a more general phenomenon. Greek myths about Diomedes' presence in Daunia were found acceptable by the non-Greek population there. Thus the people of Luceria maintained that they still had votive offerings made by Diomedes in their temple of Athena. Indeed, they even claimed to have the Palladion, which according to one version of the myth Diomedes stole from Troy, a claim which they made in competition with several other cities, including Rome, Argos, and Athens.[49] The heroic past of the area also included sanctuaries of the famous seer Kalchas and of Podaleirios, the son of Asklepios; in both cases there were stories that the hero was buried there.[50] Further west Odysseus' sojourn with Kirke was celebrated by the people of Circeii on the southern border of Latium, where they had a temple of Kirke. As evidence they would show visitors a bowl that allegedly belonged to Odysseus. Here too was the tomb of Odysseus' companion Elpenor, which was already known to

---

[47] Strabo 6. 1. 3, schol. on Lycoph. 911, *Etym. Magn.* 58. 4, [Arist.] *Mir. ausc.* 107, Just. *Epit.* 20. 1. 16, Bérard 1957: 345–6, Giannelli 1963: 162–7, cf. Ampelius 8. 5, Scheer 1996 for Teukros' arrows in Sikyon.

[48] Cf. Bickerman 1952: 73–4, Cornell 1975: 2–3, Dench 1995: 38–44.

[49] Strabo 6. 3. 9, 6. 1. 14, cf. Dion. Hal. *Ant. Rom.* 1. 69. 2, where the stolen Palladion is said to have been one of two. On Palladion and Diomedes, Gantz 1993: 642–6; in other cities, Strabo 6. 1. 14, *RE* 18. 2 s.v. Palladion; cf. also Ch. 4 n. 109. Diomedes in Daunia: Giannelli 1963: 53–9, Malkin 1998: 234–57.

[50] Strabo 6. 3. 9 (heroa), Lycoph. 1047–66 (tombs, one false), Bérard 1957: 376–8; Kalchas also associated with Klaros oracle, where he is said to have died, Strabo 14. 1. 27, 14. 4. 3. For Kalchas and his followers as ancestors of the Pamphylians, Hdt. 7. 91, Strabo 14. 4. 3.

Theophrastos in late-fourth-century Athens.[51] The Segestans had probably long claimed Trojan ancestry by the time of their first diplomatic encounter with Rome in the third century BC.[52] Non-Greek acceptance of Greek myths is not limited to Italy and Sicily. Jason's travels in the Black Sea find an echo among the non-Greek peoples of Media, Armenia, and their neighbours, where sanctuaries of Jason could be found.[53]

4. The Trojan Myth in Latium

It is in this context that the appearance of the Trojan myth in Latium should be understood. Myths of all sorts were introduced by Greeks and adopted by non-Greeks. Whether the peoples are Greek or non-Greek, they produce evidence for their mythical past, Diomedes' votive offerings in Luceria, Odysseus' bowl in Circeii, Epeios' tools in Lagaria and Metapontion, Philoktetes' arrows in several cities. And so it is in Latium. The city of Lavinium seems to have had a particularly strong association with the Trojans; several sources suggest that Aineias was claimed as its founder.[54] There was a story that Aineias died in battle near here, but that his body was never found; some suspected that he had fallen into the river, and a heroon, or hero-sanctuary, was set up beside the river to honour him. Dionysios of Halikarnassos appears to have seen the shrine, although he was not unduly impressed: 'it is a small tumulus, not large, surrounded by a row of trees which are worth seeing'. Nor was the identity of the hero secure; there were some, reports Dionysios, who believed it to be a heroon not of Aineias but of his father Anchises.[55] In 1968 archaeologists found a seventh-century tomb, remodelled in the fourth century, which was enthusiastically, if somewhat optimistically, interpreted

---

[51] Strabo 5. 3. 6, Theophr. *Hist. pl.* 5. 8. 3, Pliny *HN* 15. 119, Cic. *Nat. D.* 3. 48, Braund 1994: 19–20, Wiseman 1995: 45–50, 136, Ampolo 1994. The Romans sent a colony to Circeii in 393, but whether this was a cause of, consequence of or nothing to do with the local myth is unknown.

[52] See Ch. 7. 2.

[53] Strabo 1. 2. 39, cf. 1. 3. 2, Braund 1994: 27–8, Georges 1994: 6–8.

[54] For Aineias, Dion. Hal. *Ant. Rom.* 1. 59, Plut. *Cor.* 29. 2, *OGR* 12. 4, Livy 1. 1. 10, Just. *Epit.* 43. 1. 12, cf. Lycoph. 1259–60, Val. Max. 1. 8. 7. For Lavinium as the first Trojan foundation in Latium, Varro *Ling.* 5. 144. In Strabo 5. 3. 2 the founder is Latinos.

[55] Dion. Hal. *Ant. Rom.* 1. 64, cf. Livy 1. 2. 6, *OGR* 14. 4, *Schol. Veron.* on *Aen.* 1. 259. Dionysios may, however, merely be reporting someone else's impressions of the heroon, Timaios perhaps (cf. 1. 67. 4). A heroon of Anchises implies a version of the story that brings Anchises to Italy, cf. Strabo 5. 3. 2.

as the heroon of Aineias that had been described by Dionysios.[56] Like so many other cities Lavinium professed to have a statue of Athena Ilias, which was to be identified with the famous Palladion of Troy.[57] Here the local rivalries already witnessed in the case of Philoktetes' arrows are again apparent. For the Lavinian Palladion was ultimately dwarfed by the claims of the Romans, whose Palladion, protected by the virgins in the temple of Vesta, was the authentic one.[58] Trojan relics are, however, less in evidence in Rome since it was usually said to have been founded not by Aineias but by a descendant.

The Sicilian historian Timaios, writing in the first half of the third century BC, seems to have visited Lavinium. Here he learnt from conversations with local residents about the sacred objects that were kept locked away in their sanctuary. Among these there was, he was told, 'a Trojan earthenware vessel', further confirmation of the Trojan roots of the Latin people. Dionysios, who reports Timaios, understands him to be talking about the Penates supposedly rescued by Aineias from the flames of Troy and brought to Italy, although it is not clear that Timaios himself had these in mind.[59] Dionysios prefaces his citation of Timaios with a list of Greek words for the Penates, which suggests that whatever Timaios wrote it was not 'Penates'. In contrast to the Palladion the Penates do not figure in the Greek tradition about Troy, but are very much a Latin addition to the myth; at what stage they were added is controversial.[60]

For some time this Trojan mythology may have coexisted in Rome with stories of other wanderers from Greek mythology. Herakles, Odysseus, and the Arkadian Evander all feature in accounts of Roman prehistory. The Fabii boasted of descent from Herakles, and significantly there was a place for the hero in Fabius Pictor's history.[61] As Hercules, he was worshipped at the Ara Maxima in the Forum Boarium, the object of what may well have

---

[56] Sommella 1974, followed by Castagnoli 1982: 13, Galinsky 1992: 100–1, Holloway 1994: 138, rejected forcefully by Cornell 1977 and Poucet 1983*b*, both of whom also cast doubt on a *cippus*, supposedly inscribed with a dedication to *Lar Aeneas*; on the number of tombs of Aineias, Dion. Hal. *Ant. Rom.* 1. 54.

[57] Strabo 6. 1. 14, quoted sect. 3 above.

[58] *RE* 18. 2, s.v. 'Palladion', col. 182–5, Austin 1964: 83–5, Dubourdieu 1989: 460–7.

[59] Timaios in Dion. Hal. *Ant. Rom.* 1. 67. 4 (*FGrH* 566F59), κέραμος Τρωϊκός.

[60] Wissowa 1887, Perret 1942: 338–44, 351–4, Bömer 1951: 50–117, Weinstock *RE* 19.1 s.v. 'Penates', col. 417–57, Dubourdieu 1989.

[61] Festus 77L s.v. 'Fovi', Plut. *Fab.* 1. 2, Ch. 1 n. 105.

been the oldest foreign cult in Rome; according to some sources the altar was set up by Evander, then dwelling on the Palatine hill.[62] Greeks had associated Odysseus with central Italy since at least the sixth century, when he fathers Latinos in a passage to be found in Hesiod's *Theogony*. Several writers even gave Odysseus a role in the foundation of the city, either through eponymous descendants or most controversially in the company of Aineias.[63] Odysseus certainly did become part of the local traditions of central Italy as the case of Circeii demonstrates, but there is little evidence to suggest that the Romans themselves ever adopted him. One family, the Mamilii, did claim descent from Odysseus and Kirke, but this may reflect the traditions of the family's home town of Tusculum rather than those of Rome.[64]

Various suggestions have been made to explain Rome's ulti-mate preference for Aineias and the Trojans. It may, for instance, have been the result of a desire to be part of the Greek world and yet simultaneously distinct.[65] Nevertheless, descent from Kirke would surely have been enough to establish distinctiveness. Certainly, the Greeks would not have thought that Odysseus' liaison with Kirke would make the Romans Greek any more than Herakles' liaison with Echidna made the Skythians Greek. Other factors that are now lost to us could also be responsible. The predominance of the Trojan myth may have been the result of the political rivalries of various families; just as the Mamilii favoured Odysseus and the Fabii Herakles, so the Iulii and the Memmii favoured the Trojans. Aineias' martial prowess could perhaps have appealed to the militaristic Romans more than Odysseus' cunning, or maybe the attraction lay in Aineias' piety.[66] Alter-natively, it may simply have reflected the strength of the tradition of Trojan wanderers in Italy as a whole.

[62] On Herakles and Evander, Livy 1. 7, Dion. Hal. *Ant. Rom.* 1. 39–43, with succinct remarks of Cornell 1995: 68–9. See also Poucet 1985: 287–9, Coarelli 1988: 60–77.

[63] Hes. *Theog.* 1011–16, Hesiodic authorship of these lines is doubted, but they probably date to 6th cent., Poucet 1985: 46 n. 27, Cornell 1995: 210. Role in foundation through descendants: Dion. Hal. *Ant. Rom.* 1. 72. 5 (Xenagoras *FGrH* 240F29), Plut. *Rom.* 2. 1; with Aineias: Dion. Hal. *Ant. Rom.* 1. 72. 2 (Hellanikos *FGrH* 4F84), Horsfall 1979*b*: 379–83, 1987: 15–16, Solmsen 1986, Ampolo 1992, who also points out that Festus 432L and *OGR* 12. 2 have Odysseus in central Italy at the same time as Aineias, cf. Ch. 1 n. 50; Gruen 1992: 8–11, 16–22 in particular emphasizes the role of Odysseus.

[64] Livy 1. 49. 9, Dion. Hal. *Ant. Rom.* 4. 45. 1, Ogilvie 1965: 199, Crawford 1974: 219–20, 375–7, Wiseman 1974: 155.

[65] Gruen 1992: 29–31.

[66] Aineias the warrior: Galinsky 1969: 34–5; piety: Bömer 1951: 39–49, esp. 47–9.

Although the Romans and other Latin peoples were influenced by the stories of the Greeks, they nonetheless produced their own versions of the Trojan myth, interweaving the Trojan saga with local traditions. In Lavinium, for instance, Aineias seems to have received the cult name 'Indiges', which suggests that he may have been identified with a local deity of some sort.[67] In Rome itself Romulus was probably already a familiar figure by the time his ancestor Aineias arrived in Latium.[68] The enigmatic Penates, too, are likely to have represented an indigenous Latin tradition.[69] By the late first century BC the Trojan myth in Latium had become focused on three interlinked cities, Rome, Lavinium, and Alba Longa, the latter supposedly destroyed in the seventh century BC, if indeed it ever existed as a city at all.[70] The nature and development of the Trojan myth in Latium have been the subject of numerous hypotheses: the myth enters Latium either via Etruria or through direct contact with the Greeks; once there, by whichever route, it finds acceptance first in Lavinium and then spreads to Rome, or it happens the other way round, being adopted by the Romans and exported to Lavinium; this all takes place somewhere between eighth and third centuries BC.[71] The exploration of these often intricate hypotheses is beyond the scope of this chapter. It is enough to say that the myth was present in Latium.

In adopting a Greek view of their origins the Romans are behaving like other non-Greeks when faced with Greek myth-making. What impelled non-Greek peoples to accept the Greek interpretation of their past is unclear. The suggestion that it filled their own mythological vacuum is less convincing than it used to be.[72] It is more appropriate to consider this development in the context of interaction between non-Greek native and Greek

---

[67] Indiges (or Pater Indiges, or Jupiter Indiges): Festus 94L, Verg. *Aen.* 12. 794–5, *OGR* 14. 4, Livy 1. 2. 6, Cornell 1995: 68.

[68] Cornell 1975, rejecting the strongly argued case of Strasburger 1968. For the priority of Romulus see also Carandini 1997: 107.

[69] Dubourdieu 1989, esp. 292–307.

[70] Poucet 1985: 284–7, Horsfall 1987: 20, Cornell 1995: 70–3; on non-existence of Alba: Grandazzi 1997: 103–7.

[71] Etruria: Alföldi 1965: 278–87, Galinsky 1969: 139–40; Greeks: Cornell 1995: 66, Dury-Moyaers 1981: 163–9, Castagnoli 1982: 14–15; Lavinium first: Alföldi 1965: 246–87, Dury-Moyaers 1981: 173–7, Cornell 1995: 68; Rome first: Perret 1942: 320–44, Galinsky 1969: 141–62. Discussion up to the early 1980s is well surveyed by Poucet 1983*a*.

[72] Wiseman 1989: 130, Grandazzi 1997: 189–92, Carandini 1997: 35–84.

intruder. The myths provide Greeks with a means of making sense of an alien environment. The native population adopt the myths, not because the myths give them a past which they did not previously have, but because they give them a past which they can share with the Greek interlopers. Thus, for the non-Greek the myths are part of an accommodation with the Greek, a coming to terms with the intruder. At the same time the acceptance of the myth by the non-Greek population makes a statement to the Greeks about their willingness to accept or tolerate the Greek presence. It is also part of a wider cultural exchange, in which the Greeks, too, absorb and adapt the culture of their non-Greek neighbours.[73]

Such a thesis would suggest that the acceptance of the myth in Rome and Latium came at a fairly early date in their contact with the Greeks. Certainly the story of the Trojan War and of Aineias' escape from Troy was known in central Italy in the sixth century BC; Etruscan cemeteries have disclosed many vases that depict the flight of Aineias and Anchises.[74] Greek influence is already apparent in Latium in the sixth, or even seventh, century BC, as evidence for the cult of the Dioskouroi, Castor and Pollux, at Lavinium demonstrates.[75] This may, however, be too early. Knowing who Aineias is does not mean believing him to have been an ancestor.[76] If the Roman myth of its Trojan past did have its origins in interaction between Greeks and Latins, or more specifically Greeks and Romans, then the vaguer, perhaps sometimes rather indirect, early influences may be an inappropriate context. It had surely, however, taken shape by the fourth century, by which time direct contact between Greeks and Romans is clearly attested.[77]

Some may sense a contradiction between the argument of Chapter One, 'The Recovery of Trojan Rome', where the importance of Trojan mythology in Rome prior to the first century BC was played down, and the argument of the present chapter.

[73] See n. 29 above.

[74] Schauenburg 1960 on the vases; the evidence for Aineias in Etruria is summed up by Horsfall 1987: 18–19. Etruscan interest in the Trojan myth continues into the late 4th cent. BC, as the wall-paintings of the François tomb indicate, Cornell 1995: 135–8.

[75] Poucet 1985: 24–9, Ampolo 1990, Cornell 1995: 81–118, Grandazzi 1997: 175, 188–90; more cautious is C. J. Smith 1996, who summarizes his conclusions on pp. 225–8. For Castor and Pollux: *ILLRP* 1271a.

[76] A point well made by Poucet 1989a: 245.

[77] Cornell 1995: 397–8.

The contradiction is, in fact, more illusory than real and reflects the two different perspectives from which the myth can be viewed. Aineias' role and importance change with the context. For Romans engaging with the Greek world outside Rome or for Greeks approaching Rome, the myth is part of their shared past. Thus, as suggested in Chapter One, the myth will be most visible where there is some form of interaction between Greeks and Romans. It is to be found in history or poetry where cultural borrowings from the Greeks are most evident, or in diplomatic exchanges, or in Greek accounts of Rome. But, as the general absence of any mention of Trojan ancestry in the surviving republican material helps to demonstrate,[78] it did not play a central role within the state itself or in the Roman self-image until Caesar gave it one.

5. SCHOLARS AND ANTIQUARIANS

The West was where the Greeks first came into contact with the Romans. It was in the cities and towns of South Italy and Sicily that the first stories about Rome emerged and images of Rome began to be formed. This may seem an obvious point to make, but the importance of the western Greeks is often underplayed in modern discussions of Rome's mythical past. There are two principal reasons for this. First, there is a tendency to speak of 'the Greeks' as if they were a monolithic group, a single undifferentiated mass.[79] Yet, in any century the inhabitant of Lesbos, Athens, or Pontos, is unlikely to have viewed Rome in the same way as his contemporaries in such Italian cities as Neapolis or Taras. Secondly, there is also a tendency to privilege ancient scholars over local tradition. These two tendencies are to a certain extent a consequence of the nature of the evidence that is available, but the result is that the western Greeks are almost removed from a picture which they were instrumental in formulating.

In much modern scholarship, therefore, the progress of the myth in the Greek world is often reconstructed through a jigsaw of fragmentary passages, enigmatic references to lost writings.[80]

---

[78] See Ch. 1.

[79] It would be invidious to pick out examples, but a glance at any number of books and articles would confirm this.

[80] The best survey of this lost literature is Cornell 1975: 16–27.

In an effort to attain some degree of chronological precision, possible citations of early writers and scholars are made the subject of seemingly endless debate. The fifth-century historian and mythographer, Hellanikos of Lesbos, may or may not have associated Aineias and Odysseus with the foundation of Rome, but given the appallingly inadequate quality of the evidence neither case appears provable. All that can be acknowledged is the possibility.[81] Many have believed that the sixth-century poet Stesichoros brought Aineias to the West. It is an attractive proposition that a Sicilian poet should be interested in Aineias' western travels, but unfortunately the only evidence is a small white tablet from the Augustan period. Known as the *Tabula Iliaca Capitolina*, it illustrates in relief the sack of Troy and appears to claim to follow the *Iliou Persis* of Stesichoros, although its emphasis on Aineias, who is depicted several times with accompanying captions, seems very Augustan. In his final scene Aineias is shown escaping by sea with Askanios and Anchises, the latter clutching a box of sacred objects: according to the caption they are heading 'to the West'. Whether this is a genuine echo of Stesichoros or a rather banal Augustan addition remains an insoluble problem.[82]

Then there is a 'fragment' of Herakleides of Pontos which has been introduced into the discussion in order to demonstrate that a fourth-century Greek could imagine Rome to be a Greek city. It occurs in the context of Plutarch's account of the capture of Rome by the Gauls in 390 BC:

An obscure report of the disaster and capture of the city seems to have reached Greece straightaway. For not long afterwards Herakleides of Pontos in his treatise, *On the Soul*, said there was a story from the West that an army of Hyperboreans coming from abroad had seized a Greek city called Rome, which was located somewhere on the Great Sea. I should certainly not be surprised that Herakleides, a man prone to storytelling and invention, embellished a true story about the capture of the city with 'Hyperboreans' and 'the Great Sea'.[83]

---

[81] Dion. Hal. *Ant. Rom.* 1. 72. 2 (Hellanikos *FGrH* 4F84) with Horsfall 1979*b*: 379–83, 1987: 15–16 (against); Solmsen 1986 (for), and n. 63 above. Damastes (*c.*400 BC) is said by Dion. Hal. to agree with Hellanikos, but in what respect is unclear.

[82] It is 1 of 20 tablets, collectively known as *Tabulae Iliacae* and published by Sadurska 1964; Horsfall 1979*a* provides a thorough and sceptical discussion of the relationship between Stesichoros and the *Tabula Iliaca Capitolina*, cf. Castagnoli 1982: 7–8, Gruen 1992: 13–14.

[83] Plut. *Cam.* 22. 3 (*FGrH* 840F23), cf. Gruen 1992: 10. Wiseman 1995: 58 wonders whether the Pythagorean Herakleides was influenced by 6th-cent. Italian Pythagoreans.

But how much is an inhabitant of Pontos, even one who has lived in Athens, likely to have known about central Italy? Herakleides' talk of the mythical Hyperboreans suggests that he did not know much, and Plutarch was certainly unimpressed. In a treatise entitled *On the Soul* this story was surely not intended to be a well-researched piece of recent history. Indeed it is quite possible that Herakleides' story of Hyperboreans and the Great Sea made no mention of Rome at all and that Rome only entered this story as part of a later rationalizing interpretation of his story. It is, however, the western Greeks that are most important in these early years and their conception of Rome is likely to have been different.

Yet, in some ways, it is an illusion that there is little evidence for the West. What we are lacking are dated texts or fragments with authors' names attached, but as the first part of this chapter suggests there is abundant evidence for western stories and traditions. A certain haziness in chronology has to be accepted; sometimes an early witness such as Thucydides or the *Theogony* can be given, sometimes not. The overall impression, however, is clear. Both Greek and Trojan wanderers played an important part in the West and in the interaction between Greeks and non-Greeks. In what has preceded I have tried to give a sense of the vitality and variety of its traditions and myths, while avoiding an undue emphasis on lost writings. The local western traditions are essential to the understanding of the Trojan myth in Latium.

A very different interpretation, one that highlights the role of the ancient scholar, has found clear expression in two recent and important books. For Erich Gruen 'the conception and development of traditions that linked the origins of Rome with Troy came from the workshops of Greek historians, writers and intellectuals', and for T. J. Cornell 'the legends were manufactured by literary men and form a body of pseudohistorical tradition which originated not in popular memory but in the lamplit studies and libraries of Athens and Alexandria'.[84] To focus attention on the scholars in this way rather than on the cities themselves is surely to misplace the emphasis. The stories may not have been historical, but they were a very real presence in the collective consciousness of so many cities, as this and the previous Chapter have

[84] Gruen 1992: 20, Cornell 1995: 41, both following the influential article of Bickerman 1952.

sought to demonstrate. The ancient scholars are certainly important for the ultimate transmission of these stories, but they are
reflecting the maze of myth rather than creating it.

It is frequently pointed out that there were between twenty-five
and thirty different Greek versions of the origins of Rome, the
product, it is argued, of scholarly wrangles and learned discussion.[85] Rome is at different times a Trojan, Etruscan, Pelasgian
city; Rhomos, Rhome, Romulus feature as eponymous founders,
sometimes with Trojan ancestry, sometimes not.[86] Yet, this multiplicity was surely not merely the result of argumentative scholars
and antiquarians. Just as there were among the cities of south Italy
and Sicily countless often inconsistent traditions about the past,
each city with its own version, or versions, so too would each city
have told its own story about the origins of Rome.[87] There were at
least as many different ways of thinking about Rome as there were
different cities.[88]

Nevertheless, it is useful to consider the available western
scholarship, almost all of which has a Sicilian background. The
lost Sicilian writers, Alkimos, Kallias of Syracuse, and Timaios
of Tauromenion, are on record as discussing Rome's origins and
all supply a Trojan component. Alkimos' version of Roman
prehistory includes both Aineias and Romulus, but neither is
the founder of Rome. That honour goes to Rhomos, son of
Alba, grandson of Romulus, and great-grandson of Aineias and
Tyrrhenia. Alkimos' date is unfortunately unknown, although a
plausible case can be made for the fourth century BC. In contrast,
Kallias, who wrote twenty-two books on the Syracusan ruler
Agathokles, can be dated with certainty to the early third century
BC. He told of a Trojan woman Rhome, who married Latinos and
had three sons by him, Romulus, Rhomos and Telegonos. The
sons built Rome and named the new city after their mother.[89] In

---

[85] 25–30: Bickerman 1952: 65, Cornell 1975: 16–17; wrangles: Bickerman 1952: 67,
Gruen 1992: 51.

[86] Etruscan: Dion. Hal. *Ant. Rom.* 1. 29. 2; Pelasgian: Plut. *Rom.* 1. 1; see Cornell 1975:
16–27 for numerous examples of founders, and Ch. 1 n. 41. For clarity I latinize Ῥωμύλος.

[87] Cf. Fabius Pictor in Sicily, Ch. 1.4.

[88] For other examples of variety in Greek perceptions of Rome, A. Erskine 1994, 1997a.

[89] Alkimos: Festus 326L, 328L (*FGrH* 560F4), which probably occurred in his *Sikelika*,
Athen. 7. 322a (*FGrH* 560F1); the MS reading 'Rhodius' is usually emended to 'Rhomus'.
Kallias: Dion. Hal. *Ant. Rom.* 1. 72. 5 (*FGrH* 564F5). On these passages, Perret 1942: 386–7,
who sums up the arguments for Alkimos' date, Classen 1963: 448–50, Strasburger 1968:
12–13, Cornell 1975: 6–7, Gruen 1992: 15–16, Wiseman 1995: 52–7.

both Alkimos and Kallias there are familiar names, but in unfamiliar combinations, none resembling the orthodox Augustan picture of Rome's foundation.

The most significant and influential western historian, Timaios of Tauromenion, who lived from the mid-fourth to the mid-third century, is somewhat better known, but his writings too are lost. Much of his long life was spent in exile in Athens, where he wrote voluminously on the history of Sicily and the West, including the wars between Rome and Pyrrhos.[90] Nothing survives of his account of the foundation of Rome, but it is clear that he thought Rome to be of Trojan origin. Just as the heroic past could be seen in the landscape, shrines, and temples of Sicily and South Italy, so Timaios looked at central Italy for similar confirmation of Rome's Trojan past. He found it in the Trojan earthenware of Lavinium which was noted in the last section and in the ritual of the October Horse in Rome. The annual killing of a horse in the Campus Martius was done, Timaios believed, in memory of the fall of Troy and was intended to recall the Wooden Horse. Our sole witness for this suggestion is Polybios who reported it only to ridicule it in his lengthy assault on the Sicilian historian's credibility:

For it would then be necessary to say that all barbarians are descended from the Trojans. For almost all of them, or certainly the majority, whenever they are about to go to war or embark on some perilous campaign, sacrifice a horse and interpret the future from the way the animal falls. In his discussion of this irrational practice Timaios seems to me to display not only ignorance but also intellectual immaturity, in the way that he jumps from the sacrifice of a horse to the conclusion that they do this because a horse was thought to have been responsible for the capture of Troy.[91]

Timaios as a Sicilian was accustomed to a world in which myths of migrating Greeks and Trojans were a vital part of local traditions. For him such an argument made sense, but it offered little to convince a Peloponnesian such as Polybios who had been reared in a different mythological environment.[92]

One text, however, does survive complete and it is pervaded by

[90] Pearson 1987, Meister 1990: 131–7.

[91] Polyb. 12. 4b (*FGrH* 566F36); ὀψιμαθία is here translated as 'intellectual immaturity' rather than 'pedantry' (W. R. Paton, Loeb trans.) or 'pedantic irrelevance' (Walbank 1967); on the word, see J. Rusten's note in Loeb edn. of Theophr. *Char.* (p. 180).

[92] Significantly what little is known of Polybios' account of Roman prehistory mentions Arkadia, reported in Dion. Hal. *Ant. Rom.* 1. 32, cf. Gruen 1992: 35, 42.

the mythological world of south Italy. This is the *Alexandra* attributed to the third-century BC poet Lykophron, a work alive with
stories of wandering heroes, both Greek and Trojan. This obscure
and problematic poem purports to be a record of the prophetic
utterances of Priam's daughter, Kassandra. The fates of the warriors at Troy are predicted, many of whom end up in the west, in
Italy, and Sicily. In Italy are to be found the Greeks Odysseus,
Diomedes, Philoktetes, Epeios, and the seer Kalchas, in Sicily
the Trojans Aigestes and Elymos, and in central Italy Aineias
himself.[93]

Here Lykophron has the opportunity to tell Rome's foundation
story. Although enigmatic and elliptical, it is the earliest substantial account to survive. Kassandra introduces it in this way:

> My descendants will in time to come increase immeasurably the fame of
> the race of my ancestors, carrying off the foremost crown with their
> spears and obtaining kingly power over earth and sea. Nor, my unhappy
> fatherland, will you hide your glory in darkness, forgotten and vanished.
> A certain kinsman of mine will leave a pair of lion cubs, offspring
> excelling in strength (*rhome*), the son of Kastnia called also Cheiras, best
> in counsel and not to be scorned in battle.

The kinsman is not named, but there can be little doubt that he is
Aineias and the lion cubs are surely Romulus and Remus, the
Roman connection being reinforced by the pun on *rhome* as the
Greek word for 'strength' and for Rome.[94] Kassandra tells of
Aineias' journey from Thrace, through Macedonia, and then
Etruria, until he meets up with a former enemy, usually identified
with Odysseus. Certain features are shared with the later Augustan
versions: Aineias travels widely, protects the ancestral gods, and is
faced with similar prophecies, such as edible tables and the sow
that gives birth.[95] Important differences, however, can also be
observed. Whereas Vergil and Dionysios of Halikarnassos gave

---

[93] Odysseus: 805–11, 1242–5; Diomedes: 594–632, 1056–66; Philoktetes: 911–29; Epeios:
930–50; Kalchas: 1047; Aigestes and Elymos: 951–77; Aineias: 1226–80. In general Italian
and Sicilian passages include: 594–632, 688–737, 805–11, 911–1010, 1027–33, 1047–86,
1128–40, 1181–88, 1226–80, among which other lesser heroes can be found. Lines 31–386
prophesy the fall of Troy.

[94] Lycoph. 1226–35; on Kastnia for Aphrodite, *RE* 10 s.v. 'Kastnia'; on the pun, A.
Erskine 1995*a*. Copious scholia help with the interpretation of this poem, collected in
Scheer's edn. of Lykophron.

[95] Ancestral gods: Lycoph. 1262; tables: 1250–2, Verg. *Aen.* 3. 394, 7.107–34, Dion. Hal.
Ant. Rom. 1. 55; sow: Lycoph. 1255–8, Verg. *Aen.* 3. 389–93, (cf. 8. 81–5), Dion. Hal. *Ant.
Rom.* 1. 56.

Aineias a route via Sicily, Lykophron brings him through north Italy, or at least through Etruria. In contrast to the Augustan versions there is no obvious interval of time between Aineias and the twins Romulus and Remus. A collaboration between Aineias and Odysseus may have been mentioned by Hellanikos, but it is otherwise unknown. Lykophron interprets the sows' litter of thirty as representing thirty towers rather than the more usual thirty years between the foundation of Lavinium and that of Alba Longa. The thirty towers have been taken to stand for the thirty towns of Latium.[96] Lykophron thus gives some idea of the stories circulating among Greeks about Rome. How much reflects Roman tradition is unclear. Even Romulus and Remus, who are not mentioned by name, are here referred to as lion cubs, not wolf cubs.

As befits a prophecy of Kassandra, it is clearly important, but no one knows quite how much attention to pay to it, or indeed what sort of attention. Lykophron himself is dated to the first half of the third century BC, largely on the basis of his association with the philosopher Menedemos of Eretria and his work in the Library of Alexandria.[97] The Roman verses, however, have caused problems for some. How could someone at the court of a Ptolemy possibly have been so tactless as to describe the Romans as 'carrying off the foremost crown with their spears and obtaining kingly power over earth and sea'? Indeed how could anyone in the third century BC use such words of the Romans? Surely, it is argued, Rome did not achieve this degree of power until well into the second century BC, after it had defeated both Macedon and Antiochos. Some scholars, therefore, have preferred to detach the poem from its alleged author and place it in the second century BC. Others have chosen to regard the controversial verses as interpolations.[98]

The lines may well appear a little odd in the context of the third-century eastern Mediterranean, especially if delivered in a

[96] Lycoph. 1255–8, contrast Dion. Hal. *Ant. Rom.* 1. 56. 5, 1. 66. 1, Varro, *Ling.* 5. 144, *Rust.* 2. 4. 18, Diod. Sic. 7. 5. 4, where it is attributed to Fabius Pictor (*FGrH* 809F2); on 30 towns, Ogilvie 1965: 43.

[97] A. W. Mair in the Loeb edn., 303–6, sums up what is known about Lykophron, cf. also Fraser 1972: ii: 649 n. 17, Hurst 1991: 17–27, G. Weber 1993: 423–4.

[98] A strong argument was made for keeping the poem in the 3rd cent. by Momigliano 1942 and 1945*b*, but not all were convinced. The redating case is best put by P. M. Fraser in *OCD*³ s.v. 'Lycophron', the interpolation case by S. West 1984. The very obscure lines 1435–50, apparently about Rome and Macedon, are also considered problematic; solutions are concisely summarized by Hurst 1991: 25.

Hellenistic court, but there is in fact no need to assume that they were written there at all. It is difficult to say anything precise about Lykophron, because so very little is known about him. For instance, we do not know when he went to Alexandria, how long he stayed there, or when or where he died. The biographical tradition associates him with three places, Euboia, Alexandria, and the city of Rhegion, a Chalkidian colony on the toe of Italy. This last city was the home town of Lykos, described variously as the father or adoptive father of Lykophron, a distinguished historian of Sicily. Sokles of Chalkis in Euboia was also and more plausibly described as Lykophron's father, but the important point to note here is that Lykophron appears to have some form of family links with Rhegion.[99] Usually the Lykophron problem has been solved by moving the whole poem or merely the awkward lines to a more suitable date. I wish to suggest here that an alternative would be to move them to a more suitable location, namely south Italy.

What is at issue in these controversial lines about Rome is not the reality of power but the perception of power. From the perspective of the Greeks of south Italy in a post-Pyrrhic world Rome *was* enormously powerful and that could be summed up by talking of rule over 'land and sea'. They had seen Pyrrhos, the ambitious king of Epiros, humiliated and expelled from Italy by the Romans. It mattered little to these Greeks that the Ptolemies or Seleukids might be more powerful than the Romans; they were not more powerful in south Italy. Rhegion, in particular, was a city which had consistently supported Rome from as early as the war against Pyrrhos.[100] Whether or not Lykophron ever actually lived in south Italy, his family ties may have enabled him to share its outlook. It is even possible that the poem was written in the aftermath of Rome's victory over Carthaginian naval power in the First Punic War, by which time Rome had clearly conquered the sea.[101] Such a south Italian context would explain not merely

---

[99] In Tzetzes (Scheer edn. of Lycoph. ii: 4) Lykophron is a Chalkidian, son of Sokles or Lykos the historian; in the *Suda* s.v. *'Λύκος'* Lykos is described as 'the father of Lykophron the tragedian', while in the entry on Lykophron the poet is 'a Chalkidian from Euboia, son of Sokles, and of Lykos of Rhegion by adoption'.

[100] Pyrrhos: Polyb. 1. 7. 3, Livy 31. 31. 6–7, Livy *Per.* 12, App. *Sam.* 9, Dion. Hal. *Ant. Rom.* 20. 4–5, the latter two suggesting that it may have been incipient Rhegian disloyalty that led to the seizure of the city by its Campanian garrison. For loyalty in 2nd Punic War, Lomas 1993: 67–8.

[101] As noted above we do not know when Lykophron died.

the importance of Rome in the poem but also the whole emphasis on the cults and heroes of Italy and Sicily.[102]

The rich mythological world sketched in this Chapter offers a
basis for understanding the development of Rome's Trojan myth
and its role in the interaction between Greeks and Romans.
Where names and dates can be determined, the fragmentary evidence of lost scholars can add valuable precision to this somewhat
impressionistic picture, but it is important to remain aware that
this precision may be illusory. Alone, however, these fragments
are merely tantalising glimpses of lost scholarship, deprived of
context and frequently at odds with each other in ways which cannot be forced into a pattern. Lykophron, on the other hand, can
contribute something more substantial, although even here there
is uncertainty. Nevertheless, whether or not he represents a rare
and authentic voice from third-century BC southern Italy, the
poem provides important evidence for south Italian traditions.

As Greeks spread out around the Mediterranean, so they incorporated the non-Greek natives that they encountered into their
world view, identifying them as descendants of figures from Greek
myth, such as Herakles, Odysseus, and the Trojans. The native
peoples in turn often adapted these stories for themselves. In
doing so they were entering into dialogue with their Greek neighbours and recognizing their presence. The myths reflected and in
some sense expressed the economic and cultural interaction between Greek and non-Greek. The Roman acceptance of a Trojan
past was no different. From the outset, then, Rome's Trojan myth
was not purely Roman but rather a myth that operated between
Greek and Roman.

---

[102] S. West 1984, on the other hand, would simply remove much of the Italian material as interpolations perpetrated in southern Italy, but this fails to explain how this Italian
version so quickly became part of the standard *Alexandrian* text; by the end of the 1st cent.
BC the Roman lines were already being treated as the work of Lykophron by the
Alexandrian scholar Theon, Steph. Byz. s.v. 'Αἴνεια', scholia on line 1236.

6

Pyrrhos, Troy, and Rome

An Interlude

In 280 BC Pyrrhos, the Molossian ruler of Epiros, landed in South Italy to assist the Greek city of Taras against the Romans. His early victory at Herakleia may not have been decisive, but it did allow him to win over non-Greeks as well as Greeks. Bruttians, Lucanians, and Samnites all supported him. Rome, however, rejected any attempts at a negotiated settlement. Finally, in 275, after a two-year diversion in Sicily and a poor showing in battle against the Romans, Pyrrhos returned to mainland Greece, leaving the Italian Greeks to succumb to the growing power of Rome.[1]

It is a commonplace of modern scholarship that anti-Trojan polemic formed an essential feature of Pyrrhos' propaganda during his time in Italy. He highlighted, it is said, Rome's Trojan origins, in order to boost the confidence of the Greeks and to stir up anti-Roman feeling among them. He was the new Achilles and the Romans were his Trojans. The Greek achievement at Troy could be repeated in Italy. Jacques Perret, in a thesis that has won few converts, even went so far as to argue that Pyrrhos had invented this Trojan ancestry especially for his war against Rome. There is, nevertheless, widespread agreement that Pyrrhos offers the earliest evidence for the exploitation of Rome's Trojan past in a diplomatic or military context and that its use on this occasion was far from friendly.[2]

However appealing this view is, it is more likely to be the product of later literary imagination than the inspiration of Pyrrhos himself. The entire argument is based on little more than a sentence of Pausanias. As Pyrrhos is listening to the Tarantine

---

[1] Franke 1989.
[2] Perret 1942: 409–34, Bömer 1951: 44, Alföldi 1957: 28, Musti 1963: 236, Kienast *RE* 24 s.v. 'Pyrrhos', col. 131–2, Forte 1972: 9, E. Weber 1972: 214, Momigliano 1984: 449–50 (Momigliano 1945: 99–100 is more cautious), Franke 1989: 465, Galinsky 1992: 103, Gruen 1992: 44, Malkin 1998: 206, C. P. Jones 1999: 46.

ambassadors his mind wanders: 'While the ambassadors were speaking, the memory of the fall of Troy occurred to Pyrrhos and he hoped for a similar outcome in this war; for he who was a descendant of Achilles would be campaigning against the colonists of the Trojans.'[3] This is a statement about Pyrrhos' *thoughts*; nothing is said about anything he did. But for Erich Gruen this is the substance of propaganda directed at his Italian allies; Pyrrhos' daydreams have become official policy.[4] Ekkehard Weber accepts the propaganda interpretation and takes it back a stage further when he suggests that the idea originated with the ambassadors; this at least would explain why Pyrrhos was thinking about it while they were speaking.[5] Thoughts and intentions, however, are notoriously elusive and difficult to establish even among contemporaries. Yet Pausanias was writing some four hundred years later. Appeals can be made to the quality of Pausanias' now lost sources: 'obviously using a good source' (Momigliano), probably Hieronymos of Kardia (Alföldi), or, better still, ultimately derived from Pyrrhos' own commentaries (Perret).[6] Pausanias does not in fact give any source for this statement. He may or may not have been using a contemporary source, but, even if he had been doing so, Pyrrhos' thoughts on the Trojan War could just as easily be the product of authorial interpretation. Thoughts and speeches in historical works are literary devices and suitable occasions for the exercise of imagination. Pyrrhos' Trojan musings offered an attractive way of giving his Italian campaign a certain epic quality. Their creator could have been a contemporary, an intermediary, or even Pausanias himself. All that this passage of Pausanias allows us to conclude is that someone at some time drew an analogy between the Trojan War and Pyrrhos' war with Rome.

Pausanias' survey of Pyrrhos' career is merely a digression,

---

[3] Paus. 1.112.11: ταῦτα λεγόντων τῶν πρέσβεων μνήμη τὸν Πύρρον τῆς ἁλώσεως ἐσῆλθε τῆς Ἰλίου, καί οἱ κατὰ ταὐτὰ ἤλπιζε χωρήσειν πολεμοῦντι· στρατεύσειν γὰρ ἐπὶ Τρώων ἀποίκους Ἀχιλλέως ὢν ἀπόγονος.

[4] Gruen 1992: 44: 'He announced to his allies the expectation of a successful outcome; as descendant of Achilles, he would recreate the Achaean victory at Troy by subduing the colonists of Troy. The propaganda may or may not have had effect, but it was Hellenic propaganda.' There is no evidence for such a pronouncement.

[5] E. Weber 1972: 214, cf. C. P. Jones 1999: 46.

[6] Momigliano 1984: 449; Alföldi 1957: 28 (cf. E. Weber 1972: 214 n. 4); Perret 1942: 412–16, who traces the material through Hieronymos to Proxenos right back to Pyrrhos' commentaries. Pausanias may not even have read Hieronymos, J. Hornblower 1981: 72–4 (rejected by Habicht 1985: 85 n. 72).

admittedly a full one, prompted by his description of a statue of the king in Athens. It is valuable to contrast it with other versions of Pyrrhos' reign, especially Plutarch's *Life of Pyrrhos,* which is by far the fullest surviving account. Here the Trojan origins of the Romans make no appearance whatsoever, neither as daydreams nor as propaganda. Plutarch's silence on the matter is all the more significant because he knew the work of Hieronymos of Kardia, the alleged source of Pausanias, and refers to it several times in his *Life of Pyrrhos.*[7] Clearly Pyrrhos' commentaries, if they ever existed, would give the greatest insight into the king's thought processes, but none of the writers who mention the commentaries confirm Pausanias' Trojan analogy.[8] A considerable amount of writing on Pyrrhos survives, but the use of this analogy is limited to Pausanias.[9]

Pyrrhos' desire to emulate Achilles, on the other hand, is recorded by Plutarch.[10] This aspiration can readily be understood without any reference to the Trojan origin of Rome. He bore the name of Achilles' son; his family claimed descent from Achilles; it was Achilles who personified the heroic ideal and the warrior ethos. Most of all, imitation of Achilles involved imitation of Alexander, something of vital importance to a man who sought to replace Alexander as ruler of Macedon.[11] This comes out most strongly in Plutarch's description of Pyrrhos' invasion of Macedonian territory under Demetrios Poliorketes. Pantauchos, one of Demetrios' generals, challenges Pyrrhos to single combat. Pyrrhos accepts the challenge, stirred by a desire to 'attach the glory of Achilles to himself more through his courage than his ancestry'. His success against Pantauchos leads to an Epirote victory in the battle, in consequence of which the Macedonians are said to have been in awe of Pyrrhos and to have compared him to Alexander. Whereas other kings merely impersonated Alexander, Pyrrhos in

[7] Plut. *Pyrrh.* 17.7, 21.12, 27.8.

[8] Dion. Hal. *Ant. Rom.* 20. 10, Plut. *Pyrrh.* 8. 3, 21. 12 (via Hieronymos); also Jacoby (*FGrH* 229) is sceptical about the existence of the commentaries.

[9] Apart from Plutarch and Dion. Hal. there exist Just. *Epit.* 16–18, 23–5, Zonar. 8. 2–6, Diod. Sic. 22 (fragmentary), Dio bks. 9, 10 (fragmentary), Polyb. 1.6–7, 2. 20 and for the recently enlarged Ennius fragments, Suerbaum 1995.

[10] Plut. *Pyrrh.* 1, 7. 7, 13. 2, cf. 22. 8, Diod. Sic. 21. 21. 12.

[11] Ancestral claims of Molossian royalty: Ch. 4. 3 (Zakynthos and Epiros); imitating Alexander: Plut. *Pyrrh.* 8. 1–2, 11. 4–5, Just. *Epit.* 18. 1. 2, Kienast *RE* 24 s.v. 'Pyrrhos', col. 131–2, Stewart 1993: 284–6; Alexander as Achilles: Ameling 1988, Stewart 1993: 78–86.

battle captured the spirit of the great Macedonian king.[12] Coins minted by Pyrrhos suggest that he continued to stress his affinity with Achilles after his arrival in the west. The helmeted head on the coins is usually interpreted as Achilles, although it has some similarities with Alexander portraits and may have been deliberately ambiguous. There is, however, no need to invoke the Trojan character of Rome to explain any of this.[13]

Pyrrhos would anyway have been a rather unsuitable leader for an anti-Trojan crusade. Not only did the Molossian kings of Epiros claim descent from Achilles, they also placed considerable emphasis on their Trojan ancestry, which they traced back to Andromache, as was seen in Chapter Four, 'Trojan Past and Present'. Pyrrhos was no exception; he named his sons Helenos and Alexander, the one recalling the tradition that Priam's son Helenos came to Epiros, while the other could allude both to the great Macedonian king and to Paris, son of Priam. The Trojan flavour continues in the name of Pyrrhos' sister, Troas. Troy, then, was as much part of the Epirote public image as Achilles was.[14] It was for this reason that the Zakynthian proxenos of the Molossians chose to emphasize Trojan Kassandra when making his dedication at Dodona.[15]

Pyrrhos' heroic character, part Achilles, part Trojan, had developed out of the politics of Epiros and Alexander's empire, but it is likely to have had a special resonance in the mythological world of south Italy and Sicily, home to so many Greek and Trojan refugees. Here there were peoples who maintained Trojan connections and others who maintained Greek connections; both could look to Pyrrhos as a leader. Pyrrhos' heroic ancestry was an affirmation of his status as king, of his right to rule and lead, just as it had been earlier for Alexander.[16] The Trojan myth in this area represented not hostility between Greek and non-Greek but a shared past, albeit one that recognized the possibility of tension between the two. Where else could Aineias and Odysseus be

---

[12] Plut. *Pyrrh.* 7. 4–8. 2.

[13] Head 1911: 323 (Achilles), Lücke 1995 (Alexander); Achilles is identified via the nereid with a shield, presumably Thetis, on the reverse. Kienast *RE* 24 s.v. 'Pyrrhos', col. 132, and Franke 1989: 465 see the coins as confirmation of Pyrrhos' Trojan War propaganda. Franke also wonders whether Achilles might have the features of Pyrrhos.

[14] Sons: Just. *Epit.* 18. 1. 3, Plut. *Pyrrh.* 9; sister: Plut. *Pyrrh.* 1. 7. For a full discussion of Trojan traditions in Epiros, Ch. 4.3 above.

[15] Ch. 4.3 above.

[16] On Alexander, see Ch. 9.1 below.

found collaborating with each other? Together the Greek and Trojan traditions of the west were well suited to a monarch who himself embodied such a combination. For the rulers of Epiros the Trojan myth represented not some archetypal conflict but on the contrary compatibility and collaboration.

7

Greek States and Roman Relatives

In the 190s ambassadors from the Greek city of Lampsakos in the Troad arrived in Rome to seek Roman protection. Coming before the Senate they informed their aristocratic audience that the people of Lampsakos were kinsmen of the Romans. This is no isolated instance. Several other states also invoked ties of kinship when making approaches to Rome. The numbers may be few but the mere fact is significant. For many scholars the Greeks were exploiting Rome's Trojan ancestry to win favours for themselves. The implication is that they said these things because they thought that the Romans would be pleased to hear them.[1] This, however, distorts what was happening by focusing on the relationship between the Greek states and Rome while at the same time failing to take account of the Hellenistic context.

Two aspects in particular need to be emphasized. First, the Romans are not being singled out for special treatment. On the contrary, arguments based on kinship were an important feature of Hellenistic diplomacy. The Romans, therefore, are being treated like any other Greek state, something that is interesting in itself; the Romans after all were not Greek. Secondly, there has been a tendency to generalize about 'the Greeks' on the basis of only a small number of examples. Closer scrutiny, however, reveals that there were usually specific, local reasons why some states claimed kinship with Rome and others did not. This Chapter will be concerned to approach the subject from the Greek perspective, focusing especially on the traditions of individual states in so far as they can be determined. But first it is useful to establish the context by examining the Hellenistic practice.

[1] Cf. Gruen 1992: 49, 'Exploitation for concrete advantage remained a Greek, rather than a Roman, objective . . .'; 'This [a Greek oracular pronouncement, Plut. *Mor.* 399C] may represent another instance of Hellenic efforts to curry Roman favour by endorsing the Trojan legend' (49 n. 203); Perret 1942: 283, 'Mais cette tradition nouvelle [Aineias and Segesta], créée pour flatter les puissants du jour . . .' On the Peace of Phoinike Errington 1972: 281 n. 28 says that Ilion may perhaps 'have been deliberately introduced into the war by Attalus to flatter Rome's pride in her Trojan origin'. Such views tend to adopt the Roman view of the Greeks as sycophantic, cf. A. Erskine 1997*c*.

1. KINSHIP DIPLOMACY IN THE HELLENISTIC WORLD

In the many diplomatic exchanges that took place in the Hellenistic world, an appeal for assistance was often reinforced by reference to the kinship that existed between the two states. As a result of the colonial past there were extensive links between cities; a city may have been related to another city as colony to founding city, that is to say mother-city or *metropolis*, or two cities may have shared the same mother-city. But the links between cities included not only those which we would consider to be historical; they also included the mythical, based, for instance, on common heroic ancestors. Both forms of kinship could be drawn on in diplomatic initiatives and the language for each appears to have been identical.[2] It is epigraphy that provides much of the evidence, and this is largely Hellenistic, but literary sources such as Herodotos and Thucydides make it clear that the phenomenon of kinship diplomacy stretches back to the fifth century at least.[3]

The role of kinship in Hellenistic diplomacy comes out vividly in an important series of inscriptions from Magnesia-on-the-Maiandros in the late third century BC. The Magnesians had established a festival of Artemis Leukophryene and sent embassies throughout the Greek world seeking recognition for their festival. Many of the letters from kings and the civic decrees which they received in reply were inscribed.[4] The decree from Same on Kephallenia is of particular interest. It records how the Magnesian ambassadors 'explained about the *oikeiotes* which existed between the Magnesians and the Kephallenians on the basis of the *syngeneia* of Magnes and Kephalos, son of Deïon'.[5] The obscure genealogy offered by the Magnesian ambassadors here is only intelligible to us because Apollodoros' *Bibliotheca* reveals that Magnes and Deïon

---

[2] Discussions can be found in Musti 1963, Elwyn 1993, Giovannini 1993, 1997, Curty 1995, Will 1995, S. Hornblower 1996: 61–80, L. G. Mitchell 1997: 23–8, A. Erskine 1997*b*, C. P. Jones 1999. S. Lücke 2000. *Syngeneia: epigraphisch-historische Studien zu einem Phänomen der antiken griechischen Diplomatie.* Frankfurt, appeared too late to be taken into account. For discussion of Louis Robert's influential but scattered work on the subject see Curty 1995: xiii–xiv. For mythical founders and eponyms under the empire, Weiss 1984, Strubbe 1984–6.

[3] Hdt. 5. 97, Thuc. 1. 95. 1, 3. 86. 2–3, S. Hornblower 1996: 64–70, Curty 1994.

[4] *I.Magn.* 16–87, cf. also Curty 1995: no. 46. For similar dossiers that again show the emphasis placed on kinship in the diplomatic exchanges, Kos: Curty 1995: no. 24, Rigsby 1996: 106–53; Teos: Curty 1995: no. 43, Rigsby 1996: 280–325.

[5] *I.Magn.* 35, lines 13–14 (Curty 1995: no. 46c).

were both children of Aiolos.[6] Of this series of over sixty Magnesian inscriptions thirty mention kinship terms such as *syngeneia* and the looser *oikeiotes*,[7] but the decree from Same is the only one in which the arguments used by the Magnesian ambassadors were reported. The extensive use of kinship terminology in the replies is a reflection of the numerous genealogical arguments which the ambassadors must have presented to the states they visited.

A rare insight into the nature of these arguments is provided by a late-third-century inscription from Xanthos in Lykia. The city of Kytinion in Doris, an area that was reputed to have been the metropolis of all the Dorians, had suffered serious damage from a combination of earthquake and invasion. Ambassadors came to Asia Minor seeking financial assistance and armed with detailed genealogical arguments. They no doubt visited several cities but the Xanthian inscription is now the only evidence for their mission. The Xanthians passed a decree that not only recorded their decision but also contained a very full summary of the Kytinian appeal:

[The ambassadors] asked us to remember the kinship (*syngeneia*) which we have with them through gods and heroes and not to be indifferent to the destruction of the walls of their native city. For Leto, the founder (*archegetis*) of our city, gave birth to Artemis and Apollo here among us. Asklepios, son of Apollo and of Koronis, who was daughter of Phlegyas, descendant of Doros, was born in Doris. In addition to the kinship which they have with us through these gods they recounted their intricate descent from the heroes, tracing their ancestry to Aiolos and Doros. They further pointed out that Aletes, one of the Heraklids, took care of the colonists who were sent from our city by the command of Chrysaor, son of Glaukos, son of Hippolochos. For Aletes, setting out from Doris, helped them when they were under attack, and when he had freed them from the danger which surrounded them, he married the daughter of Aor, son of Chrysaor. After demonstrating with additional examples the goodwill based on kinship which has joined them to us from ancient times, they asked us not to remain indifferent to the obliteration of the greatest city in the Metropolis but give as much help as we can to the building of the walls, and make clear to the Greeks the goodwill which we have towards the league (*koinon*) of the Dorians and the city of the

[6] Apollod. *Bibl.* 1. 7. 3, 1. 9. 4; for Kephalos, son of Deïon as eponym of Kephallenia, see also Arist. in *Etym. Magn.* 144. 26.

[7] Elwyn 1993: 263, who takes *I.Magn.* 79–80 (= Curty 1995: no. 46b) as two separate texts, cf. also Will 1995: 318. The 11 mentioning συγγένεια are collected in Curty 1995: no. 46, some of these use both terms, e.g. Curty 1995: no. 46 b, c, e.

Kytinians, giving assistance worthy of our ancestors and ourselves; in agreeing to this we will be doing a favour not only to them but also to the Aitolians and all the rest of the Dorians, and especially to King Ptolemy who is a kinsman of the Dorians by way of the Argead kings descended from Herakles.[8]

This was no mere diplomatic formality but a substantial part of the Kytinian appeal; such kinship imposed a moral obligation on the Xanthians to help. With an impressive amount of detail the ambassadors laid out the basis of the kinship which they claimed existed between the two states. Considerable care had been taken to develop this complex network of interrelations, all of it mythical. The enormous significance of the Dorian metropolis gave them considerable mythological resources. Not satisfied with one proof of kinship they introduce example after example to reinforce their claim, in a manner that resembles Dionysios of Halikarnassos' attempt to prove that the Romans were Greek.[9] Perhaps the Kytinians overdid it. The Xanthians recognized their claims and expressed sympathy but pleaded poverty and only awarded the Kytinians a meagre five hundred drachmas.

The Xanthian evidence is exceptional in its detail. The type of material found at Magnesia is far more common. Here often complex genealogical arguments, such as that presented by the Kytinians, may lie hidden behind apparently formulaic phrases, such as 'friends (*philoi*) and *syngeneis*' and 'friends and *oikeioi* '.[10] The precise meaning of the terms, *syngeneia* and *oikeiotes* and their cognates, has been the subject of much discussion.[11] *Syngeneia* suggests blood kinship, while *oikeiotes* is something looser, including connections through marriage and perhaps even guest-friendship.[12] Thus the two terms are overlapping rather than mutually exclusive,[13] but it is perhaps unwise to seek too much precision. The

---

[8] Published in Bousquet 1988: 12–53, also *SEG* 38.1476, Curty 1995: no. 75; lines 14–42 quoted here; cf. also S. Hornblower 1996: 78–80. On the translation of τῶν ἀποικισθέντων, C. P. Jones 1999: 139–40.

[9] Dion. Hal. *Ant. Rom.* bk. 1, see Ch. 1.2 above.

[10] φίλοι καὶ συγγενεῖς: *I.Magn.* 33. 5, *I.Priene* 54. 35; φίλοι καὶ οἰκεῖοι: *I.Magn.* 31, lines 23–4, 36–7, and 37, line 7.

[11] For the debate see Curty 1995: 224–41, Will 1995, S. Hornblower 1996: 64–7, Giovannini 1997 (who argues that Curty overemphasizes mythical kinship), C. P. Jones 1999: 13–14. Curty collects all epigraphic texts which deal with συγγένεια.

[12] For similarities between kinship and guest-friendship (or ritualized friendship), Herman 1987: 16–29.

[13] Cf. S. Hornblower 1996: 64–7, in contrast to Will 1995 who seeks too sharp a dis-

decree of Same makes it clear that *oikeiotes* is something that can be based on *syngeneia*, while the decree of Gonnos begins by describing the Magnesians as 'friends and *syngeneis*' and ends with the renewal of the long-standing friendship and *oikeiotes* between the two peoples.[14] This is more likely to be the result of the over-lapping nature of the terms than of a subtle redefinition of the relationship.

Such kinship claims are yet another sign of the importance and vitality of local tradition in the Hellenistic world. Each city was distinctive and exploited its own mythical past to form bonds with other communities. Ambassadors highlighted the manner in which myths were shared and intersected. They may have elabo-rated these traditions to suit their audience, but they appear to have worked within the mythical and genealogical framework of their community rather than engaging in random invention.[15] The Magnesians do not affect to have been founded by Kephalos when approaching the city of Same on Kephallenia. Instead they find some way of bridging the kinship gap between Kephalos and their own eponym Magnes. Sometimes, too, cities could in differ-ent ways share the same mythical figure, as Tegea and Pergamon shared Auge. Daughter of the Tegean king, Aleos, she became mother of the Pergamene hero, Telephos, and was, by one account at least, buried in Pergamon.[16] The claims had force and value because they were rooted in the accepted mythical past of the cities in question.

It might seem that the purpose of claiming kinship is simply to persuade. Certainly, it is noticeable that in interstate relations kin-ship claims and kinship language feature especially when one state is requesting something of another.[17] They would appear to put moral pressure on the other state to assist by drawing attention to

tinction between συγγένεια and οἰκειότης: they are located 'sur des plans différents de la pensée, la *syngeneia* sur le plan de l'érudition mythologique, l'*oikeiotès* sur celui des relations temporelles' (321), or the 'plan mythique' and the 'plan historique' (318 n. 37).

[14] Same: *I.Magn.* 35, lines 13–14 (Curty 1995: no. 46c); Gonnos: *I.Magn.* 33 (Curty 1995: no. 46e).

[15] Cf. Curty 1995: 242–53, cf. also Zakynthos Ch. 4.3 above.

[16] *I.Perg.* 1. 156; Auge is not explicitly cited as the link but her mention in line 24 renders it highly likely, see Curty 1995: no. 41; on tomb, Paus. 8. 4. 9; on Telephos and Pergamon, Hansen 1971: 5–6, 338–48, Scheer 1993: 71–152.

[17] Elwyn 1993: 263–7, Curty 1995: 254–5; cities in distress turn to the founding city like a child to parents, so Diod. Sic. 10. 34. 3. Apart from the examples discussed in the text, note Polyb. 9. 42. 5–8, the captured Aiginetans ask the Roman commander to allow them to obtain ransom money from kindred cities.

family ties and the obligations that go with them.[18] Nevertheless, it is hard to understand why an elaborate genealogical argument should convince. No doubt the visiting embassy often left disappointed. Cities tend not to engrave their failures on stone, but literary sources suggest that such an appeal was as likely to fail as succeed.[19] To focus solely on the persuasive capacity of kinship might be to view the question too narrowly. If a state claims kinship, it incorporates the other state as part of the family and thus legitimates the request that is being made. It is better to seek favours from relatives than from strangers. To approach strangers for help could be considered akin to begging.[20] How else could Kytinion in mainland Greece justify an approach to Lykian Xanthos? Thus kinship, real or mythical, sets up a framework in which an appeal is possible.

Kinship is not a temporary condition lasting for the duration of the appeal but a permanent and reciprocal relationship. The documents from Magnesia demonstrate that the acceptance of the kinship claim was as important as the claim itself. The replies do not merely promise recognition of the festival of Artemis Leukophryene, they also affirm the existence of the kinship between the two states. Acceptance of the kinship claim establishes a bond between the two communities that goes beyond the simple acceptance of the appeal. It provides a basis for future trust and a way of relating to one another for both communities. This is an important restraint on wild invention. A Pergamene decree concerning *isopoliteia* between Pergamon and Tegea made provision for the inscribing of relevant documents, including one about the kinship which existed between them. It makes clear that this is being done so that future generations do not forget.[21] The Xanthians, by dwelling at great length on the *syngeneia* between themselves and the Kytinians, appear to be making clear that in spite of their paltry donation they do not reject the claims of the Kytinians.[22] The people of Lampsakos, as we shall see, seem to

[18] Dover 1974: 273–8, Millett 1991: 127–39, cf. also 109–12 on Arist. *Eth. Nic.* 1165ᵃ14–35.

[19] Elwyn 1993: 265–7 reviews the literary evidence, mostly classical.

[20] On attitudes towards beggars and begging: Hands 1968: 63–6, 77–9, Garland 1995: 25–6, 39, cf. Philostr. *VA* 4. 10 for mass hostility to beggars. For the legitimating character of kinship, cf. Chariton 2. 5. 8, 'Tell me your story, Kallirhoe; you will not be talking to a stranger, for there exists a *syngeneia* of character too' (following G. P. Goold Loeb trans.).

[21] *I.Perg.* 1. 156. 17–23 (Curty 1995: no. 41)

[22] See above n. 8; the Xanthians make clear that they accept the Kytinian claims in lines 46–9 and 65–8, which also makes reference to future generations.

have been almost as concerned to confirm that the Romans accepted their kinship argument as they were about their appeal.[23] So kinship claims in diplomatic initiatives should not be understood simply in terms of persuasion. They create a bond that both legitimates the request and defines the relationship for the future. Kinship implies that each city is willing to assist the other if the need arises. It may be that there will be no further contact between the two communities, but the diplomatic exchange is grounded in the idea that this is part of a long-term, indeed permanent, relationship.

Each relationship was individual and important, but together they formed a complex web joining numerous cities scattered throughout the Mediterranean. So such kinship ties became an expression not only of bonds between particular cities but an expression of Greek identity as well, yet one that was flexible and could allow the incorporation of Hellenized communities such as Xanthos. For although colonial kinship would tend to exclude, mythical kinship could embrace all who were prepared to embrace it.[24]

2. KINSHIP WITH ROME

Any instances of Greek states claiming kinship with the Romans should first be understood within this Hellenistic context.[25] Repeatedly it can be seen that far from conjuring up Trojan ancestry to win the Romans over, these states are drawing on established local traditions. Consequently such claims are not widespread, rather they are concentrated in those areas with a strong sense of a Trojan past, notably the Troad itself and north-western Sicily. By incorporating these traditions into their appeal they are following contemporary diplomatic practice. A modern preoccupation with dating has tended to focus attention on the early examples to the neglect of later instances and indeed of the phenomenon itself.

---

[23] *I.Lamp.* 4; kinship: lines 18–25, 29–31, 56–62; lines 29–31 note their pleasure at Roman acceptance of their kinship argument.

[24] Giovannini 1997 has suggested that mythical kinship was more commonly used in diplomacy between Greeks and non-Greeks (e.g. Kytinion and Lykian Xanthos) than between Greek and Greek. The evidence, however, is slight; the Same–Magnesia example explicitly uses mythical kinship between Greeks, *I.Magn.* 35, lines 13–14 (Curty 1995: no. 46c).

[25] Cf. Musti 1963: 236–7, Elwyn 1993, Curty 1995: 78–82, 251, 258–9.

Individually the cases may often be problematic and hard to date but taken together they offer a valuable insight into the role of Troy in Greek–Roman relations.

It is appropriate to begin with the Troad, where the Trojan past was very much part of the present. The people of Ilion claimed that their city was on the site of old Troy. At Skepsis they could tell of once being ruled by the descendants of Hektor and Aineias. At Ophrynion there was the tomb of Hektor; elsewhere in the Troad the locals could point to the tombs of Paris, Hekabe, Anchises, and Memnon.[26] There was considerable potential here for any state that sought to make Rome aware of the kinship that existed between them. It is perhaps no coincidence that it was an author from the Troad, Polemon of Ilion, who produced a work entitled *Foundations of Italian and Sicilian Cities*. This book, long since lost, is believed to have been composed in the early second century, just as Rome was beginning to exert its influence in Asia Minor.[27] Its title suggests that it would have been an invaluable source of information for any state pondering the prospect of kinship diplomacy with the West, not merely with Rome but with any potential intermediaries in the West.

From Lampsakos in the northern Troad comes a very important and much discussed inscription, a decree honouring Hegesias who went as part of the embassy to Rome.[28] The Romans had recently defeated Philip V of Macedon at Kynoskephalai and were in the process of negotiating a settlement with him. The embassy sought Roman protection and in particular inclusion in any treaty that was made with Philip. Although the decree makes no mention of Antiochos III, the Seleukid king's expansionist activities in Asia Minor almost certainly prompted the embassy; by early 196 he had launched an attack on the city.[29] In support of their appeal the ambassadors cited their kinship with the Romans. The Lampsakene document provides valuable evidence for several reasons. First, it can be securely dated to the mid-190s. There are

[26] On all this, Ch. 4. 2.
[27] On Polemon, K. Deichgräber *RE* 21, cols. 1290–1, with 1301 on this work, cf. Ferrary 1988: 224.
[28] *I.Lamp.* 4 (*SIG*³ 591), on which Bickermann 1932, Schmitt 1964: 289–95, Desideri 1970–1: 501–6, Ferrary 1988: 133–41, Curty 1995: 78–82, Canali de Rossi 1997: 194–8.
[29] Livy 33. 38. 1–7, 35. 42. 1–2, App. *Syr.* 2, Polyb. 21. 13. 1–5, Diod. Sic. 29. 7; Schmitt 1964: 289–95; Gruen 1984: 542–3 expresses doubts about the influence of Antiochos, cf. Ferrary 1988: 135 with n. 12.

several earlier examples of Trojan themes being used in diplomacy with Rome but all are controversial. The Lampsakene decree has the advantage of immediacy and is uncontaminated by later events. Secondly, it is not a solitary line in a history; instead it is a fairly detailed description of what happened, from the perspective of the appellant. As such it offers a model for the understanding and interpretation of less well-recorded incidents.

What it does not reveal, however, is the basis for the *syngeneia* that existed between the Romans and the Lampsakenes. As the city lies in the Troad it is plausible to assume that the ambassadors drew attention to their shared Trojan ancestry, but the detail must be a matter of conjecture. The Lampsakenes could have claimed kinship with Rome through membership of the Ilian Confederation, which was centred upon the temple of Athena Ilias at Ilion,[30] but there may have been no need for them to use Ilion as an intermediary at all.[31] Like so many cities in the Troad they may have had Trojan traditions of their own, unknown to us now, which they could use. Askanios and Skamandrios, for instance, were reputed to have founded, or more accurately re-founded, with the help of Akamas, at least two cities in the vicinity of Lampsakos—Perkote and Arisbe. Both cities had sent contingents to fight at Troy and, it was argued, both were Trojan cities. By the time of Strabo they had long since disappeared, which opens up the possibility that they had been, or could be said to have been, incorporated into Lampsakos.[32] That certainly was the fate of nearby Paisos, which unlike Lampsakos did feature in the *Iliad*.[33] Lampsakos may have been a relative late-comer to the Troad, but it could absorb the myths and traditions of the territory and make them its own.[34] We have only the merest glimpses at the local history, out of which the ambassadors fashioned their arguments. Perhaps they did use the Ilian confederation, but, if they did, that is likely

---

[30] Magie 1950: 869–71 n. 53, 943 n. 40, E. Weber 1972: 220, Will 1982: 185, Elwyn 1993: 273, C. P. Jones 1999: 96; Frisch in *I.Lamp.* suggests Tros as the common ancestor, and would thus restore lines 25–6. For the confederation, see Ch. 9.1.

[31] Cf. Holleaux 1921: 54 n. 2.

[32] Askanios: Lysimachos *FGrH* 382F9, Steph. Byz. s.v. Ἀρίσβη, see Ch. 4.2; contingents at Troy: Hom. *Il.* 2. 835–9; argued to be Trojan: Strabo 13. 1. 7; disappearance and proximity to Lampsakos: Strabo 13. 1. 19–20.

[33] Strabo 13. 1. 19, Hom. *Il.* 2. 828–9, 5. 612–14, on which Kirk 1990; the city survived at least as late as the Athenian empire, Meiggs 1972: 561.

[34] For this phenomenon elsewhere, Curty 1995: 252–3, L. Robert 1969: ii. 1321–2, cf. i. 359–61.

to have been only part of their argument. The Kytinian speech at Xanthos shows that ambassadors need not restrict themselves to just one proof of a relationship.

Kinship played a major part in the long and tortuous journey of the Lampsakene embassy. After making their case to L. Quinctius Flamininus, the commander of the Roman fleet in Greece, they travelled the entire length of the Mediterranean to the important Greek city of Massalia, modern Marseilles, a long-standing friend of Rome.[35] Like Lampsakos Massalia was a colony of Phokaia; the Massaliotes were, as the decree puts it, 'their brothers'.[36] So Lampsakos, a city from Asia Minor with no experience of Rome, turned to a western relative who was familiar with the Italian city and its ways and who could make the necessary introductions. The Lampsakenes may have dwelt upon their common mother-city when addressing the council of Massalia but its value was not limited to this exchange. Their kinship with the Massaliotes was perceived as an additional argument with which to win the Romans over; it reinforced the Trojan kinship and demonstrated how very close the Romans and the Lampsakenes were. The relationship between Lampsakos and Massalia is raised in meetings with both L. Quinctius Flamininus and with the Senate. Anyone who thinks that Greek cities used Trojan kinship claims simply in order to flatter the Romans has to explain why this embassy should imagine that the Romans would be at all impressed to know that the Massaliotes and Lampsakenes were brothers. The Hegesias decree also presents striking testimony to the way in which seemingly incompatible traditions could coexist; Lampsakos could have a Trojan past and yet at the same time be a Phokaian colony.[37] Without the ambassadors' speeches we cannot know how they coexisted, but there is no sign that it was considered to be problematic for any of the threesome.

The Lampsakene claim of kinship with Rome was an integral part of their diplomatic initiative. Indeed the summaries of the addresses to L. Quinctius Flamininus and to the Senate contain little more than repeated appeals to the obligations to look after

[35] Their friendship may not have been as long-standing as Just. *Epit.* 43. 5 suggests but it was long enough to impress the Lampsakenes, cf. Momigliano 1975: 57.

[36] *I.Lamp.* 25–6, 54–6 (ἀδελφοί); Lampsakos as Phokaian colony: Charon *FGrH* 262F7, Ephoros *FGrH* 70F46, Pomponius Mela 1. 97, Steph. Byz. s.v. '*Λάμψακος*', Magie 1950: 903 n. 118; Massalia as Phokaian colony: Thuc. 1. 13. 6, Isoc. *Arch.* 84, Paus. 10. 8. 6, cf. Momigliano 1975: 51–2.   [37] Cf. Curty 1995: 251–3.

and help one's kin. But, as was argued in the last section, it was not simply about persuading the Romans. It was also about establishing a relationship in which it was proper to make a request. As well as recording Flamininus' promise of help, the decree also records that 'he made clear that he accepted the relationship and kinship which exists between us and the Romans'.[38] Moreover, there is the long-term nature of the relationship; the people of Lampsakos wish to give substance to their mythical kinship by being included in the treaty that the Romans are negotiating. Whether or not they succeeded is arguable; the Lampsakenes thought they had, but many modern scholars disagree with them.[39]

So Lampsakos, a city in the Troad with a Trojan past to draw on, approached Rome with a request, citing kinship. Here is the perspective of the small Greek state, so often absent from Romanocentric sources. It permits us to suppose that, where Rome is said to have treated a city favourably because of Trojan kinship, the initiative may have come from the city itself, appealing to Rome just as Lampsakos had done.[40]

In the early 50s AD the emperor Claudius gave the people of Ilion exemption from tribute in perpetuity because they were the ancestors of the Roman race. In support of this he read out an old letter from the Senate and People of Rome to King Seleukos, promising friendship and alliance if he were to allow the Ilians, kin of the Romans (*sui consanguinei*) to be free from every burden.[41] Which Seleukos received the letter is not specified, but even so it is possible to draw some conclusions about the likely circumstances, if not about the recipient. The letter is surely a Roman response to initiatives from the east. The conditions imposed suggest that it was Seleukos who had requested the alliance. Similarly the Ilians, knowing of Seleukos' approach to Rome, may have sent their own embassy, citing their Trojan past in the manner of the Lampsakenes and asking the Romans to intervene on their behalf with Seleukos. They could have argued that they were

---

[38] τὴν οἰκειότητα καὶ συγγένειαν, lines 30–1.

[39] Lines 63–7, cf. 31–3, see Bickermann 1932: 286–8, Magie 1950: 947 n. 51, Gruen 1984: 542–3, though contrast Desideri 1970–1: 501–6, Ferrary 1988: 135–41.

[40] Cf. Ilion in Suet. *Claud.* 25. 3, Dardanos and Ilion in Livy 38. 39. 10, and similarly the Akarnanians in Just. *Epit.* 28. 1–2, Dion. Hal. *Ant. Rom.* 1. 51. 2.

[41] Suet. *Claud.* 25. 3, cf. Nero's speech on behalf of the Ilians, Suet. *Nero* 7. 2, Tac. *Ann.* 12. 58, which dates the speech to AD 53, though Suetonius puts it a couple of years earlier in the consulship of Claudius. The exemption is possibly reflected in the honours to Claudius and his family, *I.Ilion* 90–1, though these may be earlier.

seeking the tribute-free status that had been bestowed on them by Alexander.[42] Whatever affinity the Romans felt with Ilion, they are only likely to have learnt about its fiscal situation from the Ilians themselves. Nor should we imagine that these two embassies were the only visitors to Rome; this may have been an occasion when many Greek states were approaching the Romans with requests.

This letter has proved to be highly controversial. Whether scholars accept it or reject it, none seem especially comfortable with it.[43] There are two main reasons for this. First, it is hard to find a Seleukos who had sufficient control over Ilion to fulfil the Roman request. Seleukos I (312–281) seems too early and anyway is assassinated within a year of acquiring Ilion.[44] Seleukos II (246–226/5) lost control of Ilion to his brother Antiochos Hierax and never recovered it. Seleukos III (226/5–223) never possessed it. It was regained by Antiochos III but lost again before Seleukos IV came to the throne, the defeat at Magnesia in 189 effectively ending Seleukid power and aspirations in the Troad. When a date for the letter is selected, it is generally around 240, after the Third Syrian War (246–241) between Seleukos II and Ptolemy III Euergetes, and before Seleukos was defeated by his brother Antiochos, probably in 240. The dates are not certain but on any reckoning it does not leave Seleukos II much time. Even before his defeat de facto control of Ilion and Asia Minor as a whole was in the hands of his brother Antiochos.[45] The second reason for unhappiness is the feeling that the letter just does not fit satisfactorily within the context of the mid-third century; this is especially the case with scholars such as Maurice Holleaux who would minimize Rome's involvement in the East prior to the Second Macedonian War. On the other hand, Rome had already established friendly relations (*amicitia*) with the Ptolemies by the 270s.[46]

---

[42] Strabo 13. 1. 26.

[43] Against authenticity: Niese 1899: 153, Holleaux 1921: 44–60, Magie 1950: 943–4 n. 40 (with 829–32 n. 14 on taxation), E. Weber 1972: 217–18, Will 1979: 296, Walbank 1979: 182; for authenticity: Beloch 1925: 663, De Sanctis 1967: 269, Derow 1970: 94–102, Rizzo 1974: 83–8, Gruen 1992: 46 (cautiously), Coppola 1994: 180–2; Elwyn 1993: 280–2 is non-committal.   [44] Mehl 1986: 301–7, esp. 306.

[45] On the problem of date of letter, Holleaux 1921: 46–8 with nn. 2 and 3, Derow 1970: 94–8, Rizzo 1974: 85–7. On relations between Seleukos II and Antiochos Hierax, Will 1979: 294–6, Heinen 1984: 420–1, 428–9. There is considerable uncertainty about dates of reigns and wars in this period; this paragraph has followed *CAH*[2].

[46] App. *Sic.* 1, Eutrop. 2. 15, Dio frag. 41, Livy *Per.* 14; Holleaux 1921: 60–83; Heinen 1972: 633–7, Gruen 1984: 62–3, 673–6.

Since Claudius did have a letter in his hand, some have felt compelled to impugn the letter; it was, they say, a forgery. The responsibility for the forgery has been variously attributed: to the Romans themselves, wishing to give extra weight to their Trojan ancestry, to the Ilians, wanting to bolster their case in front of Claudius, or to Nero, seeking to enliven his speech in support of the people of Ilion.[47] Forgeries did exist, even on the subject of kinship,[48] but it seems rash to dismiss a now lost document as a forgery simply because we cannot make sense of it.

There is, however, another possibility: that the recipient of the letter was not Seleukos but Antiochos III. It is often overlooked that the letter was written in Greek, while our account is in Latin, a circumstance that offers much scope for confusion. Various possibilities can be imagined. Perhaps the letter was addressed to King Antiochos, son of Seleukos, and at some stage, either in translation or later transmission Antiochos disappeared.[49] Perhaps a Seleukos was much the same as an Antiochos. It would not after all have mattered in the first-century AD Roman Senate which long-dead king of a defunct dynasty received the letter. Certainly such a letter would fit well into the context of the latter half of the 190s. At that time Antiochos III was in a position to levy tribute on Ilion.[50] He did make several approaches to the Romans about friendship and alliance, beginning as early as 195.[51] The Romans responded by citing the freedom of the Greeks of Asia and Europe which they had proclaimed at the Isthmian Games in 196; all Greeks were to be free, without garrisons, subject to no tribute and living under their own laws.[52] The Romans had by this time established relations with the Troad; Ilion had been included

---

[47] Romans: Holleaux 1921: 58; Ilians: Magie 1950: 944 n. 40: Nero: Mottershead 1986: 103.

[48] *I.Magn.* 20, and perhaps 1 *Maccabees* 12. 5–23, correspondence between the Jews and Sparta, cf. Gruen 1996.

[49] Cf. βασιλεὺς Ἀντίοχος βασιλέως Σελεύκου in *I.Ilion* 32. 2–3 (*OGIS* 219), probably Antiochos I, see C. P. Jones 1993; cf. also *OGIS* 239, 240, for examples of the form, Antiochos, son of Seleukos; these examples are not letters, but kings so rarely inscribed their correspondence.

[50] Schmitt 1964: 293 would go as early as autumn 197 BC for Antiochos' occupation of Ilion; Livy 35. 43. 3 for Antiochos' sacrifices there in 192.

[51] Livy 34. 25. 2 (Corinth); Livy 34. 57–9 with App. *Syr.* 6, Diod. Sic. 28. 15. 2 (Rome, early 193); Livy 35. 15–17, App. *Syr.* 12 (follow-up meetings in Apameia and Ephesos). On negotiations between Antiochos and Rome, Badian 1964: 112–39, Gruen 1984: 620–36.

[52] Response to Antiochos: Polyb. 18. 47. 1, 50. 7, Livy, 33. 34. 3, 34. 57–9, 35. 16; Isthmian proclamation: Polyb. 18. 46.

among the *adscripti* to the Peace of Phoinike in 205, most probably because of its kinship with Rome, though whether the initiative came from Rome, Attalos, or Ilion is uncertain.[53] Lampsakos had used kinship in its appeal to Rome shortly before. Everything is there in the 190s except the enigmatic Seleukos.

It may be possible to be even more specific and locate the letter within the context of the negotiations of 193. Menippos and Hegesianax, ambassadors from Antiochos, were in Rome to arrange an alliance. Rome was also full of representatives of Greek states, including many from Asia, all with a case to make; Ilion may well have been among them to plead for its freedom.[54] According to Livy Menippos complained about the way in which the Romans 'thought it right to lay down terms for Antiochos, dictating which cities of Asia were to be free and exempt from tribute, which cities were to be tributary to the king, and which cities they forbade the king and his forces to enter'.[55] Had the Romans specified Ilion? Because Antiochos' ambassadors did not have the power to make territorial concessions, Roman ambassadors were sent out to Antiochos in the East. Here is a context for the letter: either Menippos and Hegesianax were given a letter spelling out Roman conditions which they were to hand to Antiochos, or the Roman ambassadors carried such a letter with them.[56] In Suetonius' letter there is only one demand, but that is the only demand which is relevant to Claudius' decision on Ilion. No doubt there were others.

Not long afterwards Antiochos was defeated and the Romans could make their own decisions about Ilion. In the settlement of Asia in 188 the Ilians got their immunity from tribute and in addition received two towns, Rhoiteion and Gergis. Ilion was favoured in this way, according to Livy, not so much on account of any recent services as in memory of Rome's origins. Nor was it only Ilion that benefited from its Trojan past; Livy adds that nearby Dardanos was granted its freedom for the same reason.[57]

---

[53] Livy 29. 12. 14; doubts about Ilion's place here are surely mistaken, see Ch. 8.3 with n. 94.

[54] Livy 34. 57. 1–3, 59. 4–5, on attendance of Greeks from Asia.

[55] Livy 34. 57. 10–11, cf. also 35. 17. 3–7 for Seleukid complaints about Roman conditions.

[56] On letters in diplomacy, Welles 1934: pp. xxxvii–xli, Sherk 1969: 186–9; note also the importance of letters for the ambassadors in *I.Lamp.* 4, lines 28–9, 39, 48–9, 62–3, 75–7.

[57] Livy 38. 39. 10, on the settlement in general, Walbank 1979: 164–75; in his account of the settlement Livy follows Polyb. 21.45 closely but Polybios has no mention of either Ilion

If Livy had only mentioned Ilion, it might be imagined that the initiative was Rome's, seeking to highlight its Trojan ancestry in the Greek world, or at least in the Troad. The Romans, however, were hardly likely to have been aware of the Trojan significance of a city as obscure as Dardanos unless the Dardanians had explicitly pointed it out to them. This city was so unimportant, wrote Strabo, that the kings were constantly shifting the population to Abydos and back again.[58] Such contempt was doubtless a good reason to demand freedom. It is possible to speculate on the arguments put forward by the Dardanian representatives, for instance that their city was named after Dardanos, ancestor of the Trojan people, or that Aineias had been commander of the Dardanians in the Trojan War.[59] The Roman victory had caused confusion in Asia and resulted in numerous Greek cities sending representatives to the Romans who were arranging the post-war settlement.[60] In such a competitive environment cities like Ilion and Dardanos that could make use of ties of kinship would be bound to do so. Rome in turn by making its acceptance of the claims clear could draw the cities of the Troad closer.

In a world in which interstate kinship mattered, Ilion's links with Rome gave it influence, if not in Rome, at least in the eyes of other states. The Lykians, fearing that the Romans would not look kindly upon their support for Antiochos, turned to Ilion for help. The Ilians pleaded the Lykian case before the Roman commissioners responsible for the reorganization of Asia. They asked that the Lykians be pardoned 'on account of the *oikeiotes* with themselves' (διὰ τὴν πρὸς αὐτοὺς οἰκειότητα). There is an ambiguity here: is this referring to the relationship between the Ilians and the Romans or to one between the Ilians and the Lykians? Both are possible.[61] Only a few years earlier in 196 a decree of the Lykian

or Dardanos. Either Livy introduced material from another source or the Byzantine excerptor of Polybios omitted this section, cf. Walbank 1979: 164; on the benefits to Ilion, Magie 1950: 950–1 n. 50, Schmitt 1964: 292, J. M. Cook 1973: 350–1, Gruen 1992: 48–9.

[58] Strabo 13. 1. 28.

[59] Dardanos: Hom. *Il.* 20. 215–41, Gantz 1993: 557–61; Aineias: Hom. *Il.* 2. 819–20; that the city of Dardanos may have nothing to do with the Dardanians of the *Iliad* is not relevant.

[60] Polyb. 21. 41. 1, 41. 6, 46. 1.

[61] Polyb. 22. 5; translated 'for the sake of the kinship between Ilium and Rome' by W. R. Paton in the Loeb, a translation which would seem to have the support of Walbank 1979; Perret 1942: 504 and Curty 1995: 192–3 prefer Lykian kinship; one might compare the Rhodian appeal on behalf of its 'sister' city, Soloi, Polyb. 21. 24. 10–5.

city of Xanthos honoured an Ilian rhetorician who among other virtues was 'worthy of the kinship (*syngeneia*) which exists between us and the people of Ilion'.[62] Such kinship might explain why the Lykians thought they could ask Ilion for help. But it is only Ilion's kinship with Rome that explains why anyone should think that Ilion should be a suitable advocate. The Romans, however, were not overly impressed. The Ilian intervention failed to achieve the desired result and the Lykians became the discontented subjects of the Rhodians.[63]

The Lykians were not originally a Greek people but in common with other peoples of Asia Minor such as the Karians they had come to adopt many aspects of Greek culture and can conveniently be termed 'Hellenized'. An important manifestation of this is the gradual replacement of the Lykian language by Greek in public documents, a process that was probably complete by the end of the fourth century BC.[64] To an outsider they might be indistinguishable from Greeks; in the first century BC Cicero could describe them simply as Greeks.[65] Their use of kinship in their relations with other states is a further sign of their participation in the Greek cultural world.[66]

An inscription survives from Rome showing a Lykian dedication to the Roman People made on some occasion between the 'liberation' of Lykia from Rhodes and the time of Sulla in gratitude for an unspecified benefaction.[67] It is not clear whether the dedication was made by a single Lykian city or the Lykian League as a whole. Strikingly the Roman People are not only friends and allies but also kin (*cognati*). Lykia may have been far from the

---

[62] Robert and Robert 1983: no. 15B, *SEG* 33. 1184, Chaniotis 1988: 305–6, Curty 1995: no. 76.

[63] On Ilion and Lykia, Schmitt 1957: 91–2 (with a full discussion of Lykian–Rhodian relations, 81–128), Berthold 1984: 168–71; Gruen 1990: 15 says a successful intervention which gained concessions, though he might not convince a Lykian.

[64] Bryce 1986: 50 on datable inscriptions, 42–54 on language use in general, 214–15 on survival of Lykian culture and language; on the diffusion of Greek culture see the succinct remarks of S. Hornblower, *OCD*³ s.v. 'Hellenism, Hellenization'. For Hellenization in neighbouring Karia, S. Hornblower 1982: 332–51, elsewhere in Asia Minor, S. Mitchell 1993: i. 80–6.

[65] Cic. II*Verr.* 4. 21, *Lycii, Graeci homines*.

[66] Cf. Curty 1995: nos. 75–80.

[67] *ILS* 32, restored text in Degrassi 1951–2: no. 2. Magie 1950: 109–10 dated this text and related inscriptions to the mid-2nd cent., Degrassi argues that all the inscriptions formed part of a monument erected in the late 80s BC. Both arguments have problems which Mellor 1978 seeks to resolve by accepting Degrassi's date for the monument but arguing that some of the inscriptions were earlier ones reinscribed.

Troad but it was still an area with strong Trojan associations and traditions. The Lykian heroes, Sarpedon and Glaukos, had fought at Troy alongside Hektor and the Trojans, an alliance that had the authority of Homer to support it.[68] Both were the objects of cult in Lykia.[69] One story, apparently going back to the sixth-century BC poet Stesichoros, finds Hekabe, wife of Priam, carried away to Lykia by Apollo after the fall of Troy.[70] None of these traditions as they survive provide the degree of kinship that would seem necessary to support a claim of *cognatio*, where some form of blood relationship is implied. But the people of Xanthos in 196 had spoken of their *syngeneia* with Ilion, so local mythology may have intersected in ways now lost to us. One such overlap is found in the person of Pandaros, archer on the Trojan side in the *Iliad*, and likely recipient of cult honours at the Lykian city of Pinara.[71] His origins are ambiguous; often considered a Lykian, he is nevertheless described as coming from Zeleia in the Troad. For Strabo Pandaros' troops are both Trojan and Lykian: 'The Lykians under Pandaros, whom Homer also calls Trojans.'[72] Here there is an argument for Lykian kinship with the Trojans and thus the Romans, using Homer as evidence. Whatever ingenious mythological arguments were developed, the claim of kinship did not come out of nothing; there was a considerable Trojan past on which to build. The Lykians, like the cities of the Troad, already had an affinity with the Trojans.

Outside Asia Minor explicit claims of kinship with the Romans are rarely recorded. One of the better documented is the case of Segesta in north-west Sicily. This city was something of a cultural amalgam; a Hellenized Elymian city, it was also influenced by years of Punic occupation.[73] The kinship between Segesta and

---

[68] Hom. *Il*. 2. 876–7. The Lykians are 'the most prominent of Troy's allies', Bryce 1986: 12.

[69] Sarpedon: Hom. *Il*. 16. 673, *TAM* 2. 1. 265, Janko 1992: 371–3, Keen 1998: 186–92, 208–10; Glaukos: *TAM* 2. 1. 265, Steph. Byz. s.v. *'Γλαύκου Δῆμου'*, cf. Quint. Smyrn. 10. 147–66, *I.Magn*. 17. 38.

[70] Paus. 10. 27. 2, Stesichoros F198 Davies *PMGF* (F21 Page *PMG*); for Apollo in Lykia, Bryce 1986: 182–5.

[71] Hom. *Il*. 2. 824–7, 4. 85–126, 5. 95–296, 795; cult: Strabo 14. 3. 5, Keen 1998: 212.

[72] Strabo 13. 1. 7, on Hom. *Il*. 2. 824–7, cf. Hom. *Il*. 5. 105, 173 (Lykian origins); Kirk 1985: 254, 339–40, Bryce 1986: 14, 35–7 on Pandaros and his mixed origins. Note also Steph. Byz. s.v. *'Ζέλεια'* on Pandaros' grave in the Troad.

[73] For Segesta's cultural background and discussion of its temple and theatre, Coarelli and Torelli 1984: 10–6, 49–54, see also Galinsky 1969: 99–101. Epigraphy can offer some indication of cultural identity, although only a few inscriptions are known from Segesta,

Rome first enters the literary record in 70 BC when Cicero prosecutes Verres for misconduct during his governorship of Sicily: 'Segesta is a very ancient town in Sicily, gentlemen, which they say was founded by Aeneas when he fled from Troy and arrived in this area. Therefore the Segestans consider themselves to be bound to the Roman People not only by permanent alliance and friendship but also by kinship (*cognatio*)'.[74] In this way Cicero introduces the story of the statue of Artemis at Segesta. This beautifully crafted, bronze statue had been seized by the Carthaginians in an earlier war and taken off to Carthage. It was only recovered when P. Scipio Aemilianus captured Carthage in the Third Punic War. He returned it to Segesta where it was placed on a pedestal inscribed with Scipio's name and *beneficium*. There it stayed until spotted by Verres.

In 70 Cicero wanted a successful prosecution; the Segestans wanted their statue back. Kinship played its part in the arguments of both, but in different ways. Cicero structured the story to begin with the kinship between the Segestans and the Romans. It was further evidence of Verres' criminal nature that he was prepared to confiscate a statue and abuse the ties of kinship. For Cicero this was of only limited importance; it was unlikely to impress many Roman nobles. It did, however, neatly and innocently introduce the theme of kinship which he would shortly employ in a forceful attack on a member of the defence team, P. Scipio Nasica. Cicero consistently refers to him as simple 'P. Scipio' to draw attention to his kinship with P. Scipio Aemilianus, who had reclaimed the statue for the Segestans. How, argues Cicero, could P. Scipio so forget his duties to his family that he defends the very man who had despoiled an ancestral monument? The removal of the statue, then, was not so much an offence against the Segestans as an offence against Scipio. So by introducing the theme of kinship Cicero manages to turn the Segestan incident from yet another minor provincial matter into a Roman matter, an aristocrat's

---

some Greek (Dubois 1989: 271–4 with *IG* 14. 287–92), and some non-Greek (Agostiniani 1977). But the neighbouring Elymian city of Entella has produced 9 bronze tablets in Greek from *c.*300 BC, Nenci 1982, with the ninth in *ASNP*[3] 17: 119, cf. also Dubois 1989: 253–71, Nenci 1993: 35–50, *SEG* 30. 1117–23, 32.914 for texts.

[74] Cic. II*Verr.* 4. 72, cf. 5. 83, 125; discussion of Segesta runs from 4. 72 to 4. 83. The *Actio secunda* from which this comes was never delivered because the case had been effectively won by then, but it was published.

betrayal of his family.[75] This was something that would interest a Roman senatorial jury.

Underlying this part of Cicero's speech is the Segestan appeal for the return of their statue of Artemis. Representatives of the city had discussed their complaints with Cicero and doubtless with other Roman politicians as well. Segestans were present in Rome for the trial; they acted as witnesses for the prosecution, and Cicero envisaged them as sitting in court to hear his denunciation of P. Scipio.[76] Segesta's kinship with Rome and foundation by Aineias would have played an integral part in their appeal, grounding their request in the duties and ties of kinship. The occurrence of this idea as the starting point of Cicero's treatment of the events in Segesta is a reflection of his discussions with the Segestan representatives. It is clear that this shared heritage of Segesta and Rome was not familiar to Cicero's audience; indeed he himself had probably heard of it only recently.[77] Cicero exploited it for his own purposes, but the Segestans were here following the precepts and customs of Hellenistic diplomacy. The ill-treatment that they had received from Verres may have made them all the more eager to establish, or re-establish, the kinship relation which would have reassured them of their place in the Roman world, confirming that recent events had been an aberration.

In claiming kinship with Rome the Segestans were drawing on traditions that went back at least as far as the fifth century BC, when Thucydides had commented on the Trojan roots of the Elymians: 'At the time of the capture of Ilion some of the Trojans, escaping from the Achaians, sailed to Sicily, and living alongside the Sicanians they were together called the Elymians and their cities were called Eryx and Aigesta [Segesta].'[78] The Trojan origin of the Segestans was also adduced as one explanation for the

---

[75] Cic. II *Verr.* 4. 79–81; for importance of ancestors, cf. Polyb. 6. 53, though strictly P. Scipio Nasica was in a different branch of the Cornelii Scipiones rather than a direct descendant of Scipio Aemilianus. It is noticeable that in the course of his attack Cicero shifts from the broader *genus* to language that ties Nasica more closely with Aemilianus, thus *familia* and *domesticae laudis patrocinium*.

[76] Demand for statue: Cic. II *Verr.* 4. 79; discussions: 4. 138; witnesses: 2. 156; in court: 4. 80, cf. also other Segestan complaints: 3. 92–3, 5. 111, 4. 59.

[77] Possibly Cicero knew of it as early as his visit to Segesta as quaestor in 75, II *Verr.* 4.74.

[78] Thuc. 6. 2. 3, though, contrary to Cornell 1977: 77 and Momigliano 1984: 444, there is no mention of Aineias here or anywhere else in Thucydides. For the context of the development, see Ch. 5; on Trojans in Sicily: Bérard 1957: 352–6.

failure of the Athenian expedition to Sicily in 415–13. Herakles, still bitter at the injustice he had suffered at the hands of the Trojan king Laomedon, was angry that the Athenians should assist the descendants of a city he had destroyed and therefore gave his support to the Syracusans. This story was present in the Sicilian historian Timaios in the early third century and may date back to the fifth century.[79]

A belief in the Trojan past of Segesta, then, was long-standing, but when and how it was first adopted in an approach to the Romans is not so clear. It is likely to be fairly early when, lacking any alternative basis for their relationship, they turned to myth. Ironically it is the latest literary source that provides the earliest occurrence. In the opening years of the First Punic War, a war that was largely fought in and around Sicily, the Segestans massacred their Carthaginian garrison and went over to the Romans. According to Zonaras, who relates the incident, this decision was influenced by their kinship (*oikeiosis*) with the Romans; they said, he writes, that they were descended from Aineias.[80] Zonaras limits himself to the Segestan motivation, but if the Segestans were at all conscious of such common ancestry at the time, they might be expected to have raised it when they met with the Romans to discuss their new allegiance.[81]

Zonaras, however, was a twelfth-century Byzantine compiler, who would have excerpted this material from the third-century AD Greek historian Cassius Dio. He is reckoned to be a faithful excerptor,[82] but nevertheless both writers are far distant from the events in question and neither may have had a very firm grasp of the role of kinship in Hellenistic diplomacy. So doubts might be raised about the value of this evidence.[83] The story is given plausibility by the special interest the Romans paid to north-western Sicily in the third century, most particularly the introduction of the cult of Venus Erycina to Rome in 217.[84] There is also the very

---

[79] Plut. *Nic.* 1, criticizing Timaios, *FGrH* 566F102b; the 3rd-cent. Lykophron is also familiar with the Trojan past of the Elymians, Lycoph. 951–77.

[80] Zonar. 8. 9; Diod. Sic. 23. 5 confirms that the Segestans did go over to the Romans; for possibility of earlier relations between NW Sicily and Rome, Momigliano 1945a: 101.

[81] Awareness of Rome would have been increased by the recent wars with Pyrrhos; for contact, note also the garrison at nearby Entella which in *c.*300 BC appears to have been commanded by a Tiberius Claudius of Antium, possibly a mercenary put there by Agathokles, G. Nenci, *Kokalos* 28–9: (1982–3) 290, *SEG* 30.1120.

[82] Millar 1964: 2–3.   [83] As they were by Perret 1942: 452–3.   [84] Ch. 8. 1 below.

clear evidence of the *Verrines* that the Segestans did later believe themselves to be related to the Romans.[85] Some have sought to support Zonaras with a Segestan coin that depicts Aineias fleeing with Anchises. They date the coin to the third century BC, shortly after the end of the First Punic War in 241 BC. The date, however, is not so certain and may even be as late as the first century BC. Nevertheless, the coin does demonstrate the importance of Aineias for the Segestans, even if it reveals nothing directly about the third century BC.[86]

There are further complications. Aineias is not the only Trojan said to have founded Segesta; there is also Aigestes.[87] This eponymous founder seems to have represented an older tradition, not merely because of his early cryptic appearance as founder in Lykophron's *Alexandra*, but also because, in those versions that include both Aigestes and Aineias, Aigestes is present in Sicily before Aineias, as if Aineias has been superimposed upon an existing story. For Dionysios of Halikarnassos, Aineias' dilatoriness needs explaining, or excusing; Aigestes reached Sicily first from a combination of luck, favourable winds, and less baggage. In the accounts of both Dionysios and Vergil Aineias lands in Sicily, meets fellow Trojan Aigestes (or Acestes in Vergil), helps Aigestes out by founding one or two cities, leaves some of his forces there, and then sails off.[88] Aineias provides the brains and Aigestes the name. So in the foundation story of Segesta Aigestes made way for Aineias but he did not disappear altogether.

It would be in keeping with the practices of contemporary kinship diplomacy that the Segestans should elaborate their Trojan traditions in order to bring themselves into a closer relationship

---

[85] Cic. II*Verr.* 4. 72, cf. also Tac. *Ann.* 4. 43. 4, where the Segestans seem to have appealed to kinship between themselves and the Romans, or perhaps with Tiberius in particular, to obtain assistance for repairs to the temple of Aphrodite at Eryx, cf. Elwyn 1993: 279 with n. 57.

[86] *BMC Sicily*, p. 137, nos. 59–61; it has been dated to the 1st cent. BC by Fuchs 1973: 625–6, cf. also the cautionary remarks of Perret 1971: 40 n. 1. Head 1911: 166–7 simply says 'After B.C. 241', but this seems to have been interpreted to mean in or soon after 241, thus Alföldi 1957: 29, Galinsky 1969: 68.

[87] Aineias: Cic. II*Verr.* 4. 72, Dion. Hal. *Ant. Rom.* 1. 52. 3–4, Verg. *Aen.* 5. 711–8, 749–58, Festus 458L; Aigestes: Lycoph. 961–4 with schol. on 952 and 964, Strabo 6. 1. 3, 6. 2. 5; schol. on *Aen.* 1. 550; schol. on *Aen.* 5. 73 has Elymos as a Trojan founder; Diod. Sic. 4. 83. 4 presents Aineias as landing in NW Sicily but not founding Segesta.

[88] Dion. Hal. *Ant. Rom.* 1. 52 (with 52. 1 on Aigestes' speed), Verg. *Aen.* 5. 35–41, 700–827, esp. 711–18, 49–58; Festus' brief notice (458) also combines the two with Aineias as founder. For priority of Aigestes, Kienast 1965: 480–1.

with the Romans. Again, it is important to note that they did not invent their Trojanness for the occasion; rather they operated within the framework of existing local traditions. A reading of Zonaras would suggest that Aineias was already present at the first Segestan approach to the Romans in the late 260s, although the sceptical might feel that by the time of Zonaras or even of Dio the distinction between Trojans and descendants of Aineias had become a little hazy, especially in the context of kinship with Rome. Perhaps their initial contact emphasized merely that the two peoples shared common origins in Troy. On the other hand, they may have gone further and pointed to a landing made by Aineias on the coast of Sicily, such landings are recorded by Strabo and Diodoros. Suggestions that Aineias left part of his expedition behind in Sicily would have reinforced the kinship claim. Neither of the last two possibilities requires Aineias to have founded a city and they could have been part of the local lore for years before the arrival of the Romans in Sicily.[89] A further argument may have been provided by the story that Elymos, eponym of the Elymians, was the bastard son of Anchises, therefore half-brother of Aineias.[90] These stories may reflect different stages of a developing tradition, but there was no need to base a kinship claim on only one argument.[91] A Segestan embassy to the Romans could have presented all these and more. Aineias the founder, however, may have been a later development as the Trojan leader came to be increasingly incorporated into local tradition.

Evidence for the grounds of any kinship claim is fairly scanty; the Kytinians in Xanthos are very much the exception.[92] We can imagine a set of core traditions exploited in different ways on different occasions. Sometimes, as seems to have happened at Segesta, a state would build on these traditions and myths to suit the audience, or at least their perception of the audience. Usually such elaboration would have no significant impact on that core set

[89] Landing: Strabo 13. 1. 53, Diod. Sic. 4. 83. 4; leaves part of expedition: Dion. Hal. *Ant. Rom.* 1. 52. 4, Verg. *Aen.* 5. 712–17; cf. also story that Anchises was buried in the area, Verg. *Aen.* 5. 760–1, if it is not Vergil's own contribution.

[90] Schol. on *Aen.* 5. 73, where it is also said that Elymos founded Egesta, Asca and Entella; Lycoph. 965 writes that Aigestes brought 'the bastard son of Anchises to the furthest point of the three-necked island', interpreted by the scholiast as a reference to Elymos, although Lykophron may intend ambiguity here; the bastard son could be Elymos or Aineias, depending on the status of Anchises' relationship with Aphrodite.

[91] Cf. Kytinian appeal to Xanthos, Sect. 1 above.

[92] Much of Curty 1995 is devoted to hypothesis.

of traditions, but an appeal to Rome was very different. The power of Rome kept the relationship at the forefront; so once Aineias was introduced, he would have to stay. He may have begun on the periphery of Segestan local tradition but by the time he appeared with Anchises on Segestan coinage he had moved into the centre. Whether Aineias is on the coins as Segestan founder or merely as an important Trojan, his presence there symbolized the kinship that bound Rome and Segesta. These coins are in fact the only true *Segestan* evidence for any Segestan belief in a Trojan past; otherwise we are relying on the evidence of outsiders. The importance of Aineias in Segesta is attested also by a temple of Aineias, erected, so it was said, by those he left behind.[93]

The main examples of cities that claimed kinship with the Romans are from the Troad or are the 'Hellenized' communities of Lykia and north-western Sicily.[94] Evidence for such overtures among other cities is much scarcer and less explicit.[95] Possibilities, however, do suggest themselves. Both the Zakynthians and the Teneans may have adapted and developed existing Trojan traditions to suit the new political environment of the second century BC. The Zakynthians who had earlier promoted kinship with Kassandra in their relations with the Molossians appear later as kin of Aineias, perhaps a response to the political crisis of the 190s when they were found aligned with Antiochos.[96] The people of Tenea in the Peloponnese had long claimed kinship with Tenedos, an island off the coast of the Troad. Nevertheless, it may only have been a desire to distance themselves from Corinth during the Achaian War of the 140s that turned them into Trojans.[97] Other cities, such as Aineia or various of the Arkadian cities, had stories of Trojan founders that would lend themselves readily to any

[93] If Dion. Hal. *Ant. Rom.* 1. 53. 1 is correct. Unfortunately his grasp on the topography of NW Sicily was less than adequate as his confusion over Erice/Elymos/Elyma indicates, 1. 52. 4–53. 1.

[94] Perhaps the Sicel city of Kentoripa can be added to the list of Hellenized states; it is referred to by Cic. II*Verr.* 5. 83–4 as a *cognatus* of the Romans and an inscription which may date to the time of the Second Triumvirate mentions the συγγένεια between it and the Latin city of Lanuvium, Manganaro 1976: 88, cf. Elwyn 1993: 276–8. There is, however, no evidence for Trojan ancestry among the cities of E. Sicily, so perhaps the source of this kinship lies elsewhere; on Kentoripa in the late Republic, Wilson 1990: 151.

[95] For discussion of this, see Sect. 4 below.

[96] Kinship: Ch. 4. 3 above with Dion. Hal. *Ant. Rom.* 1. 50 on Aineias; 190s: Livy 36. 31–2, 36. 42. 4–5, Plut. *Flam.* 17, Plut. *Mor.* 197b.

[97] Paus. 2. 5. 4, Strabo 8. 6. 22, see Ch. 4. 3.

diplomatic approaches to the Romans.[98] It would be surprising if they made no use of them, but there is no evidence that they did do so.

3. DISTANT RELATIVES AND FAMILY FRIENDS

All the states discussed in the last section could point to fairly strong Trojan ties; in some way or other they were descended from Trojans, a few even lived in the Troad. Such a community of blood was an ideal basis for *syngeneia*, but not all states could make such claims if indeed they wanted to. It was, nevertheless, still possible for them to look to the mythical past to establish a relationship in the present. It is at this point that *oikeiotes* diverges from *syngeneia*. The quasi-kinship of guest-friendship might count as *oikeiotes*, incorporating each party within the *oikos* (household) of the other, but could not easily be described as *syngeneia*.[99] Relationships by marriage were one remove away from blood-kinship, although they were perhaps open to interpretation, either as *syngeneia* or as *oikeiotes*, especially if there were children involved. Excessive concern with terminological distinctions, however, can be counterproductive and distracting. This section looks at two further examples, Delos and Akarnania. Here the Trojan myth creates a bond between Greeks and Romans but does not involve any claim that the Delians or the Akarnanians are themselves of Trojan extraction. The precise terminology might be arguable but the bond is there.

Sometime in the first thirty years of the second century BC the Delians sent an embassy to Rome. A rather damaged inscription still honours the embassy if not the ambassadors. The exact purpose is unclear, but it seems to have been concerned with the celebrated temple of Apollo on the island, perhaps with obtaining Roman recognition of the sanctuary's inviolability (*asylia*).[100] Enough of the decree survives to know that the ambassadors

---

[98] See Ch. 4. 1 (Aineia), 4. 3 (Arkadia).

[99] Herman 1987: 16–29, well summed up in his entry in *OCD*[3] s.v. 'Friendship, ritualized'.

[100] *IG* 11. 4. 756, Durrbach 1921: no. 65, A. Erskine 1997*b*, which the next few pages shamelessly plagiarize; on Delian diplomatic initiatives at this time, Baslez and Vial 1987: 281–312, esp. 305–12, with p. 299 on date; it is suggestive but no doubt coincidental that so many of the places outside the Troad which are discussed in this ch. also had strong associations with Apollo who had supported the Trojan cause in the *Iliad*, thus Delos, Lykia, Tenea, Zakynthos and Leukas.

sought to renew *oikeiotes* and friendship with the Romans. The Delians made no claims to Trojan descent but there is substantial evidence linking Delos with Trojans, in particular with Aineias.

Aineias' landing on Delos is well attested in ancient authors.[101] Dionysios of Halikarnassos tells of Aineias' visit to Delos in the reign of Anios. Traces of his sojourn there remained for centuries: 'there were many signs on Delos of the presence of Aineias and the Trojans while the island flourished and was occupied'.[102] What these signs were is left obscure; perhaps Aineias or one of his Trojan companions was the object of cult, or maybe the temple of Apollo displayed some relics allegedly left by the Trojans.[103] There is no explicit kinship here but these signs alone may have been enough to justify a claim of *oikeiotes*.

Later in the same book of the *Roman Antiquities* Dionysios provides far stronger grounds for such a claim. The Romans, he says, relate how Lavinium was named after Lavinia, the daughter of Latinus, but he adds that there is another version of the founding of Lavinium told by some Greek mythographers. They say that the city was named after the daughter of the Delian king Anios, because she had been the first to die of illness when the city was being built. This woman, who is described as 'a prophetess and a wise woman', joined the expedition after 'she was given by her father to Aineias who asked for her'.[104] The phrase strongly suggests marriage, and the anonymous author of the *Origo gentis Romanae* has also heard a story in which Aineias marries Lavinia, a daughter of Anios, now priest of Delian Apollo.[105] Whether Lavinia was a wife of Aineias or merely a daughter of Anios who was lucky enough to become eponym of Lavinium, in both cases she would give the Delians a basis for some form of kinship claim. Indeed a daughter of Anios, priest of Apollo, was an ideal choice if the purpose of the embassy to the Romans was to further the interests of the temple of Apollo. It would be a good beginning to remind the Romans of their long-standing links with the temple.

Servius' commentary on the *Aeneid* preserves a curious variation on these stories; here an unnamed daughter of Anios is secretly

---

[101] Perret 1942: 31–4, Vanotti 1995: 153–4.

[102] Dion. Hal. *Ant. Rom.* 1. 50. 1.

[103] Cf. the cult of Aineias at Aineia, Livy 40. 4, Ch. 4.1 above, or the shield of Aineias supposedly in the temple on Samothrake, Serv. on *Aen.* 3. 287, Ch. 4 n. 80 above.

[104] Dion. Hal. *Ant. Rom.* 1. 59. 3, δοθεῖσαν ὑπὸ τοῦ πατρὸς Αἰνείᾳ δεηθέντι.

[105] *OGR* 9. 5; for sources on Lavinia, *LIMC* Lavinia.

seduced (*occulte stupratam*) by Aineias and gives birth to a son.[106] The force of *stupratam* is not clear, but even if the daughter did consent Anios did not. The difference between the two stories, from the consent of Anios in Dionysios to the illicit and secret seduction or even seizure in Servius, neatly symbolizes the change in relations between Delos and Rome that took place during the course of the Third Macedonian War. In the 160s, some years after the embassy, the Romans handed over the island to the Athenians who removed the population and replaced them with Athenian colonists.[107] Whereas the stories of consent and marriage reflected Delian aspirations for good relations with Rome, the alternative with its *stuprum* reflected the reality and the resulting bitterness.

Daughter Lavinia appears in no other version, although both Vergil and Ovid do include a visit to Delos in Aineias' itinerary.[108] The *Aeneid* makes no mention of any daughters of Anios; Ovid's *Metamorphoses*, on the other hand, has a digression about the children of Anios, but in this case his daughters have been turned into snow-white doves long before the arrival of Aineias.

In both these Roman poets, however, Anchises is treated as an old friend of Anios. In the *Metamorphoses* Anchises, recalling his earlier visit, asks Anios how his children are and thus learns of their unfortunate transformation. In Vergil's account Aineias recounts his party's arrival on Delos: Anios 'recognized his old friend Anchises. We clasped right hands in *hospitium* (hospitality) and entered the building'. Thus there appears to be a relationship of guest-friendship between the two men and their families.[109] Indeed Servius quotes the late Roman commentator Palaiphatos as saying that Anios was a *propinquus* (relative) of Anchises.[110] Here then it is Anchises and Anios who are kin. Could this have been another argument used by the Delians in their pursuit of a relationship with the Romans? Nevertheless, even without kinship between the two men, the suggestion of guest-friendship may have been sufficient to establish *oikeiotes*.

[106] Serv. on *Aen.* 3. 80.
[107] Polyb. 30. 20, 32. 7; Laidlaw 1933: 130–4; Bruneau 1970: 419 is surely mistaken to think that the stories about Delos and Aineias in Dionysios date from the time of the Athenian colony. Perret 1942: 33–4, prefers the early 2nd cent. BC.
[108] Verg. *Aen.* 3. 69–120, Ovid *Met.* 13. 632–704, cf. Bömer 1982: 370–3.
[109] Ovid. *Met.* 13. 640–2, Verg. *Aen.* 3. 82.
[110] Serv. on *Aen.* 3. 80.

The origin of these stories about Aineias and Delos is obscure. The evidence for them is later than the embassy so it would be easy to say that the Delians, in need of an argument to persuade the Romans to help them, invented a specious kinship.[111] It is, however, more likely that the Delians developed their claims out of local traditions that were already in existence. Anios was a purely local myth and there must have been many stories about him that are now unknown.[112] This is not to suggest that the Lavinia story itself was already present on Delos, but rather that the potential for it may already have been there, perhaps in the story that Anios was a friend of Anchises, perhaps in some objects or places that local tradition associated with the Trojans.[113] Faced with the elaborate kinship claims of the Delians and their implicit obligations, a Roman who knew his mythology could, if so inclined, point out that Anios also provided his daughters, the so-called Oinotropoi, to aid the Greek expedition *against* Troy.[114]

There were, therefore, several arguments that the Delian ambassadors could have put forward to the Romans to support a claim of *oikeiotes*. The strongest would have been Aineias' marriage to Anios' daughter and/or her role as the eponym of Lavinium. Strong, too, would have been the very late suggestion that Anios was a *propinquus* of Anchises, but the weaker proposition that the two men were guest-friends might have been found convincing, not least by the Delians. The weakest argument would have been the Trojan landing on Delos, but even this demonstrated long-standing good relations between the two peoples.

The Trojan past also figures between Rome and Akarnania on the west coast of Greece. Again kinship, if it is involved at all, is very distant, but nevertheless the Trojan War and its repercussions do underpin Akarnanian diplomatic initiatives. Three separate accounts survive, in Justin, Strabo, and Dionysios of Halikarnassos, possibly reporting three separate incidents, possibly reflecting different aspects of the same one.[115] In each case the Romans grant some kind of favour that either explicitly or implicitly is a response to an Akarnanian request. Justin reports an Akarnanian

---

[111] So Bruneau 1970: 418–19.

[112] Full testimonia can be found in Bruneau 1970: 413–30.

[113] Cf. the πολλὰ σημεῖα of Dion. Hal. *Ant. Rom.* 1. 59. 1.

[114] Bruneau 1970: 413–18, and the scholia to Lycoph. 570, which traces the story back to the *Cypria* of the epic cycle.

[115] Just. *Epit.* 28. 1–2, Strabo 10. 2. 25, Dion. Hal. *Ant. Rom.* 1. 51. 2.

appeal for help against the Aitolians. The Romans agreed to send an embassy to tell the Aitolians 'to leave free those who in former times were the only ones not to send help to the Greeks against the Trojans, the ancestors of their race'. In a highly rhetorical speech the Aitolians scornfully dismiss the Roman intervention. The incident is usually dated to the early 230s by those who treat it seriously enough to date it.[116] A similar theme occurs in Strabo; the Akarnanians are said to have obtained 'autonomy' from the Romans by cunningly arguing that they had not participated in the expedition against Troy. In contrast to the rather negative argument found in Justin and Strabo Dionysios is very different and more positive. Because of the help the Akarnanians gave Aineias and his men on their way to Italy the Romans rewarded them with the cities of Leukas, Anaktorion and Oiniadai and some form of joint rights over the Echinades Islands to be shared with the Aitolians. Neither Strabo nor Dionysios sets his story within a chronological framework, so the date of each is left vague.

The historicity of all three cases has been questioned, but disputes about dating and authenticity must not allow what is valuable in these stories to be overlooked. True or false, all three stories combine Rome, Akarnania and Troy. None may be wholly true, but the cumulative effect is clear enough. At some point the Akarnanians did use the Trojan past when making an approach to Rome. Before considering the question of historicity, therefore, it is important to examine the arguments themselves and not allow them to be sidelined.

Both Justin and Strabo offer the non-participation argument, that is to say that the Akarnanians did not take part in the expedition against Troy. Justin includes it in the Roman address to the Aitolians, though few Romans are likely to have had sufficient knowledge of Homeric scholarship to have observed for themselves the absence of the Akarnanians from the catalogue of ships and the rest of the *Iliad*. What the Akarnanians said to the Romans we are not told. Strabo, on the other hand, explicitly attributes the argument to the Akarnanians; that was how they succeeded in persuading the Romans. The observation that the Akarnanians had not taken part in the war was not a new one; their absence had, according to Strabo, already been noted by the

---

[116] Alföldi 1957: 33, E. Weber 1972: 218, Rizzo 1974: 59, Gruen 1990: 13, Coppola 1994: 179 (between 242 and 239), Canali de Rossi 1997: 4–5 (*c*.240).

fourth-century historian Ephoros.[117] It was, nonetheless, an odd argument for the Akarnanians to use, for two reasons.

First, the non-participation argument does not appear to be one that would reflect well on the Akarnanians. To say that they were the only people in Greece who did not fight in one of the greatest wars was hardly such a tremendous boast.[118] This could lead one to suspect that others (Aitolians perhaps), knowing that the Akarnanians did not appear in the catalogue of ships, maliciously used this to explain Roman favours;[119] or that, as Strabo implies, the Akarnanians opportunistically exploited their absence from the *Iliad*. Certainly an alternative to non-participation was conceivable; Strabo himself rejected Ephoros' contention and argued that the Akarnanians did fight in the war but were not yet called Akarnanians.[120] But instead of resorting to malice or opportunism it may be possible to locate Akarnanian non-participation within the Akarnanians' own traditions. This is not to suggest that there may not have been times when the Akarnanians preferred to represent themselves as participants but rather that any claim they made to the effect that they did not fight in the Trojan War was rooted in their own local history.[121] They may even have prided themselves on not having fought because by doing so they distinguished themselves from those who had fought, in particular the neighbouring Aitolians, who do feature in the catalogue of ships.[122]

Moreover, Ephoros did not merely say that the Akarnanians did not join the expedition against Troy; he gave a reason for it. This explanation concerns an otherwise unknown variant on the Alkmaion story, which strongly suggests an Akarnanian perspective. Alkmaion together with Diomedes captured Aitolia and after handing it over to Diomedes moved on alone to take control of a territory which he named Akarnania after his son, Akarnan. In the meantime Agamemnon who had taken advantage of their absence to seize Argos was planning his expedition against Troy,

---

[117] Strabo 10. 2. 25–6 (Ephoros *FGrH* 70F123a).

[118] Cf. Thuc. 1. 1.

[119] Cf. Xenophon's unfavourable picture of Thebans at the Persian court, *Hell.* 7. 1. 34.

[120] Strabo 10. 2. 8, 10. 2. 24.

[121] For use of myths in this way, Buxton 1994: 196.

[122] A point made to me by Oliver Dany as I was coming out of a general anaesthetic in Rotkreuzplatz Krankenhaus. If one were to accept that Pyrrhos did use anti-Trojan propaganda against Rome, then the Akarnanians could also be trying to contrast themselves with Pyrrhos.

but anxious for the security of his empire sought to protect his rear by returning Argos and offering the two a place in his expedition. Diomedes accepted but Alkmaion, angry with Agamemnon, declined.[123] This conflict between Alkmaion and Agamemnon does not appear elsewhere. Could it be an Akarnanian myth justifying their otherwise shameful non-participation by reference to a cunning, treacherous Agamemnon? The seizure of Aitolia in the story is striking if the constant conflict between Akarnania and Aitolia is remembered; it not only asserts Akarnanian authority over Aitolia but also implicitly rejects any Aitolian claims to Akarnania.[124] In this way the case made by the Akarnanians in Rome would have been no mere opportunism but rather a product of their own traditions.

Nevertheless, the non-participation argument is odd in another way. It is simply a statement of inaction. There is nothing positive in it, no evidence of goodwill. This marks it out as different from the kinship examples considered earlier in this Chapter, because there is no sense that the present relationship is modelled on or building on a relationship in the past. The myth, as reported by Ephoros, may help here. If this was presented to the Romans, it could change the claim from plain non-participation to shared animosity towards Agamemnon. Moreover, the non-participation argument is all Justin and Strabo record but it can hardly be all that the Akarnanians said. In focusing on this there is perhaps something critical, if not malicious, as is evident from Strabo's use of *sophisasthai* to describe the Akarnanian approach to the Romans, implying cunning, trickery, sophistry.[125]

The goodwill lacuna might, however, have been filled by an argument such as the one to be found in Dionysios, where the Akarnanians do take positive action in support of the Trojans. Dionysios describes Aineias' route along the west coast of Greece and across the Ionian Sea to Italy. To make the crossing Aineias has the assistance of some Akarnanians led by Patron of Thyrreion.[126] After the crossing most of the Akarnanians return home,

[123] Strabo 10. 2. 25–6 (Ephoros *FGrH* 70F123a) cf. also Strabo 7. 7. 7 (Ephoros F123b), 9. 3. 12 (Ephoros F122b). For other stories of Alkmaion and Akarnania, Thuc. 2. 102. 5–6, Apollod. *Bibl.* 3. 7. 7, Paus. 8. 24. 9, [Scymnus] 461–3 (in *GGM* 1).

[124] Oost 1954: 93 notes that both Justin and Dion. Hal.'s story concern Akarnanian–Aitolian conflict.

[125] Strabo 10. 2. 25.

[126] Dion. Hal. has Θουρίῳ which could also refer to Thurioi in Italy but it is clear from

but Patron and some others are persuaded by Aineias to stay; according to some accounts, writes Dionysios, Patron eventually settled at Alontion in Sicily, a remark which might imply that there were other versions in which Patron continued with Aineias. This is the only occurrence of this story, although there is an allusion in Vergil's *Aeneid*, where an Akarnanian called Patron is a participant at the funeral games for Anchises held in Sicily.[127] Here, then, are the help and goodwill absent from the non-participation argument; if they were used together they would have made a good combination, but there is more to the Patron story than this. By joining Aineias' expedition Patron and his followers merge the Trojans and Akarnanians, providing some justification for a claim of *oikeiotes*. In this respect the Akarnanian example is similar to the Delian one. The maritime assistance is analogous to the hospitality given by Anios; Patron, like Lavinia, becomes part of the expedition, and both at the instigation of Aineias. Although no evidence exists for Trojan cults or other associations in Akarnania before the appeal to Rome, the west coast did have Trojan traditions that were independent of the Romans, namely in Epiros and Zakynthos.

These two mythological arguments, perhaps together with others, could have offered a basis for Akarnanian relations with Rome, not least from the Akarnanian prospective. The above has tried to probe the nature of the arguments themselves, while if possible staying clear of the difficult question of their specific historical context.

The Justin passage has been the subject of considerable debate, with scholars arguing for and against the historicity of an Akarnanian appeal in the 230s, followed by a Roman embassy to the Aitolians.[128] Here it will suffice to say that they are more likely to have taken place than not. It is, however, another question whether Troy played any part in the affair. What casts doubt on the Trojan aspect of the appeal, that is to say the use of the non-participation argument, is the context in which it appears. After a

the context that these are Akarnanians, cf. also Steph. Byz. s.v. 'Θυρέα'; the story would not make sense otherwise; on this and other textual problems, Vanotti 1995: 166–8. Martin's suggestion (1971: 169) that there is an allusion to Augustus here is far-fetched.

[127] Verg. *Aen.* 5. 298.

[128] Holleaux 1921: 5–22 makes a forceful attack on authenticity, followed by Perret 1942: 65–6, 450–1, Oost 1954: 92–7; there have also been several detailed refutations of Holleaux, see Derow 1970, Corsten 1992, Dany 1999: 98–119.

brief statement of the Roman case, the Aitolians respond with a lengthy speech usually dismissed as a fiction; it is rhetorical in nature and historically muddled.[129] Significantly it matches the points made earlier by the Romans. The Romans had demanded that the Aitolians leave the Akarnanians alone; the Aitolians in reply tell the Romans to deal with the threats posed to Rome by the Gauls and Carthaginians before threatening others. The Romans had referred to their Trojan ancestry; the Aitolians give a quick review of early Roman history in which there are no Trojan heroes; instead it is the Rome of shepherds, thieves, rapists, and fratricide. The two positions, therefore, balance one another. This interdependence means that the reference to the Trojan War need be no more reliable than anything in the Aitolian speech. Nor are the brevity and simplicity of the Roman case an argument for authenticity, especially as they may only be a result of the epitomizing process. Trogus' original work may have contained a Roman speech which Justin drastically abridged because what interested him was the Aitolian speech, and even that speech may have been edited.[130] Nevertheless, while literary context may make the Trojan reference suspect, historical context might be adduced in its favour. Akarnania was on the west coast of Greece, a location that gave it special access not only to the political currents of Italy and Sicily but also to their religious and mythical world.

The Roman alliance with the Aitolians in 212/11 marked the end of any friendly feeling that may have developed between the Romans and the Akarnanians. The alliance had two targets, Philip V of Macedon for the Romans and Akarnania for the Aitolians.[131] In consequence, the Akarnanians spent the first two Macedonian Wars alongside Philip and stubbornly supported him right to the end of the second war, as much out of fear and hatred of the Aitolians as loyalty to Philip.[132] In spite of repeated Aitolian protests the Romans returned to the Akarnanians the chief city of

---

[129] Holleaux 1921: 7 with last part of n. 3, Oost 1954: 96–7, Coppola 1994: 185–6, Dany 1999: 112–15.

[130] On the one occasion when Justin does admit to giving a complete speech of Trogus (that of Mithridates) it is about 5 times longer than the Aitolian speech, 38. 4–7; on Justin's method see his preface with Alonso-Núñez 1987, esp. 61–2 , Richter 1987: 17–23, Develin 1994; for pairs of speeches: 14. 3. 4–6 (Eumenes) with 14. 3. 7–10 (Agyraspids), 30. 4. 6–7 (Philip V) with 30. 4. 8–14 (Flamininus, who gets a much longer speech).

[131] Livy 26. 24. 1–14, Schmitt 1969: no. 536; Oost 1954: 333–5, Gruen 1984: 439.

[132] Livy 33. 16. 2.

Leukas which had been captured in the closing stages of the war.[133] This incident is surely the subject of Dionysios' statement that Akarnania was awarded Leukas and Anaktorion.[134] The Akarnanians argued for these places, drawing attention to the assistance they had given to Aineias and probably also to their stance in the Trojan War in contrast to the Aitolians who were there at Troy with the rest of the Greeks. There is an additional argument that the Akarnanians may have used. Earlier in his account of Aineias' voyage to Italy Dionysios describes how Aineias landed on Leukas and set up a temple of Aphrodite Aineias there. That would appear to have been all that needed saying but Dionysios adds that the place was at that time already occupied by the Akarnanians.[135] This seemingly irrelevant remark may have been part of the Akarnanian appeal for the return of the island. If Aineias had recognized Akarnanian possession of Leukas, should not his descendants do the same? Here the desired situation in the present is modelled on and justified by the heroic past.

Strabo's vague reference to the Roman grant of autonomy is probably best understood in the context of the generous treatment to Akarnania following the Second Macedonian War, a time when Rome was proclaiming the freedom of the Greeks.[136] Among the benefits bestowed on the Akarnanians by the Romans in return for their help to Aineias Dionysios also included the granting of Akarnanian requests for Oiniadai. This was a city that had formerly been held by the Akarnanians but that had been in Aitolian hands since the outbreak of the First Macedonian War. Since this

---

[133] Capture: Livy 33. 16–17; its status as 'capital' city: Livy 33. 16. 3, 17. 1, Larsen 1968: 269; Aitolian demands: Polyb. 18. 47. 8, Livy 33. 34 .7, 33. 49. 8; Livy 36. 11. 9 makes clear that the Akarnanians were given the city. They finally did lose it as a result of their conduct in the Third Macedonian War, Livy 45. 31. 12; *OCD*³ s.v. 'Acarnania' is wrong here.

[134] Dion. Hal. *Ant. Rom.* 1. 51. 2, though nothing is known of Anaktorion at this time.

[135] Dion. Hal. *Ant. Rom.* 1. 50. 4; the founding of the temple of Aphrodite at Leukas also appeared in Varro according to Serv. on *Aen.* 3. 279 (=Varro *RH* II, frag. 13, P. Mirsch), though there is no mention of Akarnania. The significance of the epithet 'Aineias' for Aphrodite is unknown; it only occurs in Dion. Hal., cf. 1. 50. 4 (Aktion), 53. 1 (Elymos/ Eryx), cf. Perret 1942: 60, Bömer 1951: 33–4.

[136] Strabo 10. 2. 25; freedom of the Greeks: Polyb. 18. 44–7; Oberhummer 1887: 148 n. 2, however, combined Strabo with Justin, though Justin is about autonomy aspired to, Strabo about autonomy attained, cf. also Holleaux 1921: 13 n. 4 for criticisms of Oberhummer. Oost 1954: 137 n. 21 is wrong to suggest that αὐτονομία precludes 197/6; his view is based on its meaning at Strabo 10. 2. 23, but ignores other uses in Strabo, e.g. 4. 1. 5, 9. 1. 20, 16. 1. 11, which are consistent with a more limited autonomy.

was not handed over to the Akarnanians until 189, after the Aitolian defeat in Rome's war with Antiochos, it must have been the subject of a separate, later appeal.[137]

If the Akarnanians did use the Trojan myth in the 230s, it would have been to establish some common ground during a tricky initial approach to an unfamiliar state. The later emphasis on their pro-Trojan stance would have served to offset their lack of enthusiasm for the Roman cause in more recent times.[138]

4. THE LIMITS OF KINSHIP

Kinship claims with Rome were not widespread. The diplomatic initiatives that most clearly make use of Trojan kinship arguments were undertaken by the Greek cities of the Troad and 'Hellenized' communities such as Segesta and Lykia. The existence of Trojan traditions is an important explanation for this distribution; these are states where there had long been a strong sense of a Trojan past.

But further factors may also have contributed. Other states did have traditions which could have been exploited or adapted; these traditions may have been less significant than in the Troad, but in combination with the many genealogies available they would have given scope for incorporating the Romans into their mythological world view.[139] There is, however, little evidence that these states did put them to use when making approaches to Rome. The modern picture of Greeks using Troy to flatter the Romans and thus gain political advantage is not easy to discern here.[140] Even where evidence does exist, they appear to be holding back; they are prepared to acknowledge ties or on occasion even limited kinship but unwilling to go the whole way. Delos and Akarnania both attest to this hesitation.

The limited number of examples permits only some tentative remarks. The very nature of the Trojan War meant that states in Asia Minor could identify with the Trojans more easily than

---

[137] Dion. Hal. *Ant. Rom.* 1. 51. 2; occupied: Polyb. 9. 39. 1–2, Livy 26. 24. 15; given to Akarnania: Polyb. 21. 32. 14, 38. 11. 9, Livy 38. 11. 9, cf. Vanotti 1995: 169–70. Dion. Hal. also mentions the Echinades Islands but there is no other evidence for this.

[138] Even in the war with Antiochos they were lukewarm, cf. Livy 42. 38. 3–4, Gruen 1984: 476.

[139] See Ch. 4.

[140] See n. 1 above.

others could. Much of mainland Greece, on the other hand, could see itself in the catalogue of ships opposing the Trojans. For this reason their relationship with the Trojans would have been more distant, even if they did have a local Trojan hero. In Asia Minor it is significant that any affinity with the Trojans is concentrated in the Troad and among Hellenized peoples and is not evident among Greek cites outside the Troad, such as those of Ionia. Hellenized native populations, however, often traced their origins back to allies of the Trojans; in imperial times the people of Abbaeitis honoured as ancestor Chromios who had been king of the Mysians in the *Iliad*, while the Phrygian cities of Otrous and Stektorion had as heroes Otreus and Mygdon, who were Phrygian kings and allies of Priam against the Amazons.[141]

This introduces another factor. There appears to have been a greater willingness among Hellenized peoples to embrace Trojan ancestry, or, to look at it from another perspective, a greater reluctance on the part of Greek states. The Hellenized/Greek distinction employed here may be rather sharp and artificial, but in this case it may offer a useful tool for understanding the differing responses to the Romans. The Hellenized Lykians, for instance, are prepared to claim kinship with both Trojans and Romans in a way in which the Akarnanians and Delians are not. They had fought under the leadership of Sarpedon and Glaukos at Troy and so could have presented themselves merely as old friends and allies of the Romans as the Akarnanians had, but their claim of *cognatio* indicates that they went further than that. The more cautious Akarnanian appeal, however, appears to open them up to disapproval from at least some of their fellow Greeks.[142] A reluctance to claim kinship with the Romans may say something about Greek attitudes to the Trojans, a desire to maintain a certain distance, but it is likely to say as much about their attitude to the Romans. Greeks may simply have had more difficulty claiming kinship with the Romans than Hellenized peoples did. It was clear

[141] Abbaeitis: *OGIS* 446, Hom. *Il.* 2. 858, 17. 218, 494, 534, Strubbe 1984–6: 259, cf. L. Robert 1990: 419–20, for possible appearance of Chromios on a bronze coin from Kadoi in the Abbaeitis. Phrygia: Hom. *Il.* 3. 186–9, Carrington 1977: 123, Strubbe 1984–6: 259–60, L. Robert 1990: 193. Cf. also the emphasis on Troy in Aphrodisias, Reynolds 1996: 41–4. The introduction of the Panhellenion under Hadrian may have indirectly discouraged professions of Trojan ancestry since Greek ancestry was a criterion for membership; the Phrygian city of Kibyra claims to be a Spartan colony and related to the Athenians, *OGIS* 497, Spawforth and Walker 1985: 82.

[142] See Sect. 3 above.

that the Romans were not Greek and did not speak Greek; language was an important signifier of Greekness.[143] It was easier to conceive of kinship with non-Greek peoples who took on the trappings of Greek culture; thus kinship between Kytinion and Lykian Xanthos was acceptable, since the Lykians appeared Greek and spoke Greek. It is interesting to note that when Dionysios of Halikarnassos argued that the Romans were Greeks he also contended that Latin was a dialect of Greek.[144] The Lykians, on the other hand, among whom Lykian was probably still spoken even if no longer used in public documents, had less difficulty accommodating the Romans in their kinship networks, since their own ethnic identity was that much more fluid.[145]

Local traditions were the most significant influence on claims of kinship with the Romans, but location and cultural background were important secondary factors, effectively limiting the number of possible claims. While in many areas Rome's Trojan ancestry would have met with indifference, in areas such as the Troad it would have generated a strong positive reaction.

[143] Language and Greekness: Hdt. 8. 144. 2, Dion. Hal. *Ant. Rom.* 1. 89–90, Strabo 14. 2. 28, Livy 37. 54, though note Hall 1995*a* who argues against exaggerating the importance of language; kinship and language: Strabo 1. 2. 34, Dion. Hal. *Ant. Rom.* 1. 29–30.

[144] Dion. Hal. *Ant. Rom.* 1. 90, Gabba 1963.

[145] Bryce 1986: 42–54 on language, 214–15 on survival of culture, cf. also n. 64 above.

8

Old Gods, New Homes

The Second Punic War introduced two new gods into Rome, Venus Erycina from Sicily and the Magna Mater from Asia Minor.[1] Both came on the recommendation of the Sibylline books, both were mountain goddesses who found homes on the hills of Rome, and both are something of a puzzle. Viewed from one angle these cults appear to have no Trojan character at all, but from another angle the Trojan content is all too obvious. Livy who provides the fullest, and apparently most reliable, account of the introductions of these two goddesses has nothing whatsoever to say about Troy or Trojan ancestry in either case. Yet, other presentations of these cults, for instance by poets such as Ovid or Vergil, lay considerable stress on it. Various explanations can be put forward for this striking contrast: Livy knew, but did not think it relevant; Troy was more appropriate to poetry than to prose; the Trojan character was a later accretion on a Troyless episode, perhaps even a product of Augustan ideology. There may be truth in all these but in themselves they seem rather inadequate. The answer should be sought again in the relationship between Rome and the outside world. Although certain patterns will be found to recur, it is useful to look at each goddess separately.

1. Venus Erycina

In 217 BC after Rome's unexpected and crushing defeat by Hannibal at Trasimene the dictator Q. Fabius Maximus Cunctator advised the Senate that the Sibylline books should be consulted. Inspection revealed that much was to be done if the gods were to be appeased, including the establishment of two temples, one to Venus Erycina, the other to Mens. These temples were built alongside each other on the Capitol and dedicated in 215. The temple of Venus Erycina was both vowed and dedicated by Fabius Maximus himself, while for its partner, the temple of

[1] For the receptivity of Rome to new gods, see North 1976, Orlin 1997.

Mens, these services were performed by the praetor T. Otacilius Crassus.[2]

This, in summary, is the account of Livy, our only substantial source for the introduction of Venus Erycina into the city of Rome. She came, although Livy does not tell us this, from Mt. Eryx in north-west Sicily, site of a major cult centre, hence the epithet. The deity worshipped there was variously called Astarte by the Carthaginians, Aphrodite by the Greeks, and Venus by the Romans.[3] Like Segesta Eryx lay in the territory of the Elymians.

Troy is noticeably absent from Livy's tale of these events. Modern scholars, however, have searched for Trojan explanations to account for the presence of Venus Erycina in Rome, suggesting for instance that Venus takes her place on the Capitoline Hill, as ancestor of the Roman people, and as part of the national heritage.[4] There are two principal reasons for adding a Trojan interpretation to Livy's rather bald account. First, ancient authors who write about the cult of Aphrodite on Eryx often associate it in some way with Aineias and Rome. The earliest surviving writer to do so is Diodoros, who speaks with pride of this distinguished sanctuary in his native Sicily. Founded by Eryx, son of Aphrodite, it numbered among its early visitors that other son of Aphrodite, Aineias. Of all the rulers of the area, he says, it was the Romans who showed the most respect for the goddess:

Finally the Romans, when they had taken control of the whole of Sicily, surpassed all their predecessors in the honours which they paid to her [Aphrodite at Eryx]. For, since they traced their lineage back to her and on account of this were successful in their enterprises, such thanks and honours were appropriate recompense to offer one who was responsible for their rise to power.[5]

Ovid too draws attention to the kinship between the goddess and the Romans, although in a manner that would no doubt have displeased Diodoros; Venus was transferred from a Sicilian hill to Rome, because 'she preferred to be worshipped in the city of her

---

[2] Livy 22. 9. 7–11, 22. 10. 10, 23. 30. 13–14, 23. 31. 9; in general on Venus, Schilling 1954, on Mens, Mello 1968. Orlin 1997: 175–6 notes how unusual it was for vowers and dedicators to be the same people.

[3] Schilling 1954: 233–9.

[4] Schilling 1954: 233–66, Alföldi 1957: 29, Kienast 1965, Galinsky 1969: 169–90, Momigliano 1984: 453, Gruen 1992: 46–7. The chief exception is Perret 1942: 300–1, 453, but he denied Trojan traditions at Eryx altogether, despite Thuc. 6. 2. 3, Lycoph. 958 with schol. on 952 and 964.   [5] Diod. Sic. 4. 83, esp. 4–6.

offspring'.[6] Equally displeasing would have been Vergil's *Aeneid*, in which the sanctuary in Sicily was founded by Aeneas himself.[7] These writers are all active in the first century BC, and Ovid and Vergil especially would have been influenced by the Iulian emphasis on Venus. But even so, and this is the second reason, the Trojan tradition of the area, and of Eryx in particular, stretches back at least as far as the fifth century BC when it is mentioned by Thucydides.[8] The essence is, thus, independent of the Iulian appropriation of the Venus myth.

It is plausible, therefore, to imagine that Troy has a role in the events of 217, even if it is absent from Livy's account. Rather than supplementing Livy with Trojan material, however, it is preferable to consider some of the possible perspectives that are involved. For the meaning of Venus Erycina will change with context and perspective. Although the evidence is relatively late and much of it is the product of a Rome in which the emperor claimed descent from Venus,[9] the present section will consider how Venus Erycina may have been viewed in the late third century BC. It will focus on the meaning of Venus Erycina first within Rome and then in the context of Rome's relationship with Sicily. In each the establishment of the temple in Rome meant something different. The relevance of the Trojan myth must be argued for and defined in each case.

In the aftermath of Trasimene Rome was a city in crisis.[10] The initiative lay with Q. Fabius Maximus Cunctator who had just been appointed dictator. On his first day in office he recommended the inspection of the Sibylline books, arguing that the disaster was largely due to negligence in matters of ritual. This step marked a new start for Rome, one that highlighted the past successes of the Fabii and promised fresh success under the Fabian dictator. There had been an earlier temple of Venus in Rome; it was the temple of Venus Obsequens, established in 295 by none

---

[6] Ovid, *Fasti* 4. 872–6, where Venus' move to Rome seems to be mistakenly linked with M. Claudius Marcellus' capture of Syracuse in 212, cf. Frazer 1929, Bömer 1958.

[7] Verg. *Aen.* 5. 759–60, where she is called Venus Idalia, thus alluding both to her Cypriot background (for Idalion in Cyprus see *RE* 9. 1, s.v. 'Idalion') and to the Mt. Ida of the Troad; cf. also Dion. Hal. *Ant. Rom.* 1. 53. 1. Serv. on *Aen.* 1. 720, discussing cults of Venus, offers the enigmatic statement, 'est et Erycina, quam Aeneas secum advexit', which sometimes is given the authority of Cassius Hemina due to Solin. 2. 14, the interpretation of which is obscure, see Galinsky 1969: 115–17.

[8] Thuc. 6. 2. 3; for full account of Trojan myths in this area, Ch. 7.2.

[9] Cf. Ch. 1 above.   [10] Cf. Polyb. 3. 85. 7–10, Livy 22. 7–8.

other than Cunctator's grandfather, Q. Fabius Gurges. This, too,
was a year in which the Sibylline books were consulted; they may
even have recommended the building of the temple of Venus
Obsequens.[11] But echoes of the year 295 do not end here. 295 was
also the year of the battle of Sentinum, in which Rome crushed
a Samnite and Gallic army in the Third Samnite War. On the
battlefield the victorious commander vowed a temple to Jupiter
Victor; the commander was the consul and former dictator,
Q. Fabius Maximus Rullianus, great-grandfather of Cunctator.[12]
It is surely no chance matter that the inspection of the Sibylline
books advised by Fabius in 217 led not only to a temple of Venus
but also to the holding of games in honour of Jupiter. Moreover,
the conjunction of the temple of Venus with that of Mens, the
personification of good sense, signalled that under Fabius wise
counsel would replace the recklessness of Flaminius, the commander at Trasimene.[13] So in a year marked by military disaster
the Romans could look back to past achievements of the Fabii
under the prescient leadership of their descendant, Q. Fabius
Cunctator. Venus functioned as a reminder of this past.

Even the epithet Erycina may not have been without significance to a Roman audience. The closing years of the First Punic
War had been fought around Mt. Eryx, a struggle vividly described by Polybios. The Romans held out on the summit in the
face of intense pressure from Hamilcar below.[14] Now in 217 in
severe difficulties at the hands of Hamilcar's son, Hannibal, the
Romans introduce the goddess of Eryx into their city, perhaps
hoping that her divine favour will protect the city and bring
similar success.[15] She would have met with a receptive audience in
Rome; almost all veterans of the First Punic War would have
done service in Sicily.

In several ways the goddess embodies the Roman attitude to

[11] Livy 10. 31. 8–9, Serv. on *Aen.* 1. 720; Schilling 1954: 27, 93–6, 200–2, Ziolkowski 1992:
167–71; Livy does not say what the Sibylline recommendations were but the temple does
follow the consultation in his narrative. Possibly Gurges was the father of Cunctator rather
than the grandfather; on the problem see Münzer *RE* 6 'Fabius (no. 116)', cols. 1814–15,
Broughton *MRR* 1. 201–2.
[12] Livy 10. 29. 14, 19; 10. 42. 7; Ziolkowski 1992: 91–4; see also previous note; his colleague P. Decius Mus died in the battle.
[13] Cf. Dumézil 1970: 473–4 ; on Flaminius' recklessness: Polyb. 3. 80–1, Livy 22. 3. 7–14,
4. 4, 9. 7.   [14] Polyb. 1. 55–9.
[15] Schilling 1954: 242–3; for the importance of the Roman stand at Eryx, Livy 21. 10. 7
(speech of Hanno set in 219), 21. 41 (of Scipio in 218).

Sicily at the time. Hannibal's arrival in the north had pushed Rome onto the defensive. T. Sempronius Longus, the consul, who had been allocated the province of Africa with Sicily, was instructed by the Senate to leave Sicily and go to the assistance of his colleague in the north.[16] In this context of apparent weakness the incorporation of a Sicilian deity could be seen as a reaffirmation of Roman mastery of the island, acted out on a religious plane. Nor was it any Sicilian deity, but the goddess of Mt. Eryx, a strategic point crucial to the control of western Sicily, an area where Carthaginian influence had been at its strongest before the First Punic War. Rising out of the plain, about 750 m. above sea level, it gave whoever occupied it a clear view of the coast and of the approaches by sea out to the Egadi Islands. The loyalty of the goddess could have been seen as questionable; she was after all supposed to slip off to Africa for nine days every year, escorted by her doves, and may already have had a cult centre there.[17] By introducing Venus Erycina into Rome the Romans could win the favour of the goddess for themselves and accordingly reduce the divine assistance that might be provided to any Carthaginian attempts to reclaim the island.[18] In this last respect Trojan kinship may have been a factor; it meant that the Romans had a better right to the goddess than the Carthaginians.

Roman goals in Sicily and Fabian success merge in the person of T. Otacilius Crassus, the dedicant of the temple of Mens, companion to Venus on the Capitoline Hill. Otacilius' father and uncle had both served in Sicily during the First Punic War and both are believed to have owed their political advancement to the Fabii. Otacilius himself continued these family links; he married a niece of Fabius Cunctator and after the vowing of the temples of Mens and Venus Erycina he went south to command the fleet in Sicily until his death in 211.[19] Venus and Mens together would

[16] Province: Livy 21. 17, Polyb. 3. 41. 2–3; instructions: Polyb. 3. 61. 9, Livy 21. 51. 5.

[17] African visits: Athen. 9. 394f, Aelian *VH* 1. 15, *NA* 4. 2; for cult centre at Sicca Veneria, Solin 27. 8, Schilling 1954: 238, Kienast 1965: 480, Galinsky 1969: 71–2, Wilson 1990: 283–5. On the doves, Pollard 1977: 146. The Athenaios passage is repeatedly and incorrectly attributed to Aristotle (Schilling 238 n. 6, Kienast 480, Galinsky 71 n. 26). It is true that Aristotle is given as the source for the previous sentence, but the statement there about feeding pigeons can be traced to the extant *Historia animalium* (8. 613ᵃ1–6), a work used several times by Athenaios at this point.   [18] Cf. Palmer 1997: 66–7.

[19] Service in Sicily: Polyb. 1. 16. 1, 1. 20. 4; Fabii and Otacilii: Münzer 1920: 62–78. Marriage: Livy 24. 8. 11; Sicily: Livy 22. 31, 37, 56; 23. 21, 32, 41; 26. 1, 23; Scullard 1973: 59, 64–5; Briscoe 1989: 66–7, 70.

watch over a successful campaign in Sicily and at the same time symbolized Roman aspirations.

Within the Roman context the introduction of the cult of Venus Erycina must be understood as one of a number of Sibylline religious prescriptions. Together these prescriptions made up a complex and hazy set of symbols, harking back to past military success and fortitude, promising good sense and victory in the future under Fabian guidance. The coming of the goddess also assured the Roman populace of additional divine favour. There seems little need to introduce Troy into the equation; Trojan ancestry was not yet an integral part of the Roman self-image and popular familiarity with the notion was likely to have been limited.[20] Recollections of the First Punic War will have had greater popular impact than any purported Trojan heritage.

The location of the temple, however, has furnished an influential argument that Trojan ancestry was an important factor in the introduction of Venus Erycina: it was situated on the Capitoline Hill, and therefore within the *pomerium*, the religious boundary of the city. It is a commonplace of modern scholarship that foreign cults were not allowed within the *pomerium*. Therefore, it is argued, Venus Erycina must have been admitted because of her family connection with the Romans. Not only is the latter argument rather tenuous but the very foundation upon which it rests is questionable. Recently Ziolkowski has forcefully shown that the whole thesis that foreign cults were excluded from the area within the *pomerium* is a modern construct with little to support it.[21]

The traditions, memories, and preconceptions of Sicilians, however, will have been very different from those found among Romans. So it is necessary at this point to consider the significance of Venus Erycina in relations between Romans and Sicilians. As this was one of the more important sanctuaries in Sicily, described by Polybios as 'the most outstanding in wealth and general magnificence of all the holy places in Sicily', the establishment of a temple of the goddess in Rome could hardly have escaped notice.[22] It created a bond between the Romans and the

---

[20] Ch. 1 above.

[21] Ziolkowski 1992: 268–83, esp. 275–9; against Wissowa 1912: 45–6, Schilling 1954: 250, 1979: 94–102, Galinsky 1969: 174, 176–7, Dumézil 1970: 487, Gruen 1992: 47, and subsequently Beard, North, and Price 1998: i. 82–4; Graillot 1912: 56–7 is more cautious, seeing a change from 217.

[22] Polyb. 1. 55. 8, cf. Diod. Sic. 4. 83, Paus. 8. 24. 6, Strabo 6. 2. 6.

people of north-western Sicily, and by extension with the rest of Sicily. This is the appropriate context for the Trojan myth.

Religion and kinship were closely entwined in the Greek world. From Herodotos through to Dionysios of Halikarnassos one of the defining characteristics of the Greeks was considered to be their common religious customs.[23] More specifically daughter-cities would frequently echo the cults, rituals, and myths of their mother-city.[24] A corollary of this was that the presence of similar religious practices could be taken as evidence of kinship between two cities. Strabo, for instance, finds confirmation of the kinship between Tenea and Tenedos in the similarities in their worship of Apollo.[25] So, from the perspective of Greek and Hellenized peoples with their strong sense of kinship, both real and mythical, the establishment of a temple of Venus Erycina would have been but a manifestation of the kinship that already existed between the Elymians and the Romans. Both had Trojan blood. Rome's acquisition of the cult could be explained and justified on the basis of kinship and in the process this kinship would be reinforced.

That would be the Greek interpretation of what was happening, but there would also have been another aspect, which brought both Greeks and Romans into more direct contact with one another. The mechanics of how the cult was introduced to Rome are unknown. The case of Aesculapius in 291 and the Magna Mater in 205 can furnish comparisons; in both cases, after a Roman delegation is sent to make the arrangements, a cult object is brought to Rome and placed in a new sanctuary, Aesculapius requiring a sacred snake and the Magna Mater a sacred stone.[26] It is not known whether any cult object had to be transferred to the new temple of Venus Erycina, but it is probable that some contact or negotiations took place between the temple authorities and the Romans. As each explored the position of the other, Trojan kinship would have provided common ground. Acceptance of kinship would be a sign of good faith, a necessary prelude to the religious transaction that would follow.

Thus public ties of kinship and religion bound Rome and western Sicily together at a crucial moment in the war against

---

[23] Hdt. 8. 144. 2, Dion. Hal. *Ant. Rom.* 1. 89. 4.

[24] Graham 1964: 14–15, Malkin 1994: 145–7, S. Hornblower 1996: 62.

[25] Strabo 8. 6. 22, cf. Paus. 2. 5. 4, and Ch. 4.3 (Tenea) above.

[26] Aesculapius: Scullard 1981: 54–6, Livy 10. 47. 6–7, *Epit.* 11, cf. Ovid, *Met.* 15. 622–745; Magna Mater: sect. 2 below.

Carthage. The Romans had been anxious about the loyalty of western Sicily, where long-standing Carthaginian connections fuelled Roman insecurity. Even before Trasimene the Carthaginians had made an attempt on Lilybaeum, which along with other cities on the coast was rumoured to be plotting revolt.[27] Nor had the Roman record at Eryx been beyond reproach in the First Punic War; the sanctuary had, it was said, been looted by some Gauls in the Roman service.[28] Respect for such an important sanctuary and affirmation of kinship would have been valuable means of winning support and remedying past mistakes, whether by design or merely as a by-product of their need for the Sicilian goddess.[29]

Rome's Trojan ancestry, then, could play a major role in the exchange between Romans and Sicilians and in Greek perceptions of events, yet at the same time have little significance in Rome itself. Livy, albeit briefly, reflects the way in which the introduction of Venus Erycina was projected in third-century Rome. Diodoros, on the other hand, offers the Sicilian perspective: Roman success was due to their Sicilian ancestor, Aphrodite of Eryx.

2. MAGNA MATER COMES TO ROME

The Magna Mater was welcomed into Rome in 204, in what with hindsight we can call the closing years of the Second Punic War. The Mother Goddess was widely worshipped in Asia Minor, where she went under a variety of names, though modern scholarship tends to know her as Cybele. The focus of ecstatic cult, overseen by eunuch priests, she is associated with mountains and nature, appearing in art flanked by lions.[30] The Romans main-

[27] Livy 21. 49–50, Polyb. 3. 75. 4.

[28] Polyb. 2. 7. 9–10; some attempt to put matters right may already have been made if it is correct that after the first war the Romans had taken some responsibility for the supervision of the cult, so Kienast 1965, using Diod. Sic. 4. 83. 7, but Diod. gives no indication of date, cf. Gruen 1992: 45 n. 182; K. Ziegler (*RE* 7A.1780, s.v. 'Tyndaris') would place it after the Second Punic War.

[29] Scheid 1985: 97–8 on introduction of Aesculapius as 'une sorte d'*evocatio* pacifique' in relation to Greek cities of Magna Graecia.

[30] Graillot 1912 is the classic study, cf. more recently Vermaseren 1977, Borgeaud 1996; L. G. Roller, *In Search of God the Mother: The Cult of Anatolian Cybele* (Berkeley, 1999), a substantial work, appeared too late to be taken into account. The evidence is collected in *CCCA*, vol. i of which is concerned with Asia Minor. For classical Greek background, Burkert 1977: 276–8.

tained a certain distance from the more extreme aspects of the cult; the personnel, for instance, remained eastern. Noisy and colourful processions in honour of the goddess continued, but public celebration in Rome centred on the annual Megalensian Games, a festival that was restrained and more traditionally Roman.[31] The temple itself, dedicated in 191, was located on the Palatine Hill, near where Augustus was later to have his home.[32]

The introduction of the Magna Mater to Rome is in some ways more problematic than that of Venus Erycina, because it generated so many, often contradictory, accounts.[33] Whatever happened in 205–4 is buried beneath extensive later elaboration and conflicting perspectives. Even the earliest evidence, Cicero and Varro, dates to as late as the mid-first century BC. There are more than twenty authors who mention the arrival of the Magna Mater; of these only two, Ovid and Herodian, introduce Troy into their accounts. So, again, like that of Venus Erycina, the story of the Magna Mater can be told with Troy or without it. Livy's account is the fullest and contains a substantial amount of detail, for instance the names and status of all the ambassadors to Attalos. So it is useful to begin with Livy and the other writers who say nothing of Troy, before considering the value and significance of Ovid and Herodian.

According to Livy frequent showers of stones prompted a consultation of the Sibylline books, which in turn revealed that,

---

[31] Dion. Hal. *Ant. Rom.* 2. 19. 4–5, Cic. *Har. resp.* 24, *Sen.* 45. Roman discomfort can be exaggerated, e.g. it was 'repugnant to Roman religious sensibilities', the Romans 'did not know what they were getting', so Thomas 1984: 1504, cf. Bömer 1964: 132–3 and Scullard 1981: 98–9, whose description of the priests as 'effeminate fanatics' may itself betray a certain lack of sympathy; it may be more appropriate to compare it to the complex attitude to the Mother Goddess in Athens, Parker 1996: 188–94.

[32] Livy 36. 36. 3, Wiseman 1984. Bömer's 1964 argument that the Romans rapidly lost interest in their new cult until it was revived by Augustus is effectively refuted by Thomas 1984: 1508–12 with Gruen 1990: 20 n. 74.

[33] The more substantial accounts can be found in: Livy 29. 10. 4–11, 29. 14 (cf. 34. 3. 8, 35. 10. 9, 36. 36. 3); Cic. *Har. resp.* 26–8 (with surrounding chs. on Magna Mater, cf. also *Brut.* 79, *Fin.* 5. 64, *Sen.* 45, *Cael.* 34); Ovid *Fasti* 4. 247–349 (cf. *Pont.* 1. 2. 140–2); App. *Hann.* 56; Herodian 1. 11; Diod. Sic. 34/35. 33. 1–3; Arnob. 7. 49 (cf. 5. 7–17, 6. 11); Silius Italicus 17. 1–47; Julian *Or.* 5. 159A–161B; Amm. Marc. 22. 9. 5–7; [Aur. Vict.] *De vir. illust.* 44, 46, *CIL* 1. 1²: p. 235; more fleeting references can be found in: Varro *Ling.* 6. 15; Strabo 12. 5. 3; Prop. 4. 11. 51–2; Val. Max. 7. 5. 2; Vell. Pat. 2. 3. 1; Juv. 3. 137–8; Dio frag. 57. 61 (Loeb, bk. 17), Solin. 1. 126; Suet. *Tib.* 2. 3; Arr. *Tact.* 33. 4; August. *De civ. D.* 2. 5, 10. 16; Ampelius 24; Stat. *Silv.* 1. 2. 245–6; Pliny *HN* 7. 120; Lactant. *Div. inst.* 2. 7. 12; Claudian *Laud. Ser.* (30) 17–18, 28–30, Jerome *Iov.* 1. 41 (*PL* 23. 283); Sid. Apoll. 24. 41–3; Festus 268L, Min. Felix 7. 3; on altar: *CCCA* iii. 218.

'should a foreign enemy ever wage war on the land of Italy, he could be driven out of Italy and conquered if the Idaean Mother were to be brought from Pessinous to Rome'. An impressive delegation of five senators with five quinqueremes was sent east to the Pergamene king Attalos, their partner in the war against Philip of Macedon, in order to obtain his help, which he willingly gave. Attalos accompanied the Romans to Pessinous in Galatia, where they collected the Mother of the Gods in the form of a sacred stone. Much of the rest of the account is concerned with the reception of the goddess in Rome. A Delphic oracle had instructed the Romans to appoint 'the best man in the state' ('vir optimus in civitate') to welcome the goddess; the young P. Scipio Nasica was selected. After he had received the goddess he handed her over to an assembly of Roman matrons, the most prominent of whom was Claudia Quinta. These matrons took the Magna Mater through the crowds to the temple of Victory.

A brief comparison with the other Troyless versions is valuable at this point. Cicero offers an earlier but somewhat scattered account of the Magna Mater and her introduction in his attack on Clodius in the *De haruspicum responso*; he also makes some allusions in other works. Nothing here contradicts Livy's version, even if Cicero does leave many aspects unconfirmed; he supports the date, the role of the Sibylline books, the Phrygian origin of the cult (though it is not so clear whether he believed Pessinous to be the source), and the prominence of the virtuous Scipio and Claudia.[34] The most significant point at which Livy differs from the majority of other accounts is in his treatment of Claudia.[35] She became the subject of a legend which is found in neither Livy nor Cicero. When the boat carrying the goddess reached Rome, it stuck in the River Tiber and could not be moved. Claudia, a woman whose virtue had up to this point been in doubt, proved her chastity by taking hold of the rope and guiding the boat up the river. Livy seems to know of this story but implicitly rejects it: he refers enigmatically to her previously blemished reputation, but in his account no boats run aground or are miraculously dislodged;

[34] Date: Cic. *Sen.* 45; Sibyl: *Har. resp.* 26, Phrygia: *Har. resp.* 27 (with 28–9 on Pessinous); Scipio: *Har. resp.* 27, *Brut.* 79, cf. *Fin.* 5. 64; Claudia: *Har. resp.* 27, *Cael.* 34. Cic.'s *ab Hannibale vexata* (*Har. resp.* 27) may suggest a bleaker picture than Livy, but the phrase is used more for rhetorical effect than accuracy.

[35] For full discussion of the differences between the various accounts, Schmidt 1909: 1–18.

instead Scipio sails out to meet the incoming ship and collects the goddess.[36] Yet the Claudia story captured the popular imagination and is repeatedly mentioned in later literature, whether at length or in passing allusions.[37]

Livy presents a convincing picture of the mood in Rome during this period, which goes some way towards explaining why the goddess should have been introduced. It was a time of anticipation and uncertainty. The Roman People were now hoping for victory; it had been promised by Delphi; Scipio Africanus was planning an invasion of Africa; a successful end to the war could be envisaged. But there were also reasons to be fearful: an invasion entailed risks, both for those in Rome and the citizen-soldiers who would be part of the invasion force; Hannibal may have been weakened but he was still in Italy; nor was there unanimous support for Scipio's adventurous proposal. Portents and prodigies were taken seriously; no divine assistance could be rebuffed.[38] Scholars, however, have preferred alternative interpretations. Some place the introduction of the goddess in the context of Roman gloom and crisis, others have argued that the Magna Mater arrived in a Rome confident and heading for victory.[39] Both positions tend to play down Livy's more complex presentation which combines optimism with trepidation. Internal political

---

[36] Cf. Graillot 1912: 62 for Livy consciously rejecting the story.

[37] Ovid *Fasti* 4. 247–349 (cf. *Pont.* 1. 2. 140–2); App. *Hann.* 56; Herodian 1. 11; Silius Italicus 17. 1–47; Julian *Or.* 5. 160a–d; more briefly in: [Aur. Vict.] *De vir. illust.* 46, Prop. 4. 11. 51–2; Solin. 1. 126; Suet. *Tib.* 2. 3; August. *De civ. D.* 10. 16; Stat. *Silv.* 1. 2. 245–6; Lactant. *Div. inst.* 2. 7. 12; Claudian *Laud. Ser.* (30) 17–18, 28–30, Jerome *Iov.* 1. 41, Sid. Apoll. 24. 41–3; or without the boat: Livy 29. 14. 2, Cic. *Har. resp.* 27, *Cael.* 34; Pliny *HN* 7. 120, Min. Felix 7. 3 and under the name Valeria, Diod. Sic. 34/35. 33. 2. Claudia also appears in relief on an altar pulling the boat, *CCCA* iii. 218. Wiseman 1979: 94–9 and Gérard 1980 consider the development of the Claudia story and suggest that the grounded boat was unknown to Cicero; Cicero's brevity and purpose, however, render his silence insignificant, nor can much weight be placed on its absence from the sketchy and excerpted account of Diod. Sic. 34/35. 33. 1–2. Wiseman also discusses Claudia's name and its variations, Q. Claudia, Claudia Quinta, Valeria.

[38] Livy 29. 10. 4–8, 29. 14. 1–3; these two passages together convey Livy's idea of the mood in Rome, although some might object that only the former represents the circumstances of the consultation of the Sibylline books.

[39] Crisis: Graillot 1912: 30–2, Burton 1996: 36–42, Beard, North, and Price 1998: i. 97; confidence: Gruen 1990, esp. 6–7, followed by Orlin 1997: 109–11, cf. also Borgeaud 1996: 108–10; Burton's defence of Graillot against Gruen gives Graillot a more extreme stance than he actually held, 'that the Romans summoned the Magna Mater in a spirit of anxiety during a particularly bleak phase of the Hannibalic War' (Burton 1996: 36) but this does satisfactorily sum up Burton's position. Livy 10. 31. 9 (295 BC) shows that the consultation of the Sibylline books does not require a crisis.

battles are also adduced to explain these events, but although there may have been such struggles they are hard to discern.[40]

There is less information in Livy about why this particular deity should have been chosen. The Sibylline oracle is given as sufficient explanation. Although little is known about how the Sibylline books were consulted, the interpretation can hardly have been independent of the *decemviri* who examined the books. Hannibal had been in Italy since 218 and the Sibylline books had been consulted at least seven times during that period, but this would appear to have been the first occasion on which anyone noticed that the Magna Mater would rid Italy of its invader.[41] The prodigy that had given rise to the consultation of the books had been frequent showers of stones; the response was to import a goddess in the form of a stone that had, according to some sources, fallen from the sky, a homeopathic solution perhaps.[42] It has also been argued that as part of their push for Africa the Romans wished to offset Carthaginian stone deities with one of their own.[43] Some suggestions, then, might be made for why it should be a stone deity, but why the Magna Mater?

Working on the basis of Livy it is possible to explain the importation of the Magna Mater in particular by reference to Roman policy in the east. The cult comes from Asia Minor, the intermediary is Attalos, a high-level embassy is sent to Attalos to ask for the goddess. This is all taking place at a time when the Romans are bringing to an end their war with Macedon and arranging their withdrawal from Greece.[44] The Peace of Phoinike is being negotiated with Philip, and Attalos is among the *adscripti* added to the agreement on the Roman side. To introduce an eastern cult to Rome was a sign of continuing commitment to the East, to introduce one from Asia Minor a sign of commitment to Attalos.[45]

[40] e.g. Köves 1963; for criticisms of a prosopographical approach, Develin 1978, esp. 17–19. Still emphasizing domestic politics but less prosopographical is Gruen 1990: 21–7, where the Magna Mater reception committee is a show of unity, cf. also Bömer 1964.

[41] On consultation procedure: Orlin 1997: 76–97, who also lists Second Punic War consultations, pp. 204–5.

[42] Livy does not mention that the stone had fallen from the sky, but see Herodian 1. 11. 1, App. *Hann.* 56, Arnob. 5. 5, 7. 49.   [43] Palmer 1997: 71–2, 95–100.

[44] Livy 29. 12. 8–16. For Pergamene involvement in the Magna Mater affair, cf. also Ovid, *Fasti* 4. 265–72, Arnob. 7. 49, Julian *Or.* 5. 159C, and less explicitly Herodian 1. 11. 3.

[45] Note how Livy 29. 12. 16 implies that the peace was not intended to last, 'verso in Africam bello omnibus aliis *in praesentia* levari bellis volebant' (With the war [against Carthage] now moved to Africa, they wanted to be relieved of all other wars *for the present*), cf. Derow 1979: 6–7.

The Mother of the Gods, in various guises, was much revered in Asia Minor and especially honoured in Pergamon.[46] By sharing a cult, therefore, the bond between the Romans and Attalos is given a religious form.

In contrast to the relatively straightforward presentation of Livy, Ovid complicates the picture in interesting ways. If Livy's Magna Mater is rather vacuous, Ovid's is disturbing and alien; noise and castration are to the fore. The emphasis is on the difficulties of incorporating this new goddess. Where Livy's story was smooth and unproblematic, Ovid's is a tale of obstacles overcome.[47] First, there is an obscure Sibylline oracle that has to be interpreted by Delphi, then a recalcitrant Attalos who can be persuaded to relinquish the goddess only by an earthquake and the voice of the goddess herself, and finally the ship that runs aground.[48] These may reflect rituals of delay and resistance to a new and alarming deity, acted out on the stage at the Megalensian Games; Ovid claims that his Claudia story is 'attested by the stage'.[49] How much is the result of Ovid's poetic imagination and how much the product of festival ritual in some way can only be guessed. The Claudia episode at least, if not the other obstacles, was widely known.

There is, however, a tension in Ovid's Magna Mater. Not only is she an alien goddess who experiences considerable difficulty coming to Rome, she is also a goddess deeply rooted in Rome's traditions and Rome's past. Ovid's story of the introduction of the Magna Mater begins in the Troad; the goddess had wanted to follow Aeneas to Italy, but the time was not yet right. The Delphic oracle reasserts the link: 'The Mater is to be found on Mt. Ida.' When Attalos gives up the goddess, he addresses her, 'Make your way; you will still be ours; Rome is descended from Phrygian

---

[46] *CCCA* i collects the evidence for Asia Minor, nos. 348–426 on Pergamon with Graillot 1912: 40, Ohlemutz 1940: 174–91, McShane 1964: 41–2, Hansen 1971: 438–40.

[47] For Littlewood 1981: 386 and Jope 1988 Ovid tries to romanize the cult, playing down the unsettling nature of the goddess, but that is in contrast to Lucretius, not to Livy. For a full and close study of Ovid's text, Fantham 1998: 125–64.

[48] Obscure oracle: 4. 255–65; Attalos: 4. 265–72 (earthquake as a sign of Mother Goddess, Cic. *Har. resp.* 24, Lucr. 2. 589–99, Schmidt 1909: 5 n. 5); ship: 4. 291–330; cf. Bremmer 1987*b* who finds comparable cases to the Claudia episode for resistance to the introduction of a new god or cult object.

[49] Ovid *Fasti* 4. 326, 'mira, sed et scaena testificata loquar', cf. 4. 187 for *scaena*, and Graillot 1912: 84–7 for drama at the Megalensian Games. See also penultimate paragraph of this section.

ancestors'.[50] A ship is constructed using the same pine forests that had provided the timber for Aeneas' ships. The Magna Mater is represented not so much as coming to a new home, but as finally coming home.

Yet, significantly, when Ovid does reach the story of the goddess' reception in Rome, there is no mention of Troy, a striking contrast to the Trojan theme of the preceding verses. This is no reunion after five hundred years of separation.[51] The focus instead is on Claudia. This, as will be seen, is probably a truer reflection of the Roman perspective than the Trojan emphasis of the earlier verses. There may be good reason to doubt Ovid's concern for historical accuracy, but his poetic depiction of the goddess is nonetheless revealing.[52] He presents a Magna Mater who is both Roman and alien, both Trojan and not Trojan.

The Trojan characterization of the Magna Mater is not limited to Ovid. His contemporary Vergil had earlier featured her in the *Aeneid*, where she appears as a protector of the Trojans, in particular of the fleet, which was constructed of wood from her own grove on Mt. Ida. She offers encouragement to Aeneas, lobbies Jupiter on behalf of the Trojans, saves Creusa from a fate worse than death, protects the fleet from the assaults of Turnus.[53] Vergil vividly places her in Rome's Trojan past; her introduction to Rome is not his concern. The Greek historian Herodian, writing in the third century AD, offers a less romanticized view of the Magna Mater than these poets. Here kinship diplomacy is explicit. Learning from an oracle that their empire will flourish if they bring the goddess of Pessinous to Rome the Romans send ambassadors to the Phrygians; no mention is made of Attalos. They easily acquire the statue by explaining their *syngeneia* with the Phrygians through Aineias the Phrygian. In Herodian Trojan ancestry is a reason why the Romans should be given the goddess, but it is not presented as a reason why they want her. There is no

[50] Ovid *Fasti* 4. 271–2: ' "profiscere," dixit "nostra eris: in Phrygios Roma refertur avos." '

[51] Cf. Ovid *Fasti* 4. 251–6.

[52] On the value of the *Fasti* as evidence: Schilling 1979: 1–10; North 1989: 576; Herbert-Brown 1994; for an illuminating review of recent work on the *Fasti*, Fantham 1995. Gruen 1990 treats Ovid too literally, cf. pp. 15–16, acceptance of Ovid's etymological interpretation of *Idaeus* (see below); p. 31 on Attalos and earthquake episode.

[53] Encouragement: Verg. *Aen.* 10. 218–55; lobbying: 9. 82–106; Creusa: 2. 788 (cf. Paus. 10. 26. 1); identification with fleet: 9. 77–122, 10. 156–8, 10. 218–55; cf. Graillot 1912: 108–11, Wiseman 1984. For Cybele as protectress of both Romans and Trojans, cf. also Tertullian, *Apol.* 25. 4.

attempt to depict the goddess herself as in any way Trojan or favourable to the Trojans.[54]

Faced with so much confusion, scholars have tended to merge accounts, so that they form a single story, often prioritizing one as they do so. Henri Graillot in general followed Livy, but rejected Livy's Pessinous for Varro's Pergamon as the source of the stone and partially incorporated the Trojan stance of Ovid; Erich Gruen shifts the emphasis a little further in Ovid's direction, so it almost seems as if Livy is supplementing Ovid.[55] Others simply reject the Trojan aspect altogether as anachronistic and reconstruct the events of 205–204 without it.[56] Taking the more attractive or probable elements from different sources and combining them appears disconcertingly arbitrary. In this Chapter the approach will be to accept that there is something of value in each, not necessarily hard historical facts but rather a perspective that illuminates. Instead of seeking to recover a single story it may be more useful and informative to probe the varied, perhaps conflicting, perspectives evident in our sources. Nor should it be imagined that any one account represents a single perspective; the tension already observed in Ovid suggests otherwise.

How then should the distinction between the Trojan and the non-Trojan version of the Magna Mater be explained? Several possibilities occur. It may reflect the difference between poetry and prose, or at least between poetry and history. Troy had been the subject matter of poets since Homer, so it is only appropriate that it makes its way into Ovid's mythologizing *Fasti*. On the other hand, Silius Italicus' poetic history of the Punic Wars contains no reference to Troy in 47 lines on the Magna Mater, but this is a work that combines poetry with history.[57] Nonetheless, poetic impulse is not a sufficient explanation. Herodian, after all, was not writing poetry and since Vergil's epic was about Troy the question becomes reversed: why did Vergil bring the Magna Mater into his story of Trojan exiles? The answer perhaps lies in Augustan ideology. Augustus did much to promote the Magna

---

[54] Herodian 1. 11; Burton's suggestion (1996: 41 n. 28) that this is dependent on Ovid must be rejected; the differences are too substantial; apart from those mentioned above, note also: the content of the oracle is different, the goddess is acquired ῥᾳδίως (easily) in Herodian, from a reluctant Attalos in Ovid, Claudia (unnamed) is a priestess in Herodian.

[55] Graillot 1912: 25–69 with 40–3 on Troy, 45–51 on Pessinous/Pergamon (Megalesion), cf. Vermaseren 1977: 38–41, Burton 1996; Gruen 1990.

[56] Thomas 1984: 1504, Latte 1960: 260 n. 3, Perret 1942: 453–4.   [57] 17. 1–47.

Mater. He located his house on the Palatine close to the temple which he was later to restore after it was damaged in a fire of AD 3. The Claudian background of his wife Livia offered scope for analogies with the virtuous Claudia Quinta; furthermore, on at least one occasion Livia may have been portrayed in the manner of the goddess herself.[58] Significantly the temple of the Magna Mater features prominently in the reliefs of the Ara Pietatis, an altar dedicated in the reign of Claudius and closely associated with the recently deified Livia. The earlier Augustan Ara Pacis may contain no explicit reference to the Magna Mater but allusions to the goddess have been detected in its floral frieze.[59] The Magna Mater, thus, was very much part of the family of the Pater Patriae. Whatever Ovid's own outlook on the Augustan regime may have been, something of the contemporary perspective on the Magna Mater is likely to have come through in his poem. The Trojan emphasis, then, may be in part a product of these poetic and Augustan perspectives, but there is more to the Magna Mater than this.

The most telling sign is the Roman name of the goddess. Livy's Magna Mater may come from Pessinous and Troy may make no appearance in his account, but he does call her 'Mater Idaea', a name that is surely some allusion to Mt. Ida in the Troad.[60] Her official title in public inscriptions is 'Mater Deum Magna Idaea', often abbreviated to M.D.M.I.; none of the surviving inscriptions, however, are earlier than the Augustan *Fasti Praenestini*, and many are considerably later.[61] Nevertheless, in the literary sources the title 'Mater Idaea' and the associations with Ida can be traced back further. Earliest is Cicero's invocation of the goddess at the end of his attack on Verres in 70 BC, *sanctissima mater Idaea*, whose temple at Engyon in Sicily had been looted by the governor.[62]

---

[58] Augustus: Graillot 1912: 108–15, Bömer 1964: 138–43, Wiseman 1984; temple restoration: *RG* 19, Ovid *Fasti* 4. 347–8, Val. Max. 1. 8. 11, Tac. *Ann.* 4. 64; Livia: Littlewood 1981, Jope 1988, Vermaseren 1977: 75 with Livia/Magna Mater cameo (pl. 58), cf. also Dio 58. 2. 4 for chaste Livia.

[59] Ara Pietatis: Torelli 1982: 71–2, pl. III. 20; Ara Pacis: Castriota 1995: 140–4.

[60] Livy 29. 10. 5, 14. 5, 34. 3. 8, 35. 10. 9, cf. Gruen 1990: 19.

[61] *CIL* 1.1², p. 235 for *Fasti* (abbreviated); others in *CCCA* iii (Italia–Latium), for instance, in full: nos. 228, 261, 405, 407, 457; abbreviated: 226, 229, 230, 240, 296, 357, 360; the majority date from the 3rd and 4th cent. AD.

[62] Cic. II*Verr.* 5. 186 with 4. 97, cf. *Har. resp.* 22, *Leg.* 2. 22 with 2. 40 (*Idaea mater*), Sen. 45, *Fin.* 5. 64 (*sacra Idaea*); the *Leg.* passage is written in formal legal language; for other writers, Lucr. 2. 611 (*Idaea mater*), Catull. 63, lines 30, 52, 70.

'Mater Idaea', then, is independent of any Augustan emphasis on Troy and there is no reason why the epithet should not go back to 205; so little second-century Latin literature survives that no conclusions can be drawn from the absence of examples.

What, then, is the significance of this epithet? In Ovid's *Fasti* Delphi announces that the goddess (and so presumably the cult object also) is to be found on Mt. Ida. It might be tempting to conclude that the epithet came from the location of the cult object, but it would be unwise.[63] Not only is Ovid the only writer out of many to imply that Ida is the source of the image, but more importantly he is not writing history. The Delphic oracle is as likely to be a product of his own imaginative interpretation of the epithet as the result of judicious research. He may well have derived the location of the cult object from the epithet; such etymological games were typical of Hellenistic poets. Ovid had already played on the ambiguity of *Idaeus* earlier in the section when he placed the birth of the Mother Goddess' son, Jupiter/Zeus, on Mt. Ida, but in this case it must be Mt. Ida in Crete that is intended.[64] He appears very conscious of the onomastic richness of his goddess: she is 'Idaea parens', 'Cybeleia', 'dea magna', 'Rhea', 'Berecyntia', 'genetrix deorum'.[65] This should caution against taking this text too literally. Further doubt is cast by the context of the information. It is not straightforward presentation of 'fact'. Ovid had been questioning the Magna Mater's spokeswoman, Erato. So what we read is reported speech in reported speech, Ovid reporting Erato reporting the Delphic oracle. Even without such a distorting context oracles are not noted for clarity.

The predominant tradition gives Pessinous as the source of the stone, with only Ovid and Varro dissenting, the one opting for Mt. Ida, the other for Pergamon. Pessinous is often rejected by scholars, largely because it is believed that Attalos did not have sufficient authority at the time to obtain the stone from Pessinous.[66] This view rests on the unlikely assumption that the stone had the

[63] *Fasti* 4. 263–4: 'in Idaeo est invenienda iugo'; Gruen 1990: 15–19 reaches this conclusion.

[64] *Fasti* 4. 201–14, Barchiesi 1994: 182–3, cf. Eur. *Bacch.* 120–35, Apoll. Rhod. *Arg.* 1. 1123–31 for Cretan/Phrygian ambiguity.

[65] *Fasti* 4. 182, 190, 201, 355, cf. 181, 319; note also all the places associated with the goddess, esp. lines 249–50, though no mention of Pessinous. The passage can be compared with Apoll. Rhod. account (1. 1123–31) of Jason's visit to the temple of the goddess at Dindymon.

[66] For the debate, Gruen 1990: 15–19, Burton 1996: 51–8, Borgeaud 1996: 108–17.

same value and meaning for the donors as it had in first-century BC Rome. The stone that was handed over was clearly important but it need not have been irreplaceable or unique.[67] In Rome, however, it became *the* stone. Nevertheless, the evidence for its source is so contradictory that to come to a firm conclusion may only be misleading. Pessinous' role could be as much a product of Magna Mater mythology as Claudia's boat.

In the Greek world the epithet, *Idaios*, had been applied to the Mother Goddess since at least the fifth century BC, when it is found in Euripides.[68] It was, however, only one of many possible titles, some of which were later used by Ovid. Literary sources often write as if one name was as good as another. Thus the third-century BC poet Apollonios of Rhodes can, within the space of fifty lines call her the Mother of all the Blessed, Mother Dindymia, Mother Idaia, and Rhea.[69] This should not lead us to imagine that these were interchangeable in the context of cult practice. Strabo can both adopt the syncretistic approach, identifying a series of deities with Rhea, mother of Zeus, while at the same time clearly indicating the geographical particularity of some of the names: 'The Berekynthians, a tribe of Phrygians, and the Phrygians generally, and the Trojans living round Ida, worship her with orgiastic rites, calling her the Mother of the Gods, Agdistis and Phrygia the Great Goddess, and by naming her after places, Idaia, Dindymene, Sipylene, Pessinountis, Kybele and Kybebe.'[70]

Epigraphic evidence shows that the most widespread names were Meter (Mother) and Mother of the Gods, but it also demonstrates that variations tended to be more localized than literary sources might lead us to believe. Meter Sipylene, for instance, is found only at Smyrna, Meter Zizima only in Lykaonia, Meter Basileia only at Pergamon.[71] Yet, Meter Phrygia is to be found in

---

[67] Cf. Fantham 1998: 145.

[68] Eur. *Or.* 1453, cf. also *Bacch.* 120–35 for Phrygian context. Literary sources who use the epithet of Asia Minor cults of the Mother Goddess are collected in Santoro 1974: 127–8, who also lists other literary epithets (p. 324).

[69] μητέρα συμπάντων μακάρων (*Arg.* 1. 1094), μητέρα Δινδυμίην (1.1125), μητέρος Ἰδαίης (1. 1128), Ῥείην (1. 1139).

[70] Strabo 10. 3. 12; Strabo can refer to the sanctuary at Kyzikos as that of the Dindymene Mother of the Gods (12. 8. 11) and apparently to the same sanctuary as that of the Idaian Mother (1.2.38), though here he may be reflecting the words of the 3rd-cent. Neanthes of Kyzikos (*FGrH* 84F39), or possibly Demetrios of Skepsis.

[71] Sipylene: *CCCA* i. 543 (245 BC), 544, 550, 555, 564; Zizima: 775, 776, 786, 787; Basileia: 351, 352, 354 (cf. Diod. Sic. 3. 57. 3); apart from the first example all these are from the Roman period or undated.

Ionia, Karia, and the Bosporos.[72] Meter Idaia, on the other hand, is not epigraphically attested at all in Asia Minor or Greece, but Strabo's list is sufficiently accurate to suggest that the name is not a purely literary one. Literary sources, then, may be fairly loose in their choice of terminology, but in the actual worship of the Mother Goddess the title was often significant and localized. The topographical overtones of any epithets would not have been lost on contemporaries.[73]

The goddess introduced to Rome in 204 could have been called simply the 'Mother of the Gods', her most common title. No epithet was necessary, and if an epithet was to be chosen there was a wide range of possibilities available.[74] The decision to add 'Idaea' as an epithet gave a specificity that pointed to the Troad, just as Meter Sipylene signalled Smyrna, or at least Mt. Sipylos. Such a title could be justified by the Trojan origins of the Romans, regardless of whether any direct contact had been made with a sanctuary in the Troad; if the Romans came from the Troad, then, their Mother of the Gods could reasonably be called Mater Deum Magna Idaea.[75] The Lampsakene historian, Charon, who was active in the fifth century BC, apparently spoke of the identification of Aphrodite and the Mother of the Gods among the Phrygians. Such an identification would give added meaning to the epithet *Idaea*, especially as it was on Ida that Aphrodite was said to have seduced Anchises and so become the progenitor of the Roman people.[76]

However much elaboration there may be in Augustan poets, underneath it all is not merely an Asia Minor identity of the Magna Mater but a Trojan one, or at least a Troadic one. That is the implication of the choice of *Idaea* as an epithet. But where and how was this epithet meaningful? To an Augustan poet with

[72] *CCCA* i. 591, 624, 665, 714 (3rd–1st cent. BC or undated); *CCCA* vi. 514, 560 (both 3rd cent. BC).

[73] Burton 1996: 55–8 goes too far in trying to prove that the goddess' epithets 'were no longer *geographically bound*' (his italics); it is clear from n. 71 above that local epithets persisted as late as the 3rd cent. AD.

[74] See *CCCA* i: 312–14, for Asia Minor.

[75] One need not suppose with Gruen 1990: 18 that the cult image is from Mt. Ida, a too literal interpretation of Ovid; Graillot 1912: 45–6 rather unnecessarily offers an alternative explanation, that the epithet was linked to the Sibyl of Erythrai, named the Idaian, cf. Paus. 10. 12. 7.

[76] Identification: Charon *FGrH* 262F5 (Phot. *Lex.* s.v. 'Κύβηβος') with Jacoby commentary, Burkert 1977: 241, 277, Hesychius s.v. 'Κυβήβη'; seduction: Hom. *Il.* 2. 819–21, Hes. *Theog.* 1008–10.

his vast arsenal of mythological knowledge it would have called to mind Troy, but whether it would have had a similar resonance in late third-century Rome must be arguable. In Asia Minor, however, perceptions will have been different. It will be suggested here that it was in the context of Rome's relations with Asia Minor, and with Attalos in particular, that the epithet was significant. For *Idaea* highlighted the ties of kinship that existed between Rome and Asia Minor.[77] The role of Asia Minor will be considered below, but first it is important to examine the reaction of third-century Rome to the arrival of the goddess.

In contrast to Venus Erycina there are fairly full, if often somewhat fanciful, accounts of the reception of the Magna Mater into Rome. Unfortunately none is earlier than the first century BC, but even so they offer a tantalizing insight into the internal Roman perspective, that is to say how the introduction of the cult was viewed in Rome itself. The emphasis here is firmly on Scipio Nasica and Claudia, representatives of the leading families and Roman virtue, Scipio chosen by the Senate and Claudia, if the stories are to be believed, by the goddess herself. By the first century BC this had developed into legend, the subject of numerous conflicting accounts. Consider a few of the variations on Scipio's role: he takes a boat to the Tiber, collects the goddess and hands her *to* Claudia and the waiting matrons (Livy), he receives the goddess *from* Claudia, who has tugged the boat upstream (Ovid), he goes all the way to Phrygia to fetch the goddess (Appian), he is not mentioned at all (Herodian). Claudia made the better story and Scipio may on occasion have been manipulated to fit in; Ovid reduces his role to two words, *Nasica accepit*.[78] Relative prominence may also be the result of competing Scipionic and Claudian versions of the reception, Livia giving Claudia an extra boost. Both Scipio and Claudia became part of the folklore that surrounded the arrival of the Magna Mater in Rome.[79]

---

[77] Gruen 1990: 27–33 also considers the place of Troy and the Magna Mater in Rome's relationship with Attalos but tends to focus more on Roman interests and initiative.

[78] 4. 347.

[79] Scipio appears in: Livy 29. 14. 6–11, 36. 36. 3; Cic. *Har. resp.* 27, *Fin.* 5. 64, *Brut.* 79; App. *Hann.* 56, Ovid *Fasti* 4. 347; Diod. Sic. 34/35. 33. 1–3; Silius Italicus 17. 8–17; Amm. Marc. 22. 9. 5; [Aur. Vict.] *De vir. illust.* 44, 46; Val. Max. 7. 5. 2; Vell. Pat. 2. 3. 1; Juv. 3. 137–8; August. *De civ. D.* 2. 5; Ampelius 24; Pliny *HN* 7. 120; Dio frag. 57. 61. For Claudia, see n. 37 above, also Bömer 1964: 146–51. For Claudia's celebrity, note also her statue in temple of Magna Mater, reputed to have miraculously survived fires twice, Val. Max. 1. 8. 11, Tac. *Ann.* 4. 64.

Claudia's miraculous encounter with the goddess is often assumed to have been the subject of a play staged at the Megalensian Festival.[80] Certainly plays had been performed at the festival since 194, including ones by Plautus and Terence.[81] Some form of dramatic presentation of the arrival of the goddess is very probable, but there is no need to believe that its subject matter was limited to Claudia. She merely offered the most memorable moment in a longer narrative. Rather than a particular, influential play performed on one or a couple of occasions, it is more likely that the story was acted out repeatedly as part of the proceedings. The enormous number of later references to Claudia and Scipio, both at length and fleeting, in such a wide variety of sources, argues for the influence of a strong oral tradition, one that may have been assisted, or even created, by regular performances at the Megalensian Festival.

Claudia and Scipio attracted considerable popular attention in Rome, but there is nothing here of Troy. Either the Trojan element evaporated for lack of interest or it was never there in the first place. Neither possibility suggests that the introduction of the Magna Mater was a celebration of Trojan identity, a re-establishment of Rome's Trojan heritage,[82] or, if it was, it was hardly effective. The waiting crowds had endured more than ten years of war and invasion; for them the goddess embodied the hope of victory, hence her first Roman home was in the temple of Victory. Even Ovid and Herodian restrict the Trojan character of the goddess to Asia Minor. Once she reaches Rome Troy disappears from their narrative. They launch straight into the story of Claudia and the immovable boat without a hint that there is anything Trojan or Roman about the goddess; there is no sign that the goddess is finally coming home. Her arrival in Rome lacks any Trojan resonance.

[80] Ovid *Fasti* 4. 326, see also n. 49 with accompanying text above; Graillot 1912: 64, Wiseman 1979: 94–9, Burton 1996: 55.

[81] Livy 34. 54. 3, 36. 36. 4–5; Graillot 1912: 84–7, Goldberg 1998 who is especially concerned with the physical context.

[82] As, e.g. Lambrechts 1951, Gruen 1990: 18–19; its location on the Palatine within the *pomerium* is often an important argument for Trojan identity, but see n. 21 above.

3. Attalos, Troy, and the Magna Mater

In Asia Minor a different perception of the Roman acquisition of the goddess can be envisaged. The Trojan character of the Mater Deum Magna Idaea would have meant something to Attalos I of Pergamon, a ruler who could count Ilion and Mt. Ida as falling within his sphere of influence. The exact status of the cities of the Troad has been the subject of much discussion. Probably they were allies rather than direct subjects, although this is a distinction that in practice would have been fairly fine.[83] Attalos laid claim not only to the contemporary Troad, but also to the Trojan past, or at least part of it. The prehistory of the Attalid kingdom, as represented by the heroes Pergamos and Telephos, was intricately bound up with Trojan mythology. By means of these two heroes the genealogical and ideological basis of the kingdom was able to embrace both Asia and the mainland, both the Trojans and the Greeks. The Trojan element in this prehistory would prove to be of value to Attalos in his relations with the Romans, offering a common ground that would find expression in the Magna Mater affair. First, however, the heroes themselves should be considered.

The capital of Attalos' kingdom was named after Pergamos, son of Andromache and Neoptolemos, a merging of Trojan and Greek royalty. Both Pergamos and Andromache were the objects of cult in Pergamon.[84] It is doubtless a reflection of the importance of the Trojan side of Pergamos' ancestry that the two sources who bring him from the Greek mainland to Asia Minor both give his mother as Andromache, whereas the scholia on Euripides' *Andromache* which has nothing about Asia Minor names Leonassa as his mother.[85] In Asia Minor the connection with Andromache could give valuable legitimacy to Attalid rule, while Neoptolemos could serve Attalid self-promotion in mainland Greece. When Attalos built his impressive stoa at Delphi, he sited it in the vicinity of the sanctuary of Neoptolemos. In this way he could highlight his

[83] Meyer 1925: 104, McShane 1964: 70–2, Allen 1983: 61; Attalid influence already extended to Ida in the reign of Eumenes I, *OGIS* 266. 21, Allen 1983: 22–5.

[84] Paus. I. II. 2, *I.Perg.* 219–20, see Ch. 4. 2, n. 78 with accompanying text. On Pergamos, Scheer 1993: 123–5, 130, Kosmetatou 1995; and L. Robert 1940: 95–105, on Pergamos in Epiros.

[85] Andromache: Paus. I. II. 1–2, Serv. on Verg. *Ecl.* 6. 72; Leonassa: schol. on Eur. *Andr.* 24 and 32, citing Lysimachos (*FGrH* 382 F10) who in turn is said to be citing Proxenos and Nikomedes.

relationship with the Aiakid hero and mark himself out as the new patron of the cult after the demise of the Epirote dynasty, at the same time linking the dynasty through Molossian Olympias with Alexander.[86] Pergamos thus provides the Attalids with a Greek and a Trojan past.

Much was also made in Pergamon of Telephos, a son of Herakles and Tegean Auge, who had left his native Arkadia to become king of Mysia in Asia Minor. He too was a recipient of cult honours. According to Pausanias the people of Pergamon claimed descent from Arkadians who came over to Asia with Telephos.[87] Later Attalids celebrated Telephos' heroic career in a narrative frieze on the Great Altar, which some have even argued was a heroon of Telephos.[88] Telephos was not a Trojan and did not fight at Troy. Indeed his record might not seem very good. Although he did slaughter a good many Achaians when they attacked Mysia under the mistaken impression that they had reached Troy, he also, and less admirably, agreed to show the Achaians the location of the real Troy in exchange for the cure of an especially stubborn wound. His guidance to Troy was perhaps played down by the Attalid dynasty; certainly no trace of it has been found in the fragments of the Telephos frieze. But Telephos could also offer the Attalids close ties with Troy. He was reputed to have been a relative of Priam, having married either Priam's sister Astyoche or his daughter Laodike; his son Eurypolos was therefore a blood relative of the Trojan royal house.[89] Telephos may not have joined the Trojan forces, but Eurypolos did, killed by Neoptolemos in an unfortunate clash of Pergamene genealogical strands.[90] Telephos' importance for the Attalids was thus threefold. As an Arkadian he asserted a Greek identity for the Attalids; as a Heraklid he recalled that other descendant of Herakles, Alexander; and most importantly in this context, as

---

[86] Stoa: Roux and Callot 1987, with pp. 7, 141–3 on location. Schalles 1985: 104–23, esp. 110–15, Laroche and Jacquemin 1992; Epiros: Laroche and Jacquemin 1992: 248–9. Olympias: Scheer 1993: 124.

[87] Hansen 1971: 5–7, 338–48, Hardie 1986: 137–43, Scheer 1993: 71–152. Cult honours: Paus. 3. 26. 10, 5. 13. 3; Scheer 1993: 134–5. Descent: Paus. 1. 4. 6.

[88] Frieze: Dreyfus and Schraudolph 1996, Webb 1996: 61–6, Pollitt 1986: 198–205, *LIMC* Telephos 1; heroon: Stähler 1978 (rejected by Scheer 1993: 136–7), Webb 1996: 62.

[89] Astyoche: Eustath. on Hom. (*Od.*) 1697. 32, Quint. Smyrn. 6. 136, cf. schol. on Hom. *Od.* 11. 520 (Akousilaos *FGrH* 2F40); Laodike: Hyg. *Fab.* 101; Gantz 1993: 579, 640, Scheer 1993: 148; Diktys 2. 5 makes Astyoche Priam's daughter and thus Eurypolos his grandson.

[90] For Telephos, Eurypolos, and the Trojan War, Gantz 1993: 578–80, 640–1 details the many sources, cf. also Roscher *Lex.* s.v. 'Telephos, Eurypolos (5)', *LIMC* Telephos.

king of Mysia with Trojan ties he rooted the Attalids in the mythological past of Asia Minor.

How these mythological ancestors coexisted in Pergamon is not
clear. It might be thought that they each flourished at different
times. The Telephos frieze may suggest that in the mid-second
century the Mysian king had greater prominence than Pergamos;
it has certainly helped to give him a larger role in modern
Pergamene scholarship. Nevertheless, the activities of Attalos I in
Greece offer evidence that both Pergamos and Telephos were
already being promoted by the late third century. The stoa he constructed at Delphi has been interpreted as signalling Pergamene
links both with Pergamos and Neoptolemos and with Telephos.[91]
The Telephos myth also seems to feature in his relations with
Aigina, an island he bought from the Aitolians in 210. In what
appears to be an Aiginetan inscription the Aiginetans, if they are
Aiginetans, find a mythological basis for their relationship with
Attalos in the *syngeneia* that existed between their ancestor Aiakos
and Herakles. Surprisingly it is Telephos' family tree which is
being exploited not that of the Aiakid Pergamos, but Telephos
would have been a far better known figure in Greece than
Pergamos.[92] A possible answer to the question of their coexistence
lies in a story told by Servius that Pergamos came from Epiros to
help Grynos, grandson of Telephos, against intrusive neighbours.
After the victory Grynos marked this collaboration by founding
two cities, Pergamon and Gryneion.[93] Thus the name comes from
Pergamos, but the population could be Telephos' Arkadians. Both
heroes provided the Attalids with a creditable Greek past, through
Pergamos to Neoptolemos and Achilles, through Telephos to Herakles; yet both at the same time gave the kingdom a secure foundation in Asia Minor, one that emphasized Attalid links with Troy.

Attalos could look to this Trojan background in his dealings
with the Romans. In 205/4 he was involved in two sets of negotiations with them, the Peace of Phoinike which ended the First
Macedonian War and led to the Roman withdrawal from Greece,

[91] Pergamos: see n. 86 above and accompanying text; Telephos: Bousquet and Daux
1942–3, Roux and Callot 1987: 114, though Telephos' association with the stoa may be later
than its construction.

[92] If Allen 1971 is right to attribute *IG* 2². 885 to Aigina and if the restoration is correct:
[διὰ τὴν Ἡρα]κλέους πρὸς Αἰακὸν συγγένειαν. For Telephos and Aigina text, Scheer 1993:
127–8.

[93] Serv. on *Ecl.* 6. 72; Grynos was the son of Eurypolos, so a relative of Priam, see n. 89.

and the acquisition of the Magna Mater. The two were not un-connected. Strikingly the Troad functions as the mythological and symbolic meeting place of Pergamon and Rome in both cases. When the peace of Phoinike was concluded, Attalos was there among the *adscripti* on the Roman side along with the small state of Ilion; together these two were the only parties to the treaty from Asia Minor. The presence of Ilion could only have been with Attalos' approval, perhaps even at his suggestion.[94] It is hard to see a role for Ilion here except as a representative of the Trojan past, a past to which both Pergamon and Rome could lay claim. When the Magna Mater made its way to Rome courtesy of Attalos, it came with the epithet *Idaea* attached; the cult was thus shaped to embrace both Pergamon and Troy. The Magna Mater offered a cult shared between Pergamon and Rome that could confirm and reinforce the political relationship established by joint partici-pation in the First Macedonian War and the agreement which followed it. Trojan mythology and kinship tied the whole package together. Thus the relationship between Pergamon and Rome operated on several different planes, political, religious, and myth-ological, while the shared cult and shared mythology carried over-tones of kinship. All this brought Pergamon and Rome closer together.[95]

Echoes of this may be found in several stories that seem to give mythical expression to the relationship between Pergamon and Rome, whether for the purposes of kinship diplomacy or merely for an audience in Asia Minor. Plutarch had read that eponymous Rhome was the daughter of Telephos and a wife of Aineias, a combination that brings together Rome, Pergamon, and Troy. This may have been a by-product of a story found earlier in Lykophron which appears to treat Tarchon and Tyrsenos, two sons of Telephos, as ancestors of the Etruscan people. Then there is the story recorded by the author of the *Suda*, that the Latins were originally called 'Keteioi' until Telephos renamed them, the Keteioi being a Mysian people.[96] The mythological and historical

---

[94] Livy 29. 12. 14; many have sought to delete Ilion from the list on grounds of implausibility, cf. Holleaux 1921: 258–60 and more recently Habicht 1995: 198; for a defence of Ilion, McShane 1964: 111–15, Gruen 1990: 31–3.

[95] As Graillot 1912: 41 very neatly puts it: 'la communauté de culte confirmait la communauté d'origine'.

[96] Rhome: Plut. *Rom.* 2; cf. Delos in Ch. 7. 3 for another Greek state providing a wife for Aineias; Keteioi: *Suda* s.v. 'Λατῖνοι'; on these and similar stories, Scheer 1993: 93–4; sons of Telephos: Lycoph. 1245–9.

context of these fragmentary stories eludes us. It is evident, how-ever, that they represent an Asia Minor viewpoint, one that asserts the priority of Asia Minor over Italy. Thus Telephos is at the centre while out at the periphery Rome and the Latins are in-debted to him for their names. Italy becomes but a mythological and etymological extension of Asia Minor.

In the Magna Mater affair Troy's significance and value lies in its role in the interaction between Pergamon and Rome. Troy acts as a bond between the two, but this does not allow us to conclude that Troy had any special meaning within Rome itself. There is no evidence that the Magna Mater entered Rome as part of its Trojan heritage. Whether intuitively or following a genuine trad-ition, both Ovid and Herodian adopt this pattern; Troy is present in the negotiations between the two powers, but is entirely absent from the reception of the goddess in Rome. In Asia Minor, where the exploitation of the mythical past was so regular a feature of diplomacy, the Trojan character of relations between Rome and Attalos I will have provoked considerably more interest. For many regions, notably the Troad, Troy had a special significance. The events of 205/4, therefore, may have had a particular importance for the dissemination of knowledge about Rome's Trojan ances-try in Asia Minor, as Ilion, Lampsakos, and other cities filed away the information for future use.

Where the initiative and impetus for the Trojan colouring came from is hard to determine. Attalos had the local knowledge and the respect for mythical ancestry. It may, however, be mis-taken to place the onus too firmly on one side or the other. It is, perhaps, preferable to envisage it as a collaborative effort, requir-ing acceptance by both as part of the process of developing and defining their relationship.

The new temple of the Magna Mater on the Palatine was not inaugurated until 191, a delay that has puzzled some.[97] Signifi-cantly, the inauguration occurred just as the Romans were joining forces with the Attalids in a campaign against Antiochos the Great. Was this a Roman gesture to reaffirm the bonds of religion and kinship which had been established a decade or so earlier?

---

[97] Livy 36. 36. 3–5, Graillot 1912: 320, Lambrechts 1951: 45–6.

4. Conclusion

The Greeks sought common ground with other states by establishing ties of kinship with them; the Romans, on the other hand, preferred to incorporate the cults of others. With Venus Erycina and the Magna Mater these two practices merge. Common cults open up possibilities of kinship and in these cases Trojan ancestry was there to give an extra dimension to Roman religious borrowing.[98] It offered the Greeks an explanation and a justification, a framework in which Roman practice could be understood. With north-west Sicily the relationship was direct; cult and kin existed in the same place. In the case of the Magna Mater it was more oblique, since the cult itself was more diffuse and the primary relationship was with Attalos. Nevertheless, Attalos' links with the Troad allowed the exchange to be shaped to highlight the kinship aspect of Rome's new cult, binding together Pergamon, Rome, and the Troad.

In both instances the emphasis on Trojan ancestry reflects the Greek perspective, the Greek way of looking at the transaction. While it may be Greek in origin, it is not, however, simply Greek; it is part of the exchange between Greeks and Romans, acknowledged also by the Romans. But Trojan ancestry is not yet an integral part of the Roman self-image and thus the way the introduction of these gods is perceived in Rome itself is quite different. Livy's account is probably closest to the third-century Roman outlook, in contrast to the mixture of Greek, Augustan, and poetic perspectives found elsewhere. As Troy becomes more central to Rome's own self-image, as it certainly has by the time of Augustus, so what might be called the Greek or outside perspective comes to coincide more closely with Rome's own, especially in the writings of the poets, who are that much more under Greek influence. A Roman of the time of Augustus could, therefore, locate Venus Erycina and the Magna Deum Mater Idaea within Rome's Trojan past in a way in which their third- and second-century predecessors could not.

[98] Cf. Strabo 5. 3. 5, when the Romans are negotiating with a certain Demetrios about piracy, attention is drawn to the kinship that exists between the Romans and the Greeks, kinship that seems to be based on common worship of the Dioskouroi: Demetrios complains that the Romans 'set up a temple of the Dioskouroi in the Forum to honour those who everyone calls saviours while at the same time sending men to Greece to plunder the native land of these very heroes'; for use of Dioskouroi in Roman diplomacy, see also Flamininus' dedication to the Dioskouroi at Delphi, Plut. *Flam.* 12, quoted at end of Ch. 1 above.

9

Ilion between Greece and Rome

In 190 BC the Romans were about to pursue the defeated Antiochos into Asia. C. Livius Salinator was taking the fleet to the Hellespont to prepare for the crossing of the land army under the command of the Scipio brothers. Landing at the so-called 'Harbour of the Achaians' he went to Ilion, where he offered sacrifice to Athena Ilias. This is the first recorded visit of a Roman to the ancestral home. Shortly afterwards the consul, L. Scipio, arriving with the army, also sacrificed to the goddess.[1]

Modern scholarship has tended to view these visits almost exclusively in terms of Rome's Trojan ancestry. For Erich Gruen we can observe here Roman posturing as the newcomers attempt to acquire a place for themselves in the cultural world of the Greek Mediterranean; it was, therefore, a message addressed not merely to Ilion or even Asia Minor, but to the Greek world as a whole. Nicholas Horsfall, on the other hand, would prefer more practical objectives: a display of Trojan ancestry could offer a pretext for Roman interference in Asia Minor. Jacques Perret, with his minimalist thesis, sees the sacrifice at Ilion as marking the first occasion on which the Romans themselves take the initiative in promoting their Trojan ancestry for political advantage.[2] All these interpretations have one point in common: the Romans visited Ilion, because they were, or were alleged to be, descendants of the ancient Trojans.

Trojan ancestry was surely a factor, but there is nonetheless room for caution. It is salutary to note another recent visitor to the sanctuary of Athena Ilias. Hardly two years previously Antiochos, sailing westwards, had left his fleet at the coast and travelled

---

[1] Livius: Livy 37. 9. 7; Scipio: Livy 37. 37. 1–3, Just. *Epit.* 31. 8. 1–3. In this ch. I am much indebted to Dieter Hertel for allowing me to see his *Habilitationsschrift*, soon to be published in a revised form.

[2] Gruen 1990: 14–15, 1992: 48–51; Horsfall 1987: 21–2 (cf. Momigliano 1984: 453); Perret 1942: 502–4; cf. also Bömer 1964: 133–4, Schmitt 1964: 291–2, Gabba 1976: 87–8. E. Weber 1972: 221 minimizes the whole episode, while Elwyn 1993: 282 suggests the Romans may also have been attempting to imitate Alexander.

inland to sacrifice at Ilion.[3] The Roman action at Ilion cannot be treated in isolation. Like the visit of Antiochos the visits of the Roman commanders can be satisfactorily understood only within the context of the whole history of Ilion in the politics of the Hellenistic world. The Roman presence at Ilion was both more significant and more complex than the mere affirmation of Trojan ancestry would suggest.

1. Ilion and the Great Powers

Antiochos and the Romans were only the latest in a long line of international powers to pay their respects at Ilion, a city that combined the prestige of a major sanctuary with a celebrated mythical past. Their illustrious predecessors included Xerxes and Alexander. Xerxes had honoured the goddess with the slaughter of one thousand oxen before attempting his conquest of Greece. Alexander had sacrificed there at the outset of his campaign against Persia.[4]

Much of the attraction of Ilion lay in its earlier incarnation as Troy, city of Hektor and Priam, site of the Trojan War. Alexander, it would appear, arrived there with his copy of Homer's *Iliad*.[5] But it was not only the city, or what remained of the city, that drew visitors, it was also the sanctuary of Athena, a sanctuary given a special mystique by its presence in the *Iliad*. The Ilians even claimed that the statue of the goddess there dated back to the Trojan War, although this was a claim that met with some scepticism.[6] The epithet 'Ilias' was probably already attached to the goddess in classical times, but the earliest evidence stems from the beginning of the Hellenistic period.[7] Xerxes, Alexander, Antiochos, and the Romans all sacrificed to her while at Ilion. Nor were they the only visitors; the Spartan admiral, Mindaros, is found sacrificing there in 411 while trying to win control of the Hellespont. Our knowledge of his presence is due only to a pass-

---

[3] Livy 35. 43. 3, cf. Briscoe 1981: 207.
[4] Xerxes: Hdt. 7. 43, and Ch. 3.5 above; Alexander: Plut. *Alex.* 15. 7–9, Diod. Sic. 17. 17. 6–18. 1, Arr. *Anab.* 1. 11. 7–12. 2, and Ch. 4.2 above. Instinsky 1949 argued that Alexander was imitating Xerxes, but on this see Bosworth 1980: 102, Zahrnt 1996. The history of Ilion is surveyed in Brückner 1902, Bellinger 1961, Hertel 1994.
[5] Plut. *Alex.* 8. 2, Strabo 13. 1. 27.
[6] Sanctuary: Hom. *Il.* 6. 86–101, 263–311; statue: Strabo 13. 1. 41, cf. Hom. *Il.* 6. 92, 273.
[7] *I.Ilion* 1. 48.

ing remark of Xenophon; doubtless there were many others, less important than Xerxes and Alexander, whose visits have gone unrecorded.[8] When Alexander reached the temple he saw a toppled statue of the Persian satrap Ariobarzanes, perhaps erected in honour of a visit, but, even if not, it is a sign of the importance of the temple and its relations with the centres of political power.[9]

The attention paid to Ilion by kings and military commanders could also have been a consequence of its location. The Troad was of particular strategic value. Bordering on the Hellespont, it offered control not only of the route to the Black Sea, but also of the crossing points, such as Abydos, vital to any army travelling between Europe and Asia.[10] A sacrifice to Athena Ilias would have been a means of gaining the favour of the presiding deity of the district. Moreover, a very public display of respect for Troy and its goddess could also have won the support of the local population, who would have had a very strong affinity with the Trojan past and with the sanctuary, whether they lived in Ilion itself or elsewhere in the Troad.[11]

Many of these visitors to the sanctuary of Athena Ilias were themselves making the crossing between Europe and Asia, and this may have had some bearing on their visit. This was the last or first major sanctuary in Asia, depending on the direction of travel. An army making the crossing of the Hellespont into Europe, or venturing into the new land of Asia, may have felt more comfortable after a sacrifice to Athena. The visit and the sacrifice could have acted as a form of liminal ritual, marking the transition from one continent to another.[12] The border status of the sanctuary was emphasized still further by a panorama that encompassed both Asia and Europe; anyone standing there could look across the plain of Troy and see the Chersonese stretched out on the far side of the Hellespont. Alexander appears to have treated the crossing

---

[8] Mindaros: Xen. *Hell.* 1. 1. 4; perhaps the Spartan Derkylidas in 399, Xen. *Hell.* 3. 1. 16, Diod. Sic. 14. 38.

[9] Diod. Sic. 17. 17. 6.

[10] Magie 1950: 82.

[11] See Ch. 4. 2; affinity with the sanctuary may have been stronger at the time of the Ilian Confederation, see nn. 27–32 below with accompanying text.

[12] Asia and Europe are already treated as distinct in 5th cent. BC, ML 93 (cf. Diod. Sic. 11. 62. 3), Hdt. 1. 4. 1, 4. 41–5, see further Cobet 1996, esp. 407–11. Prof. H. H. Schmitt has suggested to me a comparison with Corinthian sailors who sacrifice to Hera at Perachora, the headland being the first and last point of Corinthian territory which they pass; on the problems of Perachora, Morgan 1994: 129–35.

as especially significant; he is said to have sacrificed to Athena and other deities, both on his departure from the European shore and then again on his arrival at the Asian side.[13] Because of its position on the threshold between Europe and Asia, Ilion/Troy may seem in retrospect to symbolize conflict between East and West. This, however, was probably not the intention of the protagonists.[14]

Whatever significance Ilion had in the classical period was magnified and transformed by Alexander whose visit in 334 defined Ilion for the Hellenistic age. Others had visited and sacrificed, but Alexander was to do more than this; he also made promises and laid down the future of Ilion:

They say that the city of the present Ilians was a village with a small, plain temple of Athena, but that, when Alexander came there after his victory at Granikos, he decorated the temple with votive-offerings, gave the place the title of city, instructed those in charge to carry out building projects to restore the city, and judged it free and exempt from tribute. Later, after he put an end to the Persian empire, he sent a generous letter, promising that he would make it a great city with a most distinguished temple and that he would proclaim sacred games.[15]

The theme continues in Alexander's much disputed 'last plans'; Ilion was to have an incomparably spectacular temple of Athena.[16]

Alexander's visit follows almost 150 years in which anti-Persian propaganda had depicted the Trojans as the mythical precursors of the Persians. Nevertheless, Alexander's approach is quite different. We witness not so much an affinity with one side or another, Achaians or Trojans, but rather an evocation of the whole epic age. Alexander sacrifices at the graves of Achaian heroes and models himself on Achilles, yet at the same time he also sacrifices to Priam, claims kinship with the Trojans as well as the Achaians, and, significantly, lays plans for Troy's reconstruction.[17] Alexander's

[13] Arr. *Anab.* 1. 11. 7, also to Herakles and Zeus Apobaterios; Alexander may have had a certain penchant for sacrifices to Athena (Bosworth 1980: 102, Boffo 1985: 115 with n. 4), but he seems to have been particularly disposed to sanctuaries anyway, cf. Prandi 1990 with 351–7 on Ilion.

[14] Georges 1994: 63–5 stresses East v. West conflict.

[15] Strabo 13. 1. 26, who places this visit after Granikos whereas others authorities (Plut. *Alex.* 15, Arr. *Anab.* 1. 11. 6–12. 2, Diod. Sic. 17. 7. 6–18. 1, Just. *Epit.* 11. 5. 10–12) unanimously give Alexander a pre-Granikos visit. Either Strabo is muddled or there were two visits. Ilion is termed a πόλις by Xen. *Hell.* 3. 1. 16, cf. *SIG*[3] 188, Magie 1950: 904.

[16] Diod. Sic. 18. 4. 5; on the authenticity of his extravagant last plans, Badian 1967, Bosworth 1988: 164–5.

[17] Cf. Bosworth 1988: 38–9.

visit focuses not on the subjugation of the Trojans, but instead on heroes, reconciliation, and renewal.

The mere presence of the army at Ilion would have helped to lend the expedition an epic quality and recall the Trojan War. Yet, Alexander went further than this. Throughout his career he created the image of Alexander as Achilles, Alexander as hero. He is said to have been nicknamed 'Achilles' as a child by his tutor Lysimachos, to have lamented that there was no Homer to celebrate his deeds, to have mourned Hephaistion as Achilles mourned Patroklos.[18] According to Arrian envy of Achilles had led Alexander to compete with the hero since childhood.[19] Many of these stories may be the result of later elaboration, but they are based on the image that Alexander himself was projecting during his lifetime.[20] It is in this context that Alexander's homage at the grave of Achilles should be viewed.[21] For the Hellenistic king, a powerful leader with a large army of followers, operating outside the structure of the *polis* (city-state), the analogy with the Homeric hero was especially appealing and appropriate. Indeed later Hellenistic kings would be found depicted in the heroic manner, beardless and sometimes nude.[22] In contrast to his predecessors Alexander was not merely visiting a relic of the heroic age he was seeking to rebuild it. It is as if this were a return to the age of heroes.

For Alexander the Trojan War seems to have represented not so much a Panhellenic crusade as a battleground of heroes, a contrast that perhaps reflects the differing perspectives of *polis* and king. Consequently, although he may have been the new Achilles, the Trojans did not merge with the Persian enemy. Instead Alexander claims not only Achilles but also Troy and the Trojans for himself. The emphasis is not on conflict between Greeks and Trojans but rather it is on reconciliation, as the latter-day Achilles sacrifices to Priam at the altar of Zeus Herkeios, the very spot

---

[18] Lysimachos: Plut. *Alex.* 5. 8; Homer: Plut. *Alex.* 15. 8, Cic. *Arch.* 24, *Fam.* 5. 12. 7, Arr. *Anab.* 1. 12. 1, *Hist. Aug. Probus* 1. 2; Hephaistion: Plut. *Alex.* 72. 3–5, Arr. *Anab.* 7. 14. 1–7, 16. 8.

[19] Arr. *Anab.* 7. 14. 4.

[20] Ameling 1988, Stewart 1993: 78–86.

[21] Arr. *Anab.* 1. 12. 1–2, Plut. *Alex.* 15. 8, Diod. Sic. 17. 17. 3, Aelian *VH* 12. 7. Cf. also his homage to and imitation of Protesilaos, the first member of the Achaian expedition to set foot on Asian soil, Stewart 1993: 78, Diod. Sic. 17. 17. 2, Arr. *Anab.* 1. 11. 5.

[22] Beardless: R. Smith 1991: 21; nude: Zanker 1988: 5, Himmelmann 1990: 119–20 (on Alexander), R. Smith 1991: 19–20.

where the Trojan king met his end at the hands of the sacrilegious Neoptolemos, son of Achilles and ancestor of Alexander. The sacrifice, reports Arrian, was intended to avert the anger of Priam from the descendants of Neoptolemos.[23] Nor is this the only evidence of reconciliation. The programme of urban renewal inaugurated by Alexander points the same way, with its attention both on the sanctuary of Athena and on the city itself. Moreover, Alexander can claim kinship not only with the Greek heroes, but also with the Trojans through his ancestor Andromache.[24] Thus Alexander straddled both sides and so was able to look to the heroic age to justify rule in both spheres, Europe and Asia.[25]

Alexander's actions at Ilion would have been open to differing interpretations, depending on the perspective of the viewer. Indeed the ambiguous nature of Troy and the Trojans may have prompted a range of sometimes incompatible responses even in the same observer, at one time calling to mind the Persians, at another the Trojan ancestry of the liberator. Lack of evidence, unfortunately, means that we can here only talk in terms of probabilities. On the mainland Alexander's visit was perhaps seen as signalling a new Trojan War with the Persians as the enemy, the culmination of decades of anti-Persian rhetoric. Even so, it is doubtful whether mainland Greece was as preoccupied with the Persians as it, or at least Athens, had been in the previous century, even with the Panhellenic pretensions of the League of Corinth. Indeed, Alexander's visit to Ilion may have made no impact on the mainland at all. A speech from Athens in 331/30, only a few years later, contrasts Troy, past and present: once the greatest of cities, now it was uninhabited. Whether true or not, the statement seems curious if Alexander's Ilion pronouncements were well known.[26] On the other hand, in the Troad, and in Asia more generally, the reaction is likely to have been different. Alexander had entered Asia as a benefactor, showing consideration for the traditions of the area and promoting a revitalization of its heritage. Here, where the people of the Troad looked to both a Greek and a Trojan past, Alexander could be construed as paying his respects to both. By giving his attention in this way and assert-

[23] Arr. *Anab.* 1. 11. 8.
[24] Strabo 13. 1. 27.
[25] For a contemporary view of Troy as the ruler of all Asia, Lycurg. *Leoc.* 62.
[26] Lycurg. *Leoc.* 62.

ing ties of kinship Alexander not only laid down a justification for his rule, he also acquired valuable support for the future. The Troad was a proper place for Alexander to be.

Whether any of Alexander's promises were carried out in his lifetime is arguable,[27] but Alexander had established a blueprint for Ilion in the Hellenistic period. The first sign of an Ilian revival comes with the appearance of a confederation of cities in the Troad centred on the temple of Athena Ilias.[28] Membership included cities from throughout the Troad; Lampsakos, Abydos, Dardanos, Assos, Ilion, Parion, Alexandreia Troas, Skepsis, Gargara, Kalchedon, and Myrlea are all known to have belonged.[29] In addition to their common interest in the sanctuary of Athena the member cities also joined to celebrate a regular festival for the goddess.[30] The earliest evidence for the confederation is to be found in a late-fourth-century inscription honouring a certain Malousios of Gargara as a benefactor; he had contributed very large sums for the construction of a theatre and sanctuary buildings, although there is no sign that he sponsored a new temple.[31] Whether the confederation was set up at the initiative of a king, the cities themselves or a combination of the two is unknown; nor is there any agreement over the date of its establishment. Some suggest the last decade of the fourth century, perhaps at the instigation of Antigonos, while a case can also be made for Alexander's reign.[32] Nevertheless, the creation of the confederation was clear recognition of the importance of the temple and established a mechanism for maintaining the temple in the future, something which Ilion would have found difficult to do alone. It may, therefore, be right to see Alexander's influence here, whether

[27] Bellinger 1961: 2 considers nothing to have been done; important to such arguments is Lycurg. *Leoc.* 62, delivered in 331/0, where Ilion is described as ἀοίκητος, but it must be questionable how much Lycurgus knew about contemporary Ilion. A different picture emerges if Verkinderen 1987 is correct to date the establishment of the Ilian Confederation to the reign of Alexander, in which case the building work in *I.Ilion* 1. 4–5, 9–11, 38–40 may be a consequence of Alexander's orders, as recorded by Strabo above.

[28] Magie 1950: 869–71, L. Robert 1966: 18–46, Boffo 1985: 114–23, Verkinderen 1987, Billows 1990: 217–20, Rose 1991: 72–3. Inscriptions relevant to the confederation: *I.Ilion* 1–18.   [29] *I.Ilion* XII-III.

[30] Preuner 1926, see also n. 28 above.

[31] *I.Ilion* 1, with lines 4–5, 9–11, 38–40 on building benefactions; the inscription is usually dated to *c*.306 BC, a date not without problems as Verkinderen 1987 has recently shown, preferring instead the reign of Alexander.

[32] Arguments are reviewed in Magie 1950: 871 n. 54, L. Robert 1966: 21, Verkinderen 1987.

direct or indirect. The existence of the confederation would have increased the value of the sanctuary of Athena Ilias to the rulers of Asia Minor and any aspiring rulers, because any signs of respect for the goddess would have reverberated among the cities of the strategically important Troad, now that they all had a vested interest in the sanctuary.

Early Hellenistic Ilion must have been the site of considerable building activity. The theatre and certain sanctuary buildings were erected, courtesy of Malousios. Further work is attributed to Lysimachos, who became overlord of Troad after the defeat of Antigonos at Ipsos in 301. Eager to fulfil Alexander's promises to Ilion, he is believed to have begun the construction of a new temple. Recent archaeological work has confirmed this picture of intensive building and supports an early Hellenistic date for the temple of Athena.[33] Whether or not Strabo is right to credit Lysimachos with the building of the city wall of Ilion has been the subject of considerable controversy, but the examination of the surviving structure suggests that a date in the second half of the third century would be more appropriate.[34] Like other successors Lysimachos sought to legitimate his rule and his aspirations by associating the memory of Alexander with himself. In addition to the attentions he paid to Ilion, he also renamed Antigoneia in the Troad Alexandreia and embellished his coins with a striking portrait of Alexander, backed by an image of Athena, the latter perhaps intended as an allusion to his Ilian benefactions.[35]

Later rulers of Asia Minor show a similar respect for Ilion and its sanctuary. The Seleukids included it among the sanctuaries at which Seleukid documents were to be inscribed and publicized. For example, a record of the sale of land at Didyma to Antiochos

[33] Lysimachos: Strabo 13.1.26; for recent archaeology, see Rose's reports of the post-Bronze Age excavations in *Studia Troica* from 1991 onwards, also Hertel 1994. Early Hellenistic date for temple: Holden 1964: 1–5, 29–31, B. S. Ridgway 1990: 151–3, Rose 1992: 45; D. Hertel has informed me that as yet unpublished archaeological findings confirm an early Hellenistic date for the start of construction. Schmidt-Dounas 1991, however, prefers a 2nd-cent. date for the metopes; Goerthert and Schleif's (1962) Augustan date for the whole temple has not proved popular.

[34] Rose 1997a: 93–101 gives the archaeological evidence for the date and reviews the history of the controversy about Strabo 13. 1. 26. The wall must have been complete by *c*.216 BC, Polyb. 5. 111. 2–4.

[35] Antigoneia: Strabo 13. 1. 26; coins: Head 1911: 284–5; on Lysimachos and Alexander: Stewart 1993: 318–21, cf. also Lund 1992: 164, 167 and the rather fanciful views of Landucci Gattinoni 1992: 48–9; other successors and Alexander, Pyrrhos: Stewart 1993: 284–6, see Ch. 6 nn. 11–13 with accompanying text; Ptolemy: A. Erskine 1995b: esp. 41–2.

II's wife Laodike was to be set up in the sanctuary of Athena at Ilion, the sanctuary at Samothrake, the sanctuary of Artemis at Ephesos, the sanctuary of Apollo at Didyma, and the sanctuary of Artemis at Sardis.[36] The prestige of Ilion is likely to have made honours here especially attractive for Hellenistic monarchs. Thus, when a decree is passed honouring Antiochos I (or III?) with a gold equestrian statue, it looks very much like a direct response to the presence of Seleukid ambassadors. Another Seleukid, either Seleukos I or II, is found incorporated into the Ilian calendar as the month of Seleukeios and stayed there until at least the first century BC.[37] All this is part of the interaction between Ilion and the central power, an interaction that continues under the Attalids. Attalos II, for example, dedicated a statue of his brother Eumenes II to Athena Ilias; he also made gifts to the temple of land, cattle, and herdsmen.[38] No testimony survives for Attalid building activity at Ilion, although their patronage of building projects elsewhere suggests that it is quite possible. New, and substantial, buildings continued to be erected in the second century, a time when Attalid influence was at its height.[39] Demetrios of Skepsis may have dismissed early-second-century Ilion as rundown and neglected, but this unfavourable assessment probably reflects the prejudices of a neighbour. Archaeology, on the other hand, suggests that Hellenistic Ilion was quite prosperous for a small city.[40]

The Hellenistic monarchies, in particular the rulers of Asia Minor, thus gave special attention to Ilion and its sanctuary. Several reasons for this can be highlighted, the desire to emulate Alexander and so assert their own claim to rule, the importance

---

[36] *OGIS* 225 (*RC* 18), cf. also *I.Perg.* 245D48, *I.Ilion* 37.

[37] Antiochos: *I.Ilion* 32 (*OGIS* 219), lines 34–6 (statue), 21 and 29 (ambassadors); for the identity of Antiochos, see C. P. Jones 1993 supporting the majority opinion (for I) on Piejko 1991 (for III); Seleukeios: *I.Ilion* 31 (*OGIS* 212), appearing in *I.Ilion* as Seleukos I, but Orth 1977: 72–3 prefers Seleukos II, cf. *I.Ilion* 10. 3 (77 BC); for Seleukids and Ilion, cf. also *I.Ilion* 33 (*OGIS* 221), 34 (*OGIS* 220), Atkinson 1968, Habicht 1970: 82–85, Orth 1977: 43–75.

[38] *I.Ilion* 41, 42 (*RC* 62), cf. 43; for Attalids and Ilion, see also Ch. 8 above.

[39] Were they responsible for the monumental South Building, 'the largest Hellenistic building ever to have been found at Troia'? The building has been confidently dated to the mid-2nd cent., Rose 1995: 95, and rechristened 'Temple A' in Rose 1997a: 88–92. Rose has now (1998: 89) identified the whole complex as a sanctuary of the Samothrakian Gods and suggested that this 2nd-cent. vitality was a result of Ilion's promotion of its mythical links with Rome, drawing in this case on the story that the Penates came from Samothrake.

[40] Demetrios: Strabo 13. 1. 27 (where Strabo calls turn-of-the-century Ilion a village-city, κωμόπολις), Ch. 4.2 above; archaeology: Rose 1997a: 98.

of respecting the traditions of a strategically significant region, the wish to associate themselves with the heroes of the Trojan War, and finally something easily overlooked, the value of winning the favour of the goddess.

2. The Romans at Ilion

When the Romans marched into Asia Minor in 190 BC, they were not presenting themselves as some neo-Trojan army. Their sacrifices to Athena Ilias were as much a consequence of Greek traditions as of their own Trojan ancestry. In making the visits to Ilion and performing the sacrifices there the Romans were conducting themselves as other major powers had done before them. Even without their Trojan pedigree, therefore, a Roman sacrifice at Ilion could be envisaged.

Nevertheless, our sources for the visits, Livy and Justin, do focus on Rome's Trojan ancestry. Since both their accounts date directly or indirectly from Augustan times, a little Augustan colouring might be expected. Livy's description of the arrival of L. Scipio with his army runs as follows:

From there he proceeded to Ilium, where he laid out his camp on the plain beneath the walls. When he had gone up to the city and the citadel, he sacrificed to Athena, protectress of the citadel. During the visit the people of Ilium acknowledged the Romans as descendants of themselves with every honour, both in word and deed, while the Romans rejoiced at their ancestry.

This reads as if it were the first Roman visit, yet not long before this Livius Salinator had sacrificed here, an event reported by Livy with no reference to Rome's Trojan ancestry.[41] Perhaps Livius was simply too unimportant, or perhaps the presence of the army and the consul made it a grander occasion. Livy's account of Scipio's visit is nonetheless fairly low-key. The phrase, 'the Romans rejoiced at their ancestry' ('Romanis laetis origine sua') is somewhat reminiscent of Augustan Rome, a city in which Vergil is celebrating the Trojan origins of the Romans and Augustus and where a statue of Aeneas can be found in the Forum of Augustus. Any Augustan character, however, is not as pronounced as in

---

[41] Scipio: Livy 37. 37. 1–3; Livius: Livy 37. 9. 7.

Justin's account, which contains little information but much rhetoric:

When . . . the Romans arrived at Ilium, there was mutual rejoicing, as the Ilians recalled that Aeneas and the rest of the leaders who accompanied him had set out from their city, while the Romans recalled that they were descended from these people. The joy of all was as great as that which usually occurs when parents and children meet again after a long separation. The Ilians were pleased that their descendants after subduing the West and Africa were now laying claim to Asia as their ancestral empire; the fall of Troy, they said, was desirable so that the city might be so auspiciously reborn. The Romans, on the other hand, were seized by an insatiable desire to see their ancestral hearths, the birthplaces of their forefathers, and the temples and statues of their gods.

Here the sacrifice to Athena has completely disappeared and all attention is directed towards the family reunion. Again there is an Augustan feel to the themes expressed, the notion of rebirth, Troy renascent, the celebration of Trojan identity, the aspirations to world rule.[42] Indeed, re-establishing its Trojan empire in Asia would not have combined well with Rome's professed objective of liberating the Greeks of Asia from Antiochos.[43]

Although the Augustan accounts may reflect later elaboration by those more interested in ancient Troy than modern Ilion, the Trojan kinship that linked Rome and Ilion could hardly have been ignored at the time of the Roman visit. The Trojan character of Ilion had already played a part in diplomatic relations between Rome and Pergamon, as witnessed by its appearance in the Peace of Phoinike and by the Magna Mater episode.[44] The cities of the Troad had certainly become aware of the potential kinship arguments by the mid-190s, when the embassy of Lampsakos to Rome made much of the ties that bound the two cities.[45] Trojan kinship featured also in the immediate aftermath of Antiochos' defeat. This was the explanation, it was said, for the special treatment of

---

[42] Just. *Epit.* 31. 8. 1–3; Justin is not an Augustan writer but he is epitomizing Pompeius Trogus who is Augustan, Alonso-Núñez, 1987; Hertel 1994 sees the themes of the legitimacy of Roman rule and Troy renascent as reflecting an Augustan outlook, cf. Verg. *Aen.* 1. 256–96, where Jupiter prophesies universal rule to the descendants of the Trojans, *RG* preface and 26, Pani 1975, esp. 74–8 on Germanicus' verses at tomb of Hektor; Augustan attitude to empire: Hardie 1986: 364–6, 378–9, Brunt 1990: 96–109 with 432–68; Asia as Priam's empire: Verg. *Aen.* 2. 554–7, 3. 1–3.

[43] Polyb. 18. 44. 2, 18. 47. 1, 18. 50. 5–7, 21. 14. 8; Livy 33. 30.1–2, 33. 34.3, 34. 58–9, 37. 35. 9–10.

[44] See Ch. 8. [45] See Ch. 7.2.

Ilion at the Apameia negotiations and for the Lykian expectation that Ilion could make representations to Rome on their behalf.[46] Although this last example follows the Roman visit to Ilion, it helps to confirm the impression that Rome's Trojan origin was not unknown in the Troad of the 190s.

When Scipio sacrificed to Athena Ilias, however, he was following a tradition that had developed over centuries; it was what was expected of him. Yet, Rome's Trojan ancestry added an extra dimension, a special resonance to the Roman actions here, but it cannot be interpreted as the sole motivation; rather, it was one factor among several. Nor, indeed, were the Romans the first relatives of the Trojans to sacrifice at Ilion. Kinship claims had already been made by Alexander and probably by the Attalids as well.[47]

At Ilion Rome was in competition with kings, past and present, who had shown due reverence for the city, its sanctuary, and its traditions, most recently Antiochos himself. As the Romans crossed the Hellespont, they were seeking to establish a bridgehead in a strategically important region. Through respect for the sanctuary and through kinship they could hope to create and affirm a relationship with the cities of the Troad, cities that were united by their membership of the Ilian Confederation and their interest in the sanctuary of Athena Ilias. Outside of north-western Asia Minor Rome's Trojan ancestry may have made little impact except on those areas, such as Lykia, where Troy already played some part in local history. The sacrifice itself, however, regardless of the Trojan character of the visitors, will have signalled Roman respect for Asia and its traditions to the inhabitants of Asia Minor as a whole. This was all the more important because Rome was not a Greek city, and so some such reassurance would have been of value.[48]

Should we see the guiding hand of Pergamon here? Once the war reached Asia, Eumenes II was a constant presence on the Roman side, participating in army councils and supporting the Romans with troops, ships, and supplies.[49] He was discussing

---

[46] Livy 38. 39. 10, Polyb. 22. 5, see Ch. 7.2.

[47] Alexander: sect. 1 above; Attalids: Ch. 8.

[48] For roughly contemporary views of Rome as a barbarian city, Polyb. 9. 37. 6–8, 11. 5. 6–7, 18. 22. 8, cf. 5. 104. 1, 20. 10. 6 (whose views these represent is arguable, but someone was saying this kind of thing); Schmitt 1957–8, A. Erskine 1996: 6–8.

[49] Councils: Livy 37. 8. 6–7, 37. 15, 37. 19; troops: 37. 39. 9; ships: 36. 43–5, 37. 9. 6;

strategy with Livius Salinator shortly before the Roman commander visited Ilion, accompanied on the voyage by seven of Eumenes' ships. Whether Eumenes himself also went to Ilion with Livius Salinator is not specified by Livy.[50] Later, when Scipio's land army crossed the Hellespont, Eumenes was there making all the arrangements for the crossing.[51] He was not present at Ilion with Scipio, but there can be no doubt that he was an important influence on the early stages of the campaign in Asia.[52] For Romans unfamiliar with Asia Eumenes was a valuable source of local information as Cn. Manlius discovered the following year. About to campaign against the Gauls in Asia, Manlius realized that Eumenes' absence in Rome deprived him of the king's 'knowledge of places and people' and so summoned Eumenes' brother Attalos as a substitute.[53] Perhaps, then, it was Eumenes who made the Romans aware of the importance of a show of respect at Ilion, just as it was his father Attalos who had first introduced Ilion into Romano-Pergamene relations.

3. Troy Falls Again: Fimbria and Sulla

It is another hundred years before we can learn anything more of Rome's relations with Ilion. In the meantime the Attalid dynasty had ceased to exist and much of Asia Minor had become a Roman province. The visit of Fimbria in 85 BC during the final stages of the First Mithridatic War was dramatically different from the earlier visit of Scipio. Fimbria, it is said, razed the city of Ilion to the ground.

Fimbria's destructive visitation needs to be set in the context of the crisis that affected Rome and its eastern empire in the first half of the 80s BC. Mithridates, the king of Pontos, had invaded Roman Asia Minor, overcoming or winning over virtually all the cities there, including, most probably, Ilion and the rest of the Troad. Mithridates' general, Archelaos, proceeded to occupy the Greek

supplies: 37. 37. 5. For a necessarily exaggerated view of Eumenes' role in the Roman campaign, Livy 37. 53. 17–19 (speech of Eumenes); in general, McShane 1964: 145–6, Gruen 1984: 543–7.

[50] Livy 37. 8. 6–7, 37. 9. 6.

[51] Livy 37. 33. 4: 'omnibus cura regis Eumenis ad traiciendum praeparatis', cf. 37. 22. 1, 37. 26. 3.

[52] Not at Ilion: Livy 37. 37. 4–5, cf. Just. *Epit.* 31. 8. 5.

[53] Livy, 38. 12. 6: 'gnarum locorum hominumque'.

mainland as well.[54] Rome, meanwhile, was still recovering from a major war against its Italian allies and its response to Mithridates was confused. The command against the Pontic king was initially awarded to L. Cornelius Sulla, but this was later overturned in favour of C. Marius, prompting Sulla to make his notorious march on Rome to reclaim his command. Later, while campaigning against Mithridates, Sulla was declared a public enemy and a second army was dispatched under L. Valerius Flaccus, who had succeeded to the consulship of 86 after the death of the incumbent Marius. To add confusion to an already chaotic picture, Flaccus was killed in a mutiny, to be replaced by his legate Fimbria.[55] Thus, by 85 there were two Roman armies in the East, both fighting against Mithridates, both of dubious legitimacy, Sulla in Greece and Fimbria in Asia.

Although there is no explicit evidence, it is likely that Ilion and the cities of the Troad succumbed to Mithridates. The sources speak of widespread conquest in Asia Minor, Mithridates sweeping through the northern parts and apparently only meeting with serious resistance in the south.[56] It is hard to believe that he simply overlooked an area as valuable as the Troad.[57] Fimbria's hostile presence there would further suggest that Ilion, perhaps reluctantly, had sided with Mithridates.[58] The appearance on Ilian coins of the Pegasos motif associated with the Pontic king has been used to argue for some form of adherence to Mithridates, although coin motifs are perhaps rather dangerous and ambiguous signifiers of loyalty.[59] Sulla's grant of freedom to Ilion at the conclusion of the war offers an argument in favour of Ilian resistance to Mithridates, but this award may have more to do with loyalty to Sulla than loyalty to Rome.[60] How the other cities of the Troad fared after the war is less clear. Sulla is known to have

[54] On war, Sherwin-White 1984: 121–48, McGing 1986: 88–131, Hinds 1994.
[55] *MRR* 2. 39–60 cites the evidence for events in Rome and summarizes the political wrangles.
[56] Cf. App. *Mith.* 20–1, 61, Livy *Per.* 81 (Magnesia only city to stay loyal to Rome, a revealing exaggeration); for responses of Greek cities, McGing 1986: 109–12.
[57] As Magie 1950: 233–4 seems to think. August. *De civ. D.* 3. 7 does describe Ilion as *non rebellantem* but in such a heavily rhetorical context that no weight can be placed on it.
[58] Together with the apparent need for Ilion to surrender to a Roman commander, Dio frag. 104. 7=bk. 31. 7, App. *Mith.* 53, Livy, *Per.* 83.
[59] Bellinger 1961: 9, 34; if the arguments of L. Robert 1966: 36–41 are accepted these will have been minted not by Ilion alone, but the Ilian Confederation.
[60] App. *Mith.* 61, McGing 1986: 112. By the time of the third war both goddess and city are fully on the side of Rome, Plut. *Luc.* 10. 3, 12. 2.

imposed very severe penalties on the rebellious cities of Asia, leading to enormous levels of debt.[61] An inscription of 77 BC reveals a financial crisis in the Ilian Confederation, which may have been a consequence of Sullan punishment for the Troad, but the crisis could equally be a result of the depredations of Fimbria and the war in general.[62]

Appian offers the fullest account of Ilion's ill-fated meeting with Fimbria. Besieged by Fimbria, Ilion appealed to Sulla, probably drawing attention to its kinship with Rome. Sulla, although apparently still in Greece, seems to have been able to send a reply that he would help and that the Ilians should inform Fimbria that they had entrusted themselves to Sulla. Fimbria then demanded that as friends of the Roman People and as kin too they should grant him admittance. On gaining entry to the city Fimbria proceeded to commit one outrage after another. He tortured the ambassadors who had been sent to Sulla, massacred the whole population, even burning alive those who sought refuge in the temple of Athena. No single house, temple, or statue survived this rampage, with the possible exception of the statue of Athena, though not the temple.[63] The total, or near total, destruction is a theme of almost all the other accounts. The miraculous survival of the statue of Athena amid the ruins of her temple is also recorded by Iulius Obsequens and Augustine, the latter citing Livy, although Aurelius Victor seems to think that it was the temple of Athena itself that survived, on which point he may be inadvertently correct. Ilion's pro-Sullan stance, significantly perhaps, features in the majority of accounts, thus Dio, Livy, Orosius, and Augustine, as well as Appian. It is alluded to by Strabo where the Ilians consider Fimbria to be a 'bandit' and Sulla helps the recovery of the city. The main discrepancy between these different sources is not about the scale of destruction but about how Fimbria entered the city, by force or by deception, the latter possibly having echoes of the Trojan War.[64]

---

[61] Cf. App. *Mith.* 61–3, Plut. *Sulla* 25. 4–5, *Luc.* 20, McGing 1986: 140–2, Kallet-Marx 1995: 273–8.

[62] *I.Ilion* 10.

[63] App. *Mith.* 53; other accounts are Dio frag. 104. 7 = bk 31. 7, Livy, *Per.* 83, Oros. *Pag.* 6. 2. 11, August. *De civ. D.* 3. 7 (citing Livy), Iulius Obsequens 56b, Strabo 13. 1. 27, [Aur.-Vict.] *De vir. illustr.* 70. 3, *IGRR* 175. 16–17, cf. also Lucan 9. 964–9, where the city is presented as still burnt when Caesar visits, but this depiction is unlikely to have any historical value, see sect. 4 below.   [64] Deception: Dio, Appian; force: Strabo, Livy.

Although the events at Ilion were of only minor importance to the campaign against Mithridates, they were quite widely reported in the ancient sources. This was no doubt in part because of the emotive nature of the subject, Rome turning against its historic mother-city. Such an outrage, particularly given the level of destruction and the fame of the two cities, had an especial fascination. Ilion, wrote Appian, suffered more at the hands of its kin than it did at those of Agamemnon. For fifth-century Christian writers, such as Augustine and Orosius, it offered not merely a striking story but an argument in defence of Christianity. Concerned to prove that the disasters of the Late Empire, notably the sack of Rome by Alaric in AD 410, could not be blamed on Christianity, they turned to the internecine example of Rome inflicting such suffering on its parent city.[65] How did the defenders of the gods (*defensores deorum*) explain this sack of Ilion? As Augustine puts it: 'Why did the gods abandon Ilium, blood relatives of the Romans, a city that had not rebelled against its noble daughter Rome, but which instead remained so firmly and so dutifully true to Rome's better faction? Why did the gods leave Ilium to be destroyed not by the courageous men of the Greeks but by the foulest man of the Romans?'[66]

The destruction of Ilion does not coexist happily with Roman pride in its Trojan origins. It might be explained away as an unfortunate exception, which resulted from Fimbria's arrogance and impiety, indeed his 'foulness'. Such devastation, however, was not the work of Fimbria alone but of a Roman army. Alternatively, Fimbria's treatment of Ilion could be interpreted as further evidence for Roman indifference to the Aineias story. Perhaps in the early first century BC the Trojan past was still so insignificant an element of the Roman self-image that Fimbria saw no inconsistency between that and his treatment of Ilion. Yet, there are further reasons for puzzlement, reasons to wonder whether Fimbria's behaviour has not been exaggerated by our sources.

Destruction on the scale described by the sources should have made a noticeable impact on the archaeological record. Yet, archaeologists disagree about the effects of Fimbria's attack. While one archaeologist can place the division between Troy VIII and Troy IX at the time of Fimbria's visit, another can write: 'So

---

[65] Augustine: *De civ. D.* 1. 1–7; Orosius: Arnaud-Lindet 1990: pp. xx–xxv.
[66] August. *De civ. D.* 3. 7.

far, however, no clearly defined stratum has been identified to attach to any such destruction level.'[67] Nor is the archaeological evidence open to only one interpretation. For instance, Fimbria has been held responsible for a toppled wall in the Upper Sanctuary, which was earlier explained as earthquake damage.[68] The ancient sources are almost unanimous in proclaiming the temple of Athena to have been destroyed, but the remains of what is almost certainly an early Hellenistic temple with metopes dating to the third or second century BC suggests otherwise.[69] Clearly there is no unequivocal archaeological evidence for the Fimbria destruction and without the literary tradition to prompt them archaeologists would perhaps not be inclined to imagine that any such widespread devastation had taken place at all. A fair amount of building work did take place under Augustus, but it would be rash to assume that Augustan renovation equals Fimbrian destruction.[70]

Another contrast to the literary tradition is provided by the evidence for Ilion in the years immediately after 85 BC. With such stories of massacre and destruction we might expect Ilion to have been abandoned at least temporarily, but on the contrary it continues to function as a city. It is granted its freedom by Sulla and like so many other cities in Asia Minor begins a new era in Sulla's honour in 85.[71] Nor is there any lacuna in the city's epigraphic record. A decree has been found on the Acropolis mentioning help to the city given by C. Claudius Nero, proconsul of Asia in 80 BC.[72] Moreover, the Ilian Confederation continued to do its duty for the supposedly destroyed temple of Athena, as is attested by the inscription of 77 BC.[73] There are vague references in Strabo and Orosius to Sullan help for Ilion after Fimbria's attack, but

---

[67] Troy VIII/IX division: Rose 1992: 44; no clearly defined stratum: S. G. Miller 1991: 55 with n. 54. Contrast the extensive archaeological evidence for Sulla's capture of Athens, Hoff 1997: 37–43, though even here there may be some overinterpretation.

[68] Fimbria: Blegen 1958: 304; earthquake: Blegen 1937: 43; this wall has been described by S. G. Miller 1991: 65 n. 54 as 'the strongest archaeological evidence' for the Fimbria destruction, though since then Rose 1993: 100–4 has attributed damage to the North Building to Fimbria. D. Hertel has told me of fire damage to the South Wall which can be dated to the 1st cent. BC, also of early empire renovation of the South Portico (visible in Dörpfeld 1902: photo no. 292).

[69] Sources: n. 63; temple date: n. 33; Rose 1992: 45 notes lack of signs of destruction.

[70] See sect. 4 below.

[71] Freedom: App. *Mith.* 61; era: *I.Ilion* 10. 2–3, *RE* 1 s.v. 'Aera', col. 638.

[72] *I.Ilion* 73.

[73] *I.Ilion* 10.

they contain nothing specific and need not have involved any rebuilding.[74]

The literary tradition, therefore, appears to give a rather exaggerated view of the destruction of 85 BC.[75] The writers were aware of their epic model, Agamemnon's sack of Troy, and this may have encouraged elaboration as Fimbria's assault on Ilion is turned into a new sack of Troy. Explicit comparisons between the two were made by Appian, Augustine, and Strabo. The suffering is worse under Fimbria and there are no heroes any more. In Strabo Fimbria arrogantly compares himself to Agamemnon, boasting that he had achieved in eleven days something that it had taken Agamemnon ten years, a thousand ships, and the forces of the whole of Greece to achieve, but this is undercut by the Ilian retort that this time the city had no Hektor to defend it. This time, then, there were no heroes, but if this was to be a new sack of Troy, there had to be extensive destruction.[76]

Literary elaboration, however, may not explain everything. Fimbria himself may have been the victim of more deliberate misrepresentation. If so, the most probable culprit is his rival commander, Sulla, who had some control over the subsequent literary tradition, not merely because he was the winner, but because he wrote his memoirs, *commentarii*. These contained no cursory survey of his career as the twenty-two books testify. Unfortunately lost, they permeate later writing on Sulla's career and on the First Mithridatic War, having been used either directly or through intermediaries by Livy, Plutarch, and Appian.[77] Indeed, for the campaign against Mithridates there may have been no substantial alternative account to use.[78] The intended audience for Sulla's *commentarii* would have been Romans, to whom Sulla would have been justifying his somewhat unorthodox career. Nevertheless, it is likely that they also reflected the stance taken by Sulla while campaigning in the East. By representing Fimbria as the destroyer of one of the most historic cities in the Greek world with the added outrage that he was one of its descendants, Sulla could blacken Fimbria's name first in Asia and later, through the *com-*

---

[74] Strabo 13. 1. 27: τοὺς δ' Ἰλιέας παρεμυθήσατο πολλοῖς ἐπανορθώμασι; Oros. *Pag.* 6. 2. 11: 'reformavit'; destroyed cities could, however, regroup fairly quickly, cf. Halai, Plut. *Sulla* 26. 7–9. [75] See also Hertel 1994.

[76] App. *Mith.* 53, Aug. *De civ. D.* 3. 7, Strabo 13. 1. 27.

[77] Peter *HRR* ii. 195–204 for fragments, Badian 1964: 210–11, Ramage 1991: 95–9, Behr 1993: 9–21, 76–88. [78] So Badian 1964: 210.

mentarii, in Rome itself. There may also have been a need to counterbalance his own bloody siege of Athens, another historic Greek city to suffer at Roman hands.[79]

The portrayal of Fimbria at Ilion fits neatly with the general picture of Sullan self-representation in the East. While Fimbria was tearing down the ancestral home, Sulla was proclaiming his affinity with Aphrodite, mother of Trojan Aineias, a very different and more positive attitude to Rome's Trojan past. Sulla's promotion of Aphrodite may have begun fairly soon after his arrival in Greece, if his consultation of the Delphic oracle is rightly dated to 87 BC. After noting that Aphrodite had granted great power to the race of Aineias, the oracle instructed Sulla to dedicate an axe at Aphrodisias in Karia. The axe was duly dedicated, complete with a verse describing a dream in which Sulla saw a very martial Aphrodite. If it was this dream that prompted the consultation, then Sulla himself may have had some role in shaping the response.[80] Aphrodisias was a city that had initially taken some action against Mithridates by giving help to a besieged Q. Oppius, although whether it subsequently yielded to the king is unclear.[81] Its resistance to Mithridates and its association with Aphrodite gave the city a special symbolic value for the Romans as they sought to reassert their claim to Asia Minor. With the help of Aphrodite the Romans could challenge the usurper Mithridates, who was representing himself as the new Dionysios.[82] But, more than this, by grasping Aphrodite and the Trojan heritage for himself Sulla was also signalling to the Greeks of Asia that he, not Fimbria, was the true representative of the Roman state; it affirmed his legitimacy. This would have been all the more evident if Sulla was already styling himself 'Epaphroditos', favourite of Aphrodite, when addressing the Greeks. The title was officially conferred on him by the Senate only in 82, but that may merely have been the ratification of an existing state of affairs.[83] Even if

[79] For siege of Athens, Plut. *Sulla* 14, Hoff 1997.

[80] App. *BC* 1. 97; on date, Balsdon 1951: 8–9; for the importance of dreams to Sulla, Plut. *Sulla* 6. 10.

[81] Reynolds 1982: 4 with nos. 2–4, McGing 1986: 110; Aphrodisias was not the only Karian city to take a pro-Roman line, cf. Stratonikeia, *RDGE* 18.

[82] Volkmann 1958: 30–43, McGing 1986: 148–9.

[83] Plut. *Sulla* 34. 4, App. *BC* 1. 97, *OGIS* 441, *RDGE* 49. 2–3; on the title Balsdon 1951, Ramage 1991: 99–102, 107–10, Behr 1993: 144–70; Balsdon 1951: 9–10 suggests that it was already used in Greece, though Behr 1993: 155 thinks not. Note also Venus on coins minted by his son Faustus Cornelius Sulla (56 BC), Crawford 1974: 449.

the title were not used while he was in Greece, it would appear to have been a development of his earlier relations with the Greeks.

This image of Sulla as the one legitimate representative of the Roman state in the East is reinforced further by the stories of what happened at Ilion. Sulla, the favourite of Aphrodite, is the protector of Ilion, Fimbria is the destroyer. Their respective depictions reflect their constitutional positions. Fimbria is the mutinous legate, who kills his commander, Flaccus; this is paralleled by his destruction of Ilion and of Rome's Trojan heritage. Sulla, on the other hand, as befits a supporter of the Roman state and the Senate, looks after the interests of Ilion, the mother-city. Just as Ilion turns for help to Sulla, the true representative of Rome, so Roman senators come flocking east to Sulla, to escape the tyranny of Cinna at Rome.[84] Ilion becomes a symbol by which Sulla's legitimacy and Fimbria's criminality can be defined, represented, and contrasted.

The audience for this Ilian catastrophe could have been twofold, both Roman and Greek. Through the *commentarii* Sulla could address a Roman audience and incorporate Troy into his self-image. By equating respect for the Trojan heritage with respect for the constitution he would have an additional argument to impress upon the Romans his claim to legitimacy. If he did so, Sulla may well have been the first to bring the Trojan myth into the centre of Roman politics, albeit indirectly through his *commentarii*.[85] Troy here is being used to promote Sulla's case not in the Greek world but in Rome itself, although its focus on events in Ilion means the myth is still being understood very much in the context of interaction between Greeks and Romans. This anti-Fimbrian construction of the Trojan myth may help to explain its place in later Iulian ideology. Both Caesar and Augustus were adopting an image that was already imbued with constitutional force, one which therefore helped to legitimate their own position.

Earlier, when Sulla was out in the East, still campaigning against Mithridates, this semi-mythological presentation of the differing constitutional positions of Sulla and Fimbria would have been equally valuable. It addressed a Greek audience in the same

---

[84] Plut. *Sulla* 22. 1; Badian 1964: 210 is surely right to see the *commentarii* behind this image of a senate in exile.

[85] Note also the appearance of the *lusus Troiae* in Sulla's dictatorship (for the first time?), Plut. *Cato Min.* 3. 1, Weeber 1974, esp. 189–93.

way as that other image, Sulla, favourite of Aphrodite. There was a clear message here for the Greeks: surrender to the constitutional authority of Sulla; look what Fimbria does even to his own kin. Greek cities in Asia were thus encouraged to await the arrival of Sulla, rather than hastily offering their submission to the alternative Roman government, however close it might be. Sulla had been in Asia Minor before and may have had a better understanding of its traditions than Fimbria, who, lacking a Eumenes to advise him, clearly did not treat Ilion with the respect that was its due.[86] What exactly Fimbria did at Ilion must remain uncertain, lost as it is in Sullan propaganda and the elaboration of later writers, eager to create a vivid picture of the modern sack of Troy.

4. ILION UNDER THE CAESARS: *ROMANA PERGAMA SURGENT*[87]

Ilion had a special place in the ideology of the Iulio-Claudians, a dynasty that invoked Trojan ancestry to justify its ascendancy in Rome. The affinity between the Iulii and Ilion is celebrated in several monuments discovered in the Greek city. It would be wrong, however, to understand Iulio-Claudian favour for Ilion solely in terms of the ruling dynasty's family background. Although their attention to Ilion may be an extension of the image which they projected in Rome, it also fits the patterns already observed and can be understood as a continuation of earlier practice. In acting as patrons of Ilion Caesar and Augustus were acting in the same way as successive rulers in the east had done before them over the centuries. Nor indeed was this the first occasion on which Trojan ancestry had provided the basis for the relationship between Ilion and Rome, but now that the Roman state was embodied in one man it was no longer clear whether kinship was with the state or with the *princeps*. The circumstances of the civil wars would have offered an extra incentive to bestow benefactions on Ilion. Since both Caesar and Augustus had fought their civil wars against opponents in the east, the majority of Greek states had necessarily been on the side of their opponents.[88] Support for Ilion and promotion of Trojan ancestry may

[86] For Sulla's earlier time in Asia, Badian 1964: 157–78, McGing 1986: 78–9.
[87] Caesar's prayer at Ilion, Lucan 9. 999.
[88] Caesar: Freber 1993: 177–8; Augustus: Magie 1950: 439–45, Bowersock 1965: 11, 85–7, A. Erskine 1991.

have gone some way towards repairing relations with Asia Minor at least.

It is, nevertheless, useful to begin by reviewing the evidence for earlier Iulian interest in Ilion, none of which involves close relatives of C. Iulius Caesar the dictator. The evidence focuses on 'Lucius Iulius Caesar', a name that appears three times in the inscriptions of first-century BC Ilion. Until recently it could fairly safely be said that there were two L. Iulii Caesares associated with Ilion, father and son, the consuls of 90 and 64 respectively.[89] One inscription honours 'Lucius Iulius Caesar, censor', who was thought to be the father, the censor of 89 BC, while another notes the presence of 'the quaestor Lucius Iulius Caesar' at a meeting of the Ilian Confederation which has been dated to 77 BC.[90] This relatively straightforward picture has now been complicated by the discovery that the son also held the censorship, in 61 BC.[91]

So, perhaps the censor and the quaestor are the same after all. Lucius Iulius Caesar, then, would have been in Ilion in 77 as quaestor for the province of Asia, offering the confederation advice to overcome its financial crisis, no doubt just one instance of the economic problems that beset the cities of Asia Minor after the First Mithridatic War.[92] This concern for the well-being of the sanctuary would have continued in 61, when he acted as censor. Perhaps approached by the Ilians who remembered his earlier assistance, he assured them of the tax-exempt status of Athena's sacred land in the face of pressure from Roman tax-collectors. The controversy over the tax contracts for 61 BC and the general uncertainty in Asia following the recently concluded Third Mithridatic War would offer a suitable context for a fiscal problem such as this.[93] This L. Iulius Caesar, consul of 64, may even be identical with the author of the same name who wrote on early Roman history and was possibly the first to give Aineias a son called Iulus.[94] His book on the augurate would suggest that he had literary leanings.[95]

[89] *RE* Iulius 142, 143.

[90] *I.Ilion* 71 and 10 respectively, where Frisch presents the arguments for identification and dating as in 1975.

[91] Nicolet 1980: 111–22, cf. also *MRR* Suppl.: 110.

[92] For the effects of the Sullan settlement, McGing 1986: 140–2, Kallet-Marx 1995: 273–8.

[93] Nicolet 1980: 120–1; tax contracts: Badian 1972: 100, Bernhardt 1985: 194–7.

[94] See Ch. 1 n. 40.

[95] *RE* Iulius 143, col. 471.

The main argument against treating Caesar the censor, quaestor, and writer as one and the same is based on the third inscription from Ilion. It honours Iulia, a daughter of Lucius Iulius Caesar, because of her father's benefactions to the city. The elder Caesar, the censor of 89, had a celebrated daughter Iulia, mother of the triumvir Antony,[96] whereas no daughter is known for the younger Lucius.[97] This is not, however, a compelling argument. Women make so little impact on the historical record that it would be presumptuous to imagine that we know all the daughters of the Roman aristocracy. If the younger Lucius did have a daughter, she would have been called Iulia.[98]

There was, therefore, an active interest in Ilion on the part of at least one member of the Iulii prior to C. Iulius Caesar, perhaps prompted by the quaestorship in Asia. Its importance for understanding Caesar and Augustus, however, should not be exaggerated. First, Lucius Iulius Caesar, whether one or two people, is from a different part of the family.[99] Secondly, there is a substantial difference between the favour of an individual Roman aristocrat, such as Lucius, and that of the ruler of a state, as Caesar the dictator and Augustus effectively were. Both Caesar and Augustus showed favour to Ilion, Augustus more so than Caesar, although in both cases the details are obscure.

Strabo in his account of the Troad is the sole authority for C. Iulius Caesar's benefactions to Ilion. Caesar, he wrote, assigned the city extra territory and confirmed its freedom and immunity from taxation.[100] The extension of territory may have been a valuable prize for Ilion, but there is no information as to what or how much territory Ilion was given. It has been suggested on the basis of another passage of Strabo that it was at this time that Ilion was granted the coastal land as far as Dardanos.[101] Apart from this Caesar's benefactions appear to have amounted to no more than the confirmation of the existing situation and we might wonder

---

[96] *RE* Iulius 543.
[97] Nicolet 1980: 122.
[98] For a fatherless Iulia, who would fit, *RE* Iulius 544.
[99] *RE* 10. 1 col. 183–4 for family tree.
[100] Strabo 13. 1. 27: χώραν τε δὴ προσένειμεν αὐτοῖς καὶ τὴν ἐλευθερίαν καὶ τὴν ἀλειτουργησίαν αὐτοῖς συνεφύλαξε, καὶ μέχρι νῦν συμμένουσιν ἐν τούτοις, on which Freber 1993: 20, with Reynolds 1982: 81 on ἀλειτουργησία.
[101] Strabo 13. 1. 39, Magie 1950: 405, although Leaf 1923: 190 thinks that Ilion probably received this at Apameia in 188. Bernhardt 1985: 206–8 discusses the practice of extending territory.

whether Caesar really paid all that much attention to Ilion. It may
have been Caesar who wrote a letter on freedom and tax immunity found in Ilion, although Sulla is also a candidate for authorship.[102] Strabo has a twofold explanation for Caesar's generosity
to Ilion: first, Caesar's admiration for Alexander, secondly, his
kinship with the Ilians.[103] These benefactions are probably to be
placed during his brief stay in Asia after his defeat of Pompey at
Pharsalos, when he is said to have made some changes to the way
the province was taxed.[104] On the other hand, such action did not
require that he be present in the province, but in this period of
uncertainty, with the fate of Pompey still unknown, it would have
been in his interests to win over as many Greek cities as possible.
Caesar's relationship with Aphrodite was also clearly signalled by
his dedication of a golden Eros at the sanctuary of Aphrodite in
Aphrodisias.[105] This emphasis was not missed by the communities
of Asia who together honoured Caesar as offspring of Ares and
Aphrodite.[106] In his favourable treatment of Ilion and his highlighting of Aphrodite Caesar can be compared to Sulla, but unlike
Sulla he was able to base these actions upon personal kinship.

Modern scholarship frequently gives Caesar a visit to Ilion in
the aftermath of Pharsalos,[107] but the evidence for this is surprisingly slight. Ancient writers who might be expected to mention
a visit by Caesar do not. There is nothing in Strabo, although
he provides the only testimony for Caesar's benefactions to Ilion,
nor in Plutarch in spite of the fact that his *Life of Caesar* is paired
with Ilion's most famous visitor, Alexander, nor significantly in
Caesar's own commentaries, where it is merely said that Caesar
'delayed a few days in Asia' before proceeding to Alexandria.[108]
The sole evidence for Caesar's visit is in a poem, *De bello civili*,

---

[102] *I.Ilion* 77; Brückner in Dörpfeld 1902: 457–8 thinks it is Caesar, Sherk (*RDGE* 53)
remains undecided between Caesar, Sulla, and another.

[103] Strabo 13. 1. 27.

[104] Dio 42. 6. 3, cf. App. *BC* 5. 4, Caes. *BC* 3. 106, Plut. *Caes.* 48. 1, though he also made
some adjustments to Asia affairs after his return from Alexandria, [Caes.] *Alex.* 78. For
Caesar in Asia, Freber 1993: 16–30.

[105] Reynolds 1982: no. 12, lines 13–14; *BMCRR* ii. 469 suggests that Caesar's
Venus/Aeneas and Anchises coins were minted in the east, but Crawford 1974: 471, no.
458, has attributed them to Africa, 47–46 BC.

[106] *SIG*³ 760, cf. this combination on coins of L. Iulius Caesar, moneyer of 103, probably
the consul of 90 (*RE* 142), Crawford 1974: 325.

[107] e.g. Gelzer 1960: 225, Weinstock 1971: 84, Meier 1982: 480. Important doubts are
raised by Zwierlein 1986, esp. 465–6, cf. Feeney 1991: 274 n. 107.

[108] Strabo 13. 1. 27, Plut. *Caes.* 48, Caes. *BC* 3. 106.

Lucan's epic of the civil war between Caesar on the one hand and Pompey and the Senate on the other. Here there is a powerful and evocative scene as the egoistic Caesar strides round the site of Troy almost oblivious of his surroundings. 'No stone is without a name', but Caesar crosses the Xanthos without realizing and tramps over the burial place of Hektor.[109] Lucan, however, was writing poetry, not history, and was not averse to adjusting the historical record to suit his own sense of what was appropriate. Thus, contrary to more authoritative accounts, Cicero is present at Pharsalos exhorting Pompey to fight and Cato visits the oracle of Ammon at Siwah.[110] Could not Caesar at Troy be another such literary improvement?

Lucan's Troy scene brings to the fore two themes, the death of the Republic and Caesar's imitation of Alexander, both of which emphasize Caesar's destructive megalomania. Sated with the slaughter of Pharsalos, Caesar travels to the burnt-out city of Troy, from there to come face to face with the head of Pompey. This is a striking series of juxtaposed images, each of which, Pharsalos, Troy, Pompey, represents in a different way the end of the Republic.[111] It forms a sharp contrast to Augustan ideology, where the rebirth of Troy as Rome is equated with the restoration of the Republic after the civil wars. In Lucan's 'anti-Aeneid' Troy and the Republic are both in ruins.[112] In a prayer uttered over a makeshift altar Caesar does swear to rebuild Troy, but this is only in exchange for personal success and it is clear that Caesar has difficulty distinguishing between Rome, Troy, and himself.[113] Caesar's tour of Ilion also echoes that earlier visit by Alexander and thus helps Lucan to project an image of Caesar as a latter-day

---

[109] Lucan 9. 966–99; Peter Heslin has given me invaluable help with understanding this passage. Lucan's Caesar visits ancient Troy rather than modern Ilion, hence my use of 'Troy' here.

[110] Cicero: 7. 62–85; Cato: 9. 511–86, where significantly Cato refuses to imitate Alexander by questioning the oracle as surely Lucan's Caesar would have done. On Lucan's lack of interest in geographical and historical accuracy, Marti 1964: 186–98, with Ahl 1976: 159–63, Zwierlein 1986, Feeney 1991: 273–4. Although the modern claim that Cicero was in Dyrrhachion at the time of the battle is probably correct (cf. Plut. *Cato Min.* 55), it is not certain. Plut. *Cic.* 39. 1 merely says that illness prevented his participation in the battle while Livy *Per.* 111 records that he stayed within the camp but does not say whether this was the camp at Pharsalos or at Dyrrhachion.

[111] Ahl 1976: 212–13.

[112] On Lucan's poem as 'anti-Aeneid', Conte 1994: 443–6.

[113] Lucan 9. 987–99, cf. Feeney 1991: 294, 'a prayer which lays bare his megalomaniacal determination to see the Roman enterprise as his story alone'.

Alexander, a man as demented, murderous, and megalomaniacal as the all-conquering Macedonian king. The analogy is reinforced in Alexandria at the beginning of the following book. So great is Caesar's admiration for Alexander that the only sight that he is interested in seeing is the tomb of Alexander, which he hurries towards with complete disregard for the beauty of the city, an indifference that also recalls his earlier tour of Troy. Lucan uses the occasion of this visit to the tomb to give a short and damning portrait of Alexander, Caesar's role model.[114]

Recently it has been argued that Lucan plays with Caesar's commentaries, compressing some parts and expanding others, and thus distorting Caesar's purpose.[115] Caesar's own remark that he had 'delayed a few days in Asia' together with the knowledge that he had entered Asia via the Hellespont may have been all the prompting Lucan needed to improvise Caesar's tour of Troy, a visit that integrates so well with the structure and themes of the poem.[116] On the other hand, perhaps Lucan found it in a lost book of Livy, and perhaps Caesar did indeed follow custom and visit Ilion.

On the architrave of the temple of Athena Ilias stood the name of Augustus, a sign of another transformation and revitalization of Ilion. As building work commenced again, a new Roman Troy emerged. Augustus spent a good part of 20 BC in Asia Minor, a much longer stay than that of his adoptive father. During that time, according to Dio, he carried out a reorganization of the province of Asia and made grants to certain cities.[117] Doubtless, Augustus followed Caesar in confirming Ilion's free and immune status, something he may have done well before 20 BC.[118] The building work, however, is likely to have dated from the time of Augustus' residence in Asia and may reflect the Augustan largesse mentioned by Dio.[119] Apart from the restoration of the temple of Athena, the bouleuterion and the refurbishment of the theatre are

---

[114] Lucan 10. 14–52; both Alexander ('proles vaesana Philippi, felix praedo') and Caesar are characterized in very similar ways; both too are elemental forces, cf. as *fulmen*, 1. 151 (Caesar), 10. 34 (Alexander). On the importance of the Troy episode to Lucan's Caesar/Alexander analogy, Zwierlein 1986.

[115] Masters 1992: 13–25, esp. 20–5.

[116] Compare Caes. *BC* 3. 106, 'Caesar paucos dies in Asia moratus' with Lucan 9. 1001–2, Caesar 'avidus . . . Iliacas pensare moras'. Hellespont entry: Dio 42. 6. 2.

[117] Magie 1950: 469, Dio 54. 7.

[118] For Ilion's privileges after Caesar, Strabo 13. 1. 27, Pliny *HN* 5. 124, *Dig.* 27. 1. 17. 1.

[119] Brückner 1902: 589–90, Magie 1950: 469.

most readily attributed to the reign of Augustus.[120] There is no need to assume that any Augustan work is intended to repair damage caused by Fimbria's assault. Augustus was able to carry out extensive building work in Rome, including the 'restoration' of eighty-two temples without any such excuse.[121] Honours for Augustus included a statue erected in 12 BC by a certain Melanippides, a leading citizen of the city. Since Augustus is honoured on its base as a 'guest and benefactor' of Melanippides, it seems plausible to believe that Augustus visited Ilion, probably in 20 BC, staying in the house of Melanippides.[122] Augustus, then, continues the role of the ruler as the patron of Ilion.

Although the initiative for this renewed building activity would have come from Augustus, what we observe at Ilion is far from one-sided, as the Ilian response testifies. Here Trojan kinship is often used to give meaning to the relationship between ruler and ruled, Roman and Greek. Statues are erected of Augustus, his son-in-law M. Agrippa, his grandson/adopted son C. Caesar, and later of Antonia the younger, Tiberius, and the children of Claudius. Augustus is honoured as god, saviour, benefactor, patron, and kin (*syngenes*). Others are not exalted so much but the same themes continue; C. Caesar is kin, patron, and benefactor; Agrippa is benefactor and patron, Tiberius saviour and benefactor, both are *syngeneis*, although neither is a blood relative of the Iulii.[123] The stress on kinship is noticeable, especially as it appears in no earlier surviving Ilian inscriptions about Romans, not even the three inscriptions mentioning L. Iulius Caesar.[124] In the inscription honouring Antonia her daughter Livilla is given the remarkable title 'Goddess Aphrodite Anchisias'.[125] For the first time Aineias and Anchises appear on Ilian coins in clear allusion to their famous descendants, though it remains ambiguous whether the reference is to kinship with the Romans in general or with the ruling family in particular.[126] As in so many cities in Asia

[120] Rose 1991: 73–4, 1992: 49–54, cf. also 1993: 98–100.

[121] *RG* 19–21, cf. Suet. *Aug.* 28. 3–29; Kienast 1999: 408–49 on Augustan building, with 434–43 on Asia Minor.

[122] *I.Ilion* 83; for Melanippides, cf. also *I.Ilion* 85, 85a, [Aeschin.] *Epist.* 10. 10, L. Robert 1966: 75–8.

[123] Augustus: *I.Ilion* 81, 82, 83; Agrippa: 86; C. Caesar: 87; Antonia: 88; Tiberius: 89; children: 91.

[124] It has been restored in *I.Ilion* 77, but this is a letter to Ilion, possibly by Caesar, see n. 102 above.   [125] *I.Ilion* 88. 11–12 with Frisch's commentary for comparable examples.

[126] Coins: Bellinger 1961: 39, 41–2.

Minor a cult of Augustus is set up, in which Melanippides, the host of Augustus, serves as priest.[127]

But Roman favour need not come easily. Agrippa could quickly lose his temper with Ilion, when his wife Iulia, the emperor's daughter, was almost drowned in the Skamander. Believing the Ilian response to have been inadequate, he sought to impose a substantial fine on the city, only to be dissuaded by Nikolaos of Damascus and Herod.[128] It was, perhaps, on this occasion that the Ilians felt that honours for Agrippa would be appropriate. Later, in AD 23, when the Ilians competed with ten other Asian cities to be the host to the new provincial temple of Tiberius, his mother, and the Senate, they lost out to Smyrna and did not even feature among the front-runners. They had, observed Tacitus, nothing to offer the new cult but the glories of their past.[129] Trojan ancestry, then, was no guarantee of Iulio-Claudian goodwill. Instead the Ilians had to work hard for their special status, as the many honours for their kin, the imperial family, help to demonstrate. Augustan favour for the historic city was probably most readily bestowed in the early years of his reign when he was still establishing his dominance.[130]

With the fall of the Iulio-Claudians in AD 68 Ilion entered a period of relative imperial neglect. This change in its circumstances is not, however, to be explained solely in terms of the disappearance of its Trojan patrons in Rome. If subsequent Roman emperors paid less attention to Ilion, it was also because they had less need to do so. Hellenistic Ilion had prospered as kings and Romans competed for power in Asia Minor, but by the mid-first century AD Ilion was firmly in the Roman Empire and Asia was one of its most secure provinces. Emperors did sometimes visit, but they came as sightseers to a famous city and displayed a closer affinity with Greeks than with Trojans. When Hadrian stopped there in AD 124, he erected a monument at the grave not of a Trojan hero but of the Greek Aias.[131] Such a gesture was consistent with the creation of the Panhellenion under Hadrian, an

---

[127] *I.Ilion* 81, 85.

[128] *FGrH* 90 F134, Jos. *AJ* 16. 2. 2.

[129] Tac. *Ann.* 4. 15, 55–6, the Ilians 'nisi antiquitatis gloria pollebant'.

[130] For other Iulio-Claudian interest (apart from that discussed above): Germanicus visits in AD 18 (Tac. *Ann.* 2. 54. 2), Nero's speech on behalf of Ilion (Suet. *Nero* 7. 2, Tac. *Ann.* 12. 58).

[131] Philostr. *Her.* 8. 1 (137 Kay), cf. *I.Ilion* 93–4, Magie 1950: 614.

association of Greek cities united by common Greek ancestry.[132] This emphasis on Greek roots could have left Ilion sidelined, since membership would have represented an uncomfortable denial of its celebrated mythology. In response Ilion may have felt the need to reassert its Trojan identity; it is in the reign of Hadrian that Hektor makes his first appearance on Ilian coins, the first new Trojan hero to do so since Aineias and Anchises about 150 years before.[133] Caracalla's visit in the early third century was more a homage to Alexander and Achilles than to Troy or Rome's Trojan past.[134] Nevertheless, Rome's Trojan origins are again in evidence when Constantine is planning his new city in the East. He is said to have begun construction of the city on the plain in front of Ilion before God intervened and directed him to Byzantion. The story, however, may merely be the product of later mythologies about the foundation of Constantinople.[135]

The Romans were an occasional presence at Ilion from the early second century onwards. That they went there at all was as much to do with Greek tradition as it was to do with Roman origins. In Ilion can be seen the history of Asia Minor, as the visits, honours, and building work reflect the changing balance of power. The contrast between Scipio's sacrifice in 190 and Augustus' building projects almost two centuries later is itself revealing. The first is the act of a magistrate, the second of a king, the one transient, the other permanent.

[132] The Panhellenion has generated some disagreement; whereas Spawforth and Walker 1985 and 1986 would see it as founded by Hadrian and having fairly broad cultural and political significance, C. P. Jones 1996 would rather see Greek initiative and emphasize its religious character.

[133] Bellinger 1961: 48, cf. also Lindner 1994: 28–37 on Hektor coins.

[134] Dio 78 (77). 16. 7, Herodian 4. 8. 3–5.

[135] Soz. 2. 3. 2–3, Zos. 2. 30, J. M. Cook 1973: 158–9, Dagron 1974: 29–31.

Epilogue

Within the context of Greek-Roman relations Troy played a mediating role, one that offered Greeks and Romans a shared past, whether through kinship or less directly through joint participation in the heroic age. It was a collaborative effort that required each to acknowledge the claims of the other. As the examples studied in Part III suggest, it resonated most forcefully in those regions that themselves possessed well-established Trojan traditions, especially the Troad and the combined area of Sicily, South Italy, and the western coast of Greece.

Outside such regions Rome's Trojan ancestry may often have been a matter of indifference if it did not engage with the concerns of the local population. When Chios in the early second century BC celebrated its relationship with Rome, its focus fell not on Aineias but on Romulus and Remus.[1] Whatever reason the Chians had for preferring Romulus and his brother over Aineias, it is not a choice we would expect the people of Ilion to have made. Indifference was one possible response to Rome's Trojan ancestry, but some Greeks may simply have been unaware of it. Even at the time of Augustus Dionysios of Halikarnassos could complain about the inadequacy of Greek knowledge of early Roman history, and in particular about the ignorance of some Greek historians about Aineias' presence in Italy.[2]

Classical Athens had shown how Troy could be used to represent conflict with the barbarian, but nonetheless Rome's Trojan past appears to have made little impact on anti-Roman propaganda. Even the case for its role in Pyrrhos' Italian campaign is fairly weak.[3] It is possible that the evidence has not survived, but it is more probable that circumstances were not right. Successful

---

[1] Derow and Forrest 1982: 85–6 on lines 25–8.

[2] Dion. Hal. *Ant. Rom.* 1. 4. 2, 45. 4, 53. 4.

[3] See Ch. 6; in spite of Candiloro 1965: 171–6 and Momigliano 1984: 450 the fictitious letter of Hannibal to the Athenians in which he promises a worse fate for the Romans than their Trojan ancestors had suffered at Greek hands is surely not anti-Roman propaganda, cf. Merkelbach 1954: 54 and Leidl 1995, both of whom print the text.

propaganda needs to exploit the knowledge and prejudices of its audience. Here it required first that Greeks in general knew that the Romans were the descendants of the Trojans, and secondly that the Greeks had a negative view of the Trojans. Neither of these requirements could be said to have been satisfied. Indeed those who knew most about Rome's origins, for instance those in the Troad, were those least likely to be swayed by this form of propaganda. Moreover, the chief propagandists against Rome would have been the kings and they may have been reluctant to dwell on Rome's Trojan credentials. For they themselves often asserted at least partial Trojan ancestry, if only as an element of their inheritance from Alexander the Great, or because they laid claim to Asia and the Troad. It was better instead to emphasize that the Romans were barbarians and damn them accordingly.[4]

This book has focused on the pre-Augustan world, occasionally straying beyond. Augustus changed everything, redefining Rome's Trojan past and adding new meaning to it. Aineias became identified with the imperial family and his story became a myth of the Roman Empire as a whole; it was no longer one shared only between Greeks and Romans. The Augustan Aineias could be found from one end of the Mediterranean to the other. In Aphrodisias Aineias and his family in flight appeared among the reliefs that decorated the Sebasteion, the impressive temple complex of the imperial cult built in the mid-first century AD.[5] Far from Asia the same scene forms a statue group which stood prominently in the centre of Augusta Emerita, one of Augustus' Spanish colonies.[6] The emphasis was now more on Aineias than on Troy, and the common factor was more the emperor than Rome.

This close association with the Iulio-Claudians may have led to a certain decline in the myth after the fall of the dynasty; something of this was observed in the last chapter. Nonetheless, Hadrian could still compose verses in Greek that called his emperor Trajan 'son of Aineias'.[7] Dio Chrysostom, speaking at Ilion,

---

[4] Polyb. 5. 104. 1, 9. 37–9, 11. 5. 6–7, 18. 22.8, Dion. Hal. *Ant. Rom.* 1. 4. 2, cf. A. Erskine 1996*a*.

[5] Relief: R. Smith 1990: 98 with fig. 9, Rose 1997*b*: 167–8, who considers all the possible Aineias reliefs in the building, but perhaps underestimates the importance of Anchises, the link between the local goddess and Aineias; for instance, one panel may show Aineias facing the shade not of Palinurus but of Anchises. Imperial cult and Aineias: Reynolds 1986: 111–12; for the Aineias theme in imperial Asia Minor, esp. Troad, Lindner 1994: 25–75.

[6] De la Barrera and Trillmich 1996.

[7] *Anth. Pal.* 6. 332, Page 1981: 562, no. 1.

could praise the Romans as descendants of the Trojans in the course of displaying the brilliance of his rhetorical skills as he demonstrated that contrary to received opinion the Trojans had actually been the victors in the Trojan War.[8] The potency of the Trojan myth even continued into the later empire when Frankish tribes were discovered to have Trojan blood.[9] Later still, the twelfth-century Welsh bishop, Geoffrey of Monmouth, opened his *History of the Kings of Britain* with the story of Brutus, eponymous first king of the Britons. This king was remarkably a grandson of Aeneas, forced into British exile after inadvertently bringing about the deaths of both his parents.[10]

Augustus had made the story of Rome's Trojan ancestry well known throughout the Mediterranean, yet Greeks seem to have been able to acknowledge Rome's Trojan past while at the same time keeping it at a distance. Cities do not seem to have been unduly concerned that their own claims may have conflicted with those of Rome. The Argives, for instance, boasted of their owner-ship of the Palladion and even gave this local tradition official status by placing a representation of the statue on their coinage.[11] Perhaps this was local patriotism challenging Rome in some small way, but it is also worth considering another Argive example. In the late first or early second century AD the Argives made an appeal to the Roman governor in Greece, an appeal which had the support of an unknown but important Greek. In his letter of recommendation this man listed Argive achievements beginning with their leadership in the Trojan War.[12] That the Argives should be proud of their role in the war is hardly surprising, but that this should be a way of winning Roman favour is more so. It appears that it was possible to treat the Trojan War and Rome's Trojan origins as two entirely distinct matters, as if they existed in separate compartments.

The literary and scholarly tradition shows signs of similar compartmentalization. Roman rule did nothing to diminish the tendency of intellectuals to regard the Trojans as barbarians. The Homeric scholia were the product of extensive study of the text of

---

[8] Dio Chrys. 11, esp. 137–42, Swain 1996: 210–11.

[9] Barlow 1995, cf. Toohey 1984 : 24 n. 40 for other examples of Trojan ancestry in the later West.

[10] MacDougall 1982: 7–9.

[11] Ch. 4.3 above.

[12] [Julian], *Epist.* 198, 407bc; on date: Spawforth 1994.

Epilogue

Homer from Hellenistic through to Byzantine times. The writers of these commentaries explicitly and repeatedly turned to the barbarian character of the Trojans to explain aspects of their behaviour or culture. They were assumed to have all the faults typical of barbarians, boastfulness, irrationality, savagery, a tendency towards excessive grief and anger. When Pedaios, the son of Antenor, is described by Homer as *nothos*, a bastard, helpful commentators inform the reader that it is a barbarian custom to father children from many women, or, in another version, that it is a barbarian custom to have sex with many women.[13]

Pausanias too could term the Trojans 'barbarians' when describing a group of sculptures dedicated at Olympia by Apollonia. He observes how barbarian is fighting Greek, Helenos against Odysseus, Paris against Menelaos, Aineias against Diomedes, Deiphobos against Telemonian Aias. Here the Trojans, Aineias included, are clearly barbarians, even though Pausanias knew well Rome's Trojan ancestry.[14] Yet, it would be wrong to conclude from this evidence that any of these writers considered the Romans to be barbarians. Rather their perspective would have been common among Greek intellectuals, familiar with a literary tradition that went back to classical Athens; Rome was simply irrelevant. No doubt the atticizing tendencies of the so-called Second Sophistic gave further encouragement to this way of seeing the Trojans. When Rome did come into the story, however, the representation of the Trojans was different. Thus, Pausanias in his description of the settlement of Sardinia can write of Greeks, Trojans, and barbarians, distinguishing between Trojans and barbarians. But the context is now the western migrations and the Trojans in question are those who fled Troy with Aineias. This is Rome's world in both geography and subject matter, something quite separate from the scholarly interpretation of the Trojan War itself. The three categories, Greeks, Trojans, and barbarians, recall the way that Greeks of Pausanias' own day

[13] e.g. scholia (Erbse) to 11. 432–3, 20. 234 (boastfulness), 13. 137, 17. 248–55 (irrationality), 8. 96 (savagery), 24. 664 (grief), 18. 154–6 (anger), 5. 70 (bastard), cf. also 1. 454, 9.137, 13. 807, 14. 137; in general E. Hall 1989: 23–4.
[14] Sculpture: Paus. 5. 22. 2; contrary to Malkin 1998: 138, 203, 209 this cannot be taken as evidence that the 5th-cent. Apollonians themselves thought that the Trojans were barbarians; that Pausanias did is suggested also by 9. 9 where the Seven against Thebes is the most noteworthy war between Greeks in the heroic period. Romans: 1. 11. 7, 1. 12. 1, 2. 35. 5, Swain 1996: 350.

sometimes spoke of Greeks, Romans, and barbarians, leaving the Romans as a third category who were not quite Greek and not quite barbarian.[15]

In Rome itself it was rather different. Here Rome's Trojan past and the literary and scholarly tradition on the Trojan Wars could not so easily be kept distinct. Vergil, needing to use both in the composition of the *Aeneid*, addressed the problem of the Trojan stereotype in his ninth book. During the siege of the Trojan camp the Italian warrior Numanus delivers a speech extolling the tough and warlike Italians and belittling the effeminate and self-indulgent Trojans. Ascanius promptly shoots him dead, a forceful rebuttal, though one which is perhaps partially undercut by his use of a bow, a weapon sometimes associated with cowardice.[16]

The meaning of the Trojan War changed constantly, adapting to time and place. Especially suggestive is a representation of the fall of Troy from Dura-Europos, a city on the Euphrates which served as the empire's eastern bulwark against Parthian and Sassanid neighbours. Excavations have uncovered a painted shield of the third century AD, decorated with two scenes, the wooden horse before the walls of Troy, and the slaughter of Priam and other Trojans at a banquet. Citizens of Dura may have seen in these pictures their own rather difficult relationship with their eastern neighbours. For not only do the Trojans have a decidedly oriental dress sense but in a curious twist to the imagery of the Trojan War the Greeks are dressed as Roman legionaries.[17]

[15] Sardinia: Paus. 10. 17. 6; Greeks, Romans, barbarians: Dio 44. 2. 2, Artemidoros 1. 53, C. P. Jones 1971: 124–5.

[16] Verg. *Aen.* 9. 590–663 with 614–20 on Trojans, cf. 4. 215–17 and 12. 99–100; Hardie 1994: 185–211 with 199 on the use of bow.

[17] Fully discussed in Hopkins 1939: 326–49, who notes the Roman costume (349), cf. also Wiencke 1954: 306, Perkins 1973: 34 with fig. 9, *LIMC* Equus Troianus 12, *LIMC* Priamos 110.

References

Agostiniani, L. 1977. *Iscrizioni anelleniche di Sicilia.* i: *Le iscrizioni elime.* Florence.

Ahl, F. 1976. *Lucan: An Introduction.* Ithaca.

Ahlberg-Cornell, G. 1992. *Myth and Epos in Early Greek Art: Representation and Interpretation.* Jonsered.

Alcock, S. 1997. 'The Heroic Past in a Hellenistic Present'. In Cartledge, Garnsey, and Gruen 1997: 20–34.

Alcock, S., and Osborne, R. (eds.). 1994. *Placing the Gods: Sanctuaries and Sacred Space in Ancient Greece.* Oxford.

Alföldi, A. 1957. *Die trojanischen Urahnen der Römer.* Basle. (Republished Rome 1979.)

——1965. *Early Rome and the Latins.* Ann Arbor.

Allen, R. E. 1971. 'Attalos I and Aigina'. *BSA* 66: 1–12.

——1983. *The Attalid Kingdom: A Constitutional History.* Oxford.

Aloni, A. 1994. 'L'elegia di Simonide dedicata alla battaglia di Platea (Sim. frr. 10–18W²) e l'occasione della sua performance'. *ZPE* 102: 9–22.

Alonso-Núñez, J. M. 1987. 'An Augustan World History: The *Historiae Philippicae* of Pompeius Trogus'. *Greece and Rome,* 34: 56–72.

Ameling, W. 1988. 'Alexander und Achilleus: ein Bestandsaufnahme'. In W. Will and G. Heinrichs (eds.), *Zu Alexander d. Gr. Festschrift G. Wirth.* Amsterdam. 657–92.

Ampolo, C. 1990. 'Roma e il mondo greco dal secolo VIII agl'inizi del III a.C.'. In G. Pugliese Carratelli (ed.), *Roma e l'Italia: Radices imperii.* Milan. 583–626.

——1992. 'Enea ed Ulisse nel Lazio da Ellanico (*FGrHIST* 4 F84) a Festo (432L).' *Parola del Passato,* 47: 321–42.

——1994. 'La ricezione dei miti greci nel Lazio: l'esempio di Elpenore e Ulisse al Circeo'. *Parola del Passato,* 49: 268–79.

Anderson, M. J. 1997. *The Fall of Troy in Early Greek Poetry and Art.* Oxford.

Arafat, K. W. 1996. *Pausanias' Greece: Ancient Artists and Roman Rulers.* Cambridge.

Arnaud-Lindet, M.-P. 1990. *Orose, Histoires (Contre les Paiens).* i. Paris.

Atkinson, K. M. T. 1968. 'The Seleucids and the Greek Cities of Western Asia Minor'. *Antichthon,* 2: 32–57.

Austin, R. G. 1959. 'Virgil and the Wooden Horse'. *JRS* 49: 16–25.

References

Austin, R. G. 1964. *P. Vergili Maronis Aeneidos liber secundus*. Oxford.
——1971. *P. Vergili Maronis Aeneidos liber primus*. Oxford.
Bacon, H. H. 1961. *Barbarians in Greek Tragedy*. New Haven.
Badian, E. 1964. *Studies in Greek and Roman History*. Oxford.
——1966. 'The Early Historians'. In T. A. Dorey (ed.), *Latin Historians*. London. 1–38.
——1967. 'A King's Notebooks'. *Harv. Stud.* 72: 183–204.
——1972. *Publicans and Sinners: Private Enterprise in the Service of the Roman Republic*. Oxford.
Balsdon, J. P. V. D. 1951. 'Sulla Felix'. *JRS* 41: 1–10.
Barchiesi, A. 1994. *Il poeta e il principe: Ovidio e il discorso augusteo*. Bari.
Barlow, J. 1995. 'Gregory of Tours and the Myth of the Trojan Origins of the Franks'. *Frühmittelalterliche Studien*, 29: 86–95.
Barrera, J. L. de la, and Trillmich, W. 1996. 'Eine Wiederholung der Aeneas-Gruppe vom Forum Augustum samt ihrer Inschrift in Mérida (Spanien)'. *MDAI (R)* 103: 119–38.
Barsby, J. A. 1986. *Plautus Bacchides*. Warminster.
Baslez, M.-F., and Vial, C. 1987. 'La Diplomatie de Délos dans le premier tiers du IIᵉ Siècle'. *BCH* 111: 281–312.
Bayet, J. 1926. *Les Origines de l'Hercule romain*. Paris.
Beard, M., North, J., and Price, S. 1998. *The Religions of Rome*. 2 vols. Cambridge.
Behr, H. 1993. *Die Selbstdarstellung Sullas: ein aristokratischer Politiker zwischen persönlichem Führungsanspruch und Standessolidarität*. Frankfurt.
Bellinger, A. R. 1961. *Troy: The Coins*. Princeton.
Beloch, K. 1925. *Griechische Geschichte*. 2nd edn. iv/i. Berlin.
Bentley, J. 1985. *Restless bones: The story of relics*. London.
Bérard, J. 1957. *La Colonisation grecque de l'Italie méridionale et de la Sicile dans l'antiquité: l'histoire et la légende*. 2nd edn. Paris.
Berger, E. 1986. *Der Parthenon in Basel: Dokumentation zu den Metopen*. Mainz.
Bernhardt, R. 1985. *Polis und römische Herrschaft in der späten Republik (149–31 v.Chr.)*. Berlin.
Berthold, R. 1984. *Rhodes in the Hellenistic Age*. Ithaca.
Bickerman, E. J. 1952. 'Origines Gentium'. *C.Phil.* 47: 65–81.
Bickermann, E. 1932. 'Rom und Lampsakos'. *Philologos*, 87: 277–99.
Billows, R. A. 1990. *Antigonos the One-Eyed and the Creation of the Hellenistic State*. Berkeley.
Birge, D. 1994. 'Trees in the Landscape of Pausanias' *Periegesis*'. In Alcock and Osborne 1994: 231–45.
Blanck, H. 1997. 'Un nuovo frammento del "Catalogo" della biblioteca di Tauromenion'. *Parola del Passato*, 52: 241–55.
Blegen, C. W. 1937. 'Excavations at Troy, 1936'. *AJArch.* 41: 17–51.

References

——(ed.). 1958. *Troy IV: Settlements VIIa, VIIb, VIII*. Princeton.
——1963. *Troy and the Trojans*. London.
Boardman, J. 1975. *Athenian Red Figure Vases: The Archaic Period*. London.
——1980. *The Greeks Overseas: Their Early Colonies and Trade*. 3rd edn. London.
——1989. *Athenian Red Figure Vases: The Classical Period*. London.
Boedeker, D. 1996. 'Heroic Historiography: Simonides and Herodotus on Plataea'. In Boedeker and Sider 1996: 223–42.
——1998. 'The New Simonides and Heroization at Plataia'. In N. Fisher and H. van Wees (eds.), *Archaic Greece: New Approaches and New Evidence*. London. 231–49.
Boedeker, D., and Sider, D. (eds.). 1996. *The New Simonides*. Baltimore (=*Arethusa* 29/2).
Bömer, F. 1951. *Rom und Troia*. Baden-Baden.
——1958. *P. Ovidius Naso, Die Fasten*. ii: *Kommentar*. Heidelberg.
——1964. 'Kybele in Rom, die Geschichte ihres Kults als politisches Phänomen'. *MDAI (R)* 71: 130–51.
——1982. *P. Ovidius Naso*, Metamorphosen: *Books XII–XIII*. Heidelberg.
Boersma, J. S. 1970. *Athenian Building Policy from 561/0–405/4 B.C.* Groningen.
Boffo, L. 1985. *I re ellenistici e i centri religiosi dell'Asia Minore*. Florence.
Bol, P. C. 1989. *Argivische Schilde*. Olympische Forschungen 17. Berlin.
Bonnechere, P. 1994. *Le sacrifice humain en Grèce ancienne*. Athens.
Borgeaud, 1996. *La Mère des dieux de Cybèle à la Vierge Marie*. Paris.
Bosworth, A. B. 1980. *A Historical Commentary on Arrian's History of Alexander*. i. Oxford.
——1988. *Conquest and Empire: The Reign of Alexander the Great*. Cambridge.
Bousquet, J. 1988. 'La Stèle des Kyténiens au Létôon de Xanthos'. *REG* 101: 12–53.
Bousquet, J., and Daux, G. 1942–3. 'Agamemnon, Télèphe, Dionysos Sphaleôtes et les Attalides'. *Revue archéologique*, 19: 113–25; 20: 19–40.
Bovon, A. 1963. 'La Représentation des guerriers perses et la notion de Barbare dans la première moitié du Vᵉ siècle'. *BCH* 87: 579–602.
Bowersock, G. 1965. *Augustus and the Greek World*. Oxford.
Bowra, C. M. 1930. *Tradition and Design in the* Iliad. Oxford.
——1964. *Pindar*. Oxford.
Boyancé, P. 1943. 'Les Origines de la légende troyenne de Rome'. *Revue des études ancienne* 45: 275–90. (Reprinted in P. Boyancé, *Études sur religion romaine*. Rome 1972. 153–70).
Braccesi, L. 1984. *La leggenda di Antenore da Troia a Padova*. Padua.
Bradeen, D. W. 1952. 'The Chalcidians in Thrace'. *AJPhil.* 73: 356–80.
Braund, D. 1994. *Georgia in Antiquity: A History of Colchis and Transcaucasian Iberia 550 BC–AD 562*. Oxford.

Bremmer, J. 1987a. 'What is a Greek Myth?' In J. Bremmer (ed.), *Interpretations of Greek Mythology*. London. 1–9.

——1987b. 'Slow Cybele's Arrival'. In Bremmer and Horsfall 1987: 105–11.

Bremmer, J., and Horsfall, N. M. 1987. *Roman Myth and Mythography*. London.

Brillante, C. 1990. 'History and the Historical Interpretation of Myth'. In Edmunds 1990: 93–138.

Brink, C. O. 1972. 'Ennius and the Hellenistic Worship of Homer'. *AJPhil*. 93: 547–67.

Brinkmann, V. 1985. 'Die aufgemalten Namenbeischriften an Nord- und Ostfries des Siphnierschatzhauses'. *BCH* 109: 77–130.

Briscoe, J. 1973. *A Commentary on Livy, Books XXXI–XXXIII*. Oxford.

——1981. *A Commentary on Livy, Books XXXIV–XXXVII*. Oxford.

——1989. 'The Second Punic War'. *CAH*[2] 8: 44–80.

Brodersen, K., and Schubert, C. (eds.). 1995. *Rom und der griechische Osten: Festschrift für Hatto H. Schmitt*. Stuttgart.

Brommer, F. 1967. *Die Metopen des Parthenon*. Mainz.

Brückner, A. 1902. 'Geschichte von Troja und Ilion'. In Dörpfeld 1902: 549–93.

Bruneau, P. 1970. *Recherches sur les cultes de Délos à l'époque hellénistique et à l'époque impériale*. Paris.

Brunt, P. A. 1980. 'On Historical Fragments and Epitomes'. *CQ* 30: 477–94.

——1990. *Roman Imperial Themes*. Oxford.

Bryce, T. 1986. *The Lycians* i: *The Lycians in Literary and Epigraphic Sources*. Copenhagen.

Burgess, J. S. 1996. 'The Non-Homeric *Cypria*'. *TAPA* 126: 77–99.

Burkert, W. 1977. *Griechische Religion der archaischen und klassischen Epoche*. Stuttgart.

——1979. *Structure and History in Greek Mythology and Ritual*. Berkeley.

——1995. 'Lydia between East and West or How to Date the Trojan War: A Study in Herodotus'. In Carter and Morris 1995: 139–48.

Burn, L. 1989. 'The Art of the State in Late Fifth-Century Athens'. In C. Roueché and M. M. Mackenzie (eds.), *Images of Authority*. Cambridge. 62–81.

Burton, P. J. 1996. 'The Summoning of the Magna Mater to Rome (205 B.C.)'. *Historia*, 45: 36–63.

Buxton, R. 1994. *Imaginary Greece: The Contexts of Mythology*. Cambridge.

Camp, J. M. 1986. *The Athenian Agora: Excavations in the Heart of Classical Athens*. London.

Canali de Rossi, F. 1997. *Le ambascerie dal mondo greco a Roma in età repubblicana*. Rome.

References

Candiloro, E. 1965. 'Politica e cultura in Atene da Pidna alla guerra mitridatica'. *Studi Classici Orientali*, 14: 134–76.

Capuis, L. 1993. *I Veneti: Società e cultura di un popolo dell'Italia preromana*. Milan.

Carandini, A. 1997. *La nascita di Roma: Dèi, Lari, eroi e uomini all'Alba di una civiltà*. Turin.

Carapanos, C. 1878. *Dodone et ses ruines*. Paris.

Carpenter, T. H. 1991. *Art and Myth in Ancient Greece*. London.

Carrington, P. 1977. 'The Heroic Age of Phrygia in Ancient Literature and Art'. *Anatolian Studies*, 27: 117–26.

Carter, J. B., and Morris, S. P. (eds.). 1995. *The Ages of Homer: A Tribute to Emily Townsend Vermeule*. Austin.

Cartledge, P. 1987. *Agesilaos and the Crisis of Sparta*. London.

——1993. *The Greeks: A Portrait of Self and Others*. Oxford.

Cartledge, P., Garnsey, P., and Gruen, E. (eds.). 1997. *Hellenistic Constructs: Essays in Culture, History and Historiography*. Berkeley.

Cartledge, P., and Spawforth, A. 1989. *Hellenistic and Roman Sparta: A Tale of Two Cities*. London.

Castagnoli, F. 1982. 'La leggenda di Enea nel Lazio'. *Studi Romani*, 30: 1–15.

Castriota, D. 1992. *Myth, Ethos and Actuality: Official Art in Fifth-Century BC Athens*. Madison, Wis.

——1995. *The* Ara Pacis Augustae *and the Imagery of Abundance in Later Greek and Early Roman Imperial Art*. Princeton.

Catling, H. W. 1976–77. 'Excavations at the Menelaion Sparta 1973–6'. *Archaeological Reports* 23: 24–42.

Chamoux, F. 1953. *Cyrène sous la monarchie des Battiades*. Paris.

Chaniotis, A. 1988. *Historie und Historiker in den griechischen Inschriften*. Stuttgart.

Chassignet, M. 1986. *Caton, Les Origines (Fragments)*. Paris.

Cingano, E. 1985. 'Clistene di Sicione, Erodoto e i poemi del Ciclo tebano'. *Quaderni Urbinati di Cultura Classica*, 20: 31–40.

Clairmont, C. 1951. *Das Parisurteil in der antiken Kunst*. Zurich.

Classen, C. J. 1963. 'Zur Herkunft der Sage von Romulus und Remus'. *Historia*, 12: 447–57.

Coarelli, F. 1988. *Il Foro Boario dalle origini alla fine della Repubblica*. Rome.

Coarelli, F., and Torelli, M. 1984. *Sicilia*. Guida arch. Laterza 13. Rome.

Cobet, J. 1996. 'Europa und Asien—Griechen und Barbaren—Osten und Westen'. *Geschichte in Wissenschaft und Unterricht*, 47: 405–19.

Cohen, G. M. 1995. *The Hellenistic Settlements in Europe, the Islands, and Asia Minor*. Berkeley.

Cole, S. G. 1984. Theoi Megaloi: *The Cult of the Great Gods at Samothrace*. Leiden.

References

Conte, G. B. 1994. *Latin Literature: A History*. Baltimore.

Cook, J. M. 1973. *The Troad: An Archaeological and Topographical Study.* Oxford.

Cook, R. M. 1983. 'Art and Epic in Archaic Greece'. *BABESCH: Bulletin Antieke Beschaving* 58: 1–10.

Coppola, A. 1994. 'Memorie troiane e ambascerie romane'. *Hesperìa: Studi sulla grecità di occidente*, 4: 177–86.

Cornell, T. J. 1975. 'Aeneas and the Twins: The Development of the Roman Foundation Legend'. *PCPS* 21: 1–32.

——1977. 'Aeneas' Arrival in Italy'. *Liverpool Classical Monthly*, 2: 77–83.

——1986. 'The *Annals* of Quintus Ennius'. *JRS* 76: 244–50.

——1995. *The Beginnings of Rome: Italy and Rome from the Bronze Age to the Punic Wars (c.1000–264 BC)*. London.

Corsten, T. 1992. 'Der Hilferuf des akarnanischen Bundes an Rom: Zum Beginn des römischen Eingreifens in Griechenland'. *ZPE* 94: 195–210.

Crawford, M. H. 1974. *Roman Republican Coinage*. Cambridge.

Curty, O. 1994. 'La Notion de la parenté entre cités chez Thucydide'. *Museum Helveticum*, 51: 193–7.

——1995. *Les Parentés légendaires entre cités grecques*. Geneva.

Dagron, G. 1974. *Naissance d'une capitale: Constantinople et ses institutions de 330 à 451*. Paris.

Daintree, D. 1990. 'The Virgil Commentary of Aelius Donatus—Black Hole or "Éminence Grise"?'. *Greece and Rome*, 37: 65–79.

Dakaris, S. I. 1964. *Οἱ γενεαλογικοὶ μῦθοι τῶν Μολοσσῶν*. Athens.

Dany, O. 1999. *Akarnanien im Hellenismus: Geschichte und Völkerrecht in Nordwestgriechenland*. Munich.

Davies, J. K., and Foxhall, L. (eds.). 1984. *The Trojan War, its Historicity and Context*. Bristol.

Davies, M. 1988. *Epicorum Graecorum Fragmenta*. Göttingen.

——1989*a*. *The Epic Cycle*. Bristol.

——1989*b*. 'The Date of the Epic Cycle'. *Glotta*, 67: 89–100.

Davies, P. V. 1969. *Macrobius*, The Saturnalia. *Translated with an Introduction and Notes*. New York.

Davison, J. A. 1955. 'Peisistratus and Homer'. *TAPA* 86: 1–21.

——1958. 'Notes on the Panathenaea'. *JHS* 78: 23–41.

Davreux, J. 1942. *La Légende de la prophétesse Cassandre d'après les textes et les monuments*. Paris.

Degrassi, A. 1951–2. 'Le dediche di popoli e re asiatici al popolo romano e a Giove Capitolino'. *Bullettino della Commissione Archeologica Comunale di Roma*. 74: 19–47. Also in *Scritti vari di Antichità*. i (Rome, 1962), 415–44.

Delivorrias, A. 1968. 'News from Sparta'. *Athens Annals of Archaeology* 1: 41–5.

References

Dench, E. 1995. *From Barbarians to New Men: Greek, Roman, and Modern Perceptions of Peoples from the Central Apennines.* Oxford.

Denniston, J. D., and Page, D. L. 1957. *Aeschylus* Agamemnon. Oxford.

Derow, P. S. 1970. 'Rome and the Greek World from the Earliest Contacts to the End of the First Illyrian War'. Ph.D. Princeton.

——1979. 'Polybius, Rome, and the East'. *JRS* 69: 1–15.

——1995. 'Herodotus Readings'. *Classics Ireland*, 2: 29–51 (http://www.ucd.ie/~classics/Derow95.html).

——, and Forrest, W. G. 1982. 'An Inscription from Chios'. *BSA* 77: 79–92.

De Sanctis, G. 1967. *Storia dei Romani.* iii/i. 2nd edn. Florence.

Desideri, P. 1970–1. 'Studi di storiografia eracleota: II. La guerra con Antioco il Grande'. *Studi classici orientali*, 19–20: 487–537.

Deubner, L. 1932. *Attische Feste.* Berlin.

Develin, R. 1978. 'Religion and Politics during the Third Century B.C.'. *Journal of Religious History*, 10: 3–19.

——1989. *Athenian Officials 684–321 BC.* Cambridge.

——1994. 'Introduction'. In J. C. Yardley (trans.), *Justin, Epitome of the Philippic History of Pompeius Trogus.* Atlanta. 1–11.

Dörpfeld, W. (ed.). 1902. *Troja und Ilion.* Athens.

Dougherty, C. 1993. *The Poetics of Colonization: From City to Text in Archaic Greece.* New York.

Dover, K. J. 1974. *Greek Popular Morality in the Time of Plato and Aristotle.* Oxford.

——1987. *Greek and the Greeks: Collected Papers.* i. *Language, Poetry, and Drama.* Oxford.

Dowden, K. 1992. *The Uses of Greek Mythology.* London.

Dreyfus, R., and Schraudolph, E. 1996. *Pergamon: The Telephos Frieze from the Great Altar.* i. San Francisco.

Dubois, L. 1989. *Inscriptions grecques dialectales de Sicile.* Rome.

Dubourdieu, A. 1989. *Les Origines et le développement du culte des Pénates à Rome.* Rome.

Dugas, C. 1938. 'À la Lesché des Cnidiens'. *REG* 51: 53–9.

Dumézil, G. 1970. *Archaic Roman Religion.* Chicago (in French, Paris 1966).

Dunbabin, T. J. 1948. *The Western Greeks.* Oxford.

Durrbach, F. 1921. *Choix d'inscriptions de Délos.* Paris.

Dury-Moyaers, G. 1981. *Énée et Lavinium: A propos des découvertes archéologiques récentes.* Brussels.

Edmunds, L. (ed.). 1990. *Approaches to Greek Myth.* Baltimore.

Edwards, M. W. 1987. *Homer, Poet of the* Iliad. Baltimore.

——1991. *The Iliad: A Commentary.* v. Books 17–20. Cambridge.

Elwyn, S. 1993. 'Interstate Kinship and Roman Foreign Policy'. *TAPA* 123: 261–86.

References

Errington, R. M. 1972. *The Dawn of Empire: Rome's Rise to World Power.* Ithaca.

Erskine, A. 1991. 'Rhodes and Augustus'. *ZPE* 88: 271–5.

——1994. 'Greek Embassies and the City of Rome'. *Classics Ireland,* 1: 47–53 (http://www.ucd.ie/~classics/94/Erskine94.html).

——1995a. 'Rome in the Greek World: The Significance of a Name'. In A. Powell (ed.), *The Greek World.* London. 368–83.

——1995b. 'Culture and Power in Ptolemaic Egypt: The Museum and Library of Alexandria'. *Greece and Rome,* 42: 38–48.

——1996. 'Money-loving Romans'. In F. Cairns and M. Heath (eds.), *Papers of the Leeds International Latin Seminar,* 9. Leeds. 1–11.

——1997a. 'Greekness and Uniqueness: The Cult of the Senate in the Greek East'. *Phoenix,* 51: 25–37.

——1997b. 'Delos, Aeneas and *IG* xi.4.756'. *ZPE* 117: 133–6.

——1997c. 'Greek Gifts and Roman Suspicion'. *Classics Ireland,* 4: 33–45 (http://www.ucd.ie/~classics/97/Erskine97.html).

——1998. 'Trojan Horseplay in Rome'. *Dialogos: Hellenic Studies Review,* 5: 131–8.

Erskine, J. 1925. *The Private Life of Helen of Troy.* Indianopolis.

Ervin, M. 1963. 'A Relief Pithos from Mykonos'. Ἀρχαιολογικὸν Δελτίον 18: 37–75.

Evans, J. D. 1992. *The Art of Persuasion: Political Propaganda from Aeneas to Brutus.* Ann Arbor.

Fantham, E. 1995. 'Recent Readings of Ovid's *Fasti*'. *C. Phil.* 90: 367–78.

——1998. *Ovid* Fasti *Book IV.* Cambridge.

Faraone, C. A. 1992. *Talismans and Trojan Horses: Guardian Statues in Ancient Greek Myth and Ritual.* Oxford.

Farnell, L. R. 1921. *Greek Hero Cults and Ideas of Immortality.* Oxford.

Farrow, J. G. 1992. 'Aeneas and Rome: Pseudepigrapha and Politics'. *CJ* 87: 339–59.

Feeney, D. 1991. *The Gods in Epic: Poets and Critics of the Classical Tradition.* Oxford.

——1998. *Literature and Religion at Rome: Cultures, Contexts, and Beliefs.* Cambridge.

Fehling, D. 1989. *Herodotus and his 'Sources': Citation, Invention and Narrative Art.* Leeds. (First published in German 1971, translated with revisions.)

Ferrary, J.-L. 1988. *Philhellénisme et impérialisme: Aspects idéologiques de la conquête romaine du monde hellénistique.* Paris.

Finley, J. H. 1958. 'Pindar and the Persian Invasion'. *Harv. Stud.* 63: 121–32.

Finley, M. I., Caskey, J. L., Kirk, G. S., and Page, D. L. 1964. 'The Trojan War'. *JHS* 84: 1–20.

Forrest, W. G. 1980. *A History of Sparta 950–192 BC.* 2nd edn. London.

References

Forsythe, G. 1990. 'Some Notes on the History of Cassius Hemina'. *Phoenix*, 44: 326–44.

——1994. *The Historian L. Calpurnius Piso Frugi and the Roman Annalistic Tradition*. Lanham, Md.

Forte, B. 1972. *Rome and the Romans as the Greeks saw them*. Rome.

Fowler, R. L. 1996. 'Herodotos and his Contemporaries'. *JHS* 116: 62–87.

——1998. 'Genealogical Thinking, Hesiod's *Catalogue*, and the Creation of the Hellenes'. *PCPS* 44: 1–19.

Francis, E. 1990. *Image and Idea in Fifth-Century Greece: Art and Literature after the Persian Wars*. London.

Francis, E., and Vickers, M. 1985. 'The Oenoe Painting in the Stoa Poikile, and Herodotus' Account of Marathon'. *BSA* 80: 99–113.

Franke, P. R. 1955. *Alt-Epirus und das Königtum der Molosser*. Kallmünz.

——1989. 'Pyrrhus'. *CAH*² 7.2: 456–85.

Fraser, P. M. 1972. *Ptolemaic Alexandria*. 3 vols. Oxford.

Frazer, J. G. 1898. *Pausanias's Description of Greece*. London.

——1929. *Publius Ovidius Naso, Fastorum libri sex*. London.

Freber, P.-S. G. 1993. *Der hellenistische Osten und das Illyricum unter Caesar*. Stuttgart.

Fuchs, W. 1973. 'Die Bildgeschichte der Flucht des Aeneas'. *ANRW* 1.4: 615–32.

Gabba, E. 1963. 'Il latino come dialetto greco'. In *Miscellanea di studi alessandrini in memoria di Augusto Rostagni*. Turin. 188–94.

——1974. 'Storiografia greca e imperialism romano (III–I sec. a.C.)'. *Rivista storica Italiana* 86: 625–42.

——1976. 'Sulla valorizzazione politica della leggenda delle origini troiane di Roma fra III e II sec. a.C.' In M. Sordi (ed.), *I canali della propaganda nel mondo antico*. Contributi dell'istituto di storia antica 4. Milan. 84–101.

——1991. *Dionysius and* The History of Archaic Rome. Berkeley.

Galinsky, G. K. 1969. *Aeneas, Sicily, and Rome*. Princeton.

——1992. 'Aeneas at Rome and Lavinium'. In R. M. Wilhelm and H. Jones (eds.), *The Two Worlds of the Poet: New Perspectives on Vergil*. Detroit. 93–108.

——1996. *Augustan Culture: An Interpretative Introduction*. Princeton.

Gantz, T. 1993. *Early Greek Myth: A Guide to Literary and Artistic Sources*. Baltimore.

Garland, R. 1995. *The Eye of the Beholder: Deformity and Disability in the Graeco-Roman World*. London.

Geary, P. J. 1990. *Furta Sacra: Thefts of Relics in the Central Middle Ages*. 2nd edn. Princeton.

Gelzer, M. 1960. *Caesar, der Politiker und Staatsmann*. 6th edn. Wiesbaden.

Genière, J. de la. 1979. 'The Iron Age in Southern Italy'. In D. and F. Ridgway (eds.), *Italy before the Romans: The Iron Age, Orientalizing and Etruscan Periods*. London. 59–93.

——(ed). 1991. *Épéios et Philoctète en Italie*. Naples.

Georges, P. 1994. *Barbarian Asia and the Greek Experience: From the Archaic Period to the Age of Xenophon*. Baltimore.

Gérard, J. 1980. 'Légende et politique autour de la Mère des Dieux'. *REL* 58: 153–75.

Giannelli, G. 1963. *Culti e miti della Magna Grecia*. Florence.

Gill, D. W. J. 1993. 'The Temple of Aphaia on Aegina: Further Thoughts on the Date of the Reconstruction'. *BSA* 88: 173–81.

Giovannini, A. 1993. 'Greek Cities and Greek Commmonwealth'. In A. Bulloch, E. S. Gruen, A. A. Long, and A. Stewart (eds.), *Images and Ideologies: Self-definition in the Hellenistic World*. Berkeley. 265–86.

——1997. 'Les Relations de parenté entre cités grecques'. *Museum Helveticum*, 54: 158–62.

Goerthert, F. W., and Schleif, H. 1962. *Der Athenatempel von Ilion*. Berlin.

Goldberg, S. M. 1998. 'Plautus on the Palatine'. *JRS* 88: 1–20.

Golden, M. 1986. 'Names and Naming at Athens: Three Studies'. *Échos du monde classique*, 30: 245–69.

Goold, G. P. 1970. 'Servius and the Helen Episode'. *Harv. Stud.* 74: 101–68.

——1983. *Catullus*. London.

Graham, A. J. 1964. *Colony and Mother City in Ancient Greece*. Manchester (republished with addenda and corrigenda. 1983, Chicago).

Graillot, H. 1912. *Le Culte de Cybèle, Mère des Dieux à Rome et dans l'empire romain*. Paris.

Grainger, J. D. 1990. *Seleukos Nikator: Constructing a Hellenistic Kingdom*. London.

Grandazzi, A. 1997. *The Foundation of Rome: Myth and History*. Ithaca. (In French, Paris, 1991.)

Green, J. R. 1994. *Theatre in Ancient Greek Society*. London.

Green, P. 1997. ' "These fragments have I shored against my ruins": Apollonios Rhodios and the Social Revalidation of Myth for a New Age'. In Cartledge, Garnsey, and Gruen 1997: 35–71.

Griffin, A. 1982. *Sikyon*. Oxford.

Griffin, J. 1977. 'The Epic Cycle and the Uniqueness of Homer'. *JHS* 97: 39–53.

——1980. *Homer on Life and Death*. Oxford.

——1984. 'Augustus and the Poets: "Caesar qui cogere posset" '. In F. Millar and E. Segal (eds.), *Caesar Augustus: Seven Aspects*. Oxford. 189–218.

Gruen, E. S. 1984. *The Hellenistic World and the Coming of Rome*. Berkeley.

References

——1990. *Studies in Greek Culture and Roman Policy*. Leiden.

——1992. *Culture and National Identity in Republican Rome*. Ithaca.

——1996. 'The Purported Jewish–Spartan Affiliation'. In R. W. Wallace and E. M. Harris (eds.), *Transitions to Empire: Essays in Greco-Roman History, 360–146 B.C., in Honor of E. Badian*. Norman, Okla. 254–69.

Gurval, R. A. 1995. *Actium and Augustus: The Politics and Emotions of Civil War*. Ann Arbor.

Habicht, C. 1970. *Gottmenschentum und griechische Städte*. 2nd edn. Munich.

——1985. *Pausanias' Guide to Ancient Greece*. Berkeley.

——1995. *Athen: Die Geschichte der Stadt in hellenistischer Zeit*. Munich.

Hainsworth, B. 1993. *The Iliad: A Commentary*. iii, *Books 9–12*. Cambridge.

Hall, E. 1989. *Inventing the Barbarian: Greek Self-Definition through Tragedy*. Oxford.

Hall, J. M. 1995*a*. 'The Role of Language in Greek Ethnicities'. *PCPS* 41: 83–100.

——1995*b*. 'How Argive was the "Argive" Heraion? The Political and Cultic Geography of the Argive Plain, 900–400 BC'. *AJArch.* 99: 577–613.

Halliday, W. R. 1928. *The* Greek Questions *of Plutarch*. Oxford.

Hammond, N. G. L. 1967. *Epirus: The Geography, the Ancient Remains, the History and the Topography of Epirus and Adjacent Areas*. Oxford.

——1972. *History of Macedonia*. i. Oxford.

Hammond, N. G. L., and Griffith, G. T. 1979. *History of Macedonia*. ii. Oxford.

Hands, A. R. 1968. *Charities and Social Aid in Greece and Rome*. London.

Hansen, E. V. 1971. *The Attalids of Pergamon*. 2nd edn. Ithaca.

Hardie, P. R. 1986. *Virgil's* Aeneid: *Cosmos and Imperium*. Oxford.

——1994. *Virgil,* Aeneid Book IX. Cambridge.

Harmon, A. M. 1923. 'The Poet κατ' ἐξοχήν'. *C.Phil.* 18: 35–47.

Harrison, T. 1998. 'Herodotus' Conception of Foreign Languages'. *Histos*, 2 (http://www.dur.ac.uk/Classics/histos/1998/harrison.html).

——2000. *Divinity and History: The Religion of Herodotus*. Oxford.

Hartog, F. 1988. *The Mirror of Herodotus: The Representation of the Other in the Writing of History*. Berkeley. (In French, Paris, 1980.)

Haslam, M. 1997. 'Homeric Papyri and Transmission of the Text'. In Morris and Powell 1997: 55–100.

Hauvette, A. 1894. *Hérodote historien des guerres médiques*. Paris.

Head, B. 1911. *Historia numorum*. 2nd edn. Oxford.

Hedreen, G. 1991. 'The Cult of Achilles in the Euxine'. *Hesperia*, 60: 313–30.

——1996. 'Image, Text, and Story in the Recovery of Helen'. *Classical Antiquity*, 15: 152–84.

References

Heinen, H. 1972. 'Die politischen Beziehungen zwischen Rom und dem Ptolemäerreich von ihren Anfängen bis zum Tag von Eleusis (273–168 v. Chr.)'. *ANRW* 1.1. 633–59.

——1984. 'The Syrian–Egyptian Wars and the New Kingdoms of Asia Minor'. *CAH*² 7/1: 412–45.

Heitsch, E. 1965. *Aphroditehymnos, Aeneas und Homer: sprachliche Untersuchungen zum Homerproblem*. Göttingen.

Herbert-Brown, G. 1994. *Ovid and the* Fasti: *An Historical Study*. Oxford.

Herington, J. 1985. *Poetry into Drama: Early Tragedy and the Greek Poetic Tradition*. Berkeley.

Herman, G. 1987. *Ritualised Friendship and the Greek City*. Cambridge.

Hertel, D. 1994. 'Eine Stadt als Zeugnis ihrer Geschichte: Troia/Ilion in griechischer und hellenistisch-römischer Zeit'. Unpublished Habilitationsschrift, Universität Köln.

Hibler, D. 1993. 'The Hero-Reliefs of Lakonia: Changes in Form and Function'. In O. Palagia and W. Coulson, *Sculpture from Arcadia and Laconia*. Oxford. 199–204.

Hill, H. 1961. 'Dionysius of Halicarnassus and the Origins of Rome'. *JRS* 51: 88–93.

Himmelmann, N. 1990. *Ideale Nacktheit in der griechischen Kunst*. Berlin.

Hinds, J. G. F. 1994. 'Mithridates'. *CAH*² 9: 129–64.

Hölscher, T. 1973. *Griechische Historienbilder des 5. und 4. Jdts v. Chr.* Würzburg.

——1998. 'Images and Political Identity: The Case of Athens'. In D. Boedeker and K. A. Raaflaub (eds.), *Democracy, Empire, and the Arts in Fifth-Century Athens*. Cambridge, Mass. 1998. 153–83.

Hoff, M. C. 1997. '*Laceratae Athenae*: Sulla's Siege of Athens in 87/6 BC and its Aftermath'. In M. C. Hoff and S. I. Rotroff, *The Romanization of Athens*. Oxford. 33–51.

Holden, B. M. 1964. *The Metopes of the Temple of Athena at Ilion*. Northampton, Mass.

Holleaux, M. 1921. *Rome, la Grèce et les monarchies hellénistiques au iiiᵉ siècle avant J.-C. (273–205)*. Paris.

Holloway, R. R. 1994. *The Archaeology of Early Rome and Latium*. London.

Hopkins, C. 1939. 'The Painted Shields'. In M. Rostovtzeff, F. E. Brown, and C. B. Welles, *The Excavations at Dura Europus VII–VIII*. New Haven. 326–69.

Hornblower, J. 1981. *Hieronymus of Cardia*. Oxford.

Hornblower, S. 1982. *Mausolus*. Oxford.

——1991. *A Commentary on Thucydides*. i, *Books I–III*. Oxford.

——1996. *A Commentary on Thucydides*. ii, *Books IV–V.24*. Oxford.

Horsfall, N. M. 1972. 'Varro and Caesar: Three Chronological Problems'. *BICS* 19: 120–8.

—— 1979a. 'Stesichorus at Bovillae?'. *JHS* 99: 26–48.

—— 1979b. 'Some Problems in the Aeneas Legend'. *CQ* 29: 372–90.

—— 1987. 'The Aeneas Legend from Homer to Virgil'. In Bremmer and Horsfall 1987: 12–24.

Howes, G. E. 1895. 'Homeric Quotation in Plato and Aristotle'. *Harv. Stud.* 6: 210–37.

Hurst, A. 1991. 'Introduction'. In M. Fusillo, A. Hurst, and G. Paduano, *Licofrone, Alessandra*. Milan. 9–48.

Instinsky, H. 1949. *Alexander der Große am Hellespont*. Godesberg.

Isager, S. 1998. 'The Pride of Halikarnassos: Editio princeps of an Inscription from Salmakis'. *ZPE* 123: 1–23.

Jacoby, F. 1904. *Das Marmor Parium*. Berlin.

—— 1933. 'Homerisches'. *Hermes*, 68: 1–50.

Janko, R. 1982. *Homer, Hesiod and the* Hymns. Cambridge.

—— 1992. *The Iliad: A Commentary*. iv, *Books 13–16*. Cambridge.

Jeffery, L. H. 1990. *The Local Scripts of Archaic Greece*. 2nd edn. with suppl. by A. W. Johnston. Oxford.

Jenkyns, R. 1980. *The Victorians and Ancient Greece*. Oxford.

Johansen, K. F. 1967. *The* Iliad *in Early Greek Art*. Copenhagen.

Jones, C. P. 1971. *Plutarch and Rome*. Oxford.

—— 1993. 'The Decree of Ilion in honor of a King Antiochus'. *GRBS* 34: 73–92.

—— 1996. 'The Panhellenion'. *Chiron*, 26: 29–56.

—— 1999. *Kinship Diplomacy in the Ancient World*. Cambridge, Mass.

Jones, N. 1987. *Public Organization in Ancient Greece: A Documentary Study*. Philadelphia.

Jong, I. J. F. de. 1987. *Narrators and Focalizers: The Presentation of the Story in the* Iliad. Amsterdam.

Jope, J. 1988. 'The *Fasti*: Nationalism and Personal Involvement in Ovid's treatment of Cybele'. *Échos du monde classique*, 32: 13–22.

Jost, M. 1985. *Sanctuaires et cultes d'Arcadie*. Paris.

Jüthner, J. 1923. *Hellenen und Barbaren: Aus der Geschichte des Nationalbewußtseins*. Leipzig.

Kakridis, J. 1971. *Homer Revisited*. Lund.

Kallet-Marx, R. 1995. *Hegemony to Empire: The Development of the Roman Imperium in the East from 148 to 62 BC*. Berkeley.

Kamptz, H. von. 1982. *Homerische Personennamen*. Göttingen.

Kaster, R. A. 1988. *Guardians of Language: The Grammarian and Society in Late Antiquity*. Berkeley.

Kearns, E. 1989. *The Heroes of Attica*. London.

Kebric, R. B. 1983. *The Paintings in the Cnidian Lesche at Delphi and their Historical Context*. Leiden.

Keen, A. G. 1998. *Dynastic Lycia: A Political History of the Lycians and their*

Relations with Foreign Powers c.545–362 BC. Leiden.

Kienast, D. 1965. 'Rom und die Venus vom Eryx'. *Hermes* 93: 478–89.

——1999. *Augustus, Prinzeps und Monarch.* 3rd edn. Darmstadt.

Kirk, G. S. 1985. *The Iliad: A Commentary.* i: *Books 1–4.* Cambridge.

——1990. *The Iliad: a commentary.* ii: *Books 5–8.* Cambridge.

Knittlmayer, B. 1997. *Die attische Aristokratie und ihre Helden: Untersuchungen zu Darstellungen des trojanischen Sagenkreises im 6. und frühen 5. Jahrhundert v. Chr.* Heidelberg.

Knox, B. 1979. *Word and Action: Essays on the Ancient Theater.* Baltimore.

Köves, T. 1963. 'Zum Empfang der Magna Mater in Rom'. *Historia*, 12: 321–47.

Kosmetatou, E. 1995. 'The Legend of the Hero Pergamus'. *Ancient Society*, 26: 133–44.

Kunze, E. 1950. *Archaische Schildbänder: ein Beitrag zur frühgriechischen Bildgeschichte und Sagenüberlieferung.* Olympische Forschungen 2. Berlin.

Labarbe, J. 1949. *L'Homère de Platon.* Liège.

Lacroix, L. 1974. 'Héraclès, héros, voyageur et civilisateur'. *Bulletin de l'Académie Royale de Belgique*, 60: 34–59.

Laidlaw, W. A. 1933. *A History of Delos.* Oxford.

Lamberton, R. 1997. 'Homer in Antiquity'. In Morris and Powell 1997: 33–54.

Lambrechts, P. 1951. 'Cybèle, divinité étrangère ou nationale?'. *Bull. Soc. Belge d'Anthropologie et de Préhistoire*, 62: 44–60.

Landucci Gattinoni, F. 1992. *Lisimaco di Tracia: un sovrano nella prospettiva del primo ellenismo.* Milan.

Laroche, D., and Jacquemin, A. 1992. 'La terrasse d'Attale Ier revisitée'. *BCH* 116: 229–58.

Larsen, J. A. O. 1968. *Greek Federal States: Their Institutions and History.* Oxford.

Larson, J. 1995. *Greek Heroine Cults.* Madison.

Latte, K. 1960. *Römische Religionsgeschichte.* Munich.

Lattimore, R. 1947. *The Odes of Pindar.* Chicago.

Leaf, W. 1923. *Strabo on the Troad.* Cambridge.

Leidl, C. 1995. 'Historie und Fiktion. Zum Hannibalbrief (*P. Hamb.* 129)'. In Brodersen and Schubert 1995: 151–69.

Lévy, E. 1991. 'Apparition des notions de Grèce et de Grecs'. In S. Said Ἑλληνισμος. Leiden. 49–69.

Lindner, R. 1994. *Mythos und Identität: Studien zur Selbstdarstellung kleinasiatischer Städte in der römischen Kaiserzeit.* Stuttgart.

Littlewood, R. J. 1981. 'Poetic Artistry and Dynastic Politics: Ovid at the *Ludi Megalenses* (*Fasti* 4.179–372)'. *CQ* 31: 381–95.

Lloyd, M. 1987. 'Homer on Poetry: Two Passages in the *Odyssey*'. *Eranos*, 85: 85–90.

References

——1994. *Euripides* Andromache. Warminster.

Lloyd, R. B. 1961. 'Republican Authors in Servius and the *Scholia Danielis*'. *Harv. Stud.* 65: 291–341.

Lloyd-Jones, H. 1999. 'The Pride of Halicarnassus'. *ZPE* 124: 1–14.

Lomas, K. 1993. *Rome and the Western Greeks 350 BC–AD 200: Conquest and Acculturation in Southern Italy*. London.

——1995. 'The Greeks in the West and the Hellenization of Italy'. In A. Powell (ed.), *The Greek World*. London. 347–67.

Long, T. 1986. *Barbarians in Greek Comedy*. Carbondale.

Loraux, N. 1981. *L'Invention d'Athènes: histoire de l'oraison funèbre dans la 'cité classique'*. Paris. (English translation, 1986 Cambridge, Mass.)

Lücke, S. 1995. 'Überlegungen zur Münzpropaganda des Pyrrhos'. In Brodersen and Schubert 1995: 171–3.

Lund, H. S. 1992. *Lysimachus: A Study in Early Hellenistic Kingship*. London.

MacDougall, H. A. 1982. *Racial Myth in English History: Teutons, Trojans, and Anglo-Saxons*. Montreal.

MacDowell, D. 1960. 'Aigina and the Delian League'. *JHS* 80: 118–21.

McGing, B. C. 1986. *The Foreign Policy of Mithridates VI Eupator, King of Pontus*. Leiden.

McGushin, P. 1977. *C. Sallustius Crispus*, Bellum Catilinae*: A Commentary*. Leiden.

Mackie, H. 1996. *Talking Trojan: Speech and Communication in the* Iliad. Lanham, Md.

McShane, R. B. 1964. *The Foreign Policy of the Attalids of Pergamum*. Urbana.

Magie, D. 1950. *Roman Rule in Asia Minor to the End of the Third Century after Christ*. Princeton.

Malkin, I. 1987. *Religion and Colonization in Ancient Greece*. Leiden.

——1994. *Myth and Territory in the Spartan Mediterranean*. Cambridge.

——1998. *The Returns of Odysseus: Colonization and Ethnicity*. Berkeley.

Manganaro, G. 1974. 'Una biblioteca storica nel ginnasio di Tauromenion e il P. Oxy. 1241'. *Parola del Passato*, 29: 389–409.

——1976. 'Una biblioteca storica nel ginnasio a Tauromenion nel II sec. a.C.'. In A. Alföldi (ed.) *Römische Frühgeschichte*. Heidelberg. 83–96.

Marti, B. 1964. 'Tragic History and Lucan's *Pharsalia* '. In C. Henderson (ed.), *Classical, Medieval and Renaissance Studies in Honour of B. L. Ullman*. Rome. 165–204.

Martin, P. M. 1971. 'La propagande augustéenne dans les *Antiquités romaines* de Denys d'Halicarnasse (Livre I)'. *REL* 49: 162–79.

Masters, J. 1992. *Poetry and Civil War in Lucan's* Bellum Civile. Cambridge.

Matthews, V. J. 1974. *Panyassis of Halikarnassos: Text and Commentary*. Leiden.

Mehl, A. 1986. *Seleukos Nikator und sein Reich*. i. *Seleukos' Leben und die Entwicklung seiner Machtposition*. Studia Hellenistica 28. Louvain.

References

Meier, C. 1982. *Caesar*. Berlin.

Meiggs, R. 1972. *The Athenian Empire*. Oxford.

Meister, K. 1990. *Die griechische Geschichtsschreibung*. Stuttgart.

Mello, M. 1968. Mens Bona: *ricerca sull'origine e sullo sviluppo del culto*. Naples.

Mellor, R. 1978. 'The Dedications on the Capitoline Hill'. *Chiron*, 8: 319–30.

Meritt, B. D., Wade-Gery, H. T., and McGregor, M. F. 1939. *The Athenian Tribute Lists*. i. Cambridge, Mass.

Merkelbach, R. 1954. 'Anthologie fingierter Briefe' no. 129. In B. Snell (ed.), *Griechische Papyri der Hamburger Staats- und Universitätsbibliothek*. Hamburg. 51–74.

Meyer, E. 1925. *Die Grenzen der hellenistischen Staaten in Kleinasien*. Zürich.

Millar, F. 1964. *A Study of Cassius Dio*. Oxford.

Miller, M. C. 1995. 'Priam, King of Troy'. In Carter and Morris 1995: 449–65.

——1997. *Athens and Persia in the Fifth Century BC: A Study in Cultural Receptivity*. Cambridge.

Miller, S. G. 1991. 'Terracotta Figurines: New Finds at Ilion, 1988–89'. *Studia Troica*, 1: 39–68.

Millett, P. 1991. *Lending and Borrowing in Ancient Athens*. Cambridge.

Mitchell, L. G. 1997. *Greeks Bearing Gifts: The Public use of Private Relationships in the Greek World 435–323 BC*. Cambridge.

Mitchell, S. 1993. *Anatolia: Land, Men and Gods in Asia Minor*. Oxford.

Moles, J. 1993. 'Truth and Untruth in Herodotus and Thucydides'. In C. Gill and T. P. Wiseman (eds.), *Lies and Fiction in the Ancient World*. Exeter. 88–121.

Momigliano, A. 1942. '*Terra marique*'. *JRS* 32: 53–64.

——1945*a*. Review of Perret 1942. *JRS* 35: 99–104.

——1945*b*. 'The Locrian Maidens and the Date of Lycophron's *Alexandra*'. *CQ* 39: 49–53.

——1958. 'Some Observations on the "Origo Gentis Romanae"'. *JRS* 48: 56–73.

——1975. *Alien Wisdom: The Limits of Hellenization*. Cambridge.

——1984. 'How to Reconcile Greeks and Trojans'. In A. Momigliano (ed.) *Settimo contributo alla storia degli studi classici e del mondo antico*. Rome. 437–62.

Moreau, A. 1994. *Le Mythe de Jason et Médée: le va-nu-pied et la sorcière*. Paris.

Moret, J.-M. 1975. *L'Ilioupersis dans la céramique italiote: les mythes et leur expression figurée au IVe siècle*. Rome.

Morgan, C. 1994. 'The Evolution of a Sacral "Landscape": Isthmia, Perachora, and the Early Corinthian State'. In Alcock and Osborne 1994: 105–42.

References

Morris, I., and Powell, B. (eds.). 1997. *A New Companion to Homer.* Leiden.

Mossman, J. 1995. *Wild Justice: A Study of Euripides'* Hecuba. Oxford.

Mottershead, J. 1986. *Suetonius* Claudius. Bristol.

Münzer, F. 1920. *Römische Adelsparteien und Adelsfamilien.* Stuttgart.

Mure, W. 1854. *A Critical History of the Language and Literature of Ancient Greece.* i. 2nd edn. London.

Musti, D. 1963. 'Sull'idea di συγγένεια in inscrizioni greche'. *ASNP*² 32: 225–39.

Nagy, G. 1996. *Homeric Questions.* Austin.

Neils, J. 1992. *Goddess and Polis: The Panathenaic Festival in Ancient Athens.* Princeton.

Nenci, G. (ed.). 1982. *Materiali e contributi per lo studio degli otto decreti da Entella.* Pisa (*=ASNP*³ 12: 769–1103).

—— 1993. *Alla ricerca di Entella.* Pisa.

Nicolet, C. (ed.). 1980. *Insula sacra: la loi Gabinia Calpurnia de Délos (58 av. J.-C.).* Rome.

Niese, B. 1899. *Geschichte der griechischen und makedonischen Staaten seit der Schlacht bei Chaeronea.* ii. Gotha.

Nilsson, M. P. 1972. *Cults, Myths, Oracles, and Politics in Ancient Greece.* New York (first pub. 1951).

Norden, E. 1901. 'Vergils Aeneis im Lichte ihrer Zeit'. *Neue Jahrbücher für das klassische Altertum* 7: 249–82, 313–34 (=B. Kytzler (ed.), *Kleine Schriften zum klassischen Altertum.* Berlin. 1966: 358–421).

North, J. 1976. 'Conservatism and Change in Roman Religion'. *Papers of the British School at Rome* 44: 1–12.

—— 1989. 'Religion in Republican Rome'. *CAH*² 7/2: 573–624.

Oberhummer, E. 1887. *Akarnanien, Ambrakia, Amphilochien, Leukas im Altertum.* Munich.

Ogilvie, R. M. 1965. *A Commentary on Livy, Books 1–5.* Oxford.

Ohlemutz, E. 1940. *Die Kulte und Heiligtümer der Götter in Pergamon.* Würzburg.

Ohly, D. 1992. *The Munich Glyptothek: Greek and Roman Sculpture.* 2nd edn. Munich. (In German, *Glyptothek München: griechische und römische Skulpturen.* 6th edn. Munich. 1986. First pub. 1972.)

Oost, S. I. 1954. *Roman Policy in Epirus and Acarnania in the Age of the Roman Conquest of Greece.* Dallas.

Orlin, E. M. 1997. *Temples, Religion and Politics in the Roman Republic.* Leiden.

Orth, W. 1977. *Königlicher Machtanspruch und städtische Freiheit.* Munich.

Osborne, R. 1985. 'The Erection and Mutilation of the Hermai'. *PCPS* 31: 47–53.

—— 1996. *Greece in the Making 1200–479 BC.* London.

Page, D. L. 1981. *Further Greek Epigrams.* Cambridge.

References

Palmer, R. E. A. 1997. *Rome and Carthage at Peace*. Stuttgart.
Pani, M. 1975. 'Troia Resurgens: mito troiano e ideologia del principato'. *Annali della facoltà di Lettere e Filosofia di Università di Bari*, 18: 65–85.
Papillon, T. 1998. 'Isocrates and the Use of Myth'. *Hermathena*, 161: 9–21.
Parker, R. 1996. *Athenian Religion: A History*. Oxford.
Pearson, L. 1939. *Early Ionian Historians*. Oxford.
——1987. *The Greek Historians of the West: Timaeus and his Predecessors*. Atlanta.
Perkins, A. 1973. *The Art of Dura-Europus*. Oxford.
Perret, J. 1942. *Les origines de la légende troyenne de Rome (281–31)*. Paris.
——1971. 'Rome et les Troyens'. *REL* 49: 39–52.
Pettersson, M. 1992. *Cults of Apollo at Sparta: The Hyakinthia, the Gymnopaidiai and the Karneia*. Stockholm.
Pfeiffer, R. 1968. *History of Classical Scholarship*. Oxford.
Pfister, F. 1909. *Der Reliquienkult im Altertum*. i. *Das Objekt des Reliquienkultes*. Gießen.
——1912. *Der Reliquienkult in Altertum*. ii. *Die Reliquien als Kultobjekt. Geschichte des Reliquienkultes*. Gießen.
Phillips, E. D. 1953. 'Odysseus in Italy'. *JHS* 73: 53–67.
Piejko, F. 1991. 'Antiochus III and Ilium'. *Archiv für Papyrusforschung* 37: 9–50.
Podlecki, A. J. 1976. 'Athens and Aegina'. *Historia*, 25: 396–413.
——1989. *Aeschylus:* Eumenides. Warminster.
Pollard, J. 1977. *Birds in Greek Life and Myth*. London.
Pollitt, J. J. 1986. *Art in the Hellenistic Age*. Cambridge.
Poucet, J. 1983a. 'Énée et Lavinium'. *Revue Belge de Philologie et d'Histoire*, 61: 144–59.
——1983b. 'Un culte d'Énée dans la région lavinate au quatrième siècle avant Jésus-Christ?'. In H. Zehnacker and G. Hentz (eds.), *Hommages à Robert Schilling*. Paris. 187–201.
——1985. *Les Origines de Rome: tradition et histoire*. Brussels.
——1989a. 'La Diffusion de la légende d'Énée en Italie centrale et ses rapports avec celle de Romulus'. *Les Études classiques*, 57: 227–54.
——1989b. 'Denys d'Halicarnasse et Varron: le cas des voyages d'Énée'. *Mélanges de l'École française de Rome*, 101: 63–95.
Powell, A. (ed.). 1992. *Roman Poetry and Propaganda in the Age of Augustus*. London.
Prandi, L. 1990. 'Gli oracoli sulla spedizione asiatica di Alessandro'. *Chiron*, 20: 345–69.
Preuner, E. 1926. 'Die Panegyris der Athena Ilias'. *Hermes*, 61: 113–33.
Prinz, F. 1979. *Gründungsmythen und Sagenchronologie*. Munich.
Prinz, K. 1997. *Epitaphios Logos*. Frankfurt.

References

Pritchett, W. K. 1993. *The Liar School of Herodotos*. Amsterdam.

Raab, I. 1972. *Zu den Darstellungen des Parisurteils in der griechischen Kunst.* Frankfurt.

Radt, S., and Drijvers, J. W. 1993. 'Die Groninger Neuedition von Strabons *Geographika*, vorgestellt anhand des Abschnittes über Troia'. *Studia Troica*, 3: 201–31.

Raeck, W. 1981. *Zum Barbarenbild in der Kunst Athens im 6. und 5. Jahrhundert v. Chr.* Bonn.

Ramage, E. S. 1991. 'Sulla's Propaganda'. *Klio*, 73: 93–121.

Reinhardt, K. 1961. *Die Ilias und ihr Dichter.* Göttingen.

Reynolds, J. M. 1982. *Aphrodisias and Rome.* London.

——1986. 'Further Information on Imperial Cult at Aphrodisias'. *Studii Clasice*, 24: 109–117.

——1996. 'Ruler-cult at Aphrodisias in the Late Republic and under the Julio-Claudian Emperors'. In A. Small (ed.), *Subject and Ruler: The Cult of the Ruling Power in Classical Antiquity.* Journal of Roman Archaeology Suppl. 17. Ann Arbor. 41–50.

Richard, J.-C. 1983*a*. 'Sur une triple étiologie du nom Iulus, II'. *REL* 61: 108–21.

——1983*b*. *Pseudo-Aurélius Victor: Les origines du peuple romain.* Paris.

Richardson, N. J. 1975. 'Homeric Professors in the Age of Sophists'. *PCPS* 201: 65–81.

Richter, H. D. 1987. *Untersuchungen zur hellenistischen Historiographie: Die Vorlagen des Pompeius Trogus für die Darstellung der nach-alexandrinischen hellenistischen Geschichte (Iust. 13–40).* Frankfurt.

Ridgway, B. S. 1981. *Fifth Century Styles in Greek Sculpture.* Princeton.

——1990. *Hellenistic Sculpture I: The Styles of ca. 331–200 BC.* Bristol.

Ridgway, D. 1996. 'Nestor's Cup and the Etruscans'. *Oxford Journal of Archaeology*, 15: 325–44.

Rigsby, K. J. 1996. *Asylia: Territorial Inviolability in the Hellenistic World.* Berkeley.

Rizzo, F. P. 1974. *Studi ellenistico-romani.* Palermo.

Robert, F. 1950. *Homère.* Paris.

Robert, J., and Robert, L. 1983. *Fouilles d'Amyzon en Carie.* i. Paris.

Robert, L. 1940. *Hellenica*, i. Limoges.

——1955. *Hellenica*, x. Paris.

——1966. *Monnaies antiques en Troade.* Geneva.

——1969. *Opera minora selecta.* i–ii. Amsterdam.

——1990. *Opera minora selecta.* vii. Amsterdam.

Robertson, M. 1975. *A History of Greek Art.* Cambridge.

Robinson, E. G. D. 1990. 'Between Greek and Native: The Xenon Group'. In J.-P. Descœudres (ed.), *Greek Colonists and Native Populations.* Oxford. 251–65.

Rose, C. B. 1991. 'The Theatre of Ilion'. *Studia Troica*, 1: 69–77.
——1992. 'The 1991 Post-Bronze Age Excavations at Troia'. *Studia Troica*, 2: 43–60.
——1993. 'The 1992 Post-Bronze Age Excavations at Troia'. *Studia Troica*, 3: 97–116.
——1995. 'The 1994 Post-Bronze Age Excavations at Troia'. *Studia Troica*, 5: 81–105.
——1997a. 'The 1996 Post-Bronze Age Excavations at Troia'. *Studia Troica*, 7: 73–110.
——1997b. *Dynastic Commemoration and Imperial Portraiture in the Julio-Claudian Period*. Cambridge.
——1998. 'The 1997 Post-Bronze Age Excavations at Troia'. *Studia Troica*, 8: 71–113.
Roux, G., and Callot, O. 1987. *Le Terrasse d'Attale I*. Fouilles de Delphes 2. Paris.
Rutherford, I. 1996. 'The New Simonides: Towards a Commentary'. In Boedeker and Sider 1996: 167–92.
Sacks, K. S. 1990. *Diodorus Siculus and the First Century*. Princeton.
Sadurska, A. 1964. *Les Tables Iliaques*. Warsaw.
Said, E. W. 1978. *Orientalism: Western Conceptions of the Orient*. London.
Salapata, G. 1993. 'The Lakonian Hero Reliefs in the Light of the Terracotta Plaques'. In O. Palagia and W. Coulson, *Sculpture from Arcadia and Laconia*. Oxford. 189–97.
Santini, C. 1995. *I frammenti di L. Cassio Emina: introduzione, testo, traduzione e commento*. Pisa.
Santoro, M. 1974. *Epitheta deorum in Asia graeca cultorum ex auctoribus graecis et latinis*. Milan.
Schachter, A. 1981. *Cults of Boeotia*. i. London.
Schalles, H.-J. 1985. *Untersuchungen zur Kulturpolitik der pergamenischen Herrscher im 3. Jh. v. Chr*. Tübingen.
Schauenburg, K. 1960. 'Äneas und Rom'. *Gymnasium*, 67: 176–91.
——1969. '*ΑΙΝΕΑΣ ΚΑΛΟΣ*'. *Gymnasium*, 76: 42–53.
Scheer, T. S. 1993. *Mythische Vorväter zur Bedeutung griechischer Heroenmythen im Selbstverständnis kleinasiatischer Städte*. Munich.
——1996. 'Ein Museum griechischer "Frühgeschichte" im Apollon-tempel von Sikyon'. *Klio*, 78: 353–73.
Scheid, J. 1985. *Religion et piété à Rome*. Paris.
Schilling, R. 1954. *La Religion romaine de Vénus depuis les origines jusqu'au temps d'Auguste*. Paris.
——1979. *Rites, cultes, dieux de Rome*. Paris.
Schmal, S. 1995. *Feinbilder bei den frühen Griechen: Untersuchungen zur Entwicklung von Fremdenbildern und Identitäten in der griechischen Literatur von Homer bis Aristophanes*. Frankfurt.

References

Schmidt, E. 1909. *Kultübertragungen*. Giessen.

Schmidt-Dounas, B. 1991. 'Zur Datierung der Metopen des Athena Tempels von Ilion'. *MDAI (I)* 41: 363–415.

Schmitt, H. H. 1957. *Rom und Rhodos*. Munich.

——1957/8. 'Hellenen, Römer und Barbaren: eine Studie zu Polybios'. *Wissenschaftliche Beilage zum Jahresbericht 1957/8 des humanistischen Gymnasiums Aschaffenburg*. 38–48.

——1964. *Untersuchungen zur Geschichte Antiochos des Grossen und seiner Zeit*. Wiesbaden.

——1969. *Die Staatsverträge des Altertums*. iii: *Die Verträge der griechisch-römischen Welt von 338 bis 200 v. Chr.* Munich.

Schröder, W. A. 1971. *M. Porcius Cato: das erste Buch der* Origines. Meisenheim.

Scullard, H. H. 1973. *Roman Politics, 220–150 BC*. 2nd edn. Oxford.

——1981. *Festivals and Ceremonies of the Roman Republic*. London.

Shapiro, H. A. 1994. *Myth into Art: Poet and Painter in Classical Greece*. London.

Sherk, R. K. 1969. *Roman Documents from the Greek East: Senatus Consulta and Epistulae to the Age of Augustus*. Baltimore.

Sherwin-White, A. N. 1984. *Roman Foreign Policy in the East, 168 BC–AD 1*. London.

Simon, E. 1967. *Ara Pacis Augustae*. Tübingen.

Smith, C. J. 1996. *Early Rome and Latium: Economy and Society c.1000 to 500 BC*. Oxford.

Smith, P. M. 1981. 'Aineiadai as patrons of *Iliad* XX and the Homeric *Hymn to Aphrodite*'. *Harv. Stud.* 85: 17–58.

Smith, R. R. R. 1990. 'Myth and Allegory in the Sebasteion'. In C. Roueché and K. T. Erim (eds.), *Aphrodisias Papers: Recent Work on Architecture and Sculpture*. Journal of Roman Archaeology Suppl. 1. Ann Arbor. 88–100.

——1991. *Hellenistic Sculpture*. London.

Snodgrass, A. 1998. *Homer and the Artists: Text and Picture in Early Greek Art*. Cambridge.

Solmsen, F. 1986. '"Aeneas founded Rome with Odysseus"'. *Harv. Stud.* 90: 93–110.

Sommella, P. 1974. 'Das Heroon des Aeneas und die Topographie des antiken Lavinium'. *Gymnasium*, 81: 273–97.

Sommerstein, A. 1989. *Aeschylus*: Eumenides. Cambridge.

Sparkes, B. A. 1996. *The Red and the Black: Studies in Greek Pottery*. London.

Spawforth, A. J. 1994. 'Corinth, Argos, and the Imperial Cult: Pseudo-Julian, *Letters* 198'. *Hesperia*, 63: 211–32.

Spawforth, A. J., and Walker, S. 1985. 'The World of the Panhellenion. i: Athens and Eleusis'. *JRS* 75: 78–104.

References

Spawforth, A. J., and Walker, S. 1986. 'The World of the Panhellenion. ii: Three Dorian Cities'. *JRS* 76: 88–105.

Stähler, K. 1978. 'Überlegungen zur architektorischen Gestalt des Pergamonaltares'. In S. Sahin, E. Schwertheim, and J. Wagner (eds.), *Studien zur Religion und Kultur Kleinasiens: Festschrift für F. K. Dörner*. Leiden. 838–67.

Stanley, K. 1993. *The Shield of Achilles: Narrative Structure in the Iliad*. Princeton.

Stewart, A. 1990. *Greek Sculpture: An Exploration*. New Haven.

——1993. *Faces of Power: Alexander's Image and Hellenistic Politics*. Berkeley.

Stiglitz, R. 1953. 'Alexandra von Amyklai'. *JÖAI* 40: 72–83.

Strasburger, H. 1968. *Zur Sage von der Gründung Roms*. Heidelberg.

Strubbe, J. H. M. 1984–6. 'Gründer kleinasiatischer Städte: Fiktion und Realität'. *Ancient Society* 15–17: 253–304.

Suerbaum, W. 1995. 'Der Pyrrhos-Krieg in Ennius' *Annales* VI im Lichte der ersten Ennius-Papyri aus Herculaneum'. *ZPE* 106: 31–52.

Swain, S. 1996. *Hellenism and Empire: Language, Classicism and Power in the Greek World, AD 50–250*. Oxford.

Symeonoglou, S. 1985. *The Topography of Thebes from the Bronze Age to Modern Times*. Princeton.

Taplin, O. 1992. *Homeric Soundings: The Shaping of the Iliad*. Oxford.

—— 1993. *Comic Angels and Other Approaches to Greek Drama through Vase-Paintings*. Oxford.

Taylor, J. G. 1998. 'Oinoe and the Painted Stoa: Ancient and Modern Misunderstandings?' *AJPhil.* 119: 223–43.

Taylor, L. R. 1934. 'Varro's *De Gente Populi Romani*'. *C.Phil.* 29: 221–9.

Tenger, B. 1999. 'Zur Geographie und Geschichte der Troas'. In E. Schwertheim (ed.), *Die Troas: Neue Forschungen III*. Berlin. 103–80.

Thomas, G. 1984. 'Magna Mater and Attis'. *ANRW* II. 17. 3: 1499–1535.

Tod, M. N. 1913. *International Arbitration amongst the Greeks*. Oxford.

Toohey, P. 1984. 'Politics, Prejudice and Trojan Genealogies: Varro, Hyginus and Horace'. *Arethusa*, 17: 5–28.

Torelli, M. 1982. *Typology and Structure of Roman Historical Reliefs*. Michigan.

Trendall, A. D. 1989. *Red Figure Vases of South Italy and Sicily*. London.

——1991. 'Farce and Tragedy in South Italian Vase-painting'. In T. Rasmussen and N. Spivey (eds.), *Looking at Greek Vases*. Cambridge. 151–82.

Van der Valk, M. 1953. 'Homer's Nationalistic Attitude'. *Antiquité classique*, 22: 5–26.

Vanotti, G. 1979. 'Sofocle e l'occidente'. In L. Braccesi (ed.), *I tragici e l'occidente*. Bologna. 93–125.

——1995. *L'altro Enea: la testimonianza di Dionigi di Alicarnasso*. Rome.

References

Verkinderen, F. 1987. 'The Honorary Decree for Malousios of Gargara and the κοινόν of Athena Ilias'. *Tyche*, 2: 247–69.

Vermaseren, M. J. 1977. *Cybele and Attis, the Myth and the Cult*. London.

Veyne, P. 1988. *Did the Greeks believe in their Myths? An essay on the Constitutive Imagination*. Chicago. (In French, Paris. 1983.)

Visser, M. 1982. 'Worship your Enemy: Aspects of the Cult of Heroes in Ancient Greece'. *Harv. Theol. Rev.* 75: 403–28.

Voegtli, H. 1977. *Bilder der Heldenepen in der kaiserzeitlichen griechischen Munzprägung*. Basle.

Volkmann, H. 1958. *Sullas Marsch auf Rom: Der Verfall der römischen Republik*. Munich.

Vos, M. F. 1963. *Scythian Archers in Archaic Attic Vase-painting*. Groningen.

Walbank, F. W. 1957. *A Historical Commentary on Polybius*. i. *Books 1–6*. Oxford.

——1967. *A Historical Commentary on Polybius*. ii. *Books 7–18*. Oxford.

——1979. *A Historical Commentary on Polybius*. iii. *Books 19–40*. Oxford.

Watrous, L. V. 1982. 'The Sculptural Program of the Siphnian Treasury at Delphi'. *AJArch.* 86: 159–72.

Webb, P. A. 1996. *Hellenistic Architectural Sculpture: Figural Motifs in Western Anatolia and the Aegean Islands*. Madison.

Weber, E. 1972. 'Die trojanische Abstammung der Römer als politisches Argument'. *Wiener Studien*, 85: 213–25.

Weber, G. 1993. *Dichtung und höfische Gesellschaft: Die Rezeption von Zeitgeschichte am Hof der ersten drei Ptolemäer*. Stuttgart.

Webster, T. B. L. 1970. *Greek Theatre Production*. 2nd edn. London.

Weeber, K.-W. 1974. '*Troiae Lusus*: Alter und Entstehung eines Reiterspiels'. *Ancient Society*, 5: 171–96.

Wees, H. van. 1992. *Status Warriors: War, Violence and Society in Homer and History*. Amsterdam.

Weinstock, S. 1971. *Divus Julius*. Oxford.

Weiss, P. 1984. 'Lebendiger Mythos: Gründerheroen und städtische Gründstraditionen im griechisch-römische Osten'. *Würzburger Jahrbücher*, 10: 179–207.

Welles, C. B. 1934. *Royal Correspondence in the Hellenistic Period*. New Haven.

West, D. 1990. The *Aeneid: A New Prose Translation*. London.

West, M. L. 1992. *Iambi et Elegi Graeci*. ii. 2nd edn. Oxford.

——1993a. 'Simonides Redivivus'. *ZPE* 98: 1–14.

——1993b. *Greek Lyric Poetry*. Oxford.

West, S. 1984. 'Lycophron Italicised'. *JHS* 104: 127–51.

White, P. 1993. *Promised Verses: Poets in the Society of Augustan Rome*. Cambridge, Mass.

Whitehouse, R. D., and Wilkins, J. B. 1989. 'Greeks and Natives in South-East Italy: Approaches to the Archaeological Evidence'. In

References

T. C. Champion (ed.), *Centre and Periphery: Comparative Studies in Archaeology*. London. 102–26.

Wide, S. 1893. *Lakonische Kulte*. Leipzig.

Wiencke, M. I. 1954. 'An Epic Theme in Greek Art'. *AJArch*. 58: 285–306.

Wikander, O. 1993. 'Senators and Equites v. Ancestral Pride and Genealogical Studies in Late Republican Rome.' *Opuscula Romana*, 19: 77–90.

Will, E. 1979. *Histoire politique du monde hellénistique*. i. *De la mort d'Alexandre aux avènements d'Antiochos III et de Philippe V à la fin des Lagides*. 2nd edn. Nancy.

——1982. *Histoire politique du monde hellénistique*. ii. *Des avènements d'Antiochos et de Philippe V à la fin des Lagides*. 2nd edn. Nancy.

——1995. 'Syngeneia, oikeiotès, philia'. *Revue de philologie*, 69: 299–325.

Williams, D. 1987. 'Aegina, Aphaia-Tempel: XI. the Pottery from the Second Limestone Temple and the Later History of the Sanctuary'. *Archäologischer Anzeiger*. 629–80.

Williams, G. 1990. 'Did Maecenas "Fall from Favor"? Augustan Literary Patronage'. In K. A. Raaflaub and M. Toher (eds.), *Between Republic and Empire: Interpretations of Augustus and his Principate*. Berkeley. 258–75.

Wilson. R. J. A. 1990. *Sicily under the Roman Empire*. Warminster.

Wiseman, T. P. 1974. 'Legendary Genealogies in Late Republican Rome'. *Greece and Rome* 21: 153–64.

——1979. *Clio's Cosmetics: Three Studies in Greco-Roman Literature*. Leicester.

——1984. 'Cybele, Virgil and Augustus'. In T. Woodman and D. West (ed.), *Poetry and Politics in the Age of Augustus*. Cambridge. 117–28.

——1989. 'Roman Legend and Oral Tradition'. A review of Bremmer and Horsfall 1987. *JRS* 79: 129–37.

——1995. *Remus: A Roman Myth*. Cambridge.

Wissowa, G. 1887. 'Die Überlieferung über die römischen Penaten'. *Hermes*, 22: 29–57.

——1912. *Religion und Kultus der Römer*. Munich.

Woodford, S., and Loudon, M. 1980. 'Two Trojan Themes: The Iconography of Ajax carrying the Body of Achilles and of Aeneas carrying Anchises in Black Figure Vase Painting'. *AJArch*. 84: 25–40.

Wycherley, R. E. 1957. *The Athenian Agora*. iii: *The Literary and Epigraphical Testimonia*. Princeton.

——1978. *The Stones of Athens*. Princeton.

Zahrnt, M. 1971. *Olynth und die Chalkidier: Untersuchungen zur Staatenbildung auf der Chalkidischen Halbinsel im 5. und 4. Jahrhundert v. Chr.* Munich.

——1996. 'Alexanders Übergang über den Hellespont'. *Chiron*, 26: 129–47.

References

Zanker, P. 1969. 'Der Larenaltar im Belvedere des Vatikans'. *MDAI (R)*
76: 205–18.
——1988. *The Power of Images in the Age of Augustus*. Ann Arbor.
Zetzel, J. E. G. 1995. *Cicero, De re publica: Selections*. Cambridge.
Ziolkowski, A. 1992. *The Temples of Mid-Republican Rome and their Historical
and Topographical Context*. Rome.
Zwierlein, O. 1986. 'Lucans Caesar in Troja'. *Hermes*, 114: 460–78.

Bibliographic Addendum to the
Paperback Edition

On Troy note D. Hertel's two books, the substantial *Die Mauern von Troja: Mythos und Geschichte im antiken Ilion* (Munich 2003), and the briefer *Troia: Archäologie, Geschichte, Mythos* (Munich 2001).

On myth and local tradition in general, see the well-illustrated volume by J. Boardman, *The Archaeology of Nostalgia: How the Greeks created their Mythical Past* (London 2002), which collects testimonia for hero tombs and relics on pp. 210–40; in Asia Minor, T. J. Scheer, 'The Past in a Hellenistic Present: Myth and Local Tradition', in A. Erskine (ed.), *The Blackwell Companion to the Hellenistic World* (Oxford 2003), 216–31; on Attalids, E. Kosmetatou, 'Ilion, the Troad, and Attalid', *Ancient Society* 31 (2001), 107–32. For that recorder of local tradition, Pausanias, see the essays in S. Alcock, J. Cherry, J. Elsner (eds.), *Pausanias: Travel and Memory in Roman Greece* (New York 2001).

For Homer's later influence, F. Zeitlin, 'Visions and revisions of Homer', in S. Goldhill (ed.), *Being Greek under Roman Rule* (Cambridge 2001), 195–268, and the two articles by J. Porter, 'Homer: The Very Idea', *Arion* 3rd series, 10.2 (2002), 57–86; and 'Homer: The History of an Idea' in R. Fowler (ed.), *The Cambridge Companion to Homer* (Cambridge 2003).

For ethnic identity and culture in the west, see the essays by J.-P. Wilson, E. Herring and K. Lomas in E. Herring and K. Lomas (eds.), *The Emergence of State Identities in Italy* (London 2000) for the early period. See E. Dench, 'Beyond Greeks and Barbarians: Italy and Sicily in the Hellenistic Age', in A. Erskine (ed.), *The Blackwell Companion to the Hellenistic World* (Oxford 2003), 294–310 for later times. On the Trojan myth in Italy, T. Morard, *Les Troyens à Métaponte: Etude d'une nouvelle Ilioupersis de la céramique italiote* (Munich 2002); and for a very different view from the present book, M. Torelli, *Tota Italia: Essays in the Cultural Formation of Roman Italy* (Oxford 1999), especially the epilogue.

Index